Michael Chesher, Rukesh Kaura
and Peter Linton

Electronic Business & Commerce

Springer

Michael Chesher, BSc, MBA, MPhil, CEng
Roehampton University of Surrey, UK

Rukesh Kaura, BSc, CCM
JP Morgan Chase & Co, Singapore

Peter Linton, BA
Linton Associates, UK

British Library Cataloguing in Publication Data
Chesher, Michael, 1942-
  Electronic business and commerce
  1. Electronic commerce
  I. Title II. Kaura, Rukesh, 1971- III. Linton, Peter
  658'.05
ISBN 185233584X

Library of Congress Cataloging-in-Publication Data
A catalog record for this book is available from the Library of Congress

ISBN 1-85233-584-X Springer-Verlag London Berlin Heidelberg
a member of BertelsmannSpringer Science+Business Media GmbH
http://www.springer.co.uk

Typesetting: EPS, London W13 8DG
Printed and bound at the Athenæum Press Ltd., Gateshead, Tyne and Wear
34/3830-543210 Printed on acid-free paper SPIN 10863963

Contents

Preface

This book started as a project to prepare a second edition of *Electronic Commerce and Business Communications* published by Springer in 1998 (now out of print), but in practice has become a complete rewrite. This is because so much has changed in the field of electronic business and commerce in such a short period of time. The new title reflects the growing consensus that doing business electronically is increasingly 'just business', and covers all aspects of the business processes of the firm, both internally and externally. E-Commerce is now considered as a subset of e-Business that primarily involves the marketing, buying and selling of products and services over the Internet.

The new book is primarily intended as a student text for undergraduate courses, which include an e-Business module in the course syllabus, and for postgraduate courses where e-Business forms the main focus of the course or indeed is simply a module. It is completely self-supporting in that it includes reference chapters (Chapters 15, 16 and 17) for those wishing to understand more about the information technologies underpinning e-Business. In addition it is a valuable reference book for practitioners in the field of e-Business and includes a comprehensive glossary built up over several years.

The approach taken within the book is to provide the reader with a sound grounding in the basic concepts to enhance their understanding and learning through an extensive use of examples, case studies and schematics. Also, a companion Web site has been created which is increasingly being populated with material related to the book, including an online glossary (see **www.roehampton.ac.uk/staff/MichaelChesher**).

The chapters listed below form a logical sequence for the serious student of e-Business to follow, although the last three chapters and the glossary are likely to be more useful for reference purposes.

Chapter 1: Business Context

Business context introduces the age of turbulence and change that has resulted in a dramatic transformation in business and in home computing. From a corporate perspective, the marketplace continues to become more competitive and global in nature. Key factors influencing the business context include technology, globalization, political/legislative, customer focus, competition, restructuring of industry sectors, dis-intermediation in the supply chain, educational standards and the movement from manufacturing to service economies in North America and Europe.

Chapter 2: Framework for e-Business

Against the backdrop of the business context, this chapter explains what doing business electronically really means. A framework to help readers understand the scope of e-Business is presented, as well as clarifying its relationship with e-Commerce. The vocabulary of e-Business is explained including such terms as electronic mail, electronic data interchange, Internet commerce, B2B, B2C, C2C, m-Commerce, electronic marketplaces, etc., and how these have evolved.

Chapter 3: Financial e-Business

Conducting business electronically presents financial settlement alternatives to the traditional payment instructions such as cash, cheque and credit cards. This chapter includes electronic presentment (bill, statement, invoice, etc.) as well as links to m-Commerce. It describes how online payments can be made more secure for both the buyer and seller, as well as reviewing other payment alternatives for the cyber-shopper including digital wallets.

Chapter 4: Desktop Support for e-Business

Much has changed in the workplace since the arrival of the personal computer in the early 1980s. This chapter examines the business communications revolution and the desktop capabilities now available to assist business as well as home users. More importantly, the desktop is no longer considered as a standalone environment, but a communications portal to valuable information resources through the extensive use of internal and external networks. The chapter also examines the evolution of desktop hardware and software, and how Groupware environments are delivering strategic e-Business solutions to the desktop user.

Chapter 5: Business-to-Business (B2B)

The last 30 years have seen the adoption of robotics by manufacturing, and the spread of business computers within the back-office. This has resulted in most of the potential cost reductions being squeezed out of manufacturing and back-office operations. In a turbulent marketplace, companies are being forced to re-examine their supply chain operation as they seek further cost reductions to maintain their competitive position. This chapter examines how top management can introduce sound business practices, particularly on the buy-side of e-Business, to reduce costs, improve customer service and stay competitive.

Chapter 6: Traditional B2B – Electronic Data Interchange

Supply chain initiatives started back in the 1980s, particularly in the retail industry, in the form of EDI – Electronic Data Interchange. This chapter explains why EDI is no longer a choice in many industry sectors, and how it is used to replace paper-based business transactions between disparate companies by their electronic equivalents. The chapter provides a comprehensive introduction into the most widely used EDI standard, namely UN/EDIFACT and also introduces XML as an alternative approach for the exchange of structured business data.

Chapter 7: Evolving B2B – Electronic Business XML

This chapter examines XML – eXtensible Mark-up Language – what it is, what it offers, and why it is important. From an e-Business perspective, the main attraction is that XML promises to provide an internationally agreed standard for the exchange of structured business data based upon defined business processes. That is of course very similar to what the EDI is designed to do, so that EDI and XML can be viewed as complementary approaches. The chapter describes a number of XML initiatives that are underway and the importance of ebXML (supported by UN/CEFACT and OASIS) in channelling these initiatives into a single consistent approach.

Chapter 8: B2B Electronic Marketplaces

This chapter examines business-to-business e-Marketplaces, also known as trade exchanges or e-Auctions. Companies are continuing to recognize the importance of the buy-side of e-Business as they move from Web-based applications for the purchase of office supplies and MRO items (now is a chance to checkout the glossary) to the sourcing of direct materials for manufacture. Horizontal trading exchanges run across different industries, whilst vertical exchanges establish marketplaces in a particular industry. Despite their apparent attraction, many e-Marketplaces have not proved to be successful and the reasons for this apparent anomaly are explained. The evolution of the value propositions of e-Marketplaces is also examined.

Chapter 9: Business-to-Consumer (B2C)

In this chapter the emergence of the Web as a new sales channel to reach home consumers is explored. This aspect of e-Business has attracted a great deal of media attention and is increasingly described as e-Commerce, meaning the use of the Web to create electronic shop-fronts permitting the purchase of a very wide range of products and services. The chapter reviews the nature of what sells best over the Web and includes an extensive practical case study. Often business customers may purchase from the same Web site and in most cases the e-Tailer makes no distinction between home consumer and business customer.

Chapter 10: Wireless Commerce

The mobility provided by wireless communications offers new possibilities for the corporate nomad and scope for exciting new business applications. This chapter describes a number of wireless enabled devices, together with the emerging standards for wireless networks and the cellular technology evolution, together with a detailed case study of Japan's NTT DoCoMo i-mode Service. It also covers the use of mobile phones and personal digital assistants for SMS messaging and access to Internet WAP-based services.

Chapter 11: Dot.Com Economy

Over a relatively short period of time the Web has emerged as a dynamic new force to reach home consumers and business customers alike, giving rise to new business models. This chapter examines how new Internet start-up companies have emerged, some to succeed, yet many to fail, in what has been described as a modern day 'gold rush'. The publicity and media hype over this period has given rise to the term the 'Dot.Com Economy' regarded by many as synonymous with the term 'new economy'. The chapter also argues that the new economy should encompass more traditional 'bricks and mortar' businesses that have successfully made the transition to Dot.com company by integrating the Internet into their operations.

Chapter 12: Securing e-Business

Security concerns continue to be voiced by business customers and home users as a major impediment to the longer-term growth of e-Business over the Internet. In addition, administrations have recognized the threat of cyber-crime by the introduction of legislation and other measures to improve e-Business security. This chapter provides a comprehensive treatment of the subject including the options available to reduce the risk of security failures and an insight into future developments.

Chapter 13: Legal Aspects of e-Business

As the technical and commercial issues impacting the growth of e-Business are rapidly being overcome, administrations are realizing that existing legal frameworks dating back many hundreds of years are no longer adequate to cope with the demands of the digital age. This chapter therefore examines the measures underway within three main groupings. First, legislation that addresses the very special needs of e-Business in terms of distance selling, electronic signatures and contracts. Second the issue of data protection legislation for data captured as part of a commercial transaction and finally the legislation that governs the content of data made available over the Web.

Chapter 14: e-Business Strategies

This chapter addresses many of the questions posed by an organization seeking to develop a winning e-Business strategy. Strategy development is not intuitive and needs a disciplined approach, even if the original business idea is an inspired piece of entrepreneurial vision. The chapter covers many of the key factors to be included in strategy development and resulting business models that balance the level of integration between 'point and click' and 'bricks and mortar' businesses.

Chapter 15: Communications Fundamentals

This is the first of three reference chapters that provides the 'basic fundamentals' behind today's global information super-highway that together with local area networks form the telecommunications and data network infrastructure making e-Business possible.

Chapter 16: Standards in e-Business

Since a prime goal of e-Business involves the exchange of business data between disparate organizations, without standards this process would be anarchic and impossible. This chapter principally describes the open Internet-based standards progressively adopted by the business community over the last 10 years.

Chapter 17: Server-side Technologies

Finally, this last chapter provides the reader with a sound introduction to the information technologies employed in many of the servers that exist on the global information super-highway and provide the 'engines' to power e-Business.

Business Context

Age of Turbulence and Change

Ever more business transactions are being conducted electronically, thanks in part to dramatic cost performance advances in IT. Organizations are subject to an unprecedented pace of change in the way they operate to meet the business challenges of the 21st century. Success is determined by the ability of the workforce to absorb change, and to work to exploit new and emerging technologies. The digital or information revolution is at the heart of these changes, comparable in impact to that of the industrial revolution of the 19th century.

Many organizations have been quick to realise the value associated with information, and the potential it holds to secure competitive advantage. This results in improved financial margins, shorter times to bring new products and services to market, an enhanced emphasis on quality, and significantly improved customer service. The key is improved business productivity, together with customer oriented initiatives, through a combination of people skills and IT.

However, the ever growing inter-dependency of nation states, its impact upon the world economy and the political unrest that exists in some parts of the world erupting in terrorist action, has brought a new meaning to the 'age of turbulence' in which business must operate today.

Three Introductory Scenarios

The impact of electronic business (e-Business) may best be illustrated through practical everyday examples. Part of what happens is familiar, while part is at present mysterious to the non-specialist.

Puchasing a Gift

Simple description: A woman enters the store and goes directly to the information desk, having previously looked through the store's electronic catalogue on the Internet. Access to the Internet is made from home using her combined TV/personal computer. Her husband's birthday is just 24 hours away and she has almost decided what to buy him. "Do you still have stock of the Bosch cordless drill on special offer, as advertized in your electronic catalogue?" she asks. The store assistant moves to the computer screen to his left on the counter and enters an enquiry. Almost instantly he responds to the customer, "While we currently do not have any in stock, a shipment of Bosch cordless drills will be delivered this afternoon."

Technical description: There were several ways in which to establish a connection between their combined TV/personal computer and the Internet, but her son had chosen a simple modem connection via their existing telephone line (Public Switched Telephone Network) to an Internet Service Provider that had been recommended to him. Once connected to the Internet, she runs a computer program (called a Web browser) that displays information from a frequently accessed Web site (a computer that offers access to information). A number of other locations (Web sites) including a DIY Store have been conveniently added to a 'bookmark' list. By selecting the DIY Store from the bookmark, using a 'mouse' connected to the keyboard of the combined TV/DVD player/personal computer, the store's 'home page' is displayed on the screen with the option to select their electronic catalogue. Once an item (or items) has been chosen from the catalogue, ordering and payment screens are displayed; but since she wishes to purchase the Bosch cordless drill that same day, she decides to note the address of the local store.

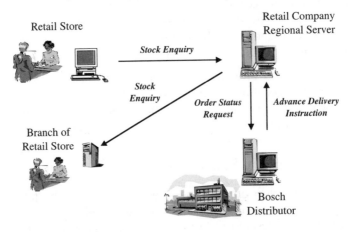

Figure 1.1 The birthday present

Responding to her question at the local store, the store assistant enters the enquiry using his computer keyboard and that is sent, firstly to the in-store computer, and then passed onto a regional server when no local stock is found. The screen displays the local stock-out condition and outstanding order information from the regional server, which indicates an imminent scheduled delivery from the Bosch distributor, as well as identifying stock availability in another local branch. The regional server, with its knowledge-based system, recognizes that this is the third enquiry made within two hours for this product, and initiates a network connection to the Bosch distributor's order processing system. A real-time Electronic Data Interchange (EDI) transaction is created and passed over the link to be processed instantly by the Distributor's order processing system. The response is returned instantly in the form of an EDI advance delivery instruction, confirming shipments that afternoon to several stores including the one in which the lady has now waited patiently for the shop assistant to respond to her simple question – which has taken just three seconds!

Sending Minutes of a Meeting

Simple Description: Due to a delay in the arrival of the in-coming aircraft, a businessman's flight is delayed by 45 minutes, which should give him just enough time to complete the minutes of the meeting held earlier that day with a prospective new client. He removes the lap-top computer from its case and proceeds to expand upon the notes he made earlier during the meeting. There are several follow-up items from the meeting which require immediate action. One such item concerns the need to establish exactly how much training is required for his prospective client to become proficient in the use of the new retail application, as well as including how much training is already a part of their standard contract. With the help of his mobile phone, which is connected to the lap-top computer, he establishes a connection to the service used by his company for information exchange and electronic mail (E-mail). While this is used both internally and externally, providing customers with access to a wide range of product information, company sensitive data related to clients is restricted solely to internal employees. In searching the database of existing clients from his lap-top computer connected to the service, he soon finds one with a similar set of circumstances to that of his prospect. He notes the E-mail address of the sales manager involved, then attaching the minutes of his meeting, creates and sends a message requesting advice on the approach to be taken. Just before the flight is called he creates a distribution list for the minutes of the meeting, noting that the recipients have a range of different types of E-mail addresses. The minutes of the meeting are sent and as he finishes packing away the lap-top computer and mobile phone, boarding commences. He can now relax on the journey home.

Technical Description: The businessman's mobile phone is using a digital cellular standard known as GSM (Global System for Mobiles) designed to replace all of Europe's analogue cellular mobile systems and provide Pan-European coverage. In practice, many other countries outside Europe have adopted this same standard. With the help of his GSM cellular phone connected into the lap-top computer via a PCMCIA card ('smart' pocket sized cards that plug into a slot in the lap-top computer providing a range of interface functions, including data communications), he establishes a connection to a network access point by entering a local telephone number. His company have put in place an Extranet (Internet-based service used for internal purposes and extended to include their own business community) based upon GE Global eXchange Services' Inter-Business Partner Service. This service is used for information exchange and E-mail. Once the 'Dial-up' connection is established to the network access point, a TCP/IP session is initiated, over which an Internet browser application is launched to help locate the required client information. Once this is completed, he prepares a short message using the E-mail client software integrated into the Internet browser application on his lap-top, creates a MIME attachment containing the meeting minutes, and sends the E-mail message to the central E-mail server for mailboxing and delivery. The distribution list (a single address that expands to a number of separate destination addresses) used for the circulation of the meeting minutes, consists of seven recipients, several with different types of addresses, including Internet mail, X.400 and facsimile.

Small Business User

Simple Description: A Sunday driver has dropped into his local AutoHelp shop for a stop-light bulb. It seems just like any other small store providing spare parts to local garages and DIY enthusiasts. There is a slight smell of oil in the air, tools on shelves, together with racks of pre-packaged components, paints and car cleaning materials. On the counter, on top of the two cash tills, are two screens, each with their own printer attached. Cables disappear into the counter to be connected to a computer no larger than a video recorder, on a shelf and protected by a wooden panel. Another cable follows a pillar on the counter into the roof only to terminate at another computer with screen and printer in a small office 10 metres away. "It's a great system," the shopkeeper explains. "It allows us to check stock availability, price each product and create a customer VAT receipt if required." The capital investment was not very high when compared to the people costs in running the business, and the considerable benefits that the system had brought in, reduced ordering time, increased stock availability, elimination of paperwork and improved customer service.

Technical Description: The cables (wireless LANs reduce the need for physical cables and are becoming increasingly popular) connecting the computers and associated equipment together form the basis of a local area network (LAN). This allows the computing resources within the store to be linked together and shared by users of the system. While there are several different types of LANs, the shop is using an Ethernet-based LAN (defines the manner in which devices transmit over the LAN and the rules that apply when multiple devices transmit at the same time) which is simple and cheap to install. In addition, Windows 2000 software (including computer network operating system) from Microsoft, is used to manage the computers and provide access to a file server (a computer together with a large amount of disk space for storing computer programs and data). One of the devices connected to the LAN is a router, which provides the means via an ISDN (Integrated Services Digital Network) line, to connect periodically to other LANs operated by regional wholesale distributors to the automotive after-market. ISDN lines are supplied by telecommunications companies in much the same way as telephone lines are provided (Public Switched Telephone Network) and can be used for both voice and data. An asymmetric digital subscriber line (see glossary for ADSL and DSL) broadband service is an alternative to ISDN connectivity. Apart from handling in-store transactions, the system used by AutoHelp also creates replenishment orders based upon sales and stock information; once confirmed these are sent electronically twice daily to several regional distributors based upon product sourcing information, with deliveries the same day for orders received before 11.30 am.

If you were unaware of such possibilities as shown by these three examples or are unclear about the use of some of the terms being used, then do not despair, just read on. This book is meant for you.

Business functions are increasingly performed electronically, whether by placing an order with a supplier, sending a message to a colleague, accessing a data warehouse for product information, or passing business transactions directly from one computer application to another. This book, with its focus upon doing business electronically, is relevant to organizations both large and small. It explains the current state of technology and how organizations can achieve significant benefits through e-Business.

We consider the complex environment organizations face today, which is having a profound effect on the way they operate, before looking in detail at e-Business. Changes over the last 30 years have been dramatic, and the business world has come to understand the value of information and how it can be exploited for competitive advantage, providing the stimulus for the emergence of a new industry centred around IT.

Organizational Change

Think about your own organization or other organizations with whom you work. What is happening to them today? They are subject to a pace of change unrivalled in business history as they compete in the turbulent environment of the new millennium. Whether they collapse, survive or prosper, will depend on how well they are able to adapt to these changes. Acquisitions, mergers, fresh legislation, new products, geographic spread, new markets, outsourcing, economic outlook, competition etc. are all symptoms of change, and illustrate its diverse nature.

The 'digital revolution' is bringing about structural changes within the economies of the more developed countries as profound as the 'industrial revolution' of the late 19th century. This is resulting in changing patterns of employment, with a decline in traditional manufacturing and a growth in the service sector. Automation has decreased the numbers required to support the manufacturing base and, due to labour costs, traditional manufacturing tends now to be transferred to the less developed countries. As more developed countries tend to base their economies around the growing services sector, the concept of the information age has emerged, based upon the rapid development and usage of IT. It is contributing to the highly competitive environment being experienced across all market sectors.

The impact of computer technology can be seen in research, its inclusion in product design for the replacement of mechanical parts, automation to displace human intervention, and within human activity systems known as business processes. Larger organizations started to show serious business interest in computers during the 1960s. Almost without exception, the point has now been reached where irrespective of organization size all new business processes incorporate a varying degree of IT content.

New Generation

Much of the process improvement achieved by organizations centres on the organization's ability to adapt to change and of finding new ways to tackle old problems. The situation continues to evolve as more and more people interact with computers as a normal part of their day-to-day lives, whether by paying at a store checkout, performing a transaction at a banking Automated Teller Machine (ATM), making a flight reservation, sending an E-mail message to a colleague or preparing a letter on their home computer.

New generations of employees are entering the business world today having a strong reliance and knowledge of IT gained from home usage, school and higher education. Their interaction with technology is natural and unflinching, initially coming from computer games, then through education where their keyboards skills rapidly become the envy of the most proficient secretary. This generation in their mid twenties are rapidly more able to embrace IT and live with change. This contrasts with older members of the organization who find it difficult to understand the technology and learn its jargon, and who often feel threatened as a result.

FunFigure 1.2 New generation

People and Information Technology

While the world has seen incredible technological advances over the last 150 years, the human race itself has remained largely unchanged for several thousands of years. The individual likes things to stay the way they are and will frequently seek to defend the status quo. We do not attempt here to define the proper corporate environment for change, but rather see it as vital to change the way the company operates and to successfully introduce a greater use of IT. Chapter 2 explores some of the techniques and programmes being adopted by the more progressive organizations as they seek to meet 'head-on' the necessity for change, and evolve as leading players in their chosen markets. The challenge is to do 'more' with less, to get 'more' out of the organization for less input.

This phenomenon is seen not only in large organizations, but is fast becoming a feature of business life for all; it is equally applicable to small start-up companies as to organizations in the public sector. However, because of their scale of operation, large organizations are generally more able to justify the IT expenditures that may accompany business process change, and to possess the people skill sets to carry them out.

In Europe, several initiatives are underway to encourage small and medium enterprises (SMEs) into undertaking the transformation necessary to secure the benefits being achieved by many of the larger organizations. In the long term, SMEs are likely to be the real beneficiaries of IT, and offer significant potential for the creation of wealth and capital.

These generalizations apply primarily to organizations that exist within more advanced or developed countries. Of the world's population, 50 per cent are still waiting to make their first telephone call, and only 10 per cent of the world's population have a basic voice telephone line. Of all telephone lines, 70% are found in countries that make up 15% of the world's population in total; but the situation is changing rapidly and the spread of global telecommunications infrastructures is forecast to accelerate over the next 20 years, providing access for a greater proportion of people in the developing countries.

The growth of global electronic business communications and its extension to commercial trading between companies (not to be confused with trading in financial markets), increasingly referred to as 'electronic business' or 'e-Business', is dependent upon the availability of basic telecommunications infrastructures. Governments of the world's leading nations are financing a number of initiatives in support of the so-called 'global digital information highway' based around the Internet.

The Business Manager

Today's business managers face increased pressure brought about by the changing environment, often requiring decisions of crucial importance to be taken within short timescales. The quality of these decisions is often affected by the availability of data, the creation of information and access to knowledge. The emphasis upon information and knowledge is illustrated in the way organizations are being re-structured, with reporting lines built around the contribution individuals make to the business. This is different from the traditional hierarchical structure that accords power to individuals based upon their relative position within the hierarchy. Power in organizations today resides where information and knowledge are located, and knowledge is seen as the most enduring asset of any organization. It is hardly surprizing that emphasis continues to be placed on computer-based applications that deliver a wide range of information to meet the varying requirements of organizations, and their extended organizations (e.g. customers, suppliers, shipping agents etc.).

This implies organizational maturity drawn from experience gained in the development and introduction of computer-based applications; or for a smaller organization, a vision of what might be achieved and a practical understanding of computing by the management team. The successful exploitation of IT by an organization throughout its many business activities requires evolution over time. It would be difficult for an organization to embark on the introduction of a fully integrated computer system, without having first already built up some experience with a number of transactional applications.

The good news is that electronic business communications does represent a starting point for many smaller organizations, by providing the 'transport' on which important 'mail enabled' applications can be introduced.

Figure 1.3 – Age of turbulence and change

Globalization

For many years, organizations in Europe and North America have relocated or acquired plants globally in an effort to lower their production costs and improve margins. Examples include Marks and Spencer (UK) taking their garment production base to the Philippines and GE (USA) acquiring a factory in Hungary for domestic lighting. In essence, while globalization has been around for some years, what is new is the concept of the global marketplace and the phenomenal rate at which it has developed, enabling firms to access geographically dispersed markets. The adoption of a globalization strategy also means that organizations are less susceptible to downturns in any specific market and effectively spreads their risk. Clearly the Internet and its ability to reach customers on a global basis has been a primary catalyst for conducting e-Business in this way.

As the world shrinks, national companies are finding themselves in competition with global forces. There are numerous examples including motor vehicles, motor cycles, white goods such as washing machines, electronic equipment including televisions and computers. However, Internet companies, such as Amazon.com, are bringing a new meaning to globalization by revolutionizing the way book and other purchases are made across continents.

Political and Legislative

Changes taking place today within organizations in the more developed countries are revolutionary in character, and challenge many of the basic concepts on which organizations have operated over the last 100 years. This has come about through the 'digital revolution'. These changes have given rise to the concept of the information society, which for many goes far beyond the establishment of a technological infrastructure supporting a service economy. The information society should also create a business environment encouraging organizations to compete on an international basis, reducing unemployment and enriching the quality of life.

European Initiatives

During 1993, the Commission of the European Communities published a White paper entitled *Growth, Competitiveness, Employment – The challenges and ways forward into the 21st Century*, which stressed that information and communication technologies (ICT) had the potential to promote steady and sustainable growth and to increase competitiveness. This document was reviewed by the European Council in December 1993, which gave it its full support and requested that a further report on the information society be prepared by a group of prominent individuals, placing emphasis upon identifying actions to be taken. The resultant Bangemann Group Report entitled *Europe and the Global Information Society – Recommendations to the European Council*, was submitted to the European Council in May 1994. It highlighted the need for an acceleration of the telecommunications liberalization process, placing initiatives with the public authorities to create public interest, and laying the financing of an information infrastructure on the private sector.

The unexpected and spontaneous growth of the Internet since the mid 1990s, with an ever increasing usage by commercial users, demonstrates that the information society is on its way and that the concept of an information infrastructure or highway is a practical and desirable objective. The Internet, apart from confirming that the latent demand exists, has illustrated several inadequacies that need to be addressed in a final model of an information highway. These include problems with security, reliability and anti-social usage.

Technology in itself is not the problem in achieving mass-market demand. Technology is frequently in search of an application and its availability outstrips market demand. The objective is to identify the applications of real value to organizations who can then exploit the uniqueness of the technology to achieve some form of competitive differentiation. A good example in Europe is the availability of Integrated Services Digital Networks (ISDN) which outstrips its deployment in North America; it represents an opportunity for European organizations to develop completely new applications, offering facilities through the use of multimedia (data, voice and image) previously not thought possible by end users. Present ISDN services are progressively moving to the even more powerful Broadband ISDN technology, based upon Asynchronous Transfer Mode (ATM), further increasing the capacity for multimedia based applications. In addition, the introduction of high speed modem technology, incorporating in-built compression and error correction, as well as the deployment of Asymmetric Digital Subscriber Lines (ADSL) to the home are further reminders that technological infrastructure is ahead of its exploitation.

US Initiatives and the Internet

Discussion of the 'information superhighway' started in the US in 1992 during the Presidential Election campaign waged by Clinton and Gore. After the election, this turned into the programme known as the National Information Infrastructure (NII). Since then a good deal of progress has been made, particularly by the private sector, with a focus towards the development of new market opportunities in home entertainment, including interactive TV and video on demand. Both in the US and Europe such services are available, but it is difficult to forecast when the mass market for these services will emerge. While initiatives are underway in the home entertainment sector, it is in the 'business-to-business' and 'business-to-consumer' sectors that most interest is focused, with projects such as CommerceNet[1], MecklerWeb[2] and Internet Shopping (see Chapter 10), where the long-term economic benefits and the impact upon society are potentially far greater.

The vision of the National Information Infrastructure (NII) as seen by the Clinton Administration provided for a seamless network, universal access, and an open competitive environment, while addressing major applications of social significance (e.g. Healthcare) and making government accessible to all. There are a wide range of participants in the process, including: Federal and State government, equipment vendors, service providers, information providers, various associations and user groups. Apart from architectural design, there are numerous technical issues including interoperability, routing (particularly with mobile computing), quality of service, security, data organization, user interfaces and heterogeneous networks (e.g. telephone, cable etc.). As well as the involvement of many existing bodies in the process (some traditionally involved with standards). A cross agency group was established known as the Information Infrastructure Task Force (IITF) to assist in gaining agreement on policy matters such as information (intellectual property rights and privacy), telecommunications (universal service and network reliability), standards and security.

During the Group of Seven (G7) Summit meeting held in July 1994 (Naples), President Clinton made a proposal for a Global Information Infrastructure (GII) and it was agreed to hold a G7 Special Committee meeting in February 1995 to agree the common rules on which the GII should be developed. Some of the issues addressed during this meeting covered intellectual property rights, interoperability, security and privacy protection. The ultimate goal for the GII is to contribute to an improvement in international trade and the worldwide economy.

The Clinton Administration took a further step in July 1997 with the release of a report entitled *A Framework for Global Electronic Commerce*, which set out the Administration's vision of the emerging electronic marketplace and, very importantly, for the first time outlined the principles that would guide the US Government's future actions to promote the new electronic age of commerce. It was both a recognition of the significant impact that the Internet and the electronic revolution has had in transforming people's lives – trading on the Internet alone is tripling every year – and an acceptance that, by their actions, governments can have a profound effect on the growth of e-Commerce. The document covered a set of principles, financial issues, legal issues (including security) and market access (including standards) to guide the evolution of commerce on the Internet. In addition, for the first time, it legitimized the use of the term 'electronic commerce' to describe the manner in which traditional paper-based commerce is rapidly moving to electronic-based commerce and the importance of the Internet in this transition.

Initiatives in the Far East

Japan is already very well advanced in the re-cabling of its telecommunications backbone network with optical fibre, which is part of a project to link all Japanese businesses and homes by the year 2010, using an advanced broadband telecommunications infrastructure. Other countries in the region have also started projects aimed at the introduction of information infrastructures.

These moves all serve to demonstrate the commitment of many of the world's leading nations to play their role in safeguarding competitive forces in the marketplace, and respond positively to initiatives that make the 'digital revolution' an economic reality.

Competition

Many organizations have been forced to look at their existing business processes, established over the years, to assess whether or not they are applicable to the way of working now demanded by the new business order. In many cases, it is clear that processes that were appropriate to the organization during the 1980s and 1990s are now irrelevant. This realization has resulted in some tough management decisions as companies seek to redefine organizational goals, calling for new levels of productivity and financial performance.

While the business world has rarely been characterized as a stable one, in past decades, organizations were allowed to develop marketing strategies which focused on competing upon price or various forms of product or service differentiation. In some market sectors, such as retailing, price still dominates the nature of competition although, when price parity is achieved, there is a need to find new forms of differentiation the customer perceives to be of value. Even in those market sectors where it is possible to achieve value differentiation, price, while no longer the key competitive differentiator, still remains an important component of the marketing mix. This in turn places a pressure on margins and a need to control cost of sales if price flexibility is to be achieved. The ideal situation is where, either the products or services marketed by the company have such a uniqueness or high perceived value to the purchaser, that price is not a key factor and the potential savings and benefits greatly outweigh the price.

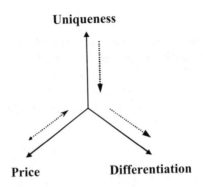

Figure 1.4   Competitive dimensions

However, for many organizations, the arrival of competition means a reduction in the uniqueness of their product or service (Figure 1.4), which in turn means that prices come under pressure and margins are eroded. There is a limit to which it is tenable to continue price discounting and, therefore, other forms of uniqueness are sought to which a purchaser attaches a value. These new forms of uniqueness are typically associated with differentiated services and heavily supported by IT innovation.

Case Study – Wincanton Logistics

Wincanton Logistics (Wincanton) is a distribution and warehousing company which during the 1990s embarked upon a major redesign of its internal business processes, geared to a much greater control of costs. Wincanton operate from 100 locations throughout the UK with 12,000 employees, 9,600 vehicles and 3 million sq ft of warehousing space. They provide services to their parent organization the Unigate group, as well as to other major companies including Tesco, Somerfield, Unipart, Texaco and Shell, operating in various industry sectors including retail, manufacturing and petroleum.

Wincanton's revenues are in excess of £450 million and, due to the highly competitive nature of their industry where profit margins are extremely cost sensitive, it has developed a corporate culture centred around the control of costs. Costing information is developed in detail when making proposals to potential clients, and wherever possible, is very closely monitored in their day-to-day operation via direct cost allocation to individual clients. This information is used for competitive advantage and is critical when negotiating the extension of contracts to ensure that the business remains profitable.

During 1992, Wincanton initiated a comprehensive internal review to establish ways in which information technology could provide greater support to the business, resulting in the development of a long-term IT strategy. By 1994, Wincanton reached the stage where it began to review how it could further improve access to financial information for control purposes and embarked upon a project known as Wincanton Information System Enterprise (WISE). The objective was to implement a new financial consolidation package which would collect and exchange information between a number of business applications, such as vehicle management, purchasing, warehousing and distribution.

Wincanton has data centres running IBM servers (RS6000, AS/400) together with PCs linked to local area networks and connected over a private TCP/IP wide area network-based upon BT leased lines and Racal switching technology. In fact, over 600 personal computers (PCs) are geographically spread throughout the UK and connected to the network. In setting out the basis for the development of WISE, it was decided to use some existing legacy applications, to introduce new development methodologies and database tools, and to place a heavy emphasis upon standard packaged software.

GE's Enterprise System – an EDI VAN gateway – was at the heart of developments being used to integrate the different legacy and new applications, some existing upon disparate platforms. Wincanton had been exchanging EDI data with some of its clients using PCs connected to GE's EDI*Express Tradanet Service. However, as part of the WISE project, work was undertaken to ensure that specific applications became EDI capable so that business information could be exchanged electronically with their clients.

WISE has proved to be highly effective, giving the following results:

▷ Cost reduction across the supply chain

▷ Improved customer service – exceeded national average for on-time delivery – Wincanton 99.8% (national average 88%)

▷ Exceeded national average for vehicle up-time – Wincanton 98% (national average 87%)

The ability to integrate information across disparate systems, including new financial software packages and legacy applications, allowed Wincanton to meet its objective of using standard software packages (with minimal customization). As Wincanton has acquired new businesses or created fresh ones associated with new service contracts, the flexibility provided by the EDI VAN gateway has allowed the integration between applications to be achieved easily and within aggressive timescales. In addition, the system architecture allows Wincanton to split their financial systems into two distinct sets of accounts, primarily for convenience and ease of management, while retaining the ability to rapidly create a consolidation of accounts when required.

Wincanton see IT as a powerful weapon which has allowed them to remain extremely efficient and, more importantly, has helped them derive a competitive advantage, as more and more business transactions are being handled electronically, both internally, and increasingly externally, using EDI with their trading partners.

A major redevelopment of systems has taken place over the last few years and several new applications have been implemented. These include:

▷ Vehicle Management System, including Workshop and Maintenance Control

▷ Sundry purchasing

▷ Warehouse Management System

▷ Site/Vehicle-based data capture systems

▷ Traffic Management System

▷ Financial Ledgers, Vehicle Costing and Contract Accounting

▷ Management reporting – utilizing business intelligence tools for database queries and EIS

The EDI VAN gateway performs the routing and interfacing of transactions between the various applications, and external links with customers and suppliers.

The current business environment demands that organizations monitor and control their costs to achieve the desired financial performance, as well as being in a position to respond positively to market price pressures. Whereas organizations could compete on price alone in the 1980s and early 1990s, this no longer applies in the new millennium where discerning purchasers expect aggressive pricing, as well as high quality, superior customer service and speed in product innovation.

It is the combination of computing power and data communications that has allowed companies to develop new business applications that provide an 'edge' over the competition. Typically this is achieved by incorporating IT, with its speedy access to information, into their products and services, offering the opportunity for improved customer service. However, this is by no means a new phenomena as the following examples illustrate:

Example AA Sabre System

Classic examples go back to the 1960s when American Airlines introduced their SABRE system, an interactive reservation system. In addition to operational improvements, including lower staffing levels and increased aircraft loading (numbers of passengers per flight), by placing their computer terminals into the travel agencies, they immediately achieved an edge over the competition, by making it much easier to book a seat with American Airlines.

Example   American Hospital Supply Company

The American Hospital Supply Company increased their sales on average by 13% per year during 1978 to 1983 largely by an innovative use of IT. They connected hospitals directly into their online order entry system. The result was to eliminate the effort involved in ordering hospital supplies and achieve differentiation over the competition.

Example   Benetton

In the mid 1980s, Benetton introduced a system that allowed its agents around the world to transmit their orders electronically. This resulted in a reduced cycle time from 10/12 days to a few hours ensuring that their distributors received goods a lot sooner; it also enabled them to react much faster to market trends than the competition.

Example   DHL

The marketplace for global physical package/document delivery has experienced phenomenal growth. As an integral part of its service, DHL needed to put in place administrative systems which would cater for fluctuations in load and improve the quality of information in response to customer queries. This resulted in the development of a global package/document tracking system that substantially improved communications between offices handling shipments and also improved the tracking of specific deliveries, enabling a positive response to customer enquires concerning delivery status.

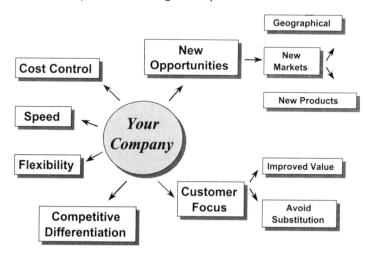

Figure 1.5   Implications: Adapting to change

Industry Re-structuring

Things are happening much faster; distance and time are contracting; customer expectations for instant service are growing; time to market is reducing; all serving to increase the pace of business. Some of this is due to improvements in logistics, particularly in air travel; much is made possible through new IT infrastructures, commonly known as 'information highways' now spanning the more developed countries.

With the pace of technology innovation and the emergence of the customer driven environment, product lifecycles are much shorter and obsolescence a continual threat. Alvin Toffler[3] comments on this fact when he says: "The forces that have made mass society have suddenly been thrown into reverse. The mass market has split into ever-multiplying, ever-emerging sets of mini-markets that demand a continually expanding range of options, models, types, sizes, colours and customizations, creating a totally new framework within which the production organizations of society will function." Another significant trend in North America and Europe is the move away from manufacturing economies to service economies with employment and wealth shifting between the two (see Chapter 11). With many more people employed in service industries this raises fresh challenges for management to find suitable ways to motivate and sustain productivity of growing numbers of office or so called 'knowledge' workers.

Example Financial Services

The Financial Services sector has energetically embraced IT, causing dramatic changes in the way that some of their services now operate. Traditional trading floors have been replaced by screens and keyboards to enable electronic trading to take place, together with links into back office systems to speed up the completion of the transaction. In foreign exchange markets, banks need to have a complete picture of their currency holdings around the world, and to set limits to such holdings minimizing risk and potential exposure by adverse fluctuations. The collapse of Barings Bank (UK) illustrated the dangers inherent when such systems are not in place. Another example is evident in the increasing use of automated teller machines (ATMs) and credit cards by the public, and the subsequent reduction in visits to their banks. This in turn has enabled some banks to re-structure their operations causing the shedding of large numbers of employees or their deployment into roles providing more direct customer contact. In a commodity marketplace such as banking, this is a deliberate strategy aimed at winning business by focusing upon customer service.

Example Fashion Industry

> The Fashion industry is heavily influenced by the need to bring new designs to the marketplace in advance of competition; the same trend also exists in the computer industry. There is an explosion of new products, where technical innovation and the ability to exploit speed of introduction, known as 'time to market,' can provide a head start on the competition.

Example Office Supplies

> New management techniques such as Electronic Data Interchange (EDI) play a key role in making this possible by speeding up the process. Brun Passot, a French company in the office supplies business, is one such example. Through EDI and other direct customer ordering techniques, it has been able to respond far more rapidly to customer demand, to help reduce customer inventories and to build customer loyalty. The result has been to capture a significant percentage of the highly fragmented French marketplace for office supplies.

Customer Service

The well-known quality initiatives of the 1980s have progressively become diffused within organizations to reflect a corporate culture in which a total quality management (TQM) philosophy is now fully established. TQM is aimed at optimizing the internal working practices of the organization to eliminate inefficiencies and hence unnecessary cost. It encourages involvement and helps motivate individuals to work together, improving upon existing practices. This has led to a growing trend among companies to seek ISO 9000 accreditation, as a means of demonstrating to customers that they follow well-established internal procedures and processes, to ensure that high levels of quality excellence are sustained. The 1980s saw a number of companies using quality for competitive differentiation, thus enabling them to secure high prices.

People and organizations have become more discriminate about the products and services that they seek to purchase, placing fresh demands on suppliers who wish to win both new and repeat business. While the 1980s were heavily influenced by the importance of quality, the continuing passion is still for customer service.

Example Domestic Insurance

> A classic example of combining strong customer focus together with a highly competitive offering is Direct Line, a UK subsidiary of the Royal Bank of Scotland[4]; it offers instant quotations and insurance for domestic

customers over the phone. Set-up in 1985, with its telephone-based and computer-supported customer contact, Direct Line insures over 2 million vehicles making it the UK's largest private motor insurance company. In many respects, it has redefined the manner in which private vehicle insurance is sold in the UK and, despite achieving a competitive edge for a period of time, it now faces strong competition from other insurance companies offering similar services. In effect this method of selling private vehicle insurance has now become the norm and it is a competitive disadvantage not to be able to operate in this manner. Having established brand recognition by nature of its operation, Direct Line is able to offer competitive pricing without sacrificing quality of service. However, having lost the initial competitive edge, it is now seeking new ways of service differentiation to stay ahead of its competition.

Example   Automotive After-market

Another similar example is Kwik-Fit, which has built up a network of workshops throughout the UK, offering replacement tyres, batteries, exhausts etc. with a very strong emphasis upon customer service, or what Kwik-Fit terms as customer delight in the service offered. This approach is complemented by a robust, but simple to operate, computer system that provides customer quotations of price and stock availability, as well as billing and payment. The address information collected from the customer at the time of payment provided the basis of a mailing list that enabled Kwik-Fit in 1995 to move into a new business venture of car insurance, using the successful formula already established by Direct Line and described earlier.

Sales Channels

Traditional means of selling has involved face-to-face interaction with the customer usually in a shop, direct mail or other promotional campaigns using the written word and finally the telephone; personified by the cold calling double-glazing salesperson. The Internet has introduced a fourth sales channel for companies to reach home consumers or their business customers. The characteristics of this fourth sales channel will be described in greater detail in later chapters. However, it is clearly an important development and with the increased market penetration of Internet access both within business and in the home, it is rapidly becoming an important means of generating additional sales volumes.

Technology

Organizational use of IT has evolved through several distinct stages over the last 30 years. Initially, there was a heavy focus towards operational improvements centred around reduced costs, followed by a tactical emphasis upon achieving improved effectiveness, particularly for the individual. More recently interest in IT has been dominated by the strategic contribution it can make towards gaining competitive advantage.

As new generations of employees schooled with a strong reliance upon IT enter the business sector, the digital or information revolution is giving rise to expectations of an Information Society. This concept is actively supported by many governments around the world through initiatives such as the building of information highways, to be used by both consumers and the business sector. A six layer model illustrates the telecommunications infrastructure required to support an Information Society, and how this links to the specific requirements of the business sector.

The steady increase in the usage of electronic business communications is being helped by several popular IT trends; these include, end user computing incorporating Local Area Networks, distributed 'open' computing, high performance networking and multimedia documents.

To compete in this new economic environment, companies will be required to extend their customer driven philosophies and adopt 'best' business practices, making the most effective use of technology. This allows them to:

▷ Reduce support costs and improve business effectiveness
▷ Use IT as an enabler to re-design business processes
▷ Swiftly introduce new and differentiated products and services
▷ Compete better on the basis of value, time, uniqueness and customer service

Efficiency Improvements

Early business computing activities tended to focus upon automating well-defined business processes, aimed at improving efficiency within the organization. Popular uses were in finance and production departments, where the computer's ability to process large quantities of repetitive information rapidly resulted in savings in time and effort. Both the technology itself, and the ability of organizations to use it, largely influenced the early uses of computers in terms of scope and impact. As part of the evolution, it became possible to achieve important new cost reductions, usually in staffing, simply by taking transactional and operational business processes and mapping these into data processing systems. It was accepted that as a precursor for computerization, the business processes themselves required restructuring and that the claimed efficiency improvements, owed as much to the resulting simplification and streamlining as the use of the computer itself. This does not diminish the importance of the resultant applications which were able to support significant increases in volume with much smaller incremental levels of staffing.

Example   Hawker Siddeley Aviation

In the late 1960s, Hawker Siddeley Aviation (now part of British Aerospace) embarked upon an ambitious programme to design and implement a company production control system for use across its six UK sites. Significant productivity improvements were a direct result from the rationalization of paperwork and procedures that took place in parallel with the design of the system; but this process took time because of the need to gain consensus across the sites. The exercise converged on a common set of documentation including engineering process layouts, work order paperwork and inter-company transfer of work. The introduction of the production control system resulted in staff savings approaching 50%, excluding the re-deployment of staff to new roles associated with the maintenance of the new system. In addition, the production control system, together with the same level of staffing, was able to support increased volumes of work as the aircraft production rate steadily increased.

Personal Effectiveness

Advantages were soon realized: with ready access to information, carried by the transactions feeding the finance and production applications, accounts receivables could be sold to factoring companies and stock availability information could improve customer service. New IT capabilities centred around data communications evolved to serve the growing requirement of unleashing information, such that information could be distributed to those in the organization that could best use it.

The period that followed in the early 1980s was orientated towards the effectiveness of the individual, brought about by the personal computer. While revolutionary at the time, dramatic price/performance improvements in computer technology now offers increased processing power and information storage on the desktop never thought possible 15 or more years ago. This has given birth to a complete new industry in software products that aims to service corporate information requirements at the desktop, including, word processing, spreadsheets,

E-mail and bulletin boards, together with the underlying operating system and network software that makes this possible. Companies such as Microsoft, Lotus and to a lesser extent Novell have emerged as significant players in this marketplace, and now exert a strong influence in much the same way that the industry was dominated by IBM (76% of the world market) in the late 1970s. IBM's acquisition of Lotus in 1995 demonstrates the power exerted by the software industry and the importance to a company such as IBM in securing its competitive position in the IT marketplace.

The most important advances in IT concern data communications and networking allowing computers, sometimes whole communities of computers, to be linked together. As organizations at the turn of the millennium seek new ways of conducting business, their ability to communicate with customers, suppliers, manufacturers, banks etc. places greater reliance upon data communications facilities. The personal computer has evolved into a communications device providing access to information, whether held on a local file server linked to a local area network (LAN), or on a corporate file server reached via a wide area network (WAN). Information access is positioned alongside the traditional desktop applications such as word processing, spreadsheets, and communications intensive applications, such as E-mail and Electronic Data Interchange (EDI).

Six Layer Model

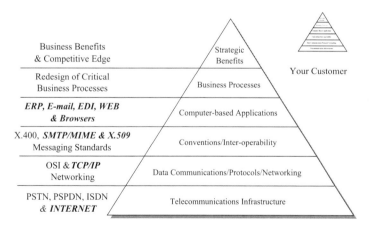

Figure 1.6 Thick architecture

Figure 1.6 shows a six layer model that has been developed to illustrate the link between the telecommunications infrastructure required to support an Information Society, with a specific emphasis to business users. Clearly conventions/rules/standards need to be adopted if different parts of an organization, or indeed completely different organizations, are to be successfully exchanging business information between their respective computer-based applications.

While there are many aspects that need to be addressed, international standards assume a new level of importance when information highways are to be extended from national to global usage. Many de jure (international) and de facto (industry) standards already exist that are entirely relevant to the various elements making up the architecture that supports the information highway. A comprehensive review of standards in e-Business is provided in Chapter 16.

Some of these terms might at first sight seem strange and for those readers keen to learn more, later chapters and the glossary provide further details. The key requirement at this stage is to understand the basic concepts. Telecommunications infrastructures are fundamental to the growth of e-Business and require support and guidance from governments to ensure that they evolve in much the same way as the inland canal, railway and road networks have done in the past. All the same analogies apply: the need to avoid congestion, road works and sufficient capacity on the trunk routes to handle the volume of traffic.

Another important observation based on research conducted by the authors is the increasing trend by organizations towards the convergence of conventions/rules/standards and even applications, with a strong preference towards those that are either open standards-based or have strong market acceptance. The resultant 'thick' IT architecture makes it easier to focus on the real use of technology, rather than worrying about interfacing issues. As an example, the Internet Protocol (IP) which defines the manner in which data is transported in containers over information highways, is being used within organizations (Intranets), between trading partners (Extranets) and as a means of reaching other organizations attached to the Internet. For the first time a homogeneous 'open standards -based highway' exists capable of being used by everyone, whether within the same building or across the world. This removes obstacles and brings much needed simplification to the use of information technology.

In Figure 1.6 the first four layers represent the 'thick architecture' referred to above and those standards in 'italics' represent the winners that are supporting the phenomenal growth of e-Business.

Public information highways use existing telecommunications infrastructures, typically the telephone (PST), packet switched (PSPDN) networks and the Internet to transport a wide range of electronic business communications. This has yet to reach mass market proportions, but without the further deployment of broadband services, will be inadequate to handle future multimedia applications that require much greater speeds. Even for organizations that build their own private networks, they still need to connect to the 'public' information highway to reach other organizations. Dramatic progress is being made both in Europe and the North America in the delivery of cost effective high speed services for both the 'business-to-business' and 'business-to-consumer' market sectors.

Business Productivity Improvements

Organizational change is needed to bring about improvements in business productivity. How can IT assist in redirecting employees' efforts into more 'value added' activities? By their very nature, many industries command a uniqueness reflected in specific business processes. Most organizations use a range of business communications facilities for internal communications within and between departments, as well as with their trading partners. Since the mid 1980s, the use of e-Business has grown at a rapid rate, and is seen as an important management tool in the fight to achieve business productivity improvements.

Assuming parity of product or service, the ability for organizations to achieve an 'edge' over the competition, combining a compelling marketing mix with innovative use of IT, will not continue indefinitely. The challenge is to extend the window of competitive edge for as long as possible, since over time competition will move to adopt the new practice, and it then becomes the 'norm' for the industry. Those organizations that do not adopt it will suffer competitive disadvantage, but for the market leaders, the search goes on to identify new forms of competitive differentiation.

Change and Information Technology

The organizational changes initiatives described earlier have set expectations on the ability of IT to serve the organization and its extended organization (e.g. customers, suppliers, shipping agents etc.) primarily through the use of electronic messaging and information technologies. The impact of technology, as described in this chapter, clearly indicates that this expectation is a reality for many organizations in the way they operate today.

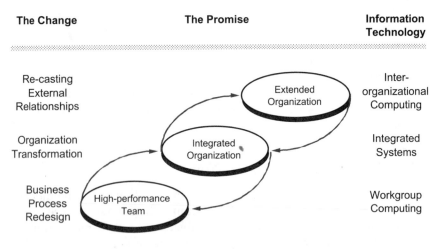

The Change	The Promise	Information Technology

Figure 1.7 Competitive pressures in the 1990s

The above schematic illustrates how organizational change may be viewed, firstly through a focus upon business process improvements, rather than respecting the traditional boundaries erected by the functional organization; secondly restructuring and cultural changes that bring about fresh ways of working and acceptance of new corporate values; and finally, recasting the external relationships away from adversarial, to integrate the extended organization fully into the overall functioning of the business. Electronic messaging and information technologies that embrace workgroup computing are ideal for this purpose, and can provide the tactical means for organizations to achieve the promise of a boundaryless operation with a free flow of information to those that need it. Organizations are realizing the critical contribution being made by their extended enterprise in being able to achieve identified business goals. At a practical level, this requires close integration of business processes between the parties, typically supported by sound business practices such as electronic data interchange (EDI). As an example, a major retailer may well be extremely effective in its own operation, but without an efficient supply chain that closely integrates its suppliers with its own internal business processes, competitive advantage will be lost.

---

[1] CommerceNet is a nonprofit consortium to jointly develop and implement new e-Commerce technologies and business practices worldwide. www.commerce.net

[2] www.mecklerweb.com is US publisher MecklerMedia's commercial Internet presence, providing daily Internet news, company announcements and a multi-storey shopping mall.

[3] Alvin Toffler, The Third Wave

[4] Royal Bank of Scotland www.royalbankscot.co.uk

Framework for e-Business

Introduction

Messaging forms the nervous system of any organization. Hardly any business activity can take place without messages being exchanged; progress reports, requests for help, arrangements for meetings, instructions to co-workers, purchase orders, delivery notes, invoices and so on ...

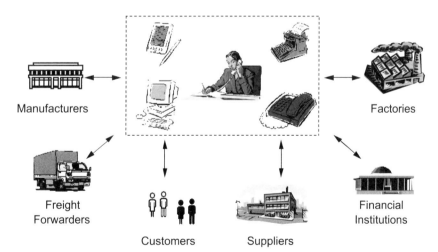

Manufacturers

Factories

Freight Forwarders

Customers

Suppliers

Financial Institutions

Figure 2.1 Business *means* communications

Until relatively recently, most businesses operated at a leisurely pace within close and well-defined geographic boundaries, and messages could be written or typed on pieces of paper and distributed by internal or external postal services. For urgent messages, or for communications where a degree of interaction between the parties was necessary, electrical devices have been available for about a century. The telegraph and its descendant, the telex, provided for expensive, rapid, long distance delivery of short written messages, and the telephone enables two people to communicate, providing they are both available at the same time and have a language in common. The remarkable degree of co-operation between national telephone companies allows telex and telephone messaging to take place, simply and without the intervention of operators, on an almost worldwide basis.

Mintzberg wrote in 1972:

> One can perhaps visualise the organization of the future with teletype terminals in the offices of each senior executive. Then, true to the manager's information needs, the transmission of instant communication would be automated. The transmitter of information would simply choose which managers were to receive a current bit of news. He would then key in the code to open the proper channels, and would enter the message which would appear simultaneously in the appropriate offices.[1]

However, during the past 40 years, this cosy world has changed:

▷ Business has become much more international in nature; for example, a product may be designed in Europe, assembled in Taiwan using components bought from a dozen countries around the world, and then packed with additional components into a complete system in Europe, ready for worldwide distribution.

▷ Competitors are no longer just the companies up the road; they are often from other continents and intent on extending their markets across the world.

▷ Customers have become more demanding, expecting immediate response to their requests, whether for goods or for information.

▷ The regulatory environment has changed – and will continue to change – as governments seek to encourage competition, and as consumer protection and environmental issues become more important.

▷ Information technology has become more pervasive, particular with the adoption by business of the Internet and its associated technologies.

To keep pace with these changes, messaging systems have had to adapt. The laboriously typed letter or memo, carried from place to place by the postman, has given way to electronic or digital messages, created in a computer and distributed by electronic means to other computers, and thus Mintzberg's prophesy has indeed come true. Some electronic messages are still typed by, addressed to and read by humans, but another class are created, addressed, received and interpreted completely automatically.

Origins of Electronic Business

A fundamental feature of business today is the need to obtain, store and communicate information, so that individuals have access to the necessary facts from which decisions can be made and actions taken. In many respects these basic capabilities tend to be taken for granted without much consideration given to the very dramatic changes that have taken place in the 'office' and across 'businesses' over a relatively short period of time. For the practitioner or student attempting to master the fundamentals of e-Business, the ongoing discussions about terminology only tends to cloud their understanding of the subject. This chapter aims to present a simple framework in which to describe the key terms and to trace the origins of e-Business to its current evolution. Remarkable as it may seem, the position has been reached whereby the use of the term 'electronic' is largely becoming irrelevant since most business is now conducted electronically.

However, before the arrival of today's electronic era, traditional business communications in most companies were dominated by the use of postal services, telex and telephone. Indeed, until the 1970s, most internal business communications within organizations was heavily paper-based and supported by a network of secretaries often grouped into typing pools. These secretarial functions created a wide range of business documents including internal and external correspondence, office forms, business records, process sheets, shop floor documentation, etc. During the 1970s with increasing use of computers by business, typing pools started their decline with a transformation into data preparation departments supporting the newly arrived computer-based applications (financial ledgers, payroll, stock, work in progress, etc.). Finally with the arrival of online processing, such functions ceased to exist in much the same way that 'secretarial functions' in offices started to disappear with the arrival of the personal computer in the 1980s.

Electronic Business Communications

During the 1970s, electronic typewriters and then word processors started to make their presence felt within the office environment. Word processors came in a variety of different configurations from single user to multi-user systems, from companies such as Wang that have long since disappeared from the computing landscape. However, the arrival of the personal computer in the 1980s heralded the most dramatic changes in the 'office' introducing desktop computing for the first time. The applications introduced were a natural evolution from the mainframe and multi-user systems, including the electronic mail (E-mail), word processing and spreadsheets. The interconnection of personal computers using local area networks (LANs) and adoption of graphical user interfaces (GUIs) increased the possibilities by re-designating the personal computer as an 'easy to use' communication device.

Much of the early experience in electronic business communications was within medium to large organizations, which were able to establish their own private data communications networks linking office locations and making electronic messaging possible. Many of the mainframe and mid-range computer manufacturers by introducing E-mail applications seized the opportunity to sell more equipment. However, since the E-mail applications introduced were based upon the vendor's proprietary messaging technology, these systems were incompatible and prevented the interchange of messages between them. This created 'islands of electronic messaging', sometimes even within organizations deploying disparate systems across different divisions of the same company. This situation naturally frustrated the growth in external electronic business communications with trading partners (suppliers, logistics companies, banks, etc.).

During this same period much was happening in the field of telecommunications with the emergence of organizations known as value added networks (VANs), offering a limited range of network based services to larger organizations, including E-mail. The services offered were largely constrained by monopolistic legislation existing in many countries outside the US. In Europe, governments within the European Economic Community (EEC) were beginning to see the real competitive potential that telecommunications could bring to their economies, resulting in the 1987 Telecommunications Green Paper. This legislation heralded the re-regulation of data communications services across Europe, eliminating the monopolistic powers of state-controlled telecommunications and introducing competition into the marketplace.

Electronic Mail (E-mail)

In this book electronic mail (E-mail) is defined as 'person-to-person electronic messaging'. It is also known as inter-personal messaging (IPM), but inter-personal messaging is a term that is diminishing in use and popularity.

After mainframe computers gained the ability to service communities of remote users, each with a simple terminal, users soon realized that the computer itself could be used to provide a personal messaging system.

All that was necessary was for the sender to type a message and leave it as a file with the recipient's name attached. At some later time the recipient could retrieve the message and, if need be, relabel the file to pass on the message to another reader or initiate a response to the original sender.

Such an informal mechanism will work perfectly well for a small, close-knit group of users who can agree upon a simple file naming convention for message addressing, but can descend into chaos when the user community grows. The result was the creation of simple E-mail systems which are built around a 'rack of electronic pigeon holes' or mailboxes. Each user is allocated a mailbox by a central administrative function, which can prevent duplication of names and handle message counting and billing activities. Simple security mechanisms were added to prevent users from peeking into other peoples' mailboxes, and the outcome was the direct precursor of the 'private' or in-house E-mailing systems available today from computer vendors and third party software suppliers. IBM's PROFS, Digital's ALL-IN-1™ system, Microsoft Exchange, Lotus's Notes and Internet Mail are well-known examples.

Ray Tomlinson, an American engineer is credited as being the 'father of E-mail' when he wrote a program in 1971 that enabled a user to send a message to a colleague, as long as the colleague was on the same computer. However, Tomlinson's real breakthrough was to invent the use of the @ symbol as part of the address to identify the particular computer on which the recipient's mailbox was located. So, a message is created with the aid of a computer terminal using a simple text editor, which usually forms part of the E-mail package. The subject, destination and copy addressees are added, and it is sent. The message is then immediately deposited into the recipient's mailbox and becomes available for retrieval.

With the growing popularity of E-mail within organizations helped by the arrival of LAN E-mail packages, greater interest was being shown in a common messaging standard that could eliminate the islands of messaging being created. In addition, such a solution would openly encourage greater external exchange of E-mail between trading partners. The public telecommunications operators, following the success of their data networks deployed on a global basis (packet switched public data networks based upon X.25), had through an International Telecommunications Union sub-committee, developed a standard for E-mail (they termed it 'inter-personal messaging') known as X.400. Public and private telecommunications operators sought to promote the X.400 standard as the basis for a global messaging environment, and indeed much progress was made in establishing both the technical and administrative infrastructure to make this happen. However, while technically an excellent specification, X.400 suffered from serious practical flaws including the addressing scheme which was viewed by many users as rather cumbersome. While still in use today across messaging backbone networks, X.400 has largely been displaced by its Internet equivalent standard known as Simple Mail Transfer Protocol/ Multipurpose Internet Mail Extensions (SMTP/MIME). For those old enough to remember the arrival and evolution of video recorders, it is a bit like comparing the struggle between Betamax and VHS, which VHS eventually won.

What is the Internet?

Unless the reader has spent the last few years on another planet it would be difficult to avoid some exposure to the Internet, although interpretations, understanding and knowledge vary. The dramatic and unexpected explosion of electronic communications in the office and home that started during the 1990s is solely attributable to the Internet. It is the subject of numerous books and continues to attract a great deal of publicity and worldwide interest. Its origins lie in the US military, and spread into the academic and research communities with government funding. As colleges and universities around the world set-up their own computing environments the Transmission Control Program/Internet Protocol (TCP/IP) architecture became a popular choice. It was not long before campus networks based upon TCP/IP suite were being interconnected or internet-worked – hence the birth of the Internet.

In 1969 the US Department of Defence (US DoD) established a 'wartime digital communications' project to understand if it would be possible to design a network that could rapidly re-route data traffic around failed network nodes. The Defence Advanced Research Projects Agency (DARPA) launched the project and by 1975 declared the resultant DARPA Internet to be a success. Its management was then taken over by Defence Communications Agency and by 1980 the major protocols, still in use today, were stable and progressively adopted throughout ARPANET.

The US National Science Foundation (NSF) started the Supercomputer Centres program in 1986 since, until that point, supercomputers such as Crays were largely the playthings of large, well-funded universities and military research centres. NSF's objective was to make supercomputer resources available to those of more modest means by constructing five supercomputer centres around the US and building a network linking them with potential users. NSF decided to base their network on the Internet protocols, and NSFNET was born. For the next decade, NSFNET would be the core of the US Internet, until its privatization and ultimate retirement in 1995.

The creation of the World Wide Web (WWW or simply Web) has been one of the Internet's most exciting developments which has propelled the Internet into the public eye and caused the business world to take Internet technologies seriously. The idea of hypertext had been around for more than a decade, but in 1989 a team at the European nuclear research laboratory (CERN) in Switzerland developed a set of protocols for transferring hypertext via the Internet. In the early 1990s it was enhanced by a team at the National Centre for Supercomputing Applications (NCSA) at the University of Illinois, one of NSF's supercomputer centres. The result was NCSA Mosaic, a graphical, point-and-click hypertext browser that made Internet usage easy.

Aside from the Internet's technical progress over the last three decades, its sociological progress has been phenomenal, becoming a prominent feature of business life, as well as having an increasing presence within the home.

Electronic Data Interchange

In this book electronic data interchange (EDI) is defined as 'the electronic transfer of structured commercial data using agreed message standards between computer applications'.

Although banks started using electronic funds transfer (EFT) during the 1970s, EDI has its origins in the early 1980s when the first of the electronic trading communities was established. These companies, sometimes forming part of an industry group or association, could see the potential that electronic communications could bring in reducing time and costs by interfacing their computer based applications. Initial progress with EDI was partly frustrated by the availability at the time of cost effective information technology, as well as the increasing recognition that it was difficult to undertake EDI without the redesign of business processes and the resultant organizational impact this caused.

More specifically it was necessary to:

▷ Formalize and document activities

▷ Streamline and adapt business processes

▷ Agree common sets of rules and standards

While management commitment was necessary for the success of E-mail, this became even more critical for EDI as the processes were not solely under the control of one organization, but many organizations. It was under these circumstances that several competing service companies emerged to act as intermediaries for the exchange of electronic business documents between community members.

For those companies engaged in EDI, it is necessary to develop an organizational culture focused upon change and an acceptance of increased dependency upon IT. While there are real tactical benefits from EDI, such as reducing costs, there are also strategic benefits to be obtained by using the technology, primarily through the business relationships which are established between co-operating organizations, and the scope for using the information exchanged more effectively, leading to increased competitiveness.

Using a similar analogy to the creation of E-mail messaging islands referenced above, electronic information cannot be successfuly exchanged between computer-based applications belonging to two separate organizations unless some pre-agreement exists on its format, which implies some form of standardization of effort being established. While EDI initially emerged as a technology to speed the exchange of business documents, it has been burdened by the complexity of agreeing electronic document formats (EDI standards) and the difficulties in implementing them (see Figure 2.2).

Electronic Mail	Electronic Data Interchange
▷ Usually unstructured messages in textual format	▷ Structured messages in a standard electronic format
▷ More Intra-enterprise than Inter-enterprise	▷ Mainly Inter-enterprise
▷ Person-to-person	▷ Application-to-application
▷ Personal messages, forms and business reports	▷ Typically business transactions
▷ Usually no data format standard	▷ Data format standards increasingly UN/EDIFACT

Figure 2.2 E-mail & EDI characteristics

Benefits of EDI

Earlier in this chapter, we saw how E-mail has evolved from a myriad of little local user communities, with a need for a certain amount of inter-community messaging, into the global Internet community that we know today. While this was happening, a second form of electronic messaging came into being and followed a roughly parallel path. Electronic Data Interchange (EDI) was invented as a means for business documents, such as requests for quotations, purchase orders, invoices, acknowledgements, etc. to be passed directly from the sender's application to the complementary application in the recipient's computer.

The driving force was a need to reduce costs and improve customer service. By transferring a purchase order, for example, through some form of electronic messaging system, several benefits would arise:

▷ The order would be available to the vendor's computerized order entry application within a matter of minutes rather than the several days taken by conventional mail.

▷ Opportunities for orders to be misdirected, or simply lost, would be virtually eliminated.

▷ With the order already in computer-readable form, the expense, delay and possibility of introducing errors, all inseparable from keying the order into the recipient's computer, would all be eliminated.

▷ The customer would receive better service and, over time, the frequency of ordering could be increased without significant addition to overheads.

The last of these benefits is, perhaps, the most important since it has permitted the introduction of 'Just In Time' inventory philosophies. This allows wholesale buyers/purchasers, such as automobile assemblers or the large 'high street' retail stores, to phase out their goods inward stock-holdings, and move incoming goods direct to point of use or point of sale, with replenishments on a daily or even shorter cycle. Successful implementation of such systems provides for order-of-magnitude improvements in end-user service, enormous one-off savings, improved flexibility in production planning (i.e., giving the ability to make what is actually needed rather than what a planner thinks might be needed), and improved cash flows.

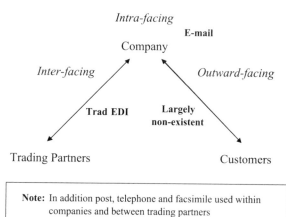

Figure 2.3 . Electronic business communications (1980s)

Figure 2.3 summarizes the situation during this period, showing how companies operated in three modes in support of their electronic messaging initiatives. First, 'intra-facing', involving the use of E-mail for internal business communications within and across the organization. The second mode involves 'inter-facing' with its trading partners using EDI linking business applications, but only adopted by a relatively small number of companies. Last, very little 'outward-facing' electronic messaging activities were undertaken with their customer base, where the relationship was dominated by traditional selling techniques of face-to-face, post or telephone.

Electronic Commerce

The term e-Commerce has been through an evolution since its initial usage in the early 1990s. This initial interpretation reflected the anticipated growth in the business-to-business market sector extending beyond EDI to other forms of electronic interaction between companies. The emergence of e-Commerce coincided with the steady growth of traditional EDI and new Web-based applications for 'inter-facing' between trading partners, and before any significant use of the Internet as a new sales channel to reach home consumers.

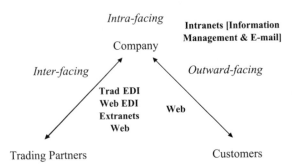

Figure 2.4 e-Commerce (early 1990s)

Acceptance of the Internet by the business world, particularly for E-mail, as well as access to information via the Web, has caused many organizations to consider applying this same model solely for internal usage. In this way organizations are able to harness the Internet's 'ease of use' and other benefits, yet avoid the security issues that figure highly in the list of concerns with open Internet access. Very simply the term 'Intranet' has evolved to describe the use of Internet technologies (although not exclusively) within an organization for enhancing connectivity and communications. Previously this may have involved the use of proprietary LAN E-mail systems together with bulletin boards or textual databases tailored to the specific needs of the organization.

Establishing an Intranet using open Internet standards makes it easier to purchase software, support users and extend its reach to trading partners at the appropriate time (see Figure 2.4).

The infrastructure, whereby specific trading partners forming part of the extended enterprise are given selective access to the organization's Intranet, is known as an 'Extranet'. Providing entry to corporate information via an Extranet introduces security issues requiring action to be taken to restrict unauthorized access to specific applications and information (normally only made available to employees) using some or all the following measures:

▷ System passwords

▷ Challenge/Response authentication

▷ Firewall techniques.

The primary motivation to implement Intranets is to improve the flow and timely access to information within an organization, as well as to facilitate collaborative working on corporate projects. Use of Internet technologies offer cost savings over competing alternatives, as well as reducing the training time for implementation. One-to-many publishing applications can significantly reduce the cost of producing, printing, shipping and updating corporate information. While two-way transaction driven applications can improve information quality and provide a highly efficient alternative to paper-based business processes. Finally, many-to-many interaction facilitates the exchange of information between interested individuals, perhaps forming part of a newsgroup, workgroup or conference.

While an Intranet serves the internal organization, and the Extranet extends the capability to major trading partners, it is quite likely that at some point open access to the Internet will be required. At this stage the software 'firewalls' mentioned above become even more critical in preventing access by the many millions of Internet users to precious proprietary corporate information. Additional security is needed when transiting the Internet to 'public' Web sites to enter sensitive information or when sending a business transaction over the Internet to a business partner via an E-mail attachment.

Various Examples

GE's Intranet includes access to information sources such as, human resources, employee benefits, hot news, travel agency, GE values, internal training, ideas forum, their public site as well as access to the individual Intranets of the separate GE businesses.

Ford developed the Mondeo (the world car) by establishing a worldwide team so that while one team slept another continued the work using common information sources, based upon an Intranet infrastructure.

Federal Express provide customers with browser-based access to their internal tracking system for shipment status enquires, which improves customer service and increases customer loyalty at reduced operational cost.

British Midland provides customers with online flight booking facilities using browser access which offers greater customer convenience at reduced costs.

Texas Instruments use Web Form based EDI for low cost customer data entry that is converted by a server into a standard format that can be processed by their internal application.

Case Study – BT

In the early 1990s BT (British Telecommunications plc) began to suffer from chronic internal problems because of paper overload. This coincided with a period when BT's business was becoming global in character and the pace of business was accelerating due to an increasingly competitive marketplace. The need to transmit information as well as support paper-based business processes resulted in major processing delays and rising costs. E-mail helped alleviate the situation, but only at the expense of major IT investments providing increased network and electronic storage media. Many electronic documents distributed as attachments were replicated and stored electronically many times over. This resulted in a Document Management System project being initiated in 1994.

In the same year BT began large-scale experimentation with the Internet's World Wide Web technology, and by early 1995 had concluded that this was the best means of improving internal access to information. In addition the same browser technology could provide a consistent front end to many of their internal applications, which at the time each required their own different client software interface. A decision was taken to proceed with a full implementation of an Intranet, and after 18 months the community of users reached over 60,000 (E-mail and Web access). BT senior management regard the Intranet as a business critical application that has major operational consequences for BT should it be unavailable for any reason. BT's 1995 business case for the Intranet projected an annual saving of £60 million, yet in its first year of full operation these savings rose to £305 million and have since grown to £663 million per annum, mainly due to the productivity improvements so far achieved. BT's Intranet includes access to:

▷ Internal Directories

▷ Job specific pages

▷ Sales & marketing information

▷ Service planning & provisioning

▷ Fault resolution

▷ Total human resource support

▷ Facilities management

▷ Voice/Data integration

▷ Group working

▷ Company news

▷ Executive information systems

▷ BT policies

▷ Tracking enquiries

The benefits cover increased speed of working, less paper, timely information, move from a 'push' to a 'pull' information mentality, less duplication, virtual/distributed team working and better morale. However, opening up the Internet connection from the Intranet can result in 'cyber skiving', access to improper information and security issues requiring appropriate company policies and firm management direction.

Case Study – Tyson Food

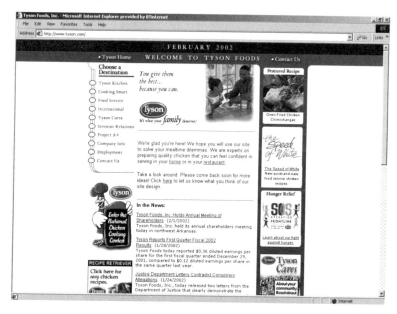

Figure 2.5 Tyson Food

At Tyson Food, the prime motivation for implementing an Intranet was to achieve efficiency improvements which would bring about internal cost reductions (Figure 2.5). As an example, the company estimated that to provide each of its 50,000 staff with an employee reference manual on an annual basis could cost as much as £7 per manual, that is well over a quarter of a million pounds just to distribute one document. Tyson Food now use their internal Web servers to publish company information by department, competitive analysis, etc.

Electronic Commerce Redefined

Companies have recognized the value of the Internet in allowing them to become more 'outward-facing' to their customers, and the establishment of a corporate Web presence for marketing purposes has usually preceded the implementation of an Intranet. Indeed, during the latter part of the 1990s, sophisticated Web-based applications consisting of 'shop-fronts' were creating an exciting new marketplace for selling directly to home consumers as well as business customers. In particular, the news media seized upon the term e-Commerce (synonymous with Internet commerce) and largely redefined it as the marketing and selling of products/services to consumers over the Internet.

However, in this book, e-Commerce is viewed as a sub-set of e-Business and concerns 'the use of the Internet and other information and communications technologies for the marketing, buying and selling of products and services'. This applies to companies marketing to business customers as well as to home consumers, which face much the same challenge, namely to establish an effective self-service sales channel that will attract customers through excellence in customer service and perceived added value.

Internet Commerce

Many organizations started their involvement with the Internet by establishing access for E-mail purposes using an Internet Service Provider (ISP). The ISP connection enabled the corporate E-mail hub/switch to be used to process incoming and outgoing Internet E-mail (POP3 and SMTP/MIME based respectively) between employees and external trading partners. In addition, the connection provided nominated employees with the ability to access the Internet's vast quantity of information, perhaps for research or competitive analysis purposes, using a Web browser.

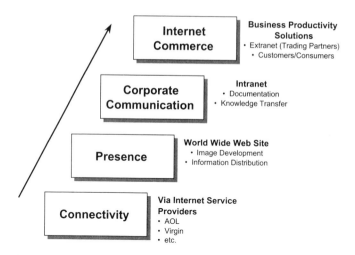

Figure 2.6 Internet commerce evolution

The next phase in the evolution was to establish a presence on the Internet by setting-up a 'public' Web site, primarily as a marketing communications exercise to promote the image of the organization and make available 'public' information, such as products and services (see Figure 2.6). Since the 'public' Web site could be accessed by anyone with Internet access, it was usual to place this outside the corporate 'firewall', either using a separate Web server or by renting space on the ISP's public Web server. The development of an external Web site was normally to provide information to potential customers and other interested parties in support of marketing or operational initiatives.

Not surprisingly, the success of an external Web site encouraged the organization to set-up a corporate Web site for internal usage. This was not a trivial exercise, as it required a culture change within the organization to support the free exchange of business information in electronic form and a complete rationalization of existing methods/processes used to support the current means of information dissemination. More importantly, procedures needed to be put in place to ensure that information was continually maintained up to date, otherwise the Intranet was doomed to failure. This stage usually heralded further rationalization of E-mail usage in the organization and a migration to a common client/server E-mail environment. End users could either use E-mail features that were integrated into their Web browsers and accessed via their desktop personal computer (e.g. Microsoft Internet Explorer or Netscape Navigator), or use a separate E-mail interface, e.g. Microsoft Outlook, which still has a Web browser 'look and feel' about it.

An Intranet implementation also provided the opportunity to extend corporate legacy applications by offering a browser-based interface, that gave the same 'look and feel' as normal Internet Web access. This was particularly well-suited for an administrative support system or where forms-based data entry was required, using the Web technologies described earlier. Other application examples included financial accounting, procurement and logistics applications, each providing a consistent interface to the end user.

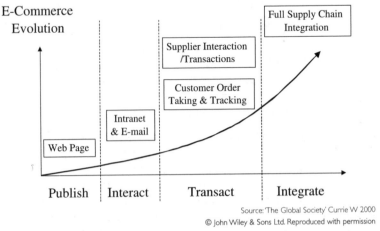

Source: 'The Global Society' Currie W 2000
© John Wiley & Sons Ltd. Reproduced with permission

Figure 2.7   e-Commerce evolution

The final phase in the Internet commerce evolution was where internal applications, including online ordering and quotations systems, were deployed (together with appropriate security measures) on the Internet for use by consumers, business customers and suppliers.

Remember, the terms 'electronic and Internet commerce' are viewed as largely being synonymous.

Currie (2000)[2] illustrates this evolution in a similar manner with an emphasis towards the business-to-business category, ultimately leading to full integration of the supply chain (Figure 2.7). While this emphasis still lies at the heart of e-Business, the publicity attracted by the Dot.Com companies in the consumer market space has placed a disproportionate emphasis towards 'electronic and Internet commerce', as referring solely to the business to consumer sales channel, which is clearly not the case.

Electronic Business

In this book e-Business is defined as 'the practice of performing and co-ordinating critical business processes such as designing products, obtaining supplies, manufacturing, selling, fulfilling orders, and providing services through the extensive use of computer and communication technologies and computerized data'.[3] This definition, by Alter (2002), provides a much broader framework in which to understand the e-Business phenomena and includes all stakeholders.

While the evolution continues, it is clear today that, almost without exception, all businesses whether large or small use some level of information and communications technology to assist them in their business operation. In consequence, it is argued that this represents the real meaning of e-Business where business process and the use of information technology are inextricably linked to encompass all aspects of a company's business operation. In this respect the terms e-Business and business are becoming synonymous, and therefore the 'e' in e-Business is rapidly becoming redundant. When surveying the thinking behind e-Business there are far more areas of overlap than difference. More than anything, e-Business is perceived as on-going initiatives aimed at doing things differently resulting in improved competitive outcomes for the company. In addition, the very significant contribution of open Internet technologies and their acceptance by the business world has created a 'thick architecture' that eliminates some the technological barriers existing before the Internet's emergence. Therefore, e-Business is about using the convenience, availability and worldwide reach of the Internet to enhance existing businesses or create new virtual businesses.

Key factors contributing to the growth of e-Business include:

▷ Opportunities to pursue customer service initiatives and improvements within the supply chain to enhance competitive positioning.

▷ The emergence of the Internet as a cost-effective alternative to costly private and value added networks.

▷ The increasing trend for employees to tele-work made possible by being networked with their colleagues, business partners and customers.

▷ Scope to secure savings through the re-engineering of business processes as companies create new Internet-based applications.

▷ Growing use of the Internet as an alternative sales channel in addition to face-to-face, post and telephone.

Figure 2.8 extends the previous schematic to show the much greater intensity in e-Business for 'inter-facing' with trading partners as well as 'outward-facing' Web applications reaching out to business customers and home consumers. In both these segments of the business, companies are deploying sophisticated applications to complement their existing traditional 'brick and mortar' businesses. However, deciding to pursue the Internet as an additional sales channel requires careful consideration and planning, since many organizations with 'bricks and mortar' expertise do not necessarily possess the necessary experience and skill sets to be successful in this new sales media.

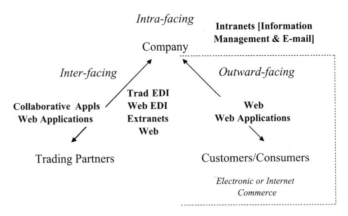

Figure 2.8   e-Business (late 1990s)

It is clear that three predominant categories of e-Business have now emerged and take their place alongside the other numerous acronyms which seek to confuse those wishing to understand this subject (see Figure 2.9).

▷ **Business-to-Employee (B2E)** – the 'intra-facing' activities that take place within an organization aimed at using information technology to significantly improve internal communications resulting in faster business processes, cost reduction and other efficiencies when responding to business change initiatives.

▷ **Business-to-Business (B2B)** – those 'inter-facing' initiatives that seek to create strategic electronic links within the supply chain to enable trading partners to improve stock turn through more effective replenishment action. Also includes a growing number of Web-based applications for smaller trading partners migrating from facsimile.

▷ **Business-to-Consumer (B2C)** – a completely new sales channel which opened up with the explosive adoption of the Internet within the home. However, the use of the Internet for the marketing and selling of products and services to home consumers has been through a rather 'roller-coaster' period since its inception and much has been learnt over a very short period of time. Often the same Web 'shop-front' is open to business customers who may need to register on the site to enjoy preferential pricing.

There are other three letter acronyms such as G2C (Government-to-Citizen), P2P (Path-to-Profit), Consumer-to-Consumer (C2C), etc. which will be addressed elsewhere in the text.

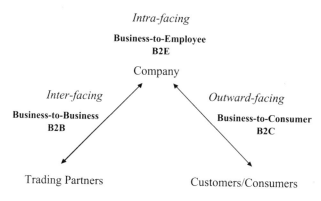

Figure 2.9 Predominant categories of e-Business

Electronic Marketplaces

The dictionary tells us that a marketplace is 'an open space where a market is held in a town'. Electronic marketplaces or 'marketspaces' are not so very different, but now extend beyond a town to reach global proportions. They represent an environment in which buyer and seller can freely come together and facilitate the exchange of products and services, usually for a payment. Similarly with traditional marketplaces, the key to their success is their ability to attract a critical mass of buyers and sellers to participate in the trading process. Aside from matching buyer with seller, there need to be processes and infrastructures that address the issues of product/service delivery and payment, as well as legal considerations such as the applicability and/or redress under contract law or consumer protection legislation. For these reasons most e-Marketplaces (also known as trade exchanges or electronic auctions) are operated by intermediaries, a consortium of companies within an industry or a large influential company (see Chapters 6 and 9 for additional information).

Evolving Scope of e-Business

The scope of e-Business has become extremely broad and now appears in many aspects of corporate and home life. With this trend the 'e' dimension has become an implicit part of the new way of doing things and is no longer viewed as being very exceptional. Simply, old processes have been discarded to make way for more effective ways of doing things that are becoming the norm in some areas of business activity. In addition, new functions have emerged in response to business needs that are only possible with the advances of technology. This section examines some of the examples of e-Business in action to illustrate its increasing relevance and scope (see Figure 2.10).

Electronic Auctions

Under normal conditions, goods are advertized and people then attend the auction of the goods at an agreed time and place. Goods often start with a reserved price set by the seller and bids are placed over and above this price until the bidding stops and the final bidder lays claim to the goods. In one model of online auctions much the same approach applies, such as Ebay.com which has a significant presence with competition from other companies including QXL.com. In addition to listing fees, Ebay charges sellers 5% of the winning bids although there is a ceiling set, while QXL's charges 4% of the winning bid, although the ceiling set is higher than Ebay. Currently Ebay has some 34 million users worldwide, compared with the 3.1 million people using QXL.

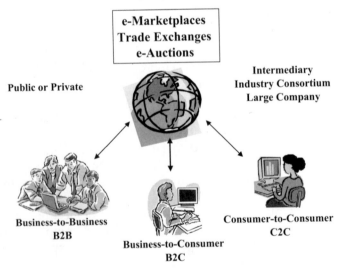

Figure 2.10 Categories of e-Marketplaces

Another variant of e-Auctions is known as the reverse auction and arises from a business strategy to improve profit margins by seeking to reduce the cost of materials by placing pressure on suppliers. This is a process in which a large organization solicits bids from other companies to supply goods, often raw materials, but unlike a normal auction, where prices rise, in a reverse auction suppliers will be tempted to lower their prices as the deadline approaches (see Figure 2.10). The actual auction itself is normally conducted over a very short period of time, e.g. several hours, although some flexibility in making extensions to the cut-off time is necessary to ensure that no further bids are likely to be made. Companies that have successfully implemented electronic auctions comment on the need for very comprehensive specifications to be prepared for the suppliers. In addition, it is critical to maintain credibility with suppliers and demonstrate that the process is fair and does not favour the incumbent supplier. Follow-up with suppliers not winning a contract is essential to ensure that they bid for future contracts and believe that they have a good chance of being successful next time.

Electronic Gambling

It is currently illegal to operate online casinos in most of Europe and North America. This has forced operators to set-up facilities in less-restrictive places in the Caribbean or South America where no such restrictions on gambling have been implemented. It is estimated that there are approximately 1,500 e-Gambling Web sites operating and growing. Indeed in the US, further legislation is being proposed which would prohibit the use of credit cards, electronic funds transfers, cheques and other similar financial instruments drawn or payable through any financial institution being used in such transactions.

In the UK the introduction of a betting tax on horse racing (since abolished) was the stimulus for setting up online betting associated with tax-free havens outside the UK (see **www.sportingbet.com**).

Electronic Banking

The banking industry was the first to operate EDI for funds transfer between banks on a global basis using the SWIFT network. It has traditionally offered a range of electronic services to corporate clients including cash management, currency risk exposure, trading services, etc. Indeed, banking appears to be an obvious candidate for e-Business, since much of its activities revolve around responding to instructions from customers and providing information in the form of confirmation and statements. Clearly, when conducting e-Business between a buyer and seller over the Internet, the settlement of payment is critical to successfully completing the transaction, and banking institutions have a key role to play.

Electronic Auctions
Electronic Banking
Electronic Gambling
Electronic Engineering
Electronic Government
Electronic Learning
Electronic Marketing
Electronic Retailing
Electronic Supply Chain
Electronic Trading

Figure 2.11 Evolving scope of e-Business

With the increasing use of automated teller machines (ATMs) and plastic credit/debit cards the character of personal banking has changed dramatically with fewer incentives for customers to visit the bank branch office. This has been compounded by telephone and Internet banking that, while seeming a great idea, has not been the spectacular success originally forecast. This is due primarily to a poor take-up by customers to a new way of conducting their personal banking, although as consumer purchases over the Internet increase, so Internet banking is growing.

Case Study – Security First Network Bank

The first entry into Internet banking in 1995 was Security First Network Bank (SFNB) in the US with no 'bricks and mortar' presence. Sometimes being first pays, but in the conservative area of banking this has not been the case for SFNB as getting the necessary critical mass of banking clients to convert to online banking has been tough. The struggling bank ultimately was taken over by the Royal Bank of Canada. This is not to say that it has been a complete failure, as in the UK several Internet banks including Egg.com, First Direct and Cahoot.com have established viable customer bases.

In many respects purely online banks should have a very significant advantage over the 'bricks and mortar' institutions since they offer instant customer satisfaction, are universally available and operate with much lower overheads. However, research concludes that despite the advancements in technology, currently the High Street branch remains the most popular channel of interaction for customers with their bank; but this could change. Other surveys indicate that Web sites of 'bricks-and-mortar' banks receive greater visits/usage than Web sites of 'online only' banks, suggesting the need for 'online only' banks to establish some form of physical presence.

Electronic Government

Administrations around the world have been quick to realize the potential the Internet can bring to improving communications between government and citizen (G2C). Already, access to numerous Web sites provide a wealth of information from legislation proceeding through governmental bodies to position papers on topics of high public interest. This not only applies to central government but to many of the administrative departments such as those dealing with income tax and state pensions. In addition, local government authorities are encouraging the use of E-mail as an effective and speedy means of communication between relevant departments and members of the public. With the high level of Internet penetration in the US, it is not surprising that a considerable programme of activities promoting e-Government initiatives exists there. This includes e-Citizen Service Awards supported by MIT and Anderson Consulting to honour best practices in electronic government. Past winners include the city of Boston (**www.cityofboston.com**), US Dept of Housing & Urban Development (**www.hud.com**) and Virginia Department of Motor Vehicles [4].

Despite the obvious benefits of e-Government there are also concerns regarding the citizen's rights to privacy and access which need to be protected within a clear ethical framework.

Electronic Learning

With the ever increasing demand for education and learning within the developed and developing countries of the world there has been a need to examine new ways of course delivery that enhance the learning experience of the student. Electronic learning is not a new phenomenon, indeed computer-based training (CBT) has been available for many years, but is generally not a preferred method of learning for many students. However, the new generation of e-Learning tools delivered over the Internet/Web offer much greater possibilities to successfully engage the student in a powerful alternative to traditional face-to-face learning, or at least to complement it.

Within the university environment, computer mediated communication (CMC) and other e-Learning software packages are progressively being introduced and include products such as Blackboard, FirstClass and WebCT. Some of these packages offer basic objective testing tools to help gauge the degree of student learning, but other packages, such as Perception from Question Mark Computing Ltd, are very sophisticated and interface with several of the conferencing products. As an aside,

Perception uses an XML syntax standard for importing and exporting questions used in the objective tests.

Typically, when introducing an e-Learning package into a university the first priority, and the easiest, is course administration which seeks to establish effective communications between the teaching team and students. This allows course announcements, syllabus, attendance details, assignments and lecture materials to be posted for student access either on Campus or from home using a Web browser. The next stage is to use the asynchronous electronic conferencing environment for group discussion, perhaps as part of an assignment. For many students forced to work part-time in order to finance their studies, time on campus can be very pressured and taken-up with lectures, lab/tutorial sessions and library visits. For these students the main benefits of e-Learning is that conference participation can be at a time when it is most convenient for them, and not even necessarily undertaken on campus, as long as they have access to the Internet from home to connect them to the campus conferencing server.

Businesses, often under considerable competitive pressures, do not look favourably at the loss of key staff members to participate in off-site training courses. For this reason there are a growing number of course modules offering an alternative to, or reduced need for, face-to-face learning. This is achieved by arranging course delivery using e-Learning tools designed to allow students to proceed at their own pace and test their understanding of the subject at key points in the learning process. Such an approach is highly suitable for skills training, but more difficult for some academic subjects.

1   Mintzberg Henry, The Myths of MIS, California Management Review Vol. 15 No. 1 (Fall 1972) P.97 (University of California) – ESS P.68

2   Currie Wendy (2000), The Global Information Society, Wiley, P.22

3   Alter Steven (2002), Information Systems – The Foundation of E-Business, Prentice Hall, P.6

4   Web site (www.dmv.state.va.us/dmvnet/online.asp)

Financial
e-Business

Financial Services Evolution

Several centuries ago, new international trade routes opened exciting new markets to entrepreneurial organizations conducting commerce with new unknown partners. Critical to this commerce was the ability to be able to exchange one good with another, or for money – legal tender representing value and backed by a national authority. Numerous financial instruments were created to facilitate this new trade, and many European and US banking institutions began to evolve into global providers of these services. Essentially these services were primarily product driven by the financial institutions, which met the need of the day and have been continuing to do that for much of the 20th century. Towards the end of the century however, this one-way relationship between financial service providers and the consumer began to transform, and worldwide commerce began putting additional stresses on existing systems. No longer were markets characterized by physical traits locked in by specific geography – new markets were electronic, global and consumers demanded multiple delivery channels. Intense competition and consumer unpredictability have forced huge consolidation and change over the last few decades. Financial institutions were merging and the number of players contracting, against a backdrop of new entrants providing services which increasingly looked like those provided by traditional banks.

These new entrants were leveraging technological advances and the increasing use of the Internet and the concept of the unmanned bank, or Internet-only bank emerged. This was no surprise to most technologists, when you consider that banking is almost completely an electronic-based product, and banks have always been large users of technology. Given this one would imagine a huge plethora of Internet-only banks to flourish, however this was not necessarily the case, and the landscape was mixed. Citibank's Internet bank, Citi f/i was to be an Internet-only stand-alone subsidiary, and was launched in 1999. However as early as 12 months later, it was absorbed back into the parent and simply provided another distribution channel instead. There are numerous other examples of international and domestic US-based banks scaling back their Internet stand-alones, or new entrants to the market failing to attract the numbers of customers initially anticipated.

At the other end of the scale, there a few startling successes. One only had to look at world's largest Internet-only bank based in the UK, the rather esoterically named Egg. In early 2001, it boasted more than a million and a half customers, a size that dwarfed most Internet-only banks in other countries at that time. Other smart new entrants were also showing how technology could potentially revolutionize the banking industry. DeepGreen Bank, launched in August 2000, provided lightening fast home-equity based lines of credit if the applicants and the underlying properties fitted its business profile. Unconditional approvals took approximately two minutes, and could facilitate an unsecured loan up to $25,000 which could then be sent to the applicant's bank account by wire transfer within 20 minutes. The platform behind the bank provided Internet-based connectivity to key systems that could validate land title, valuation, credit scoring and number of other systems allowing fast credit scoring. Furthermore, the application used PKI technology to provide a digital signature on the application allowing an end to end digital process.

Dawn of the Cash-Less Society

The Lombard bankers that were prevalent many centuries ago were very familiar with the concept of correspondent banking, with its antiquated ways and complex and often long lead time transactions. Ironically, we live in an age where everything needs to be faster and ever more efficient, yet within the walls of international banking, some of these antiquated traditions are still strong and resisting change. Banking systems still remain steeped within the constraints and practices prevalent many centuries ago – indeed the modern version of correspondent banking has changed little when compared to its ancient brethren.

Before the mass adoption of e-Commerce, the business of making a payment was predictable. Transactions were settled using a combination of instruments that had been around for decades if not centuries – a combination of cash, checks, credit and debit cards, electronic transfers etc., all usually transmitted over phone lines, magnetic tapes or dedicated electronic links. New approaches found it difficult to gain traction and critical mass, as consumers continued to be wary and industry dominants made new entry to their markets difficult.

Much has changed as a result of the rise of the Internet, and the realm of finance is no exception. The dawn of the cash-less society has become a familiar mantra, and exciting and innovative upstarts are gaining millions of users within a matter of months, compared to the closely nurtured client base that many of the global banks have built over decades. Many examples of the new order of things are already visible in many countries, such as Singapore and Hong Kong where smart cards are used for numerous transactions in lieu of cash. China is gearing itself up to have a 'smart' national identity card, with much additional functionality allowing non-cash based transactions. Mobile phone users in Germany can already use their mobile phones to pay for taxi rides. In Finland, these same devices will dispense a can of your favourite fizzy drink. Human behaviour takes time to change, although some technologies can creep into our lives without us realizing. The case of credit cards is illustrative – they were virtually unheard of three decades ago. ATM usage was highly suspicious in the eyes of consumers in the 1970s.

Cash-less transactions are already prevalent in many ways, and we compare and contrast the major initiatives and providers of these alternatives in the following sections.

e-Wallets – Virtual Cash?

The concept of virtual cash, and its associated counterpart, the e-Wallet or Digital Wallet became popular vocabulary in the 1990s when a number of initiatives were launched. The digital wallet, either stored on a physical medium such as a smart card of some kind (on a credit card, or mobile phone SIM card as examples) or sitting on a server somewhere in cyberspace, began taking form. The holistic idea behind the digital wallet was to provide a rich functionality of services that embraced digital identity through authentication (typically PKI-based), coupled with high levels of security. The technology also promised additional conveniences, such as consolidated billing presentment and payment and high levels of integration with smart mobile devices and a variety of software. The concept was appealing, and seemed very utilitarian given the promised convenience, however take up had been a mixed bag, with only some notable successes.

e-Currencies

A true e-currency does exist today. No Central Monetary or National Authority has backed and launched an e-currency. This however has not deterred many new organizations from offering alternative e-currencies. Essentially these are units of exchange that can be spent on the Internet, but somehow linked to the material world, and its associated legal tender. These e-currency alternatives achieved little success and early versions introduced in the mid to late 1990s are almost all out of business, or have changed their business plans. They never achieved the critical mass required to provide high levels of acceptance and liquidity which allows for a free and open market, with multiple parties making an exchange. The primary approaches can be categorized loosely into three broad definitions.

▷ Digital electronic currency

▷ Rewards/loyalty-based currency

▷ Person-to-person (P2P) networks

Examples of digital electronic currencies included organizations such as First Virtual launched in 1994 (closed down operations in 1998), Digicash launched in 1996 (closed down operations in 1998) and CyberCash. Essentially these approaches shared a relatively similar architecture and process as follows:

1. Consumers would utilize the services of a 'bricks and mortar' bank that supported the scheme, which facilitated the ability to download e-currencies (i.e. CyberCoins in the case of CyberCash).

2 This currency could then be spent at participating online merchants that would accept the e-currency in question.

3. The online merchant would then exchange the e-currency for legal tender that was credited to the merchant's bank account.

4. The corresponding 'spend' would be debited from the consumer's e-currency account.

The approach never caught on, with processes being complex in nature and a distinct lack of Web merchants that would accept the alternative currencies.

Reward- or loyalty-based currencies included many players, but perhaps the best known being Beenz and Flooz, which were launched in 1998. Brand recognition was fuelled by multi-million dollar advertizement campaigns but despite this, both shut down operations in August 2001. At the heart of their proposition was a rewards-based scheme not dissimilar to the age old concept of a gift certificate, which has been around for the last 100 years. Beenz had aspirations to become a universal Internet-based currency building on its roots as a loyalty program. Both functioned in a similar fashion, in that gift certificates were sold to a consumer online and the amount charged to a consumer's credit card. The e-currency could then be spent at a participating merchant, or it could be E-mailed to a friend or colleague. At its height, Beenz boasted 1.5 million customers and Flooz had some significant partners, such as Barnes and Noble. The continual success of online auctions, however, was driving significant demand for payments between unknown parties which were typically low value in nature. At around the same time as other alternative e-currencies, a new approach was emerging, and on the back of the growth of online auctions such as eBay, beginning to blossom and reach critical mass. Person-to-Person (P2P) payments were gaining in popularity, and a number of players emerged. The concept was simple – consumers could use intermediaries to pay others without disclosing their banking details. The process flow was as follows:

▷ An account is created by the user with one of the providers of P2P services. An integral element of this is linking the online account to a credit card, or bank account. This information is confidential to the P2P provider.

▷ When a purchase is made, the P2P provider debits the credit card or bank account, and transfers the funds to the beneficiary, who is notified by E-mail that their funds are ready to be received.

▷ If the beneficiary holds an account with the P2P provider, the funds are credited to their online account. If not, an account needs to be established (some providers automatically create an account) and the beneficiary can then transfer them electronically to a physical bank account (or a cheque created and mailed), or use the funds online.

These payment systems were cheap, and simple to use. Without doubt, the dominant player and one of the first was PayPal, who drove the majority of its growth with its affiliation with eBay (see Case Study). Billpoint Inc., whose online payment method was renamed Ebay Payments also derived its growth in a similar manner and these two propositions had the majority of the ever expanding user base. In early 2002, up to 90% of the P2P volume was driven by the online auction market.

What started as a person-to-person payment mechanism soon grew to a person-to-business model, with a large number of online merchants beginning to accept this mechanism to be paid for goods and services. P2P payments were showing huge projection growth curves as the technology platforms matured and other large players entered the market. A number of key competitors to market leader PayPal emerged, including:

▷ In August 2001, Citibank launched c2it. Using its international clout, it signed a distribution deal with America Online (AOL) and in May 2001 became the preferred payment system on Microsoft's Network, reaching hundreds of millions of users. An integral element of c2it's marketing plan was to tap the huge international market – there are approximately 30 million foreign workers in the US sending money home every week or month. Additionally, Citibank was looking to differentiate its product by integrating other services such as Electronic Bill Presentation and Payment (EBPP).

▷ Western Union virtually created the concept of money transfer 125 years ago, and were aggressively looking to use the Internet as another channel leveraging its established 'bricks and mortar' global network. Its MoneyZap service was establishing ground.

▷ Checkfree, a major player in the EBPP market (see later) was also launching an E-mail payments engine as one element of functionality in its broad suite of services under its WebPay umbrella. This was an ASP model which other institutions could use under their own branding.

▷ A number of Portals, such as Yahoo! offered direct payment capabilities.

As the market continues to mature, clearly interoperability between these networks will become increasingly important, yet this opens a key competitive conundrum. At the time of writing it was unclear whether a consortium of the larger players would create a 'club' much like the credit card networks, or these offerings would continue to co-exist as stand-alone entities.

Case Study – PayPal

October 1999 saw the humble launch of a simple home page that would grow into one of the Internet's major success stories – a person-to-person payment (P2P) network called PayPal. As with many success stories, the growth of this 'good' idea started with a slightly different and less successful proposition, and within a few months of its launch, had begun its heady rise in attracting millions of customers at astonishing rates.

Peter Theil and fellow co-founder Max Levchin had teamed up in 1998 (aged 30 and 26 respectively) to start a company called Field Link that specialized in providing encryption software for wireless devices. The technology had nurtured the concept of moving money using devices such as palmpilots. Thiel (CEO of PayPal) was a chess-loving intense libertarian that had studied law at Stamford University. When approached by Levchin (CTO of Paypal), he was running a hedge fund.

Demand for their initial concept was sparse and the company changed direction to other areas as well as renaming itself Confinity. It was at that point that an application called PayPal was born, allowing users of handheld devices to beam money to each other. The company had a strong start with a capital investment of $3 million from Nokia. Despite this initial success, the original idea did not blossom and in 1999, both increasingly realized that there was not an easy way of making a payment on the Internet. Additionally, not everyone had a wireless device such as a palmpilot, but almost all net users did have an E-mail address.

From these humble beginnings, a Web version of the PayPal application followed and started trading using established networks – E-mail and a universal currency, the US Dollar – whilst building a new person-to-person network platform. Without a doubt, one of the key observations and drivers were online auctions, such as eBay, which PayPal launched its service on in early 2000. Thiel had noted that as late as 1998, almost 90% of eBay's transactions were settled with checks or money orders.

The concept was simple. Money would be exchanged via cyberspace – all users needed was an E-mail address, a credit card or bank account number and an Internet connection. Recipients of funds would receive money in a new account (if they did not already have one) and PayPal would debit the sender's account (credit card or bank account) respectively. Anyone who received money therefore automatically became a new PayPal client.

The viral growth of PayPal was breathtaking. By end of 1999 there were 10,000 users. Two months later, that number was 100,000. By using savvy pricing techniques (the service was effectively free initially, with revenues being garnered from the cash locked into the PayPal system), new users were attracted to the service. Even when pricing models were introduced, these were much more attractive than those levied by the credit card companies. In March 2000, X.com merged with PayPal electing to ditch its banking business and its brand name in favour of the PayPal service.

At the time security was a continual area of focus, however Paypal was one of the propositions that forged ahead without the authentication of sellers. Although this afforded first mover advantages, the company had to work hard on enhancing risk management techniques and providing greater focus on authenticating sellers at the site.

Although eBay continued to be one of PayPal's largest partner sites (generating approx 60% of revenues), it was already connected to over 2.6 million merchants and continued to grow at a fast pace. 15th February 2002 was also a significant day for PayPal as it went public, raising another $90 million with its shares surging 54% on the first day of trading, despite the downturn in the dotcom boom. The PayPal statistics were startling:

▷ 14 million registered accounts in early 2002, signing on approximately 25,000 new accounts per day

▷ Revenues of $64.4 million for the nine months to September 2001

▷ The service was available in 36 countries around the world

▷ 625 employees with a customer service unit of 400 people

PayPal had recognized its ability to innovate and its nimbleness had allowed it to create a critical mass in a minimal amount of time. The future was in a broader base, and service offerings were being expanded. These included a Mastercard co-branded debit card (with Bank One), the ability to sweep funds from a PayPal account to a traditional bank account, a credit card from Providian and a money market fund administered by Barclays.

In the middle of 2002, the success of PayPal had attracted the attentionof eBay, which acquired the company in July of the same year – the plan being to allow PayPal to continue trading as an independent brand.

Smart Card Approaches

The use of smart card technology to house a digital wallet was introduced initially in the early 1990s. Although there have been a few variations on the theme, two of the most successful and commercial examples can be illustrated by the Mondex Card, and the American Express Blue Card.

The Mondex Card, introduced by the British Bank National Westminster in 1990, looked like an ordinary credit card, albeit with an integrated circuit housing a CPU and 512K of RAM. It was launched into the commercial market in 1994 as an electronic cash system that provided a direct electronic equivalent of cash, backed by a consortium of banking partners and Mastercard as the principal driver, with full ownership reverting to Mastercard in August 2001. At that time over 6 million cards had been distributed, with the majority being in Asia Pacific. Franchises and pilot projects were active in numerous countries including Japan, France, Latin America, Norway and the Philippines.

The microchip contained a wallet where value was held electronically, and divided into five separate domains, allowing up to five different currencies to be held on the card at any one time. The microchip also contained various security software modelled on PKI infrastructure. Additional to this technical infrastructure was Mondex's proprietary operating system called MULTOS. This facilitated a number of applications, such as loyalty point initiatives.

The approach also took another step forward when American Express launched Blue, which combined an American Express credit card with smart card technology. Much like Mondex, users could download a digital wallet and smart card readers were given away free to promote the adoption of the value added services. Unfortunately, most of the cards in use were not using the smart card technology outside a few pockets of consumers.

The other manifestation of smart card technology involved a technology platform that did not require a physical interaction between card and reader for the digital wallet to be debited, termed as contact-less interaction. Most applications of this technology were used in electronic toll road systems, excellent examples being the Network of Electronic Transfers (NETS) used primarily in Singapore and the EZPass system in America.

NETS was founded in 1985 to operate and manage an online debit payment service. Additional services were added over time, including electronic payment services such as EFTPOS, Shared ATM services, CashCards, eNETS, FEDI (Financial Electronic Data Interchange) and Trade Finance services. In 2000, NETS formed a global marketing alliance with Visa International to market the CashCard solution under the Visa Cash Brand, and the technology is now in use in the Philippines, South Korea and Thailand. The Visa alliance brought access to Visa's Common Electronic Purse Specifications (CEPS), allowing the capability to store foreign currencies for use abroad as well as online transactions. In 2001, NETS processed about 100 million CashCard transactions and 88 million EFTPOS transactions amongst a user base of approx 6 million CashCards and the technology allowed a diverse range of options, including the ability to make peer to peer payments via cellular telephone technology.

The NETS card employed both contact and contact-less technology approaches, with the latter allowing debits to be made when inserted in a reader connected to an antennae. The smart card housed an electronic digital wallet that could be used in a number of applications, such as purchases made at retail outlets, vending machines, public pay phones, car parks and libraries in Singapore. Cardholders could also pay for purchases made over the Internet using a smart card reader and the NETS E-Wallet, and many retailers (such as Internet e-grocery shopping and taxis) were adopting the approach. Additionally, the wallet was debited when entering or passing the Singapore electronic toll gateway, ERP (Electronic Road Pricing) system, providing contact-less debits. The smart cards could be topped up using direct Internet access (with a smart card and a consumer's local bank account) or via any local ATM machines.

Identification and Authentication Services

The introduction of server-based technology approaches to provide identification and authentication services together with digital wallets began to take shape in the late 1990s with a few high profile entrants, led by Microsoft's Passport Service and a competing initiative known as the Liberty Alliance. These approaches provided services that liberated the user from having to sign onto multiple sites with different user IDs and passwords (although most users recycle or re-use only a few passwords) at different Web sites. Furthermore, these services were equipped to provide a more efficient online shopping experience, with financial details and associated information on shipping and billing addresses all contained within one convenient sign on, for merchant sites that participated.

The introduction of these services were far from a huge success, and take-up from some players such as Microsoft was enforced on the back of other highly successful services, such as Hotmail. Although users did see benefit from the single sign on experience, this benefit did not outweigh their concerns on security and data privacy being compromized, with personal data stored on remote servers somewhere in cyberspace. Furthermore, the early services were criticized for the lack of security which did little to dispel these consumer fears.

Progress continued to be made however, and the introduction of a standard for digital wallets also helped propel their use in the mainstream. Electronic Commerce Modelling Language (ECML) was launched in June 1999. The approach provided a consistent format for common data fields, containing personal and financial data and a number of high profile organizations such as IBM, Microsoft and Mastercard adopted the standard.

Microsoft .net Passport

Microsoft, as part of its .NET strategy, launched its .net Passport service in March 1999. The service was essentially a digital wallet that also included some additional services, including the ability to use one sign-on service, which allowed the entrance to participating Web sites through the use of one sign on, known as Single-Sign-In (SSI). Microsoft .net Passport users create a single sign-in name and password for use across participating .net Passport sites. Once created, the user is sent a unique Passport ID (PUID) for every user, which is the authentication record used with participating sites. The service did not utilize digital certificates, and as the PUID did not authenticate the identity of the user, several 'profiles' could be established by users for anonymity reasons – much like with free E-mail services such as Hotmail, where many users have several E-mail aliases.

Once a user has provided credit card information, a shopping experience at participating sites becomes much easier via a service known as .net Express Purchase. Merchant pages requiring payment details, and associated information (such as shipping), are automatically populated via a single click.

Passport benefited from a large user base of approximately 200 million users very quickly, as all Hotmail user accounts were automatically enrolled to use the technology, although only about a third of the users were aware of the passport infrastructure and an even smaller proportion utilized the additional services such as express pay.

In late 2001, Microsoft agreed to change its proprietary Passport solution under mounting industry criticism, to allow interoperability with other approaches and services. This was facilitated via the use of Kerberos technology – a network authentication protocol allowing one computer to provide its identity to another across an unsecured network. This is facilitated via encrypted messaging.

Liberty Alliance and AOL Magic Carpet

Microsoft was not alone in this market, and a few notable competitors had formed, or were beginning to provide viable alternative services as the market matured. Sun Microsystems led a large user alliance group to form the Liberty Alliance in September 2001. This consortium was seeking to develop an open standard to support identity, authorization and authentication services, in a similar vein to the Passport service. High profile members included American Express, General Motors, Sony and AOL TimeWarner.

Liberty Alliance was looking to build interfaces allowing decentralized identity services, and collectively the alliance possessed several critical mass backers that could individually bring hundreds of millions of users. AOL had introduced an identity service initially known as AOL Quick Checkout, which was later renamed and enhanced as Magic Carpet. In many respects Magic Carpet was introduced as a defensive measure to compete with Microsoft's Passport services.

Mobile Payments

The convergence of various technologies continues, and the proliferation of functionally rich mobile devices in our lives continue to play a greater role in everyday activities. Going shopping is no exception to this embracing trend. In Chapter 11, when we examine the security aspects of Mobile e-Business, we discuss this in additional detail – the majority of the enabling technology has been available for some time; what has been lacking is a consumer friendly platform that has a good critical mass and proposition for consumers as well as potential merchants. Within this chapter, we examine which approaches are beginning to provide a viable proposition to make payments using mobile technology. The approaches are still relatively new, with only a small handful beginning to gain any traction. Nevertheless, they provide a useful foundation in terms of how the technology can be utilized. The precept is simple – where merchants are registered, a mobile device can be used to make a payment – the amount is simply billed to the consumer's account (i.e. in the case of a user subscribing to a service using a cellular phone), a prepaid mechanism such as a prepaid cellular phone card, or directly linked to 'bricks and mortar' financial accounts.

The approaches have been touted as being very well suited to micropayments, typically less than $10.00 and our examples below certainly tout this aspect also. The evolution of mobile payments has been highly successful (in all but a very few cases) such as the NTT DoCoMo i-mode service in Japan (see Chapter 10 for a case study). In this case, DoCoMo has created an 'approved' domain where m-Commerce transactions can take place, and effectively acts as the clearing house for collections on behalf of micro-billers. This low cost entry for potential content providers has been exceptionally successful in building critical mass. The Japanese community are also relatively willing to pay for content – almost half of DoCoMo's i-mode subscriber base pay for services. In contrast, other initiatives mainly centred on approaches launched in Europe, take a different model. Most applications look to take a small service charge for providing and facilitating services, with the billing usually appearing on a cellular phone bill – the Sonera Mobile Pay service in Finland serves as a good example of this.

The platforms are exceptionally useful for last minute whim purchases– forgotten birthdays, flowers sent at the last minute etc. as well as entertainment content. Financial services are important content providers, and many banks continue to evolve their functionality to evaluate revenue models using mobile payment technologies.

Paybox

Developed by paybox.net AG, Paybox was a system founded in Germany and rolled out in July 1999, and whose shareholders included Deutsche Bank, debitel AG and mobilkom Austria. Paybox had managed to attract about 750,000 clients and launched the service in a few European countries, including Spain, Sweden, Austria and the UK.

The system provided the functionality of any user with a Global System for Mobile (GSM) cellular phone to make secure payments to any merchant registered with paybox, with the linkage to a normal current/checking account. With GSM networks prevalent in a large number of countries, the platform offered the potential for robust scalable growth in other markets. Like many successful approaches, paybox was looking to exploit two simple and prevalent technologies – voice cellular technology and Short Message Services (SMS), used extensively in European and Asian markets.

Paybox operated a managed service provider approach and through its Paybox Intelligent Architecture (PIA) modular model; elements of the platform or all of it could be provided to any client. The merchant does not have to be online, and indeed any merchant (or person) requiring a payment can be supported. The process flow of its operation is as follows:

1. A consumer provides their cellular telephone number to the merchant (whether online or in the real world). The merchant had to be a member of the paybox service prior to the transaction. For users not willing to disclose cellular numbers, paybox can provide alternative IDs.

2. These 'payment' details were transmitted by the merchant to the paybox system (identified by the consumer's cellular phone number).

3. The consumer is then called back and an interaction takes place through a paybox Interactive Voice Response (IVR) system, which requests a PIN. The transaction can then be completed by the consumer entering a personal PIN number which paybox will then verify.

4. Upon verification, the monies are transferred from the consumer's account to the merchants'. A Short Message Service (SMS) message is then transmitted to the consumer.

P2P payments, as discussed earlier, can also be accommodated – the merchant in the example above is simply another person registered with paybox.

Vodafone M-Pay

Vodafone launched its M-Pay service in 2001. The service is effectively a reverse-billed one, not too different to some of the e-Wallet services that were discussed earlier, in that a user ID can be obtained and together with a PIN, online interactions can take place without a mobile device. What is different is that Vodafone's functionality provides for a larger user base than just relying on mobile devices such as cellular technology.

The service was launched in a trial in the UK, Germany and Italy. The process is very similar to that of paybox, with the added functionality of not having to have a cellular device to complete the transaction. The service uses a simple approach. Payments on the cellular payment platform are facilitated via established payment instruments such as credit cards, debit cards or electronic direct debit for larger purchases.

Consumers are identified via the cellular device. Payment and shipping details continue to be securely held in an e-Wallet. Settlement can also be via a consumer's phone bill, or prepaid cards.

At its evolutionary stage, Vodafone was still adapting its model, although its prospects looked promising. With a large subscriber base, good brand recognition and mobile networks in 28 countries, it was well placed with a core critical mass of potential clients.

Electronic Bill Presentment and Payment (EBPP)

Nobody likes to receive a bill; and there are a lot of them to have to pay. Estimates vary, although most numbers centre on approximately 25 billion bills generated in the US alone. This mammoth task costs a small fortune, with estimates on the cost of each bill being upwards of a few dollars compared with a few pennies if the process could be electronic (for B2C transactions). For B2B transactions, this number rises to an average of $10.00 per invoice in the paper world. Add to this cost all the peripheral time and associated value in consumers processing these bills, writing checks and mailing costs. With these sorts of statistics, it is no surprise that the advent of Electronic Bill Presentment and Payment (EBPP) and Electronic Invoice Presentment and Payment (EIPP) has attracted so much attention. Essentially this is simply the process of a consumer (EBPP) or organization (EIPP) receiving a bill/invoice and paying it electronically. The savings around the process also allow a user of the technology to unlock significant benefits through better management of working capital. Reducing Days Sales Outstanding (DSO), and better quality information on accounts receivables provides compelling reasons to adopt these approaches. Majority of the focus and take-up of the proposition has been centred on EIPP as organizations have been attracted to the approaches and potential advantages the technology offers.

Although much of the value proposition has historically been based on the financial cost savings, the technology is being increasingly viewed as an effective channel for more effective customer relationship management as well as a tool for increasing customer retention. With sophisticated online dispute management, and a greater penetration into the client environment, these goals are beginning to be realized. The bill or invoice has historically been a very effective touch-point with the consumer, and additional marketing channels are also introduced to cross sell to new or associated services.

As with most technologies EBPP is not that new, with initial systems having been introduced in the early 1990s. Not surprisingly, these were not very integrated, with connectivity and bandwidth usually awful. Additionally, the payment aspect was usually fulfilled by a manual paper instrument as opposed to anything electronic. However advances in processing technology and the use of the Internet is beginning to allow the technology to gain critical mass and wider adoption. The major barrier to the adoption has perhaps been the difficulties surrounding the integration of the technology to existing systems in the accounts receivable and payables departments. Clients have usually invested significant resources and investment dollars in building efficient processes. The benefits of EBPP are considerably diminished if billers still have to manage certain functions outside of automated workflows. The situation is changing however, with providers offering technology that is XML-based to allow easier integration into client legacy systems.

EBPP Processes

When examining EBPP, it is useful to categorize between retail (B2C) and corporate (B2B) implementations, as both are somewhat different. These are outlined in Table 3.1. The B2B processes are always much more complex and volumes significantly higher – for instance a corporate's telephone bill can easily run into thousands of lines, with multiple plans spanning many areas and departments. At the turn of the century, the majority of the volumes were in B2C relationships, although that disparity was disappearing fast.

Retail (B2C) EBPP	Corporate (B2B) EBPP
Smaller value payments	Larger value payments
Simple invoices	High volumes, with complex invoices
Electronic payments are typically via an individual's bank account, or low value clearing oriented√	Electronic payments tend to involve multiple settlement methods, including same day settlement systems
Simple processes usually managed by an individual	Processes involve several departments, usually requiring approval processes and audit requirements

Table 3.1   Differing characteristics of EBPP

The EBPP process has numerous terminology associated with it, and in the following sections, we provide an overview of the main aspects.

Biller

The biller starts the process by creating the original invoice or bill.

Biller Technology Provider (BTP)

Provider of billing software, usually selling to billers. This software will allow a biller to convert their paper-based environment into an electronic one.

Biller Service Provider (BSP)

BSPs provide outsourced platforms to allow billers to send bills and receive their respective payments. This negates the need to purchase EBPP software and its associated costs. A number of financial service providers have purchased or licensed applications and become BSPs themselves. JPMorganChase uses BCE Emergis and Citibank Bottomline Technologies offering.

Consolidators, Aggregators and Distributors

These institutions provide aggregation services, consolidating bills and providing distribution to various consumers. Additional services could also include the routing payments to financial institutions and payment processors. Examples include Spectrum and Checkfree. Checkfree provides numerous EBPP services, whereas a portal such as Yahoo! only provides an aggregation service. These services are usually powered by a larger player (in the case of Yahoo!, the offering is provided by Checkfree) and provide two access mechanisms. The first is a summary of the aggregated bills ('thin') usually with hotlinks to the biller's site, and the second is the presentation of the detailed bill ('thick').

Some consolidators will actually consolidate bills that are not necessarily transmitted electronically. In these cases, a consumer's bills are actually mailed to the PO Box for the consolidator, and bills are scanned where necessary. Examples of these types of providers include Cyberbills and Paytrust, and an example of the latter's service offering is illustrated in Figure 3.1.

Other entities play an intermediary role, between the bill presentment process and the payment processing aspect. Spectrum, a bank owned consortium, acts as such an intermediary, referred to as a 'switch'. Switches gather electronic bills from various billers and present them at a central source (in the case of Spectrum, this would be at the member bank's CSP offering, as discussed below).

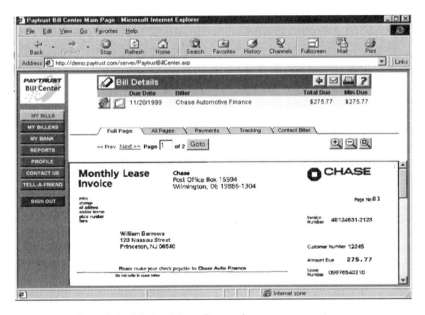

Figure 3.1 Bill detail from Paytrust's numerous services

Customer Service Providers (CSP)

These entities are the touchpoint between the consumer, and have primary contact with the consumer. This is typically used in the case of B2C structures, and in the B2B process, the biller usually has direct contact with their consumer. Examples include portals such as Yahoo! as well as financial institutions such as JP Morgan Chase and Citibank.

EBPP Systems

EBPP adoptions can take on a number of approaches, which can be usefully categorized into three broad domains:

▷ Portal Aggregation

▷ Consolidator

▷ Biller Direct

With the Biller Direct model, the biller controls the entire process and creates the bills which are then presented on their own site. The biller usually purchases the EBPP software, or outsources the process to a BSP. Once bills are ready, the consumer is notified, usually via an E-mail and the consumers can then view, manipulate and interact with the biller directly as well as pay their bills via this site. This approach is used extensively by the larger organizations such as utility, telephone and credit card companies who all have critical mass in terms of volumes processed. Additional examples are service-bureaus such as Billserv.com and Princeton eCom.

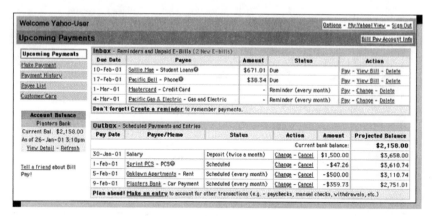

Figure 3.2 Yahoo! Aggregation Service

The consolidator model comprises of a third party that aggregates bills for consumers from a variety of sources, and presents them together in one location. This could be via a portal (the portal aggregation model) such as the offering from Yahoo! (see Figure 3.2), or service organizations that will take in paper bills as well and present them electronically once they have been scanned by the provider. Examples of this include Cyberbills and Paytrust.

Dispute Management

One of the key benefits of EBPP is the ability to provide online dispute management. This provides the ability to unlock significant savings, especially in the B2B arena where bills are typically complex, and consists of hundreds of pages. From the client perspective, online dispute management also provides numerous benefits. Although Web based customer support infrastructure will not eliminate the typical service call, which Forrester Research estimates can cost an average of $33.00, the technology does allow for these calls to be of a much higher quality.

Facilitating e-Financial Services

Newly emerging business models and increasing levels of international trade have always placed huge stress points in the financial services industry to speed up settlement processes, increase protection for the counter-parties, innovatively use new technology and reduce the burdensome and inefficient paper trails associated with the process. With the advent of the Internet, geographic borders became non-existent and the technology platforms begin to provide an opportunity to achieve some of these elusive goals.

A large number of standards exist within the financial services industry. Within the context of this discussion, we examine some of the key initiatives as well as the emerging XML-based standards which are allowing increased integration and inter-operability of financial-based systems. Other initiatives extensively use Public Key Infrastructure (PKI) approaches within financial services (as discussed in Chapter 12 – Securing e-Business). Here we examine one of the primary initiatives within financial services, Identrus, as well as a number of Trade related approaches.

Open Financial Exchange (OFX)

OFX, primarily a B2C standard, was established in 1997 by Checkfree, Intuit and Microsoft, principally to allow interoperability for personal financial management packages such as Quicken and Microsoft Money. The initial versions of the standard were SGML based until the release of V2.0 which updated it to be XML-based in December 1999. The standard was used extensively with over 1,000 banks and numerous brokerages.

Interactive Financial Exchange (IFX)

IFX, essentially an offshoot of OFX, was launched in October 1999 by a larger consortium of financial services providers, and numerous vendors. Created by the Banking Industry Secretariat (BITS), the objective was to provide a broad offering that encompassed EBPP applications as well as other application integration. IFX also incorporated a second standard called Gold, which was developed by IBM and Integrion, to support Internet banking. Compared to OFX, IFX also broadened the ability to carry richer and larger amounts of remittance information, as well as capturing a wider range of payment options. Although its adoption is still slow, a number of major players such as Spectrum have embraced the standard and are creating additional interoperability between EBPP and numerous financial systems.

e-Based Trade Services

Given the numerous documents that need to be exchanged in a typical trade related transaction, it is no surprise that XML is playing an ever greater role in this fast changing arena. A number of models have emerged, but one of the key initiatives which illustrates the trend is the one by Bolero International. This initiative is owned by SWIFT (Society for Wordwide Interbank Financial Telecommunications) and the TT Club (Through Transport Mutual Insurance Association Limited).

At the core of the Bolero proposition sits Bolero.net, a platform that allows the online exchange of trading documents centred on the Bill of Lading that use BoleroXML. Many documents have been released encompassing a number of financial categories. Other providers, such as TradeCard also rely on XML-based trade documents for electronic exchange. Bolero also utilizes a PKI infrastructure, such as Identrus (discussed below) or many of the other providers of PKI technology. This approach, used in conjunction with a robust legal structure outlined in the Bolero Rule Book provides a consistent process for dealing between participants.

The letter of credit has been around for many years, faithfully providing a level of security and comfort between a buyer and seller that essentially do not trust each other. This instrument has long been criticized for being inefficient and costly. Its long endurance has simply been the lack of a viable alternative. That was until an innovative approach was bought to market in the form of Tradecard, which does not operate within standard letter of credit rules and environments. The focus of Tradecard, established by officers who had many years experience of trade processes, was on B2B online marketplaces initially, providing a completely automated end-to-end process that was suited to e-Commerce.

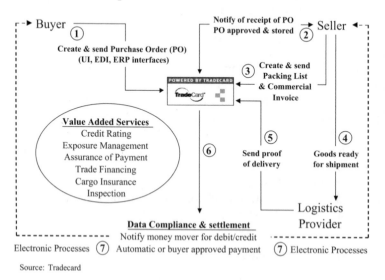

Figure 3.3 TradeCard process flow

At the heart of the Tradecard engine lies a compliance engine that takes in feeds from numerous parties (such as freight forwarders, carriers, inspection companies etc.), which the compliance engine processes prior to releasing funds to the seller (from the buyer) as illustrated in Figure 3.3.

These initiatives continue to grow as an increasing number of organizations begin to utilize their services.

Identrus

Identrus LLC was formed in April 1999 by a group of international banks. The founding institutions included ABN Amro, Bank of America, Barclays, Chase Manhattan (JPMorganChase), Citibank, Deutsche Bank and Hypo Vereinsbank. In September 2000, Identrus and SWIFT joined forces providing a broader foundation.

The system is effectively a closed group – only parties that have agreed to abide by the system's rules and regulations are allowed to participate. Participating financial institutions in the Identrus system serve as Identrus Certificate Authorities (CAs), establishing the identities of their corporate customers and certifying them as trusted trading partners on the Internet. Identrus Certificate Authorities issue unique digital IDs (digital certificates) to their customers. These Identrus Global IDs are backed by the power of a crypto-based global public key infrastructure (PKI). The system also allows the creation of non-disputable records of the transactions (refer to Chapter 12 Securing e-Business for more details on PKI infrastructure). As well as a large number of banks, a number of vendors have also supported the Identrus solution including Verisign, iPlanet and Computer Associates to name a few.

With research continually showing that the majority of consumers polled place the greatest amount of trust with on online interaction in their financial services partners, especially banks, a banking sponsored initiative such as Identrus holds much hope to gain critical mass. With its member network, which exceeded 50 banking partners at the time of writing, Identrus seemed well placed to become at least one of the dominant players facilitating e-based commerce on the Internet. Microsoft had also supported the initiative, ensuring that many of its core products (such as Windows 2000 and Net Enterprise servers) were easily integrated with Identrus-based solutions.

Identity certificates issued by the qualifying banks are secure. Root certificates are 2,048-bit keys, with Level 1 certificates being 1,024 (although Level 1 issuing banks can also use 2,048-bit keys). Putting that in perspective, most browsers today use no more than 128-bit encryption. In terms of participation, a financial institution may elect to make its own

PKI infrastructure compliant with the Identrus specifications and operating rules. Alternatively it can look to utilize the Identrus Express program. This provides a structure that has been pre-certified by Identrus, also providing established technology providers who can offer outsourcing options (such as data centres).

In early 2002, Project Eleanor was launched, aimed at providing secure direct B2B payments on the Internet, funded by fifteen global financial institutions. The project provided Web-based specifications to initiate e-payments, with the goal of integrating payment information with the e-payment itself. One of the key issues in using most payment systems is the very limited amount of reference information that can be sent together with the payment. Banking processes associated with the payment are transparent to the trading partner, and there are several tools allowing for the mitigation of risk and dispute resolution.

Once a financial institution is Identrus 'capable', its corporate customers can use the Identrus Global ID with its partners, whose financial institution is also a participant. When counterparts are certified within the system, protection is provided both ways since the global legal and risk management rules spell out precisely what happens if something goes wrong in a transaction. Furthermore, partners have usually been identified by strong established banking rules, such as 'Know Your Customer' disciplines which are employed when bank accounts are opened, or banking services extended.

A typical transaction within the Identrus network is illustrated in Figure 3.4, and an associated process flow (adapted from Identrus.com) might look like the following transaction:

1. A technology company finds a Web site of a contractor and makes an order. The manager inserts his smart card containing his global ID into his computer's reader and requests authentication of the contractor's Web site. The manager sends an RFP to the contractor confident that it will only be seen by its intended recipient.

2. The manager receives an E-mail from a distributor who is offering the required lab equipment. The price is attractive and the distributor promises delivery within 30 days. The offer contains a digital signature plus an attached performance guarantee from an Identrus member bank.

3. The manager requests authentication of the offer's origin and integrity. He receives assurance that the distributor is legitimate and the offer is intact and will not be repudiated. The response also validates both the distributor's and the bank's performance guarantees, providing financial recourse should the distributor not meet the commitments made in the offer.

4. A follow up E-mail from the company's computer vendor confirms that the required servers and workstations are in stock. The manager submits a purchase order signed with his Global ID and copies the financial institution, requesting a payment guarantee to accompany the order.

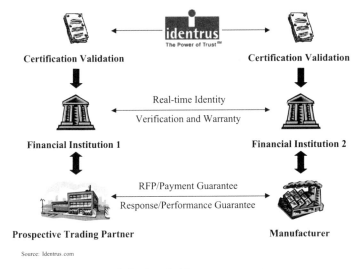

Source: Identrus.com

Figure 3.4   Sample Identrus transaction

Cash is King

Having discussed the major initiatives, despite the euphoria, when we examine the volume flows of transactions in major 'wired' economies it is clear that cash is still king. At the turn of the century, approx 82% of all transactions in the US were facilitated by the trusty old greenback (see Figure 3.5). The ability of cash to be instantly convertible and portable provides compelling reasons for its continued use and dominance. Its anonymity is universal and despite its drawbacks (it's not easy to purchase large items with cash alone, and it's easily stolen) it still represents the favoured choice for many consumers.

Despite these reasons, uses of other types of payment formats, such as cheque books and credit cards, with its relatively newer counterpart the debit card (funds are immediately debited from the underlying consumer's account), continue to gain additional volume and dominance. Additionally, credit card usage still dominates transactions over the Web, where cash is not used. Over 90% of e-Commerce transactions conducted on the Web were via credit cards in the early 2000s, although high costs continued to be a key deterrent to many online merchants, who typically had to absorb anything from 3% to 5% of the purchase price in fees in the US and Europe. The situation was worse in some parts of Asia, where fees approached up to 10% in less developed countries. These costs, coupled with the associated risk of sending credit card information (even via SSL secured systems) continues to slow down the adoption of credit card usage.

Volumes of Transactions

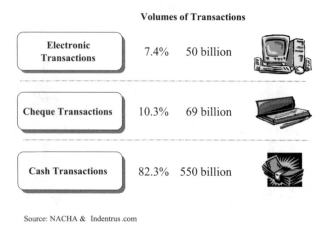

Source: NACHA & Indentrus.com

Figure 3.5 US payments in year 2000

The emergence and continued use of the Internet has opened many new distribution channels and the ability for merchants to charge for their services. In some cases, these charges are small – termed micro-payments – which are typically less than $5.00. Excellent examples include text in journals or newspapers where content is charged in pennies, or music files where a user may just want to download a few tracks costing a couple of dollars. These types of transactions have also provided an additional conundrum to the online payment challenge, and one that credit cards cannot address in a cost-effective manner. There have been a number of alternatives, including person-to-person (or P2P) payment systems. Other approaches have been very country centric – for instance, in Japan m-Commerce via the NTT DoCoMo i-mode service is the principal approach used (see Chapter 10 – Wireless Commerce).

It will still be some time before we replace cash as the dominant medium of exchange, and certainly not till National Governments begin to legally back e-Based cash alternatives.

Desktop Support for e-Business

Introduction – Desktop Computing

As new technologies come to market, and new working practices ingrain themselves into our everyday lives, the way we work and the environment we work in continues to evolve. From an aesthetic viewpoint, one can clearly see the movement away from the typing pools surrounded by offices, to more open areas, fostering the exchange of ideas and encouraging communication. Disparate global communities are linked by high bandwidth communication channels, allowing fixed topology and nomadic mobile access for its constituents.

The tools at our disposal have changed accordingly, in line with the environment they operate within. Visions of the early desktop conjure up huge machines, with little computing power compared to the ever smaller devices in today's offices. Furthermore, the significant increases in Local Area Network (LAN) technologies allowing greater bandwidth, and the ever evolving influence of the Internet environment facilitated many new ways of working, some of which we are only beginning to exploit to their full potential.

In this chapter we examine the evolution of business communications from several key aspects:

▷ The desktop's interaction with the environment that it operates in, namely internal and external networks

▷ The evolution of desktop hardware and the software that drives it

▷ Groupware environments and associated technologies

Moore's Law & Hardware Evolution

Dr Gordon Moore, the man who co-founded Intel Corporation which is today one of Wall Street's favourite companies, was an insightful man. He prophesied back in 1965 that the number of transistors per square inch (on integrated circuits) that can be fitted onto a chip doubles roughly every 18 to 24 months. Many decades later, Moore's Law, as it became known, still holds more or less true and has withstood the test of time. Amazingly, the number of transistors has increased from 2,300 in 1971 to over 42 million on Pentium 4 processors.

The technological advancements that we have seen continue to dazzle. In the mid 1960s and late 1970s, capital and especially advanced information technology was considered the scarce and expensive resource. Workers were viewed as replaceable, and IT tools were the expensive cost. Today billions of bytes of information flow at the touch of buttons 24 hours a day around the globe, tended by highly educated and competent individuals – technology hardware has now acquired the status of a commodity, and the emphasis is on satisfying the need of knowledge workers by providing tools that are not only powerful, but intuitive to use as well.

We have seen the emergence of a desktop machine, in recent years, capable of performing calculations and feats only possible by the early archetypal monolithic supercomputers. Intel Corporation, the organization responsible for the phenomenally successful 80x86 and Pentium range of processor chips, continues to work on its next generation of processor chips, leveraging new advances in silicon and other technologies. To put the power of their latest Pentium chips into perspective, its abilities outshine by several factors the processing power of a large mainframe machine, typically in use a few decades ago. Boring household appliances, such as fridges, today contain more powerful processors than most personal computers when they were first introduced.

Organizations already have the infrastructure in place to facilitate co-ordination and communication possibilities never imagined in the competitive marketplace of the last decade. The competitive factor is no longer the technology, but the availability and effective use of a skilled and competent workforce to fully utilize the tools that are available to them. A key requirement has always been the ability to 'humanise' the technology, effectively making it simpler to use for the average, non-technical user.

The changing aspects of the workplace, and how we do work, have put increasing emphasis on being able to take our work with us. Traditionally this was only feasible in a limited sense, but advanced miniaturization of complex technologies gave birth to a whole host of portable devices – as each new iteration of the technology comes to market, we are treated to ever smaller, ever more powerful machines. The shift caught the imagination of users, and the focus moved to more functionality in ever smaller units. This demand pull is still evident, even though the market emerges with ever smaller units capable of processing power that match any respectable desktop machine.

This trend is not entirely a new phenomenon. The idea of the modern portable personal computer goes back many years, perhaps more than one would originally imagine. Thirty years ago, Alan Kay working at the Xerox Palo Alto Research Centre (PARC) prophesied a notebook sized computer capable of recognizing handwriting and able to communicate with other systems through radio frequency. At the time, PCs were not widespread, and his comments seemed somewhat off the mark. His vision is today a reality in the form of advanced palmtop units, which grow richer in functionality in every release.

Costs of portable PCs have dropped considerably as their popularity continues to increase, but it is not only sizes that have shrunk, with each new model costing less and offering more. The sizes of these machines continue to decrease, and consequently the fastest growing segment of the personal computer market is the sale of portable machines. Corporations have embraced this trend for portable computing in the form of a more permanent set up in the office, or home, via a docking solutions coupled with a full size screen, which the portable unit plugs into. The user is effectively 'plugged-into' the internal corporate network, as well as access to external networks such as the Internet, easily and without hassle.

Computer Processors – The Next Era

The processor of any computer is the heart of any machine, and sophisticated advances in chip technologies bring to market ever faster and powerful variants, while every few years a new technology is spawned. Most of us are familiar with chips that use Complex Instruction Set Computer (CISC) chips, prevalent in our desktops and other mobile devices. CISC chips completed large numbers of complex tasks in ever faster cycles, but limitations prevented large back-end processing supercomputers from reaching new levels of processing performance. This led to the introduction of processing designs known as RISC (Reduced Instruction Set Computer) technology in the late 1980s, and by simplifying the number of tasks these processors needed to complete, performance was enhanced significantly. Consequently, the 1990s began to see the migration of the Unix industry to this platform with RISC-based machines outperforming their CISC brethren. In addition to the increased power, the chips were smaller and cooler, an important factor for portable machines. Despite efforts by various coalitions to bring this technology platform to the consumer market, penetration was never significantly achieved. Some notable efforts included Apple Computer, IBM and Motorola, who joined forces to attempt to exploit the technical superiority of RISC architecture, and to also attempt to compete with the dominant position Intel had achieved in the marketplace. The trio developed the PowerPC microprocessor. The first systems built using this chip were marketed by IBM back in 1993, in their RS series of workstations. It was March 1994 when Apple brought the PowerPC to the desktop, marketed under its Power Macintosh family. Despite some initial divergence from the intended common platform that the PowerPC was designed for, Apple and IBM finally agreed on the specifications of a common PowerPC Reference Platform (PReP).

Apple had been moderately successful with its Power Macintosh family of products, but this still only represented a small fraction of the desktop market that Intel controlled. The major impediment to gaining market share had never been the technical superiority of the chip architecture, but rather the lack of compatibility with the Intel series of chips which dominated the desktop market.

The never ending thirst for additional processing power continues unabated however. This is despite chips breaching processing speeds of several gigahertz. Chip performance can only be improved in a few ways:

▷ Increasing clock speeds, allowing more tasks to be completed in the same time frames. The corresponding issues with this are the increases in heat produced which have negative effects on reliability.

▷ Making chips smaller, which reduce the pathways for data to travel. Sizes are depicted in microns, with new generations reaching an incredible 0.1 microns.

▷ Processing in parallel and design chips to enable them to do so, allowing several tasks to be processed simultaneously.

The first two advances have continued in all of the architectures, but it is the latter that is beginning to come to fruition in the early years of the new century. Although these techniques were evaluated in the 1980s, these did not become commercially viable – the approaches were ahead of their time.

The next generation of architecture, known as Explicitly Parallel Instruction Set Computer (EPIC), uses design concepts that build on the parallel approaches RISC introduced with every possible operation built on parallel approaches. One of the first commercial variants of this technology was Intel's IPF architecture and its Itanium Chip.

One technology has not superseded its predecessors, and each co-exists in different applications and environments. The processing power of RISC and EPIC processors are well suited for high end processing platforms. CISC continues to evolve in terms of its processing performance and provides an excellent platform for desktop and personal computing applications, although as software applications and user requirements continue to grow, the fundamental processing superiority of RISC and EPIC approaches will dominate.

The Role of The Network

In the early 1980s, the advent of the personal computer provided the user with a means of solving problems locally, without the hassle of having to deal with a centralized MIS department. This was facilitated with tools such as Visicalc and Lotus 123. Importantly, people could buy these tools at a departmental level, with discretion of which hardware and software left to the local level.

As the number of these PCs grew, there was a logical need to share expensive resources (such as high performance printers – driven by high quality printing requirements), and the sharing of files. It was sensible to link these machines together using a Local Area Network (LAN) and the mid 1980s saw a huge growth in the number of LANs implemented. The early installations again suffered the fate of the initial PCs bought. Discretion for these installations were left at the local departmental level, and large organizations soon found themselves dealing with many different topologies, utilizing different software solutions.

The networking industry was beginning to blossom, especially with the introduction of Wide Area Networks (WANs), as LANs were co-ordinated and linked together. Many farsighted organizations were quick to see the potential of linking various users within their networks and sharing information as well as expensive resources. Organizations learnt and began to realize the possibilities that utilizing this infrastructure offered for important new applications, such as workflow and collaborative group working, especially when covering multiple geographic locations. As application functionality grew, so did the demands on network-based resources and the resulting demands on increased bandwidth for multi-media rich content.

Whilst the corporate world was going through its own small revolution, the prominence of the Internet was growing at ever phenomenal rates. By the early 1990s, some organizations were beginning to experiment and utilize Internet technology. By the middle of the decade, arguably the roles had reversed, and the majority of organizations were utilizing

Internet technologies to some extent. It was becoming more commonplace to see an Internet E-mail address adorning many business cards, and organizations now had a new headache – communication outside of the internal network.

The need to network is a necessity in organizations today, whether this is via physical or remote links, internally or externally. The marketplace has acknowledged this requirement and many machines now ship complete with networking hardware capabilities, and associated software to allow the communication and interaction between individuals. Indeed operating systems themselves are being oriented towards networked applications, with facilities to share personal storage domains and facilitating application sharing, and most releases boast 'plug and play' capabilities so that computers can link and be linked with minimal effort. This is not only affecting the way we work, but also the way we play – most machines directed to the consumer market are functionally rich in hardware specifications, Internet ready and boast high capacity modem facilities.

In the corporate world, the way departments and consequently whole organizations work and communicate has been radically changed – information is considered the lifeblood of an organization. In the contemporary organizational environment, extending the biological analogy, the network (whether LAN or Internet based) can be viewed as the veins carrying that information. Consequently, the amount of resource afforded to network technology and the importance of availability has increased dramatically.

On the hardware side, larger and larger bandwidths are being provided within the corporate environment, as new technologies such as image and voice continue to be integrated across networks. The widespread use of fibre optic cable allows the bandwidth hungry multi-media applications that are becoming commonplace on the desktop. The network itself is also taking on a new form; the concept of a LAN is being redefined as a growing army of mobile workers, armed with functionally rich devices, demand to join the network of computers from various locations around the world. These themes are further explored in Chapter 10 – Wireless Commerce.

The sheer impact of the Internet on everyday life – at work and at home – is simply breathtaking. Today, from the desktop linked into the Internet, or corporate Intranet, individuals are treated to a whole array of real time information. Searching this vast domain becomes ever easier with new browser technologies, and ever more powerful search engines and intelligent agents that can be highly customized. This with the continued trend to access corporate databases and centralized software licenses sitting on corporate servers have opened up new challenges (and potential cost savings), and posed some interesting questions on the desktop, and its associated hardware. The role of the computer continues to change and the advent of a different configuration of computing platform offers new possibilities (sometimes referred to as the Network Computer). These thin client devices promise much – being functionally simple, they can operate across a variety of networks and platforms and typically do not house any floppy disks or CD-ROMs, but come complete with high performance communication infrastructure such as Ethernet network connections. Although introduced in the market with high hopes, they have yet to gain critical mass.

Software Evolution

It has not only been hardware that has seen some fundamental changes in the past years. The supporting software options to help us work have mushroomed and we found ourselves facing difficult choices as the numbers grew. Many organizations experienced a period of decentralization, controlled and more often uncontrolled, where users were empowered to make choices according to their requirements. The widespread use of corporate networks and their growth clearly brought home the need for a homogenous set of tools, and a process of consolidation took place; the introduction of a 'suite' of software illustrated the trend.

Furthermore, software technologies fuelling the growth of the Internet continued to be propelled by Gopher (in the early days) and advanced browser technologies. Netscape, best known for its Netscape browser software, was catapulted into the mainstream when the company launched its product, instantly valuing the organization at millions of dollars.

This section of the chapter examines the evolution of the desktop Operating System (OS), the introduction of the Graphical User Interface (GUI) and its continual evolution, the role of Internet software technologies, as well as a look at popular software packages and the impact they have made on organizations.

The Emergence of MS-DOS

With the emergence of the IBM personal computer in the early 1980s, developed by a team of technical wizards, IBM gained prominence in the desktop market thanks to an aggressive marketing campaign. These machines were slow and heavy and would boast a couple of hundred kilobytes of memory, a megabyte or two of storage and operated at speeds that would send most users to sleep today. Many of us may have used, or at least seen these machines gathering dust in a forgotten room within our organizations.

The Disk Operating System (DOS) was licensed in 1981 to operate on machines that utilized the Intel 8088 processor, featured in the early personal computers, and was designed to utilize the available technologies of that day. The machines have evolved, and in latter times, we have chips which operate thousands of times faster than the 8088, yet it was some years before the use of DOS which can only perform one task at a time, diminished. For almost a decade, users were subjected to interacting with the machine via a keyboard designed to slow the individual, and an operating system, MS-DOS, riddled with unfriendly jargon and associated commands.

The emergence of the graphical user interface (GUI) and the mouse pointer device, whose progenitors can be identified as Xerox Corporation (who failed to exploit the technology) and Apple (who arguably did exploit the technology, but not to its full potential), had the potential to address this orthodoxy, and has succeeded in becoming the new popular standard. Microsoft Corporation, the original developers of DOS (for IBM), has succeeded in making their Windows GUI arguably the defacto standard on the PC platform. It is almost impossible, or at least very difficult, to even purchase a new PC machine without having Windows software pre-loaded.

Bridging the Cognitive Gap

The challenge faced by all organizations, whether in the private, public or other sectors, is effective utilization of the immense computing power that the average user has at their disposal. Organizations have invested billions of dollars in advanced technology yet white collar productivity statistics have either been stagnant, or never even get close to double figures. This paradox has been somewhat arduous to explain, and a lot more challenging in eliminating. The reasons are numerous, but perhaps the most important is the misguided belief that throwing technology at the problem was the panacea – traditionally technology has been difficult to use and understand, especially when the supporting processes were not in place.

Machines need to be made to fit into the human environment rather than attempting to force humans to conform to theirs; zealots of technology can sometimes underestimate the impact of this. Few can forget their first feelings of helplessness when switching on one of the early personal computers, only to be faced with a blank screen and blinking cursor. Those that had not mastered the arcane language of DOS, consisting of complex command lines, could not progress further. If that was not challenge enough, each application required its own competencies and language, creating the need for specialists in each area. Hardly the best way of realizing promised productivity gains from technology.

Thankfully, not all innovators subordinated the human in favour of the machine. The work at the Xerox Palo Alto Research Centre (PARC) was innovative and refreshing. Apple Computer Inc. had built its empire on the back of its user-friendly interface, inspired by the work at Xerox PARC; the machine was engineered to support the needs of the interface, completely eliminating the mysterious blinking prompt in favour of more intuitive icons and pull down menus. Microsoft had followed suit with its Windows range of operating software. For many, the Apple Macintosh interface was always seen as being more intuitive than the Windows product, although the distinction becomes increasingly blurred as new releases of Windows came to market.

FunFigure 4.1 GUIs make it easy!

The challenge of the GUI is to bridge the gap between our goals and thoughts, and the means of attaining these goals via the use of our computers. When we have achieved this, we may finally begin to see a reduction in the paper we use; when we write or communicate via paper, there is no need to think about how to enter the data, and therefore lose concentration of the problem in hand. An effective user interface can address this, and other stumbling blocks such as having to read lengthy manuals before using a piece of software: who has the inclination, or the time, to learn what the machine can achieve and cannot. *Learning by doing*, as an old Chinese proverb describes it, *is the truly effective way of learning*.

Intuitive interfaces and utilizing metaphors encourage the user to experiment and hence learn. Ensuring a consistency between applications significantly reduces learning times for new software and encourages confidence in users.

Work by US researchers has validated these[1], which compared GUI users and Character User Interface (CUI) users. An excerpt is provided below.

▷ GUI users accomplished 58% more work than CUI users in the same time period.

▷ GUI users expressed less frustration, rated at 2.7 out of 10, compared to 5.3 out of 10 for CUI users.

▷ GUI users were better able to explore and learn the capabilities of their applications, by 23% more than CUI users.

In conjunction with increased usage of GUI approaches, the trend is being augmented by speech recognition software and pen technologies such as Palm Computing's Graffiti language. The umbilical link connecting us to the computer is perhaps about to be changed, when examining recent trends. Not before time: the QWERTY keyboard was designed for the original mechanical typewriters, and the layout was governed by the over-riding need to slow the typist down, so that the mechanical keys would not get jammed. This antiquated design has endured for decades, and even with the advent of the mouse pointer, pioneered by the work of Douglas Engelbart at the Stanford Research Institute in the 1960s, the keyboard is still the primary form of input. There have been new keyboard designs that have followed a more intuitive layout, but these have not been successful in the marketplace.

On the desktop, operating systems (OS) promise to make our link with the computer more invisible and less arduous. As more software applications support these emerging technologies, such as pen computing and voice recognized inputs, implications for the way we work are unclear. As the technologies mature and become more stable, our link with the tools we work with will hopefully become easier to use and more akin to the paper and pencil, where we do not have to think about how to enter data.

As new releases of software come to market, the use of new interface technologies are transparent – this is clearly the way forward, and the latest versions of operating systems available to use attest to this trend; the challenge lies in making the user interface as transparent and as intuitive as possible.

Software Suites

The trend of decentralization brought an end to the traditional data processing and IT departments. Functional departments were afforded autonomy in controlling the way they worked and consequently the tools that they required to do their work. The emphasis had moved from proprietary written software solutions to the use of standardized 'off the shelf' software packages. Each user, or groups of users, purchased the solution that best met their needs. This usually meant buying the most advanced word processor, spreadsheet or graphics package.

Inevitably, as corporate data and information was disseminated, problems of sharing data between entities and departments became evident. Where information could be shared, retaining the integrity of data was an increasingly difficult task to manage – the underlying models and applications were all different. This situation has led to organizations being encouraged to adhere to one set of common applications throughout the company. The need led to the advent of a range, or suite, of software packages from one supplier.

With the huge take-up of the Internet and increasing uses of Internet-based technologies, suites are also being enhanced to provide these additional functionalities. Examples are Lotus including a Java-applet version of SmartSuite; Microsoft adding Internet features to their new Office Suite (Small Business Edition and Professional), including its Internet Explorer product.

The suite approach has arguably taken off not only for the integration aspect, but perhaps more importantly for the firm, the huge cost savings that could be made – essentially it made business sense. Furthermore large users could negotiate substantial discounts making the savings even more considerable. For instance, an office suite costing in the region of several hundreds of dollars, at retail list price, can be reduced down to around a third of that cost when bought in bulk quantity. Ironically we see a return to centralization with suite solutions being imposed throughout organizations.

Advantages

The advantages of going down the 'suite' path are numerous, and outlined below.

> ▷ *The Cost* – As already discussed, the cost savings can be considerable, and this is one of the primary driving forces behind the growth in buying software in this package.

▷ *Increased Integration* – Organizations are benefiting from the increased integration possibilities that suites can provide. Manufacturers are also expanding their market share on the back of promoting additional tools and technologies that facilitate easy sharing of data between applications. Inserting a graph into a word processed document is easily performed. Applications also support additional macro facilities that allow corporate users to customize functions from multiple programs to synthesize new products to meet their needs. The suite has been marketed as more than just a collection of programs collated in a convenient box.

▷ *Consistency* – With each application possessing similar menus and button bar icons, the user can adapt and learn new applications much faster. Training costs can also be reduced by employing suite software.

▷ *Control* – Large organizations have a difficult time in controlling upgrade costs, and associated problems that occur when different elements of the organization are using different versions of the same software. Corporate desktop initiatives are also much easier to implement and associated savings can be discerned when requiring support from just one vendor.

Disadvantages

It is difficult to envisage how buyers can go wrong with taking the suite approach. After all the suite concept was the biggest hit in the early to mid 1990s, with the largest market share netting almost $1 billion for Microsoft alone. Microsoft Office represented almost 50% of earnings for Microsoft Corporation in 2000. Despite the advantages, there are some distinct disadvantages associated with taking this strategic viewpoint to software acquisition.

▷ *Best of Breed* – A collection of software packages from one vendor are seldom all market leaders within their fields. Purchase the Lotus suite for example, and you get the industry acclaimed 123 spreadsheet package, but are also given a less popular word processing package. There is a trade-off, especially when users are familiar with a specific package. Enforcing a change can cause resistance, whether covertly or overtly. In some cases, the costs of the social pain greatly outweighs the financial gain.

▷ *The 80:20 Rule* – Suites are an excellent example of the 80:20 rule, where 80% of the users are really only using about 20% of the functionality in each suite – for the majority of the users, these added features are simply not required and subsequently not used.

▷ *Networking the Suite* – You cannot break up a suite – running the word processing software on one machine, and the spreadsheet on another is not permitted. If one element of the suite is being used, then typically the licenses for the other elements are also being effectively utilized. This can cause some difficult administration problems within a networked environment, and in some cases it is more sensible and cost effective to purchase individual licenses. The latter point is an important one, and can be one of the most important decisions an organization can make, when evaluating the suite approach to individual packages. Consider an organization with 1000 PCs, with 50% of users using word processing, and the rest using a spreadsheet package – only 500 copies of each application are needed. If this situation involved suite licensing, then the 500 using word-processing would effectively be utilizing the entire suite license, hence requiring the full 1000 licenses.

Evolution of the Suite – Web Services Models

The origin of the Suite concept centred around bundling discrete products from one manufacturer in a competitive package, encompassing the key software products required by an average user – word processing, spreadsheet and graphics software. Further subsets included 'Professional' suites, that included database and project management software options. Essentially, as time has gone by, each product has become more integrated with the other, reflecting the requirements and working habits of users.

Given the successful take-up of suites, this represents a significant investment and ongoing cost component to organizations. Numerous initiatives had led to Web services models, where features are represented in components and sold separately as opposed to a complete suite – in some cases, a pay as you go type of approach. These approaches were beginning to take hold, an example being Microsoft's Office.NET strategy.

Network Operating Systems

Earlier in this chapter, the prominence and growth of network infrastructures, whether internal networks typical of most corporate organizations, as well as the increasing impact of Internet influenced topologies was discussed. The software driving this trend has evolved almost as fast as the underlying hardware – especially in the area of Internet applications. Here we examine the historical evolution of the networking software, as well as taking a look at future trends that are emerging in the marketplace.

From David into Goliath

In the 1990s, Microsoft attained monolithic status within the personal computer marketplace. The company, that was founded in 1975 by Bill Gates and Paul Allen, built its foundations on its first product – a version of BASIC developed for the MITS Altair, an early personal computer. The company received its first big break when their product was chosen to supply an operating system for IBM's first PC. Since then, it has grown to become the world's largest software vendor – Bill Gates has metamorphosed from David into Goliath. Each iteration and release of Microsoft's major Windows Operating System enjoyed spectacular marketing campaigns. The sheer marketing muscle of the organization is one of the success factors of the Windows product gaining such prominence over other's offerings, such as Apple Computer's product. Since its launch in the early 1990s, the product has been continually updated and evolved to maintain its leadership position – the product line is outlined below.

Version	Characteristics
Windows	First Windows product – launched in 1985
Windows v3.1	16-bit GUI – became the defacto standard on the PC platform
Windows For Workgroups (v3.11)	Windows v3.1 superset, intended for LAN use and resource sharing
Windows NT	32-bit operating system, primarily designed for high end workstations – launched May 1993
Windows '95	Desktop system with 32-bit processing capabilities and new GUI – launched August 1995
Windows CE (Compact Edition)	Windows software environment for hand-held mobile devices
Windows '98	Launched in 1998, this expanded the functionality of '95 significantly
Windows 2000	Launched in February 2000, Windows 2000 built on the growing NT platform
Windows ME (Millenium Edition)	ME was specifically tailored for the consumer market
Windows XP	Windows XP was launched in October 2001, with versions aimed at the consumer and business segments via its Professional edition
Project Blackcomb	This is the code name for the next generation of Windows Platform, furthering Microsoft's .NET strategy

Table 4.1 Windows product line

On the desktop PC platform, Microsoft's products unquestionably have the lead and the future OS can be represented (not necessarily led) by the organization's forthcoming projects. The trend for the OS of this millennium is heavily reliant on embracing the integration of intelligent devices into existing infrastructures, as well as ensuring enhanced Internet capabilities.

Since the early releases of Windows, the product has been criticized for not being user friendly enough, and critics pointed to the advanced interface of the Apple Macintosh as the benchmark. Nevertheless the product, through Microsoft's effective strategy and marketing, entrenched itself on the majority of every desktop PC sold and used. On the server end of the market, several options have eroded the significant market share Novell enjoyed, with Windows NT/2000 platforms and open source Linux becoming popular choices.

Windows NT represented the first Microsoft product that did not rely on DOS to function, as opposed to earlier variations, hence possessing an advanced and robust architecture making it more reliable and stable. This put it in the league with other strong 'true' operating systems such as Unix solutions.

The new generation of Windows-based products (essentially evolving the NT structure introduced in the 1990s) builds on new technology integration and functionality. Additional releases, articulated in next generation releases code named Project Blackcomb (and an interim release termed Project Longhorn) are representative. It is this product that represents the real direction that operating systems may take in the next decade. The focus is on storing data as objects, descriptions of *where* to find the data rather than in files. It is this orientation on objects that represents great strength. This modular approach to an operating system, with 'independent co-operating parts' supports the trend of open systems and theoretically poses an interesting situation for vendors such as Microsoft – third party developers could easily produce elements for the OS, and hence perhaps reduce their hold.

Evolution to Web-based Components

As operating environments become more complex, advanced features begin to provide complex functionality to a wide community of differing users. This trend has led to increasingly monolithic applications. The late 1990s spawned the concept of component-based applications (with proponents such as Oracle's CEO Larry Ellison), and with the emerging use of Web-based approaches, the idea was well received. Within this context, a much broader shift is taking place within the arena of complex platforms which has a much wider context than just the network operating systems, embracing development applications, Web-based services, as well as operating and application software to bring forth a completely new strategy. As such, many of these initiatives were in their nascent stages in early 2000 and visions were shared, to varying degrees of detail, as elements were being developed with other aspects simply being a vague concept.

All of the large players were articulating this message, with heavy weights such as IBM and Microsoft perhaps having the broadest platforms with others such as SUN and Oracle providing elements. Within the scope of this chapter, we examine the holistic elements of these approaches within the context of the operating software and productivity tools, covered in detail in the next sections. We examine two main approaches by IBM and Microsoft, although there are others from players such as SUN, Oracle and Hewlett Packard to name just a few.

When examining server operating system forecasts, many advocate the dramatic rise of the Microsoft solution gaining market share at the expense of others. Within the general trend, the vendors are moving towards an environment much desired by users: a true enterprise wide distributed computing environment that would make the different platforms transparent. Desktop operating systems are evolving into powerful systems that can support object-oriented programming. The focus is very much on the development of an OS consisting of a micro-kernel representing the OS, with modular building blocks that can be developed by any third party, providing the user with a truly open and versatile OS environment.

Microsoft's .NET Strategy

In early 2000, Microsoft announced its .NET strategy – essentially its strategic blueprint of the future as it saw it. This was to be the corporate banner under which all of its products and strategies would be branded, and consequently encompassed a large number of services and areas ranging from its Windows-based software to Web-based services such as MSN and Hotmail, to its online identification efforts via Passport to name just a few. From a technological perspective, the platform was based on XML and Simple Object Access Protocol (SOAP) standards and provided the infrastructure to interchange data through public and private environments, as well as proprietary and open systems. Development tools such as Visual Studio were also embraced within the .NET platform, and provided extensive additional functionality, especially for Web services.

Services delivered as components also provided a new revenue model, with a move away from large applications. This was very evident in the suite software, where Microsoft Office would evolve to Office.NET and introduce subscription-based services. The Microsoft route to the future is just one vendor's vision, and the other players in the field are also developing their paths to the next generation of operating systems. All share large areas of overlap, and with all products the key to success will be achieving critical mass in terms of support from third party vendors.

IBM's Websphere

In many respects, IBM possessed one of the broadest platforms, with market leading positions in many of the key areas. IBM was an early proponent of Java development approaches and continued to incorporate these approaches into many of its key market leading propositions, such as Lotus Notes/Domino. Through its Lotus subsidiary, the Domino platform was evolving into a set of Java 2 Enterprise Edition components. In addition IBM was one of the earliest leaders in adopting Web services, although it was sometimes criticized for the lack of integration between its packaged applications.

Group Working

Working patterns have always been characterized by the need to communicate and share information. Business has always been a group activity, requiring several people with differing competencies to work together. Since computer technology impacted business life some decades ago, the need to communicate over greater geography and within shorter time scales has taken on more prominence. The infrastructure to allow groups to work together is already available through the networking of stand-alone machines. In past times the justification of linking personal computers centred on the sharing of expensive resources. LANs are now facilitating the use of technology in sharing information and helping individuals work more effectively with each other. The focus has become more strategic.

The late 1970s saw the emergence of the term 'Groupware'. Over the years, this has represented many different things and as the concept became more fashionable in the mid 1980s, the plethora of products purporting to be 'groupware' mushroomed, and correspondingly other terms that are similar to, or used synonymously with, groupware followed suit. Examples are collaborative computing, multi-user applications, workflow computing and computer supported collaborative working (CSCW).

There is confusion as to which terms applies to which product – throughout this book, the term groupware is generally used, although the different aspects relating to each term is discussed further. What exactly is groupware? Many definitions exist and the term means different things to different people. A good working definition is:

A collection of software programs designed to support people working in groups.

We can attempt to usefully separate this collection of programs into some distinct categories, listed below.

▷ Groupware environments

▷ Workflow software/computing

▷ Conferencing and consensus-building software

▷ Scheduling/Diary software

Examples of software would include; desktop conferencing, E-mail, bulletin boards, meeting support systems, group calendars and voice enabled applications. Many software solutions offer one or more of these elements – examples of these are discussed later.

The Evolution and Growth of Groupware

Arguably the most basic and earliest forms of groupware were simple E-mail facilities, which created the basis for a dominant messaging platform prevalent for the last three decades. Back in 1971, when Ray Tomlinson created a way for ARPAnet users to send electronic messages to one another, effectively creating E-mail, he also created one the most pervasive forms of group working.

Indeed a less glamorous and simple definition of groupware may be 'E-mail with bells and whistles', although this does not represent the newer advanced technologies available today. At the core of any groupware product is the ability to ease communication – this invariably translates into a form of E-mail. The 1970s saw the growth of computer mediated communication. At this time, groupware was defined along the lines of 'group processes and the software to support them'. The use of the term *processes* is an important one to highlight up front. The purchase of a groupware package then, and now, did not immediately lead to focused and functioning teams. There has to be emphasis and examination of processes and how they need to change.

Groupware evolved further in the 1980s when attempts were made at office automation to support workers – the theme was to help people work together. The term became popular in the mid to late 1980s, where productivity successes were being cited and lessons from successful implementations were learnt. The software was becoming more sophisticated and refined.

The groupware concept fitted in nicely with the business thinking of the early 1990s, when many organizations were expending great efforts to re-design processes, and aligning technology to these newly created work patterns. These products were being used as the building blocks for disseminating information, co-ordinating people and activities. As power is devolved further down the organization, teams require information that was historically held at the apex of the traditional pyramidal organizational structure. Groupware infrastructures were increasingly being used at the beginning of the decade, to disseminate this information to all, or subsets of employees.

The collection of groupware software addresses four main tasks performed in offices:

▷ Finding and collecting information

▷ Using this information

▷ Communicating and interacting with others

▷ Attending/initiating meetings

Some proponents of groupware also saw the technology as a means of reversing the 'productivity paradox'. This phenomenon highlighting the huge investment made by organizations in technology, but deriving only marginal improvements in productivity. By aligning technology to the way people work and the dynamics of human interplay, true benefits in productivity could be realized. Arguably, we already have enough technology on our desks to support everything we want to do.

At the turn of the century, elements of groupware were being incorporated into virtually all applications and Web-based services. Diverse approaches and supporting technologies were maturing to provide extensive benefits. Examples such as collaborative Web-based exchanges were proving beneficial for industry consortia to bringer faster cycles of product development. Applications were becoming richer in nature and more accessible.

These factors, amongst others, have contributed to the growth of the groupware market. All projected estimates concur that the market will experience healthy growth in the next 10 years.

Groupware Environments

Products that provide the basic infrastructure to build a technological group working environment, would fall into this category. Typically the actual pieces of the puzzle would be either developed by the organization purchasing the environment, outsourced to a developer, purchased off the shelf or accessed via a third party source on the Web – perhaps a marketplace the organization may be a part of.

This type of product is perhaps one of the most popular for large organizations, as it provides the flexibility to build features that address the needs of the business. This product would be categorized by possessing numerous features such as an E-mail engine, several databases, bulletin boards, and calendaring features. The emphasis is on enabling collaboration between people, regardless of their physical location or the time zone they work in.

An excellent example of this type of product would be the Notes product by Lotus, which further evolved and was renamed Lotus Domino in early 1997. Microsoft had concentrated into further developing its Exchange product, which although launched into the market after Lotus Notes, was gaining market share. As with Notes, MS Exchange is also being upgraded to support the various Internet-based standards such as XML and SOAP under the .NET strategy, and improving the cross collaboration between its other Internet-based products, such as Microsoft Explorer.

Advent of the Intranet

The role of products such as Lotus Notes/Domino and Microsoft Exchange has blurred in recent years, as organizations have increasingly continued to embrace Internet-based technologies in a more aggressive manner. The advent of the Intranet, essentially an internal information system, configured to integrate various Internet-based technologies, has begun to challenge the use of products such as those offered by IBM and Microsoft. Intranets are not new, with the early configurations consisting of various UNIX stations utilizing TCP/IP protocols. What is more recent is the widespread adoption of this type of groupware technology, and the wider scope outside of sharing files and rudimentary E-mail facilities. This rush to embrace the concept of the Intranet has also led to major manufacturers ensuring that their offerings also support these technologies.

Instant Messaging – R U Ready?

The use of Instant Messaging (IM) grew at a spectacular rate, driven mainly by the consumer market. This simple technology, which leveraged basic E-mail like technologies (essentially based on a post office type store and forward model) evolved to begin providing instantaneous messaging more akin to the telephone. Not surprisingly, as usage grew exponentially, users began informally using the technology in business environments, causing organizations to wake up to the business advantages of incorporating the approaches, effectively complementing their various communication methodologies already ingrained in everyday life.

Instant Messaging (IM) applications are all very similar when examining core functionality. Users activate a client software that interacts with a central server highlighting the user's online presence. Users identify themselves via a 'nickname' which is also used to identify who else is online at that particular moment in time. Users are then able to invite other users to enter a conversation (or can be invited by other users). The interaction is via simple text messaging that is delivered almost instantly via windows that appear on the user's screens. The interaction is almost instant, as opposed to E-mail. Messages are not routed and queued and are less reliant on the Domain Naming System (DNS), hence the enhanced performance.

Once online, buddy lists can be created which allow the identification of users when they are online (typically icons are highlighted). Users can simply click on the user icon, to initiate a discussion. This element of presence awareness – essentially an electronic in/out sign – is an exceptionally powerful aspect of IM, allowing an instant discussion that is different to using a telephone, in that it is usually more casual in nature. Indeed later generations of services allow the user to click an icon providing the ability to initiate a more traditional telephone discussion either using corporate private networks or Voice Over Internet Protocol (VoIP) based conversations.

Evolving and building on the early Internet Relay Chat and Unix-based Talk programmes, IM services when introduced in the late 1990s became exceptionally popular in consumer applications. Early manifestations were popularized and stereotyped by bored teenagers, or separated lovers and friends spending hours catching up or gossiping online. Online communities began building large user bases, with three main providers dominating – America Online, with its America Online Instant Messenger (AIM) service, Yahoo Messenger and Microsoft's MSN Messenger service. By the turn of the millennium, several hundred million user accounts were actively used in a combination of social and business contexts. In the latter, IM promises to be an important technology which like most new technology, will initiate another spectacular shift in our everyday lives.

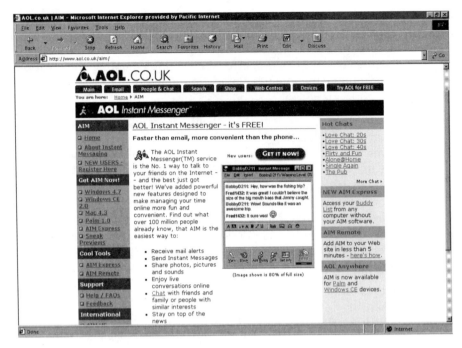

Figure 4.2 AOL's Instant Messaging Service

Since its introduction, the use and potential benefits of IM technology within the business environment has grown up, with numerous industries and applications beginning to garner and exploit it for competitive advantage. Not surprisingly, given the instant nature of the communication methodology. One may ask if we need yet another communication method, given overload by voicemail, E-mails and a variety of other communications. The technology is not replacing these well ingrained communication approaches, but rather co-existing and providing a complementary application. Its easy social fit, coupled with the fact that over half of business phone calls don't reach their intended recipients in a timely manner, are just some of the reasons the technology is easily integrating itself into our social and business lives.

Despite the success in the consumer world, there were however numerous reasons why IM usage in businesses was being impeded. These included:

▷ Businesses required strong security such as encryption and potentially authentication services. Basic IM services did not provide for this.

▷ Interoperability between systems was not evident and there was a distinct lack of integration between existing directories.

▷ Message archiving was not prevalent on all services.

▷ Usage policies within organizations were immature.

The latter posed some interesting conundrums. One of the powerful features of IM was its ability to mimic ad hoc discussions that were not necessarily as formal as E-mail or memos. Given this particular feature, IM was providing a sophisticated supplement to normal group interactions such as video or telephony conference calls. Additionally, IM was well suited to replicate the non-formal exchanging of ideas and comments typically exchanged in less formal settings.

Given the interest the business community were expressing in IM services, it's no surprise that major vendors such as Microsoft and IBM/Lotus began offering the services, as well as integrating them into their core applications such as Lotus Notes and Microsoft Exchange. The Lotus Sametime product, launched in 1999, began to offer some of the robust additional services that business interaction required, and effectively challenged some of the reasons that IM was not being utilized in a business context. These services included encryption, linkages to existing directories, store/forward/retrieval services and additional groupware services allowing more advanced collaborative activities.

Naming conventions were also not suited for business commerce. Nicknames were easily created, and as a consequence identification of users (or indeed authenticating them) was difficult. Who knows that 'Red Rooster' is Robert Jenkins in Purchasing!

Another rather startling aspect of IM services was the effective birth of a new language. As the use of IM proliferated, a rather esoteric new language was developing. Given the instant aspect of the interaction, and typically casual and informal nature of the discussions, a new shorthand had developed within its user communities. Typical examples are illustrated in Table 4.2, and these ranged from basic glossaries to more advanced communications typified by power users of the technology.

Basics		Advanced	
cu	See you	ruok	Are you okay
gtg	Got to go	bcnu	Be seeing you
nbd	No big deal	btdt	Been there, done that
ttyl	Talk to you later	?4u	Question for you
hand	Have a nice day	cid	Consider it done
pcm	Please call me	wfm	Works for me

Table 4.2 Instant messaging shorthand

Standards

IM had a major impediment that was slowing its take-up, especially in business environments. There were not widely adopted standards, and interoperability continued to be non-existent. The situation was exacerbated by the competitive stance of major providers such as AOL in keeping and maintaining its dominant position, especially against Microsoft. The political dynamics were overriding the technical capabilities that were available. Despite this, there was acceptance that this needed to change, and a few standards were beginning to emerge, as outlined below.

▷ *Session Initiation Protocol (SIP)* – SIP serves as a general standard for all real time point to point interactions such as IM, although its applicability is somewhat wider than that encompassing VoIP networks and videoconferencing, as examples.

▷ *Instant Messaging Presence Protocol (IMPP)* – As discussed earlier, one of the basic components of IM is its presence awareness capability. The IMPP working group (an element of the Internet Engineering Task Force (IETF)) was working on a standard to address this particular element of IM.

▷ *SIP for Instant Messaging and Presence Leveraging (SIMPLE)* – Interoperability of IM systems continued to be heavily challenged due to the political and competitive nature of the dominant players. The SIMPLE standard looked to address interoperability issues and both Microsoft and AOL had agreed to conform to these standards.

Wireless IM

The use of wireless Short Message Service (SMS) was widespread by the turn of the century (see Chapter 10 Wireless Commerce), and in many ways IM and SMS share the same roots. As it grew, IM technology had the basic infrastructure to liberate users from PCs and embrace the numerous rich wireless devices available, such as cellular phones, personal digital assistants or any other device capable of wireless interaction. The usage of IM's underlying technology was providing some very interesting opportunities – such as its presence awareness features. Coupled with accurate location-based information from a wireless services provider, messages could be fired to users wanting to locate a particular location – a restaurant for example or even another person when they were within a particular radius. Especially useful for crowded events.

The potential impact of the convergence of these technologies was being explored, and a forum being established. One example was the Presence and Availability Management Forum[2]. Interoperability issues within this space were also being examined, with the major players such as Ericsson, Nokia and Motorola founding the Wireless Village initiative in April 2001, which was also supported by the IEEE standards body. The effort was based on building interoperability between participant technologies, using the SIMPLE protocol.

Workflow Software/Computing

Mention workflow software or computing, and most people will immediately think of some type of imaging system, or associated software. This is hardly surprising, as these systems brought the term to the mainstream. Workflow has changed and evolved though, and many different levels of functionalities exist – this is where the confusion begins to manifest. What is workflow?

When considering any work process, groups of people and information are involved – the information flows with the flow of the work, being enhanced or added to at each stage. Whatever the job, people must have access to the relevant information, at the relevant time. Workflow computing is the act of providing the data at each step of the work process, and workflow software automates the transfer of information to support this flow. The essential principle is to examine business issues and to translate them into a solution that can be improved using technology. It is workflow's group orientation that sometimes leads to confusion with 'groupware' products. A simple example is the workflow of a document, say in an insurance company. In order to process a claim, the relevant document may be routed between several groups of people. A typical flow could be:

1. Claim case opened by administrator

2. Adjuster adds comments after viewing

3. Manager signs and validates claim

4. Accountant prepares payment of claim

5. Payment generated and sent to claimant

Although simplistic, the example illustrates the several departments that the document has flowed through. It is applications like these that early forms of workflow improved significantly – helping to tie departments more closely together, and to reduce "in-tray" delays. It is also these types of paper intensive industries that allowed imaging companies to do extremely well with workflow solutions.

Once the workflow has been established, software can automatically route information or documentation to the relevant area/person, suspend and archive information, hence cutting delays, inefficiencies and costs. The benefit to the customer is also significant, as the organization is able to complete the cycle in a much shorter time frame.

Workflow possesses some key functionalities:

▷ Routing – probably the most critical aspect of any workflow application is the ability to route information or documents

▷ Audit Trail – it is important to be able to track and report who has added or modified

▷ Integration – the ability of the software to work with, and interact with existing applications

Links with Business Process Re-engineering (BPR)

Workflow dovetails nicely with BPR initiatives. As processes are changed, workflow allows technology to increase productivity by automating the transfer of information involved in that process. Just as there are several different levels of applying BPR techniques, workflow supports BPR in different ways. At the most basic level, workflow helps to identify what does, and does not work well in the way a business operates. Productivity gains can be achieved by utilizing technology to help automate these processes. This is a basic to intermediate level of workflow application. An example of this would be the installation of document image processing to move and image documents within an organization.

At the other extreme, workflows can be completely rebuilt, and processes are not simply optimized, but completely changed. New infrastructures and technologies are established to support this new way of working, increasingly being delivered using Web based approaches or on an ASP outsourced approach. As processes are changed to meet new challenges, many organizations are demanding applications that can allow inter-departmental collaboration – whether this is just simply exchanging documents electronically, or more sophisticated needs. This is where a new and growing breed of workflow applications are being utilized.

Just as processes cannot be cast in stone, workflow has grown to possess a more supple form, where applications can be changed easily. This feature has unsurprisingly been implemented on a flexible client/server and Web-based architectures. Typically it is internal processes that are benefiting from workflow the most today. This includes financial, administrative processes and the customer service function. Much of this is due to workflow's in-ability to deal with ad hoc requirements well – this is discussed further later.

Evolution of Workflow

Today, workflow means much more. Workflow is no longer just associated with distinct products, but is distinguished by a set of features and capabilities that are being built into a variety of applications, even at the desktop.

The introduction of new features is making the application of workflow techniques more widespread. Traditionally, the technology made huge improvements in back-office applications, where the routing of information and needs of the user were within manageable boundaries. Today workflow needs to break out of fixed routing, as it was in earlier imaging systems. The emphasis is not so much on the flow, but on the management of work. Work management applications are now beginning to address the requirements of knowledge workers, whose tools are paper, fax, telephony and the desktop i.e. usually a suite of applications, including electronic mail. These needs, by virtue of their ad hoc nature, make automation a more complex issue.

Two ways that workflow is meeting these requirements, are via:

▷ Electronic forms

▷ Intelligent agents

The Intelligent Agent

Workflow is evolving to meet needs that are ad hoc in their nature. One manifestation of this on the desktop is the advent of the intelligent agent.

The intelligent agent is automated workflow, which the user can define. The results are much more proactive, rather than reactive – as opposed to receiving information and then acting on it, the intelligent agent can 'search' for the information required, and/or perform some transformation to the data before routing it on. The agent is performing a myriad of tasks, and is closely linked to the idea of the 'integrated desktop' of the future. Within work-management, a good example of this in operation may be the following.

▷ Orders are received electronically via EDI or over the Web – each order is processed via the processing manager. An intelligent agent may perform the following tasks:

▷ Credit status of customer is verified

▷ Check if present order is within credit limit

▷ Can order be fulfilled

▷ Process order

▷ Adjust inventory accordingly

▷ Send out confirmation

Each event may trigger an action that is routed to other areas within the organization. The 'intelligence' can be as complex as the user wants it to be. At another level, intelligent agents may be used to collect information. For instance, a Marketing Manager who requires up-to-date information on certain products may set up an agent to collect any clippings on these products – this information is routed automatically to the desktop. This capability of intelligent routing differentiates it from groupware (although increasingly groupware products are incorporating workflow technologies).

The Information River

Workflow is growing up – simple elements of workflow are appearing in almost every application. The introduction of workflow can range, from a core business application, typically dealing with back/front-office administrative work processes, to desktop applications. The former is expensive and usually host-driven, whereas the latter is relatively cheap and easily implemented.

With the trend of workflow taking on a 'management of work' approach, the challenge for users is to integrate this new technology into new processes. This is already evident, with re-engineering initiatives relying on workflow technology.

As the technology matures, one can see the relatively rigid simple workflow computing of yesteryear, taking on a more fluid and flexible appearance – conceptually emerging as an "information river". As data and information flows through the organization, workflow technology will route, enhance and deliver it to its ultimate destination. Users will be able to tap into this resource, directly or via personal intelligent agents. The river will be functionally rich, embracing not only text, but voice and video.

Conference and Consensus Building Software

Conferencing software promises many benefits for group working – especially for meetings with staff over geographical areas. Related to this area is the growing field of video conferencing technologies, which are discussed later in this chapter.

Software that has been around for some time, but has not yet hit the mainstream, centres on facilitating discussions and meetings using computer technology. Historically also referred to as Group Decision

Support Software (GDSS), the underlying theme is to provide an environment that constructively helps the decision making process, while reducing or attempting to nullify some of the negative aspects of group working. Consensus building software attempts to create a level playing field among people who have some input into the decision making process.

Typically, the set-up involves a series of participant terminals, which can be located in one room, or various locations using underlying technology platforms like LANs, Virtual Private Networks (VPNs) or the public Internet. Each participant in the discussion contributes, often anonymously – the argument is that because prejudices cannot be applied to the idea promoted, comments are more honest and decisions are reached in a shorter time than without the software.

Scheduling/Diary Software

Anyone who has attempted to schedule a meeting with several busy professionals immediately recognizes the value of being able to automate this tedious and iterative process. This is where group scheduling software comes into play – interest in this type of software was relatively muted until the 1990s, despite early applications being available for many years. Its popularity had grown with the increased use of E-mail and groupware products.

Group scheduling software basically scans online personal diaries for mutually free time, notifies participants of proposed meetings and automatically updates calendars if each participant is able to attend. In conjunction with this, the software may also allocate an appropriate conference room, and provide other value added features.

Users of the IBM Professional Office Systems (PROFS) will recognise this feature immediately – they have been benefiting from it for decades. Typically the new breed of calendaring and scheduling software possesses, at minimum, the following attributes:

▷ Electronic calendars

▷ Meeting scheduling capabilities

▷ Personal 'to do list' function

The key players in the market have positioned themselves to provide an integrated messaging, scheduling and workflow capability – typically seamlessly incorporated into other applications such as Lotus Notes, being one example. Indeed the ability to view diaries and schedule meetings is frequently voiced as a significant factor in the decision to proceed with a Microsoft Exchange implementation. In addition there are many smaller providers, each offering product capabilities that meet the above core attributes, as well as other value added features. Key to their success is the ability to integrate into other environments.

Challenges with Scheduling Software

The benefits of scheduling and calendaring software are apparent, but implementation does not always improve productivity. This apparent paradox is easily understood if the underlying assumptions of the technology are not realized. For instance, saving time and work when scheduling meeting necessitates everyone else involved doing some more work. For the system to work, each person needs to maintain an up-to date online diary. This is fine for those that are accustomed to maintaining an electronic schedule, but for those that are not, a new way of working is implied. This change in working style is resisted at times, due to the short-term inconvenience.

As a secretary may tell you, although a 'slot' in a manager's schedule may be open, they are not actually free during this period. Again, without the secretary, an application cannot determine this, and usually requires a re-scheduling process once that slot has been tentatively booked. New terminology and practice is required to allocate periods of time – many see this as an activity that is not only difficult, but too much hassle. This often results in the act of 'blocking out' periods of time, when in reality the manager may be available.

Many of the calendaring and scheduling products on the market today utilize an underlying E-mail facility to function. The store and forward nature of E-mail post offices can cause frustrations with the system, due to the delays experienced when different servers are being updated. This situation is exacerbated with busy schedules and rooms that are in high demand.

Scheduling software is a powerful tool. Many implementations are supporting an entry into a broader workflow approach, where the tool is being used as a delegating and directing mechanism. The software is growing up at a fast pace, and increasingly being incorporated as one piece of a broader puzzle, typically integrated into other applications and allowing users to dynamically update their diaries using remote access mechanisms, or via the Internet.

Justifying and Implementing Groupware

Groupware is considered a 'good thing', but it can be difficult to near impossible to justify its implementation using standard financial engineering tools. Groupware's greatest benefits are often intangible and therefore difficult to quantify using widely used and accepted measures. Often it is the indirect benefits that the technology brings that outweigh the original perceived benefits.

A critical point is the training, consulting and maintenance costs that groupware environments, such as Notes, necessitate. Studies have shown that for every dollar spent on software, up to five are spent on consulting services. Even having taken these costs into consideration, companies using groupware have gained from significant productivity gains.

Deployment of groupware depends heavily on addressing technical and social conditions of the organization. Groupware changes the dynamics and decision making processes of an organization. Handled badly, the implementation can be disastrous. Issues that need to be handled include:

▷ Conflict – new processes need to be built, and hence new skills. Not everyone believes in investing in these skills.

▷ Deskilling and Job Loss – there is a very real fear that jobs will be either deskilled or simply replaced by the technology.

▷ Ownership – information needs to be clearly identified as being owned by the individual or the team.

▷ Reward systems – these need to be aligned to the new group working environment being implemented.

There are numerous other social impediments to implementing groupware successfully.

Groupware – Here to Stay

Group scheduling, workflow and the groupware environment is here to stay. As with all aspects of groupware, organizations are successfully deploying this new technology as it matures – the organizational changes in the way we work cannot be fully predicted or hurried. The need to adapt to this new way of working is going to differentiate those that can derive competitive advantage and those that resist and struggle with the change.

Organizational change needs to be anticipated. The technology will replace and deskill some workers and communication and authority structures will change. This decentralized control should not dim the prospect of introducing the technology. Groupware fits in well with the new emerging organizational structures that are increasingly being implemented.

Videoconferencing

The marrying of technologies has always been a popular dream, and certainly the convergence of television and computing has been one of the most promising. Videoconferencing has been around for some time, and it has only been the beginning of this decade that advances in technology are allowing the widespread use of the technology at acceptable costs.

The roots of videoconferencing can be traced back perhaps as long ago as 1927, when Herbert Hoover used a video booth in Washington D.C. to communicate with a Bells Labs videophone in New York. More recently, in 1964, AT&T introduced its PicturePhone – since then the quest to videoconference has taken on almost a religious fervour. Evangelists include the telecommunications companies worldwide. This is not surprising when one considers the sheer amount of data being transmitted when using the technology – moving this amount of data means potentially large profits for these firms.

For instance, a colour moving image confined to a 320 by 240 pixel quadrant generates 4.8 megabytes of data a second. One minute of uncompressed colour video uses 287 megabytes of storage. It is not surprising that one of the keys to unlocking the widespread use of videoconferencing has been effective compression techniques.

Growth of Videoconferencing

In the early 1980s, a fully equipped videoconference room with all the 'extras' may have cost up to $500,000 – this also required private communication links that could amount to $50,000 a month. Videoconferencing was certainly not cheap. This has changed in recent times though, with leaps in compression and computer technologies. In the mid 1990s, quality systems could be purchased for $20,000 utilizing switched dial up public networks that cost around $10 an hour. At the turn of the millennium, these costs have dropped even further, with small entry level systems typically being less than $5,000 and up to $15,000 for a large functionally rich system. The cost justification continues to become simpler.

Market estimates agree that the technology will really take off in the latter end of the decade. Indeed, estimates in the early 1990s indicated that almost half the Fortune 1,000 companies had purchased videoconferencing systems[3]. Giga Group estimate the $550 million market in 2001 to more than double by 2005.

The technology has been dominated by a few organizations: Polycom, Compression Labs and VTEL. Standardization between these companies is still an issue, and although they have publicly agreed that interoperability is key to the success of these systems, each continues to market proprietary technology. The situation is reminiscent of the fax machine, whose growth did not really mushroom until one type could communicate reliably with other types. Since applications tend to mostly be inter-company use, end users have not been particularly concerned with this.

This lack of adherence to a standard to not due to the lack of the existence of one, but more a criticism of the low video and audio quality that the standard bodies have defined. In 1990, the CCITT standards body defined the H.261 (or Px64) international standard for codec interoperability, and compression – codecs convert analogue video signals to digital signals for transmission. This has been superseded by the H.320 standard, the international specifications for audio conferencing and video-conferencing. Typically these standards are used over ISDN-based lines, with a minimum of 128Kbps required, and 768Kbps providing TV type quality.

The H.323 videoconferencing standard provides the ability to utilize IP connectivity allowing organizations to utilize their own IP-based network or Virtual Private Network. This approach will no doubt become the dominant one over time, as increases in bandwidth technology continue to facilitate this rich data exchange.

Videoconferencing on the Desktop

The trend of the desktop becoming more multifunctional and flexible is evident – videoconferencing has been available for a desktop machine for many years, but it has been the dramatic drop in the price of powerful processors that have made it a viable business solution. A desktop videoconferencing system typically requires a Pentium-based computer as a base, and consists of a camera, microphone, speakers and video circuitry and software for compression and decompression. Prices vary according to the video quality, and continue to drop as use grows. Pushing the desktop market are players like Intel, as well as the telecommunications companies – the hook is the need for fast processors required to work with videoconferencing technologies. Typically this translates well for Intel's powerful processors, such as the family of Pentium chips. Intel itself has launched and aggressively marketed its videoconferencing system.

Desktop products are growing at a phenomenal rate, especially as units now cost less than a few hundred dollars. There is some misalignment with integrating the units with other desktop applications though. Two primary choices exist:

▷ Using a circuit switched system – this typically translates into an analogue or an ISDN connection

▷ Integration into the LAN/IP environment

Circuit switched solutions are the most popular, and as ISDN coverage worldwide increases, the option becomes increasingly practical. The latter is more attractive, but less prevalent at this time. The growing deployment and availability of ADSL broadband-based services are also playing an important role in the adoption of desktop videoconferencing. The huge bandwidths that video requires can have a dramatic impact on LAN performance, whose typical infrastructure today cannot easily meet with the demands. This will probably be addressed in two or three years time, when newer technologies boost LAN network capacities, and become the more dominant approach.

Videoconference – Glorified Videophone?

Videoconferencing, whether on the desktop or not, is more than videophone. Although the two technologies share the key components of image and voice, videoconferencing tools have a critical third dimension – that of the ability to collaborate online. This is via shared desktop applications, or the use of a whiteboard.

At its most basic, a whiteboard provides the freedom to communicate written or graphical communication between parties, and usually manifests itself in the form of a tablet. Products on the market are more functionally rich, and co-operate with desktop applications, such as Word and Excel.

It is this key functionality that provides the added value. Whiteboards and data-conferencing products have been on the market, and utilized widely for some time. Data-conferencing products allow screen-sharing of applications, allowing both users to edit documents. These products will usually operate with an external modem, or using a VPN or Internet, making them very accessible and flexible.

For many organizations, the added bonus of video is not justified even at today's relative low prices. Other reasons for not using video, for instance, is the availability of a suitable telecommunications infrastructure – i.e. South America still lacks a robust digital service. Much depends on the application.

Applications of Videoconferencing

So what applications are videoconference systems being used for? They tend to vary, but by far the most popular is meetings, internally, locally, and geographically dispersed. With business taking a more global stance, and the time taken for an executive to clear a calendar for an international meeting (up to six weeks, including an average of three days for the meeting), the use of the technology can afford some real advantages. Additional cost and safety concerns over international travel (there was a huge spike in videoconferencing after the tragic terrorist events of 11th September 2001 in the US) have further fuelled the take up of the technology.

Currently, the majority of the meetings are point-to-point but users are discovering real advantage in multi-site meetings, despite the relatively high cost, due to the switching technology. One area that organizations perceived great benefit is in saved travel expense. Companies have spent immense sums on necessary business travel, and this has increased in latter times due to the increasing globalization of organization and business needs. The potential savings that can be made by video-conferencing are therefore attractive not only from a financial perspective, but also from a resource point of view – this can include factors such as:

▷ Time savings derived from less travel

▷ Less jet lag

▷ Increased productivity

There is little quantifiable evidence to indicate that the take-up of videoconferencing technology has indeed produced significant travel savings. In fact, many cite other productivity savings as greater, but due to the difficulty in putting a figure on this, travel is used as a good cost justification.

Many are reluctant to use videoconferencing technology for key meetings, especially first time meetings. The nuances that are picked up when face to face do not translate well, especially due to the slight time lag and the fact that people can easily move away from the camera at key points – not so easy when one is physically present. After all, would you want to play poker over a videoconference link? Other important aspects are echo cancellation, fidelity and lip synchronization. Many users of videocon-ferencing have found that it is the quality of the audio, over the video, that makes for a successful conferencing session, and for this reason the PSTN may also be used in conjunction for the audio element of the interaction.

High value applications are numerous though, and include scenarios such as:

▷ Distance learning

▷ Managing geographically dispersed projects

▷ Entertainment and broadcasting;

▷ Internal meetings.

Many organizations are finding the only way to practically assess the value of videoconferencing, whether at the desktop or not, is to pilot the technology. With costs dropping every quarter as its use propagates throughout business and practice become more widespread, the technology becomes more attractive. There are a wide range of products now on the market – the key is in selecting the right solution for the needs of your organization, and how it should be implemented – whether this is via desktop use, using circuit switched technology or a larger installation.

---

[1] PV Jones, A GUI Puts a Friendly Face on Computing, *Business Quarterly*, Spring 1993, P.110–113

[2] www.pamforum.org

[3] Bane of Business Travel, Joan M. Feldman, *Air Transport World*, September 1993, P.44

Business to Business (B2B)

5

Introduction

> *"...in the years between 1870 and 1920 the cost of distributing necessities and luxuries has nearly trebled, while production costs have gone down by one-fifth... What we are saving in production we are losing in distribution."*[1]

The above quote from Ralph Borsodi (1929) still has relevance today as the proportionate cost structures within businesses, including direct labour costs, raw-material and overheads, continue to vary. These trends have been even more pronounced over the last 30 years with greater adoption of robotics by manufacturing and business computers in the back-office. When analyzing the position it is clear that most of the potential cost reductions have now been squeezed out of manufacturing, primarily due to the relentless pressure to achieve productivity and quality improvements. The progressive development and adoption of business computing that created the knowledge-worker has also contributed to streamlining back-office operation and further taking out cost. As a result companies have been forced to re-examine their supply chain operation as they seek further cost reductions to maintain their competitive position. Indeed, many have found that supply chain improvements continue to offer real scope to make a difference to their business results, but demand some drastic changes in the way they do business.

So, whilst opportunities still exist to achieve internally focused efficiency improvements, invariably it is the external processes involving the total supply chain or extended enterprise that really make a difference. Top management recognizes the importance of sound business practices, under-pinned using e-Business, to reduce costs, improve customer service and stay competitive. The change in the traditional 'win-lose'

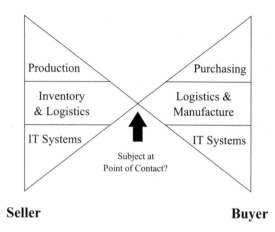

Figure 5.1 Traditional model

relationship that has existed between seller (supplier/manufacturer/ distributor) and buyer (manufacture/distributor/retailer) illustrates the dramatic manner in which attitudes are changing (Figure 5.1). In the past, once all basic product factors have been satisfied, the primary subject of contact has come down to price/delivery, with the assumption that there is a winner and a loser as an outcome of the negotiations. Several of the more innovative retailers have seen that by a greater integration of their supply chains, a 'win-win' relationship can be established with their suppliers. Since closer long-term strategic relationships are established there is a greater willingness to exchange information and co-operate more fully, resulting in efficiency and productivity improvements that can be shared between both parties. This is referred to as the e-Supply Chain model (Figure 5.2).

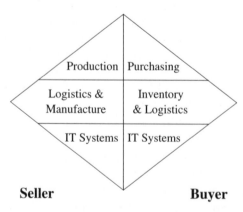

Figure 5.2 e-Supply chain model

In summary, there is a growing realization that profitably producing and selling a top quality product (or service) at the best possible market price, is not solely a function of the organization alone, but increasingly dependent upon the effectiveness in which the total supply chain is managed. Therefore, business process improvements need to extend beyond organizational boundaries to envelop and integrate with those activities of all trading partners within the supply chain.

Business Focus

All commercial organizations exist to create customers and through sales revenues and optimal management of corporate assets, deliver profits to shareholders. When trading in a competitive environment companies pursue strategies that improve profitability by increasing 'revenue' and reducing 'costs'. Clearly these two different focuses are not mutually exclusive and many organizations naturally develop action plans that seek to both maximize revenues and minimize costs.

When pursuing a 'revenue' focus some of the likely possibilities are:

▷ Increase the sales of existing products by reducing stock-outs. This requires strong customer relationships and collaboration that is based upon fast and efficient response to changes in demand patterns.

▷ Expand sales channels through alliances and explore the suitability of the Internet to reach new customers.

In contrast when pursuing a 'cost' focus, likely possibilities include:

▷ Establish strategic relationships with suppliers to secure improved prices, terms and conditions.

▷ Reduce raw material and product inventories throughout the supply chain.

▷ Reduce distribution/warehousing costs.

▷ Rationalize the supply chain to eliminate non-value added activities and intermediaries.

The Supply Chain

A typical company will comprise a core competence that is used to produce products for onward selling to customers. Production volumes are determined by sales orders received from customers as well as forecasts of likely sales demands. The production process will invariably involve the purchase of materials from suppliers, which may consist of basic supplies such as steel, plastics, sugar, cereals, etc. or components such as electrical switches, circuit boards, exhaust pipes, pumps, etc. The exact nature of the materials supplied is dependent on the complexity of the finished product sold by the company. Therefore companies obtain supplies and components, change these materials into finished products and then distribute them to their customers.

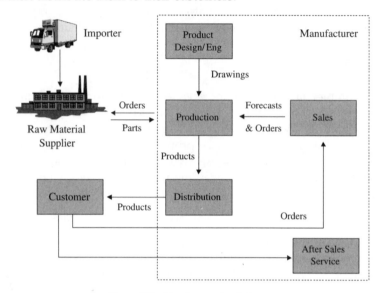

Figure 5.3 Simple supply chain

This chain of events, often likened to a pipeline, is known as the supply chain, and managing the process is known as supply chain management (SCM). SCM can be thought of as the management of upstream and downstream relationships with suppliers, distributors and customers to achieve the greatest customer perceived value at the least total cost. For this very reason, in the retail sector, supply chains compete, not just retailers. This is in recognition of the vital contribution towards the success of the retailer, made by how well business processes along the whole of the supply chain are managed. SCM activities typically include procurement, production scheduling, order processing, inventory control, distribution warehousing and customer service. A key factor is the accuracy and timeliness of information that initiates and accompanies the physical process, traditionally achieved using paper-based business transactions such as purchase orders, goods received notes, advanced shipment notifications, invoices, etc. Structured electronic messages using recognized international EDI standards for syntax have been in use for many years and are supplanting their paper-based equivalents, albeit at a slow rate.

The concept of the supply chain as a pipeline from seller to buyer is helpful in understanding that for the most efficient flow throughout the whole process, obstacles that inhibit the flow need to be removed or their effect minimized. In addition, whilst ideally the flow through the pipeline should be continuous (never stopping), in reality this is not the case. This is because of varying customer demand patterns that have their repercussions upstream within the pipeline, as all the other activities need to reflect this new upturn or downturn in customer demand. The different activities within the supply chain introduce a level of discontinuity and the further upstream they are, the less able they are to respond to the varying customer demand.

Without good knowledge of customer demand, many organizations prepare forecasts from which to plan and schedule production. As a Dutch philosopher once stated "the most difficult thing about forecasting is predicting the future". Often these forecasts are wrong and as a result either too little or too much is produced that results in under-stocking or over-stocking respectively. The points of discontinuity in the pipeline often coincide with activities where buffer or excess stocks are held merely to compensate for inefficiencies in the supply chain. By maintaining buffer or excess stocks, companies incur costs related to inventory storage, handling, damaged goods, product obsolescence, product returns and administrative and management costs. The various buffer stock holdings within the supply chain at the distributor, regional distribution centres, national distribution centre and manufacturing plant also tend to hide the real demand patterns. Other complications may also arise including the logistics lead-time constituting procurement, manufacturing and delivery frequently being longer than the order fulfilment time, also known as the customer order cycle.

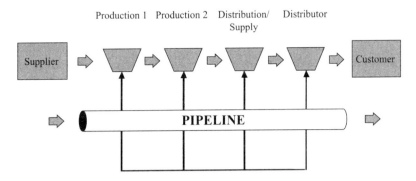

Disturbances to Pipeline Flow

Figure 5.4 Supply chain as a pipeline

Hopefully this explanation will start to stimulate some thoughts on possible ways in which efficiency along the supply chain pipeline can be improved, including:

▷ From a customer service perspective high stock levels seem to imply fewer stock-outs and happier customers.

▷ From an accountant's perspective, stock levels require funding and need to be minimized. Otherwise the cost of holding stock needs to be reflected in higher prices to maintain profitability and may adversely affect competitive edge.

▷ Rapid feedback of accurate customer demand patterns to the upstream activities in the supply chain would reduce the uncertainty.

▷ Rapid feedback of accurate customer demand patterns to the upstream activities in the supply chain and reliable advance information on the shipments of products would reduce uncertainty and enable the level of buffer stocks to be reduced/eliminated.

▷ Fewer activities would reduce the points of discontinuity in the supply chain and fewer barriers to the flow of products.

▷ Co-operation by the parties within the supply chain pipeline is not enough. The very fullest collaboration is required, without the traditional adversarial nature of the seller/buyer relationship.

The Value Chain

This approach developed by Porter (1985) [2] examines the activities performed within an organization to establish how they interact, and where improvements could be a source of competitive advantage. Porter's earlier work also examined the competitive forces within an industry and can be used as a basis for determining ways in which IT can be used by an organization to destabilize the equilibrium of a marketplace in its favour.

However, the value chain concept simply suggests that the primary activities through which a product passes within a company must add value if it is to command a higher price when sold to a customer. There are also secondary activities that add value indirectly by making it easier for the primary activities to be achieved. The value chain is a powerful concept when mirroring the activities within the supply chain, since it provides a criterion by which we can decide whether an activity is effective or not by simply asking:

▷ How does this activity add to the perceived value of the product by the customer? If the answer is that the activity contributes no added perceived value, then eliminate it.

▷ Alternatively could this activity be improved to increase the perceived value of the product by the customer? In which case, introduce the improvement.

This is expressed in an overly simplistic manner to get the point across. In practice all activities add some cost, so eliminating those activities that contribute little or no value can make a significant contribution to profitability.

Just-in-Time and Quick Response

The value chain of an organization and its extended organization that forms the supply chain can be mapped together to identify areas of potential process improvement. For example, using EDI to closely couple the information flows, between the inbound logistics function of the manufacturer and the outbound logistics function of the supplier, materials/parts can be called off with certainty of delivery, thereby achieving considerable savings in stock holdings and warehouse space.

Such an approach is more generally known as 'Just-in-Time' or JIT ordering within the manufacturing sector and 'Quick Response' ordering in the retail sector. Aside from the obvious savings achieved by closely coupling information systems in this way, a strategic and important new business relationship becomes formed between the trading partners. The Just-in-Time management philosophy originally emerged in the 1980s and strives to eliminate sources of manufacturing waste. Again, these turn out to be primarily activities that add cost, without adding value. JIT, sometimes known as lean or stockless production, provides the means to reduce inventory levels, improve product quality, reduce production and delivery lead-times, as well as reduce machine set-up times. In the JIT environment excess manufacturing capacity is used instead of buffer stocks to hedge against changes in demand patterns that may arise. JIT primarily applies to repetitive manufacturing processes in which the same products and components are produced over and over again. The implementation of JIT requires co-operation between the trading partners, using EDI as the means to exchange business transactions that are then integrated into their respective IT applications. However, the manufacturer normally initiates the process by issuing an order or the delivery request (call-off) to the supplier. JIT has had well publicized successes in several industries but none more than the automotive sector where it is the norm by which the industry operates.

Similar in concept to JIT, Quick Response is used within the fashion or apparel industry as a strategy for linking retailers and manufacturers to achieve increased responsiveness. Again EDI is usually the means by which the retailer calls-off deliveries of garments based upon sales trends within the retail outlets. In both North America and Europe some companies have been moving to a concept known as 'apparel-on-demand' whereby retailers send their point of sale information directly to the manufacturing floor to eliminate downtime and create sales-driven manufacture. This concept which is a logical extension of Quick Response has resulted in significant savings within the supply chain by reducing stock levels as well as the need for mark-downs, and is a good lead into the next section on e-Collaboration.

Example   Benetton

Benetton, based in Treviso, some 20 miles from Venice, is one of the world's largest clothing producers and distributes its products largely through independently owned shops in over 60 countries. It was one of the first companies to appreciate the potential of rapidly acquiring details of the products selling through its shops, and the impact that this information could have in influencing what best to manufacture. Initially orders were placed by shops around the world using a Value Added Network that triggered replenishment action from distribution centres. Subsequently point of sale (POS) information was sent electronically to Benetton, where it was analyzed by geographic region and together with plans for new ranges determined future manufacturing schedules.

e-Collaboration

An important phase in e-Business B2B evolution has been the movement from trading partner co-operation to collaboration that has been driven by intense competition found in today's markets. Collaboration is an opportunity for firms to move away from the traditional adversarial position of buyer/seller to seize competitive advantage by optimizing the whole supply chain network, not just their link in the chain. e-Collaboration is fundamentally changing the way businesses interact; it is not only individual companies continuing to compete with one another, but in the retail sector entire supply chains compete against one another. To remain competitive in today's turbulent economy, supply chains need to adopt collaborative approaches that enable all trading partners to work more closely together.

The success of most high street retailers relies on the ability to meet varying customer demand and using the old adage means having the "right product, in the right place, at the right time". Decreased stock-outs not only improve customer satisfaction but also contribute to increased profitability and market-share. At the same time, lowering costs by reducing buffer stocks and excessive stock levels as well as lowering distribution costs all add to the range of benefits achieved by e-Collaboration.

Example UK Food Retailer

UK food retailer Sainsbury reported that when jointly working on new promotions with Nestle using data provided by a new collaborative application supplied by Eqos, availability on the shelves rose by 2% to 97% and at the same time overstocking fell by a quarter.

e-Procurement

Earlier in this chapter it was suggested that the last three decades have seen costs squeezed out of manufacturing and the back-office, causing companies to re-examine the supply chain for new ways of taking out costs. Since material purchases constitute a significant proportion of the cost of goods sold, organizations have been generally keen to pursue improvements in the procurement process and in particular to negotiate better prices and conditions with suppliers. To achieve this much attention has been focused on business-to-business (B2B) trade using the Internet as many of the world's largest firms announce plans to automate their procurement processes, with massive repercussions for suppliers across all industries.

Trade Exchanges or Electronic Marketplaces

This section seeks to position electronic marketplaces in relation to the B2B trading and a more exhaustive treatment of the subject can be found in Chapter 8.

When thinking about effective forums for bringing buyers and sellers together, it is natural to reflect upon the experience of stock exchanges that manage financial marketplaces around the world in which stocks/shares, as well as other financial instruments, are traded online. The movement to online trading and the disappearance in many stock exchanges of the dealing floor or 'pit' has created a far more efficient process where settlement times are dramatically reduced. However, these changes have not been achieved without some resistance from the parties involved. Through the introduction of online trading exchanges or electronic marketplaces, the broader business community is now applying a similar philosophy. Horizontal trading exchanges run across different industries, whilst vertical exchanges establish marketplaces in a particular industry and frequently are able to reduce the fragmentation found in vertical market sectors. Examples of horizontal trading exchanges exist in a range of industries including aerospace, petroleum, chemicals, energy, pharmaceuticals, etc.

Example   Automotive Industry

In February 2000 a consortium of automotive manufacturers led by General Motors, Ford and Daimler-Chrysler created a vertical trading exchange called Covisint planning eventually to be capable of handling up to $300 billion of automotive business. This unprecedented joint effort aims to mesh together back-end systems from the automotive manufacturers and their suppliers to create a Web-based exchange to automate the time-consuming and costly process of acquiring direct materials and parts, and sourcing contracts from suppliers. Covisint appears to have established itself with a strong online presence with its quote-and-auction services and technology. General Motors conducted about $98 billion in procurement transactions via the online exchange during 2001, of which procurements of direct materials, such as steel and plastics, made up about $96 billion of the total. General Motors also spent $200 million on indirect goods through Covisint's catalogue system. General Motors was able to reduce its transaction costs and to process more orders by using Covisint.

To tackle other critical parts of the supply procurement process, such as inventory management, collaborative design and quality assurance, Covisint relies on several third-party vendors.

Example   Wal-Mart's Retail Link

Irrespective of the number of industry specific 'public' trading exchanges still operating in the future, 'private' exchanges such as Wal-Mart's Retail Link are almost certain to play a major role. All suppliers that deal with the world's largest retailer are required to do so over Retail Link that has links only to Wal-Mart and no other retailer.

Electronic marketplaces and collaborative initiatives such as Collaborative, Planning, Forecasting and Replenishment (See Chapter 8 for further details) are having a major impact upon the supply chain, particularly in retailing, where sustainable moves to eliminate costs are crucial for maintaining market leadership. Supporters of these initiatives point to the long-term potential of trade exchanges as a means for taking significant costs out of the distribution system. It is argued that whilst larger companies have built IT infrastructures enabling them to reap the benefits from dealing with their big trading partners through the use of EDI, smaller businesses have been unable to afford the capital investment. EDI requires highly specialized knowledge that relies primarily on IT personnel rarely found in small businesses and as a result SMEs have been forced to continue using costlier and more time-consuming paper-based processes. Since the trading exchanges are based on the Web, a more affordable and simpler technology, they provide industry-wide data-sharing platforms that offer the opportunity even for the small supplier and the one-store retailer to participate. For many of the larger food manufacturers/distributors, the small retailer is still an important part of their total service strategy and currently they do not have a satisfactory way of connecting to them in a real-time fashion. However, trading exchanges can address this problem with a range of options, from Web browser to less complex forms of application integration, using XML technologies. In addition for manufacturers in some industries a high proportion of cost lies in using a distributor to reach the marketplace. As it becomes feasible to reach customers in sufficient numbers using the Internet, either as an alternative or complementary approach to conventional distribution, then supply chain composition will need to be re-examined; resulting in important cost savings and improved customer service.

External Buying and Supply Chain

Companies such as Dell and Cisco sell significant volumes of their business sales over the Internet making good use of similar 'electronic shop-front' technology to that used in the B2C marketplace to improve the way in which their business customers interact with them. These Internet centric applications increase customer intimacy through the use of information technology allowing business customers to have personalized set-ups on the Web browsers as they enter the site. Not only can they obtain a wide range of product information, but they can also place orders and subsequently track delivery status. Figure 5.5 below illustrates a new breed of sophisticated application build upon Web technology, that can act as a front-end to the customer ordering module of an enterprise resource planning system such as SAP, Oracle Applications or Baan.

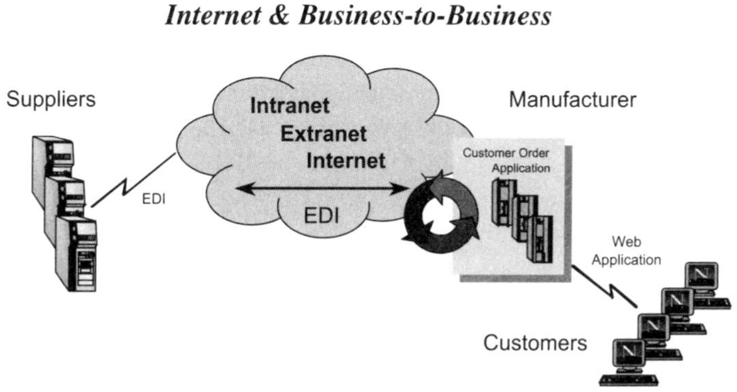

Internet & Business-to-Business

Figure 5.5   External buying and the supply chain

While such an approach is clearly not suitable for fast moving consumer goods, the use of a Web browser is ideal for business customers ordering more specialized products such as computers. The Web browser offers intuitive functions that minimize training, electronic catalogues to speed-up product choice and a shopping cart analogy for comfort and ease of use. An organization operating this type of electronic shop-front, could in theory be a virtual distributor, where orders are sent electronically to suppliers using EDI and it is the supplier that maintains the inventory and actually fulfils the customer order.

Example   Sun Microsystems

Sun Microsystems, which helped pioneer the commercial Internet, has been well behind e-Business leaders such as Cisco, Dell and Intel. Sun set a number of goals to change this situation that included conducting a greater number of auctions to boost online sales and procurement, as well as push more supply chain business online. Sun believes that buying and selling over the Internet is a far more complex business re-engineering task for them as an established high-end systems vendor than it would be for a start-up e-Business or a maker of commodity products. However, since Cisco are selling approximately 87% of their high-end network products on the Internet, Sun believe that they could sell considerably more over the Internet and EDI valued added networks than at present.

Internal Buying Requests

A variant on direct customer ordering using a 'selling' application is external purchase ordering using a 'buying' application. This arises from internal buying requests, that are raised within an organization and results in the placement of purchase orders upon suppliers. Many organizations have realized that improvements in their internal buying process, coupled with direct links to suppliers, offers great scope for cost reductions, by more effective purchasing, and increasing customer service to the internal buyer. Preferred suppliers are usually chosen on the basis of product availability, best price and delivery performance and they provide the information to populate the internal buying application. Direct EDI links to these suppliers may also exist as shown in Figure 5.6, once internal approval has been given for the purchase order to be placed. Companies are continuing to recognize the importance of the buy-side of e-Business as they move from Web-based applications for the purchase of office supplies and MRO items to the sourcing of direct materials for manufacture.

Example – Volkswagen AG

> Volkswagen AG, the world's fifth largest automotive manufacturer, having rejected the invitation to join Covisint (see above), opted to build its own private electronic marketplace known as Supply.com. During its initial year of operation, the marketplace conducted over 600 auctions for strategic parts valued at $12 billion with more than 4,000 suppliers. In addition Supply.com provides the means by which VW workers world-wide can select from some 360,000 MRO (maintenance, repair and operation) items using an electronic catalogue-based application offered by 200 approved indirect suppliers, thereby eliminating the need for manual ordering.

Internet & Business-to-Business

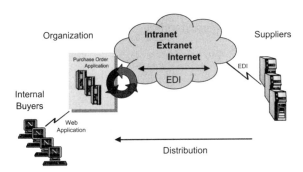

Figure 5.6 Internal buying & sourcing

In late 1996, several leading Fortune 500 organizations within the US, together with their key suppliers, formed the Internet Purchasing Roundtable. Their goal was to provide access to easy-to-use, open, standards-based Internet purchasing solutions for the procurement of high-volume, low cost indirect goods and services. Through discussion and close consultation with both technology providers and financial institutions, the Roundtable participants developed the Open Buying on the Internet (OBI) standard. This is based upon current Internet standards including SSL for secure communications, HTML for the user interface, SET for credit card transactions and X.509 for digital certificates. Once the initial version of the OBI standard had been completed, a non-profit making users' consortium was created. While the OBI Consortium aims to improve and promote use of the standard, it is also keen to develop other standards and share business practices for conducting e-Commerce business-to-business. GE is a member of the OBI (Open Buying on the Internet) Consortium[3] and the following case study provides a practical example of 'business-to-business' purchasing using the Internet.

Efficient Consumer Response

The Efficient Consumer Response (ECR) initiative began in the mid 1990s and was characterized by the emergence of new principles of collaborative management along the supply chain. In reality it is little different to earlier sections within this chapter, but whilst building upon initiatives in the North American marketplace it has strong European foundations. Similar to e-Collaboration it is based upon the premise that trading partners can serve their customers better and at less cost by working together in a collaborative manner. The business environment in which ECR emerged was characterized by dramatic advances in information technology, shifts in consumer demand and the increasing movements of goods across international borders within the European Economic Community.

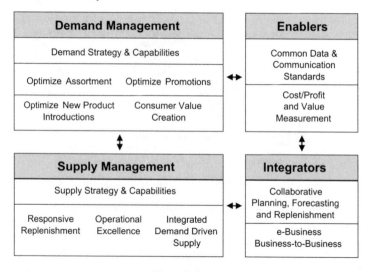

Figure 5.7 Global ECR scorecard

The highly competitive marketplace demanded fresh ideas and approaches to increasing the efficiency of the supply chain. In Europe, as in North America, it became clear that the traditional adversarial relationship and rigid separation of roles between manufacturer and retailer threatened to stifle improvements within the supply chain. In addition this situation also failed to take the fullest advantage of valuable information now becoming available at points within the supply chain as greater use of information technology became deployed. In consequence ECR Europe, a joint trade and industry body, supported by many high profile companies present in the European retail market, sought to change the status quo and develop far reaching approaches to improve performance throughout the supply chain.

ECR Europe is headquartered in Brussels and works in close co-operation with national ECR initiatives in most European countries. Participation in projects at European and national levels is open to large and small companies in the grocery and fast moving consumer goods sectors, including retailers, wholesalers, manufacturers, suppliers, brokers and third-party service providers such as logistics operators.

FunFigure 5.8 Continuous replenishment in action

The real value of ECR Europe[4] has been its work in bringing the various stakeholders together and developing a comprehensive model that provides the strategic direction and practical knowledge required to establish an ECR environment. The model, known as the Global ECR Scorecard, also acts as a reference point to gauge progress towards implementing the goals of ECR (see FunFigure 5.8).

The scorecard focuses on four key areas and stresses their interdependence:

▷ Demand Management includes all the factors associated with understanding and managing the demand for products and primarily covers assortment rationalization, optimizing promotions and improving new product introductions.

▷ Supply Management naturally focuses upon the different aspects of the need for rapid and efficient replenishment within the overall supply chain and includes operational excellence, responsive replenishment and integrated demand driven supply.

▷ Enablers focus upon the data and information management aspect of the supply chain. This includes product identification, data management and processing capabilities that are required to ensure timely and accurate communication and monitoring of product flows between trading partners. EDI and data warehousing are two key information technologies that are employed.

▷ Integrators represent the move towards a standards-based environment that forms the foundation of e-Business. These including collaborative planning, forecasting and replenishment (CPFR) and the wider use of open standards-based data communications networks.

Example   Wal-Mart and Procter & Gamble

As the concepts surrounding ECR were emerging, Wal-Mart, a leading and highly innovative player in the North American fast moving consumer goods marketplace, introduced a continuous replenishment programme (CRP) with one of its suppliers Procter & Gamble. CRP was characterized by:

▷ Operations supported by information technology and EDI applications

▷ Changing from a batch mode of supply to a continuous flow of products

▷ Without CRP replenishment action was triggered by the retailer's order

▷ With CRP the supplier takes replenishment action based upon known retailer inventory data

Procter & Gamble (P&G) received daily electronic data on Wal-Mart's sales of P&G products, which was used for forecasting purposes that initiated the automatic shipment of products to Wal-Mart. Wal-Mart were able to maintain lower inventory levels yet still reduce the number of stock-outs, since P&G also increased its on-time deliveries from 94% to 99.6%. In addition P&G's sales volumes at Wal-Mart grew by 40% over a one-year period, due to the success of the CRP process and resultant preference by Wal-Mart to deal with P&G.

Supply Chain Evolution

The supply chain has developed dramatically over the last 20 years from its origins characterized by trading partners dealing with one another in a rigid paper-based environment usually in adversarial manner. This evolution is diagrammatically shown in Figure 5.9, moving from a starting point of separate internal departments to departmental functional integration, e.g. Purchasing and Material Control became merged into Materials Management. There then followed a period in which the internal functional departments become integrated through transparency and sharing of data and information made possible by Enterprise Resource Planning (ERP) packaged applications or similar. This provided manufacturers with considerable cost savings through process improvements and lowering of inventory levels, but still left inefficiencies within the total supply chain. The more recent phase concerns full external integration with trading partners across the total supply chain, resulting in further reductions in inventory levels.

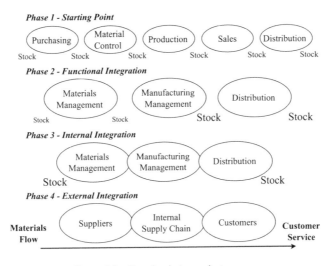

Figure 5.9 Supply chain evolution

e-Business Evolution

In Chapter 2 a framework for e-Business was presented based upon the idea that as the progress of doing business electronically proceeds, e-Business is becoming 'business as usual', rather than anything very exceptional (Figure 5.10). Therefore the scope of e-Business was defined in these broad terms as 'the practice of performing and co-ordinating critical business processes such as designing products, obtaining supplies, manufacturing, selling, fulfilling orders, and providing services through the extensive use of computer and communication technologies and computerized data'. In addition, within the new collaborative environment it is becoming increasingly more difficult to separate out intra-company (intra-facing) and inter-company (inter-facing) processes, which is an added reason to broaden the definition. Interest in e-Business has been driven by companies wishing to increase revenues and lower both operating and capital costs. Indeed for many industry sectors there

127

is no going back as 'doing business electronically' is no longer a choice – the trading community mandates its use as a norm and therefore a condition of trading community membership.

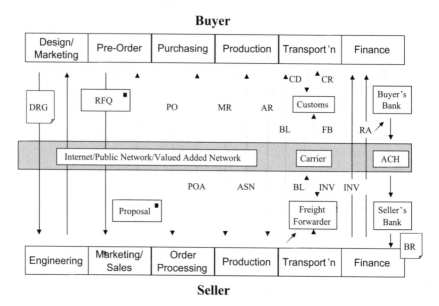

Figure 5.10 – Across the whole business cycle

Equally e-Commerce is considered as a sub-set of e-Business that covers the use of the Internet (and other technologies) for the marketing, selling and servicing of products and can equally apply to either business-to-business or business-to-consumer, although more generally it is associated with the B2C category. Business customers and general consumers are interested in e-Commerce since it can:

▷ Lower prices for existing products

▷ Offer new products and services previously not thought possible

▷ Deliver greater convenience and improved customer service through a self-service approach to the buying experience

While forecasts vary between the different market watchers, today's business-to-business purchases over the Internet have risen sharply, some suggesting that business volumes are doubling every 4 months. The B2B marketplace is believed to be a much larger marketplace that the B2C marketplace although in many of the developed countries around the world B2C revenues are rising steadily as Internet access within the home continues to increase.

The following chapter considers in detail the traditional B2B environment that has been dominated for many years by EDI. Although other alternatives are emerging that will simplify the data syntax and presentation, EDI continues to be popular amongst larger trading partners as a means of conducting business electronically in conjunction with an EDI Value Added Network (EDI VAN) service or alternatively direct connection over the Internet. Several EDI VAN services have introduced new ways that allow smaller trading partners to take fullest advantage of the Internet. TradeWeb from GE Global eXchange Services is an example of such a service that is based upon EDI Web forms and allows subscribers to this service to become members of the world's largest trading community of more than 40,000 trading partners. All the traditional back-end EDI requirements, such as mapping and translation services, are hidden and transparent to the subscriber, who simply works with a Web browser that displays a business document as a form for completion. Services such as TradeWeb are extending the participation of those involved in EDI based trading partner networks beyond larger organizations to smaller businesses (SMEs).

Quantifying the Benefits

Several of the examples quoted in this chapter provide either a qualitative or quantitative statement of benefits achieved by the companies conducting e-Business B2B. Research undertaken by AMR Research (2001)[5] provides an indication of the likely benefits to be achieved for manufacturers and retailers employing collaborative planning, forecasting and replenishment (CPFR) in the fast moving consumer goods marketplace.

Benefits achieved by retailers include:

▷ Lower stock levels with typical improvement of 10% to 40%

▷ Higher sales volumes with typical improvement of 5% to 20%

▷ Lower logistic costs with typical improvement 3% to 4%

Benefits achieved by manufacturers include:

▷ Faster replenishment action with typical improvement of 12% to 30%

▷ Higher sales volumes with typical improvement of 2% to 10%

▷ Better customer service with typical improvement of 5% to 10%

Intangible e-Business B2B benefits that have been identified in practice include for the seller (supplier, manufacturer or distributor):

▷ More time for customer service

- ▷ Reduced order entry times

- ▷ Faster turnaround/response

- ▷ Lower buffer stocks levels

- ▷ Strategic trading relationship established

And for the buyer (manufacturer, distributor or retailer):

- ▷ Fewer exceptions/mistakes means reduced progressing effort involving telephone calls and E-mails

- ▷ Increased accuracy of replenishment information

- ▷ Higher stock turn

- ▷ Reduced warehouse space, yet fewer stock-outs

- ▷ Improved tracking and handling

- ▷ Dramatically reduced replenishment cycle times

e-Business B2B Summary

The Internet now provides access to an online global marketplace, which operates on a 24-hour basis, with millions of customers and thousands of products and services. It provides organizations with new, more cost effective and time efficient means of working with development partners, suppliers, manufacturers, distributors, retailers and customers; plus, the opportunity to purchase products and services from new supply sources in parts of the world that they would otherwise not have thought of approaching. While this may change in the future, currently the Internet provides little assistance in the 'discovery' stage of new supply sources around the world. This is partly due to the trend towards private rather than public trade exchanges, in which nominated or approved supply sources are invited to 'bid'. The main contribution of the Internet comes once contact has been established and business communications start to be exchanged.

e-Business B2B is enabling companies to:

- ▷ Shorten procurement cycles times through use of online catalogues, ordering and payment

- ▷ Cut costs on a range of materials and products through competitive bidding

- ▷ Reduce development cycle times and accelerate time-to-market through collaborative engineering and new product introduction

▷ Gain access to worldwide markets at a fraction of traditional costs

In summary traditional EDI enabled supply chains have delivered benefits through the use of Just-in-Time for manufacturing and Quick Response in the retail sector. New collaborative applications such as e-Procurement and ECR offer scope for even greater benefits throughout the supply chain. These collaborative applications are allowing companies to share data and information from both sides of the trading relationship. Companies are making this easier by the use of enterprise application integration (EAI) software tools based upon XML to ease the integration of the many different applications used. Lastly ebXML (see Chapter 7), though in its infancy, offers the promise for EDI to finally realize its full potential that could result in significant future B2B growth.

1   Quote by Ralph Borsodi (1929), The Distribution Age

2   Porter ME (1985), Competitive Advantage – Creating and sustaining superior performance, The Free Press

3   OBI Consortium www.openbuy.org is a non-profit organization managed by CommerceNet

4   See www.ecrnet.com Electronic Commerce Europe

5   AMR Research Inc www.amrresearch.com

Traditional B2B – Electronic Data Interchange

Introduction to EDI

As outlined in Chapter 2, e-Business has been around for longer than you might think. The first moves in that direction started back in the 1980s, particularly in the retail industry, in the form of EDI – Electronic Data Interchange. Then, as today, one of the main drivers for this development was the so-called 'supply chain', starting with the raw materials through to the finished goods. For most organizations, particularly in retail, this is where the heaviest costs are – in buying, distributing and warehousing the stocks of goods to go on the shelves. It is often said that in retail, the key to success lies not so much in selling, but in buying wisely. That is why the supply chain is so important. Before e-Business, many organizations had large numbers of staff occupied solely in sending out orders by letter, telex, phone or fax – a very expensive, time-consuming and error-prone operation. This also made it essential to keep large stocks in warehouses, at great expense, in order to provide a buffer for the delays and uncertainty in the whole logistics process. As one of the pioneers of EDI, Tom McGuffog, put it: "Uncertainty is the mother of inventory, and the grandmother of under-utilized resources"[1].

By today's standards, the first steps towards e-Business were very crude – a mainframe computer would be used to generate a list of orders on magnetic tape, one tape for each supplier. In the days when networking was slow and expensive, the tapes would then be delivered overnight by lorry or van to the suppliers.

EDI Value Added Network Services

In the 1980s came the first moves to distribute such data over networks, and various independent Value Added Network Services (VANS or simply VAN) came into being. These are modelled closely on the familiar postal system, in that VAN users connect to the service either via a dial-up connection or a leased line, and send in commercial messages such as orders and invoices. These are then sorted and placed in the recipients' mailboxes on the VAN, ready for collection later by the recipients – rather like sending letters to a post office Box Number, where they are stored until collected by the recipient. (It might seem a better idea to send the data directly to the recipient's computer system, but many organizations prefer to collect data as and when it suits them, rather than to have it delivered directly).

Pros and Cons of VANs

One obvious question is why an organization should want to use a VAN instead of simply sending commercial messages directly to their trading partners, for example via E-mail or some other communications method. There are several reasons:

▷ Administrative overheads. Making sure that perhaps hundreds or thousands of separate orders have all been delivered successfully to perhaps hundreds of suppliers requires a lot of checking. It is also critical to know – particularly with perishable goods – whether the order has been received by the supplier, whether it has been accepted, and when the goods will arrive.

▷ Managing the networking and communications requires specialist skills – ideal for outsourcing.

▷ E-mail is not suited to structured data.

The attractions of VANs are:

▷ One-stop shop – batches of orders can be sent at one go to a VAN, to be collected later by multiple recipients.

▷ VAN networks are relatively secure, certainly compared to E-mail.

▷ VANs provide an audit trail – senders can find out if and when messages were received by the VAN and later collected by the recipient.

On the other hand, VANs are relatively expensive, and E-mail systems are cheap and easy to use. There has been plenty of work going on in the Internet community to provide effective and secure ways of sending structured data via E-mail or other means. There is more about this later in this and subsequent chapters.

EDI and SMEs

During the 1980s and 1990s, EDI traffic over VANs grew rapidly, as large organizations, particularly in the retail industry, took advantage of the substantial cost savings available. However, these savings could only be obtained after fairly substantial investment in the IT facilities needed, and many SMEs (Small and Medium Enterprises) found the costs prohibitive. As a result, many of them did not use EDI, while others were forced into it by their large and demanding trading partners. Figures show that only a fairly small percentage of all the companies across the world have adopted EDI, though that conceals the fact that the bigger the company, the more likely that they are using EDI – even today, when XML is more in vogue. But from their point of view XML is just another form of EDI, and several large organizations are already sending XML data through traditional EDI VANs. The basic decision is horses for courses – using whatever format and method their trading partners prefer. The overriding objective is to speed up and strengthen the supply chain, in order to remove that expensive uncertainty.

Hubs and Spokes

This common pattern of large organizations adopting EDI, and smaller ones then joining, or forced to join, can be summed up in the phrase 'hubs and spokes'. Think of a large retail organization with perhaps several hundred different suppliers, ranging from other large organizations to very small specialist producers. This can neatly be visualized as looking rather like a bicycle wheel, with a central hub representing the large buying organization, and the suppliers connected as spokes. Of course some of the suppliers will be big organizations in their own right, with their own suppliers, and therefore may be both spokes and hubs.

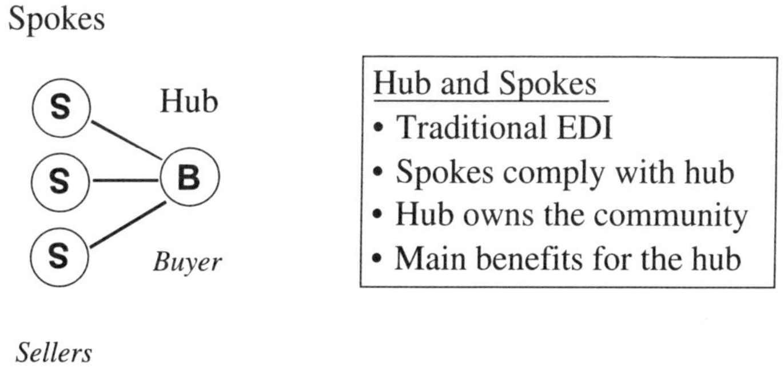

Figure 6.1 Hubs and spokes

Delivering EDI by Other Means

Because of the problems for SMEs, there are a number of hybrid uses of EDI – for example, some VANs will accept data in EDI format, but convert it and deliver it as fax messages or E-mail messages to small trading partners. Since the growth of the Internet, and the growing number of companies with access to a browser, most VANs also provide what is called Web-based EDI, in which small trading partners can receive orders and send invoices interactively through Web-based forms on a browser. In many cases, there is special software on the browser that will accept an order, print it out neatly, store the details, and later generate an invoice. It is a mostly manual operation, but in that way SMEs gain most of the benefits of traditional EDI at low cost.

All this underlines a key point – traditional EDI and today's Internet solutions, particularly XML, are not opposites, but just different ways of sending and receiving commercial data. XML does have one substantial advantage over traditional EDI – it is easy to generate an attractive display of XML data on the browser. But browsers require human intervention, and a key objective in e-Business is to reduce human intervention as much as possible.

Comparison between E-mail, EDI and XML

EDI has a lot in common with both E-mail and XML – all three involve the sending and receiving of data over a network. But there are some significant differences as well, and a comparison between them will highlight these:

E-mail	EDI	XML
Person-to-person	Computer-to-computer	Mainly computer-to-computer
Free format text	Structured text	Free format text, within tags
Commercial and private use	Commercial use only	Mainly commercial use
Human-readable	Hard to read	Fairly human-readable
Verbose	Condensed	Verbose
Optional attachments	Single file	Often with related files (DTD, CSS)
Binary data only in attachments	Binary data option (rarely used)	Text, with optional graphics
Normal punctuation	Pre-defined delimiters only	Normal punctuation in text
No metadata needed	Metadata in documentation	Metadata included in tags

Table 5.1 Comparisons between E-mail, EDI and XML

Free Format or Structured Text

E-mail is all about sending free format text messages between individuals. It must therefore be human-readable, with normal punctuation and normal words in any language you like. You can send binary data (for example a word-processed document or a graphic), but only as a separate attachment. There are rules about addressing E-mail, but that apart, pretty well anything goes.

EDI in contrast is designed to exchange commercial documents (such as orders and invoices) between organizations. So it does not need to be human-readable at all, and at first sight EDI looks pretty off-putting (see the EDIFACT example later in this chapter). However, that is not really a problem. EDI data is designed to be sent, not by a person, but directly from one computer system to another without any human intervention. In the case of an order from a shop to a food manufacturer, the idea is that the shop's stock control system prepares the order and then (after approval by a human buyer) sends it automatically to the food manufacturer's production planning system. In computer jargon, such programs are called 'application programs' or just 'applications', to distinguish them from 'system' programs used by the operating system. This distinction is important. Applications can also be described as 'end-user programs'. Hence also the expression A2A, meaning Application-to-Application, and the more formal phrase 'Enterprise Application Integration' (more about this in Chapter 15).

Experience has shown that, once systems like these have been installed and tested, they are quicker, more efficient and less error-prone than the equivalent manual ordering system run by human beings by telephone or fax. This improves the supply chain, one of the prime goals of e-Business.

XML is somewhere in between – it carries free format text, but with tags containing definitions of what the text is or means. The text itself therefore is human readable, but the definitions contained in the tags may or may not be so obvious. Nevertheless, XML files containing commercial data such as orders and invoices tend to be much more readable than the EDI equivalents. That is only an advantage if humans need to handle the data at some stage. In large organizations that have invested time and money to handle EDI, that is irrelevant. But for SMEs the readability of for example an XML order or invoice can be a significant advantage, and that is part of the current appeal of using XML for this sort of commercial data. There is more about XML in Chapter 7.

Structured Data

It is worth looking in a bit more detail at what we mean by 'structured' data. Take some typical E-mail messages – most of them are 'unstructured', meaning that they cannot be processed by a computer, because a computer does not have the language skills of a human being. For that reason, both EDI and XML messages have to be structured in such a way that a computer can process the contents. For this, the computer needs to understand:

▷ The punctuation ('delimiters') used to separate the elements

▷ The elements and their type, by using metadata

▷ The hierarchy of elements in the data

To illustrate the issues of structured data, let's take a typical example – a commercial order from a shop to a manufacturer for a particular product. The order will define various things, such as the product names, quantities, perhaps with item numbers and descriptions of the goods ordered. These elements must be in a defined order or structure, so that the processing computer can make sense of them. There may be multiple such order lines in an order, to be shipped to various addresses on various dates. In EDI, this hierarchy of elements is defined in a separate document, called a 'Message Standard', and obtainable from the standards authorities (more about this below). In XML, the hierarchy is defined in the tags that surround the data. An XML file must have a so-called 'root' element (such as <Order>), with a hierarchy of tags below that (such as <OrderDate>, <Item>, <Price> etc.). So, one way or another, the structure of both EDI and XML data must be known to both sides in advance for this sort of commercial data. That is why standards are so important, and we shall look at that question in more detail further on.

Punctuation and Delimiters

Punctuation is also vital, in order to distinguish the various elements from each other. In E-mail, it is very simple – we use the normal conventions of language, namely spaces to separate words, and the familiar punctuation signs such as commas and full stops. But this is not precise enough for EDI or XML – for example, a full stop is also used as a decimal separator. EDI standards specify particular characters to be used as punctuation to separate elements and segments (roughly the same as words and sentences in E-mail). The EDIFACT standard specifies the use of the characters : + ' to be used as these delimiters, performing the same role as commas and full stops in text. These characters therefore must not be used in the data (though there is provision to use them together with a release character). These delimiters are one reason why EDI looks so unreadable, but it is also why EDI data is easy for computers to process.

What is a Line?

You may wonder why such data cannot be separated into lines. The reason, as explained in more detail in Chapter 15, is that the concept of a 'line' is not as straightforward as it looks. We are used to recognizing lines visually on a page, but different computers have different definitions of what constitutes a line. So for safety, most EDI standards do not split data into lines. That way, they are platform-independent – a key requirement for open standards.

In XML, punctuation is much simpler – the data is free format (up to a point) and always has to be surrounded by opening and closing tags like this: <Description>Widget</Description>. Generally, XML data is split into separate lines, but that is purely for the convenience of humans. XML specifies that what is called 'white space' (spaces or tab characters) between tags is to be disregarded, so therefore data can be split into lines without causing a problem. Overall, the result is that XML is more verbose than EDI, but has the advantage that it is readable by both humans and computers.

Release Characters

Both EDI and XML have ways of getting round the problem of reserved characters used as delimiters. In EDI, one character is always defined as the release character. In EDIFACT, this is by default the ? (question mark). Without that, an expression like +44 123 456 789 (where +44 is the convention for an international telephone call to the UK) would cause havoc in an EDI message, because the software would interpret the + as a delimiter. But if you turned it into ?+44 etc., it will be handled correctly, because at the receiving end the software will strip out the release character, leaving +44 etc. And before you ask, if you really want to send a ? you send ??

Similarly in XML, you can display any reserved character by using &. So to put the 'greater than' sign into text you have to enter the characters > and the browser shows that as >

Metadata – Data about Data

Another key difference between E-mail on the one hand, and EDI and XML on the other, it is that E-mail does not need any metadata – data about data that tells you what the original data means. In E-mail, none is needed – we take it for granted that the recipient will understand the language, words and punctuation used in our message.

In contrast, EDI can only be understood with the help of documentation that explains in detail the standards used, right down to very precise detail about each individual element in an EDI message. XML is a halfway house – it contains free format text, but the tags explain and define what the free format data means. In XML, there may also be additional files, such as a DTD (Document Type Definition) that specifies the elements contained in an XML file, and their attributes. Either way, you need this metadata in order to make sense of both EDI and XML.

Sometimes even E-mail needs metadata. If you receive an E-mail written in an unknown foreign language, you need metadata (such as a dictionary) to make sense of it.

EDI, XML and SMEs

All these features make EDI very condensed and efficient, ideal for computers, but hard for humans to read and handle. For organizations that don't have the resources to integrate EDI into their in-house systems, the result is that EDI can be difficult and labour-intensive, and this lies behind the relatively low level of uptake of EDI among small and medium enterprises (SMEs). The hope is that XML will make life easier for SMEs. However, there is such a large investment in EDI by large enterprises that it is likely that EDI and XML will co-exist for some time yet, and be integrated. In any case, XML does not solve all the integration problems, particularly when dealing with systems that do not understand XML. This integration issue is fundamental for e-Business, and one we will return to.

The rules and standards are determined in advance, and are laid down in documentation published by the various standards authorities, such as the UN/EDIFACT organization.

EDI Standards

There are numerous EDI standards in the world, mainly because EDI started in the 1980s mostly on a national basis. Though different in detail, they share most of the features described above. The basic purpose of such standards is to enable trading partners to exchange data in a common format – like a common language. In some ways, therefore, these standards play the same role that, for example, Latin played in the Middle Ages, when it was the normal language for spreading information because it was so widely understood. More recently, there have been attempts to develop the use of world languages such as Esperanto.

For a formal definition of EDI, see glossary entry for Electronic Data Interchange.

Standards Authorities

When e-Business started, the need for common standards was clear – there were many different types of computer systems, and different ways of storing data. Trade organizations started to devise such standards.

In EDI, the structure of a document is defined in a standard prepared by some central authority, working in co-operation with industry experts. In the case of UN/EDIFACT (EDIFACT), now the most widely used international EDI standard, the structure is defined in a document published by ISO as ISO 9735 (with subsequent additions; they can all be downloaded from the EDIFACT Web site). The original document specifies things like the character sets to be used, the structure of a message, and a number of rules about including or leaving out data.

In the United States, there is a widely used EDI standard called ANSI ASC X12 (X12) developed by the American National Standards Institute. They have announced their intention to converge on EDIFACT, but progress is slow.

In the United Kingdom, a national standard called TRADACOMS was developed before EDIFACT, and is still widely used. Similarly, in France there is a standard called GENCOD, and there are various other standards in other countries, such as VDA in Germany. There is also a standard used in the European automotive industry, ODETTE. The details are not too important, because they all work on roughly the same principles, even though in many cases they look very different.

In order to explain in general how EDI works, we shall take a more detailed look at the main international standard, EDIFACT. However, for full information refer to ISO 9735.

EDIFACT

In the 1980s, the United Nations Economic Commission for Europe in Geneva began to develop EDIFACT, with the aim of facilitating trade. EDI standards need these basic components:

▷ A syntax for messages which specifies the structure and sequence of elements in the data. Just as syntax in language defines where to place the subject, verb and object in a sentence, so in EDI, syntax defines where to put things like the sender's address, date and time, reference number and other such values.

▷ An encoding scheme to identify the character set being used.

▷ A data dictionary that defines the standard business data elements, such as sender, product code, address, currency, etc.

▷ Combinations of data elements to be used for standard messages.

A paper invoice, for instance, normally consists of a header containing the name and address of the company sending the invoice, the company to make the payment, the invoice reference number, date etc. There are details of the goods supplied, which may consist of a series of lines, each containing such details as product code, expiry date, unit price, etc. Each of these items and lines has an equivalent in an EDI electronic format with data elements combined into segments, and segments combined into messages.

EDI Message Structure

Using EDIFACT as an example, we shall explore the EDI message structure in more detail. Firstly, before any effective dialogue can take place between either human beings or computer systems a common language or dictionary of terms is needed. These terms are the information-conveying elements that form the basis of any language. In EDI these terms are called data elements and form the vocabulary. Each data element will identify an individual field or item of data designed for a specific purpose; e.g. product code, expiry date, unit price, invoice number, postal code, etc. Individual data elements may be combined to form composite data elements. For example, in the EDIFACT orders message below, the line starting 'COM' has a composite element containing +44 123 456 789:TE where TE means it is a telephone number (as opposed to a fax number). Note also the use of the release character ? mentioned earlier to send +44. The 'dictionary' that holds all these data elements together is referred to as the data element directory.

```
UNA:+.? '
UNB+UNOA:1+SENDER+RECIPIENT+010203:1234+SNRF01+PASSWORD+ORDERS'
UNH+1+ORDERS:D:97A:UN++1'
BGM+105+RS1+9'
DTM+137:20010203:102'
NAD+BY+++ABC+HIGH STREET 123+ANYTOWN++XX1 1YY+GB'
CTA+OC+:J. SMITH'
COM+? +44 123 456 789:TE'
NAD+SU+++XYZ PLC+SIDE ST+++ZZ1 1AA+GB'
CTA+SU+:JOHN BROWN'
COM+? +44 789 456 123:TE'
LIN+1++BF01:BP'
IMD+F++:::BRASS FITTING'
QTY+21:21'
MOA+146:1.75'
LIN+2++PF02:BP'
IMD+F++:::PLASTIC FITTING'
QTY+21:4'
MOA+146:0.50'
UNS+S'
UNT+19+1'
UNZ+1+SNRF01'
```

For convenience, this interchange has been split into separate lines – in real life it would of course be just one long continuous string. In EDIFACT, unprintable line control characters (like Carriage Return and Line Feed) are not valid and are removed. They are platform-specific, and the whole point is to avoid that.

EDI Segments

In the same way that a sentence contains information about a specific topic, there is a requirement in EDI to provide logical groupings of data. These logical groupings are called segments. A segment is a functionally related group of data elements or composite data elements which describes a certain aspect of the overall dialogue, e.g. an address segment, a goods description segment, a payments segment, etc. Each segment starts with a three-letter name or 'tag'.

Some of these segments may be applicable to many types of EDI dialogue, e.g. all documents require the same address segment, and hence they can be grouped together in a segment directory. So an EDIFACT message is just an assembly of suitable segments. That is how new messages are created – by picking and choosing from the segment directory.

There are two types of segments - Service segments and Data segments.

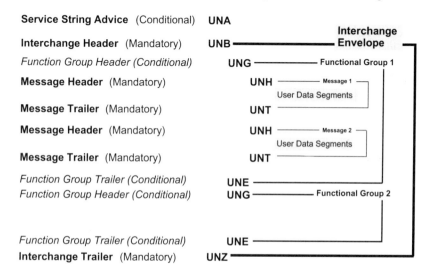

Figure 6.2   Service segments

In basic EDIFACT, all service segments start with the letters UN. In the example above, the first service segment is called UNA, and defines the delimiters to be used. It is Conditional – meaning optional. If you do not define it, the default delimiters are used. It is frequently omitted.

The second service segment, UNB, contains addressing details in the same way that a paper envelope has a name and address on it. It also contains other things you would expect to find on an envelope – the address of the sender, and a date and time stamp. It also includes a few things not normally found on envelopes, notably a value called the 'Interchange Control Reference' also called 'Sender's Reference'. This is a unique reference number or value assigned by the sender. This follows normal commercial practice – every paper order or invoice has a unique reference number, so that it can be tracked. It also means that duplicate orders or invoices can easily be detected. Some trading partners take that a stage further and verify that the Interchange Control References are in strict numerical sequence.

The UNB segment can also contain other optional values, including a value called an 'Application Reference'. This is either a user-defined name, or more often the official name for the kind of data being sent in the whole interchange. In EDIFACT, each message type is given a unique six-character name. For example, an order message is called ORDERS, and an invoice is called INVOIC – truncated because the names are always six characters. Other names are less memorable – for example, INVRPT is the Inventory Report Message. There are dozens of such defined messages.

The UNH segment UNH+1+ORDERS:D:97A:UN++1' is the message header, and defines in more detail exactly which version is being used. Over the years, many new messages have been introduced, with revised versions of older messages. This UNH segment tells us that we are using the 1997 version, developed by the UN. You might expect people to use the latest versions, but unless there is a good reason for doing so, such as additional segments to carry important data, there is no advantage in using a later version, and it is quite common for organizations to go on using older versions, because they serve the purpose, and there is nothing to be gained by changing. As they say, "If it ain't broke, don't fix it". This is particularly important in EDI, because a trading partner cannot change a standard or a version unilaterally – it has to be by mutual agreement between all the trading partners, otherwise confusion and problems result.

Full details of all the messages and their versions can be found on the EDIFACT Web site.

Data Segments

After these initial service segments come the data segments. The names, or three-letter 'tags', must always be the official ones, but the data in the elements after the tag is user-defined. Quite often, the tag name is reasonably intuitive – for example the letters BGM in the BGM+105+RS1+9' segment stand for 'Beginning of Message', and DTM stands for 'Date and Time of Message'. This closely resembles the corresponding paper versions of such documents.

Looping Segments

If you think of a moment about a paper versions of an order, it will normally have some standard information at the top, such as name and address, followed by several order lines for individual items. Each of these order lines might have a name, a code number, the quantity ordered, and perhaps a description. An order from a large shop might contain thousands of such order lines. In computer terms, these lines form a loop – we cycle through the various elements in each order line until we have processed all the items. The maximum number in a loop varies, but often runs to five or six digits. There are also loops within loops.

This introduces an aspect of EDI, and particularly of EDIFACT, that makes life hard for humans but easy for computers. In an EDIFACT message, these loops, not to mention loops within loops, are not very obvious. It only becomes clear if you read the EDIFACT documentation. As we see in the EDIFACT example above, the LIN segment occurs twice, and each is followed by a number of other related segments, namely IMD (Item Description), QTY (quantity) and MOA (Monetary Amount). So there is a top-level segment, in this case LIN, and below it are grouped a number of related segments. This looping structure is very characteristic of EDI.

At the end of all these user data segments, it is often convenient to put in a special service segment, UNS, to divide a message into sections, if so required.

After that, we get the message trailer UNT+19+1' which includes a checksum, in this example 19, which is just a count of the number of segments in the message starting with the previous UNH and including UNT. Each UNH must have a matching UNT.

Finally, we get the interchange trailer UNZ+1+SNRF01' which includes another checksum showing the total number of messages UNH-UNT in the whole interchange – in this example just 1, and then repeats the Sender's Reference for confirmation. If the checksums don't agree, an error is raised, because the interchange is incomplete and may have lost some data, or been tampered with. Each UNB must have a matching UNZ. If groups are being used, then each UNG must have a matching UNE.

EDI Interchange

The EDI interchange forms a single unit to be sent to a trading partner. In concept, an interchange is just like a paper letter sent to that trading partner, consisting of an envelope with address (UNB segment) plus one or more messages (orders, invoices etc) inside the envelope. Note that though strictly speaking there is a valid and useful distinction between 'interchanges' and 'messages', these terms are sometimes used interchangeably.

The syntax rules effectively specify the grammar for the EDI dialogue. It is these rules that will define how the components (data elements, segments, EDI messages, functional groups and EDI interchange) are formed together to produce a logical and coherent communication that can ultimately be correctly interpreted for the receiving application.

Message design guidelines allow working groups engaged in designing new EDI messages or modifying existing messages to do so in a consistent manner, which will allow other users to understand them.

EDI Interchange Hierarchy

An **interchange** is therefore just like a traditional paper envelope, containing an address on the front, and one or more messages inside. Optionally, it can contain one or more functional groups, which are groups of messages of the same type to different trading partners. The group cannot consist of different types of messages to the same trade partner. However, groups are little used.

A **message** contains one complete commercial document, for example an order or an invoice of any of the predefined message types. A message is made up of a number of segments, starting with a header segment, a variable number of data segments, and a trailer segment. Related data segments are often placed in segment groups. Segment groups can contain further **segment groups**.

A **segment** consists of a tag (three-character name) plus a number of elements, which can either be:

▷ a **simple (component) data element** with a single value, such as the value 105 in the BGM+105+RS1+9′ above, or

▷ a **composite data element** consisting of one or more component data elements, each with a single value, e.g. DTM+137:20010203:102′.

Data Elements and Qualifiers

The EDIFACT terminology is a bit confusing, so it is worth remembering that a composite data element always consists of two or more component data elements, and that a component data element is the same as a simple data element. Unless there is a need to be very precise, it is usually enough to talk just about a "data element".

A typical example of a composite data element is the date field in the DTM segment above:

DTM+137:20010203:102′

This segment contains just one composite data element with three component data elements (delimited by :). Of those, two component data elements (the values 137 and 102) define the meaning and the format of the date more precisely. In this example, we can look up the code values in the EDIFACT documentation, to find that 137 means 'document/message data/time' and that 102 is the 'data/month/time/ period format/qualifier', which in this case tells us that the format is YYYYMMDD, also known as CCYYMMDD.

As these three values (two qualifiers and an actual date) always need to go together, it makes sense to link them as component data elements within one composite data element. This is a very typical example of EDIFACT construction. In particular, the use of qualifiers like 137 and 102 is very common in EDIFACT. Qualifiers provide a very efficient and versatile way of conveying information, particularly to other countries with different languages, but at the expense of readability. In E-mail, and to a lesser extent in XML, it is very hard to achieve this conciseness and efficiency – but then, those advantages are less important when the priority is to be human-readable.

Omitting Data

EDIFACT has rules about omitting data. Conditional (meaning optional) data can always be omitted. In addition, insignificant characters such as leading zeros in a variable length number, or trailing spaces in a variable length alphabetic or alphanumeric element should be removed. A price like this – MOA+146:0000.75' – is incorrect because it has unnecessary zeroes. It should be 0.75.

EDIFACT Messages

There are now a large number of different EDIFACT messages, of which an increasing number are for specialised purposes or particular industries. Details are on the EDIFACT Web site. There are also subsets – for example the European Article Numbering Association have issued a selection of EDIFACT messages adapted and simplified for their members called EANCOM messages. Among other things, EANCOM do not recommend the use of functional groups in EDIFACT interchanges. EANCOM currently has a user base of some 30,000 organizations round the world.

Acknowledging EDIFACT Messages

Another way of providing an audit trail is for the recipient to send back an EDI message. In many cases, suitable messages have been defined – for example, an Order Response (ORDRSP) to confirm, vary or reject line items in an order message. This sort of message gives a commercial, not just a technical, acknowledgement. There is also a generic syntax and service report message, called the control message CONTRL. This does not give any sort of commercial acknowledgement, but does confirm receipt, and if necessary gives details of any syntax errors.

EDIFACT Enhancements

One perhaps surprising aspect of EDI is that most EDI data round the world is sent without encryption. A notable exception is the finance industry, where it is common, but most other industries do not give it high priority. One reason is that VANs maintain a high level of network security and data integrity – enough for routine commercial data. However, encryption is available, and the EDIFACT authorities have published detailed standards. There is also a special message called AUTACK – secure AUThentication and ACKnowledgement message. This gives secure authentication, integrity or non-repudiation to messages or interchanges.

Another interesting EDIFACT enhancement is Interactive EDI, called I-EDI. There is a useful distinction in computing between 'batch' systems and 'interactive' systems. A typical batch system is a payroll program, which runs weekly or monthly. Once the program starts running, there is no dialogue between the user and the computer. In contrast, an interactive system is one where there is a dialogue, with a request/response pattern, and processing therefore has to be done in real time. A good example is an airline ticket reservation system, which must work as an online, real-time dialogue, for example between a travel agent and the ticket system. Such systems are sometimes also described as 'transaction processing' or 'TP systems'.

Traditional EDI is therefore basically a batch system, dealing with files or interchanges one at a time. In contrast, I-EDI uses EDIFACT syntax to maintain an interactive dialogue. However, there are many other existing ways of doing this, so batch EDI remains far more common than I-EDI.

Other EDI Standards

To illustrate the differences between EDI standards, below are shortened examples of an X12 message, called a 'transaction set', and then a TRADACOMs interchange.

ANS ASCI X12 (X12)

X12 at first sight looks quite different from EDIFACT, but it is based on the same concept of segments, each identified by a tag at the beginning (ISA, GS etc.) and delimiters:

```
ISA* 00* ORDERS      * 00* PASSWORD   * 09* SENDER           * ZZ* RECIP
     * 020131* 1249* U* 00200* 123456789* 0* P* *
GS* PO* 88* X0000X0* 020131* 1310* 123070001* X* 002003
ST* 850* 0001
. . .  more
IEA* 1* 123456789
```

The delimiter by default is the * character, but that apart, there are many similarities. The ISA line contains addressing details, similar to the EDIFACT UNB segment and TRADACOMS STX.

TRADACOMS

TRADACOMS was developed before EDIFACT but uses similar conventions. There are various mostly minor differences. For example, the 'envelope' is labelled STX, not UNB:

```
STX=ANAA:1+SENDER+RECIPIENT+010203:101112+ORD1++ORDHDR+B'
MHD=1+ORDHDR:6'
. . . data segments'
. . . data segments'
. . . data segments'
END=4'
```

Among other minor differences, TRADACOMS supports only one currency (whereas EDIFACT, by using a value plus a qualifier, is more flexible). TRADACOMS requires capital letters only. TRADACOMS supports an STX time field of only HHMM, whereas EDIFACT has HHMMSS. But for most commercial purposes, such as orders and invoices, specifying time down to the second is irrelevant. TRADACOMS continues to be used quite widely in the UK, but relatively little in other countries.

Case Study – Lightweight Designs

Lightweight Designs is a small business based in London, UK that was started by two art graduates in 1996 to design, print and distribute greeting cards, including complementary products such as gift wrap. The company markets a range of retro image greeting cards based upon TV characters popular in the UK during 1970s and 1980s and sells its products through sales agents to independent retailers and multiple store chains. Lightweight Designs operate a networked version of the Sage Line50 software package that provides sales order processing and inventory management in addition to financial and management accounting. Sales orders are received either by post or facsimile and entered into the Sage Line50 system for processing.

In Spring 2000 the company ran a successful test marketing of their greetings cards in a number of stores belonging to WH Smith, a large UK multiple store chain that sells papers and magazines, books, stationery, music CDs, etc. The subsequent sales agreement with WH Smith required Lightweight Designs to implement EDI for the receipt of purchase orders and subsequently for the return of invoices. Since most of WH Smith's suppliers were using the TRADANET EDI VAN service operated by GE Global eXchange Services, Lightweight Designs decided to subscribe to this service and purchased the necessary GE EDI software to manage the exchange of EDI messages with WH Smith.

The GE EDI software (Interact for Windows), enables Lightweight Designs to connect to the GE TRADANET service two/three times a day to retrieve any electronic purchase orders in TRADACOMS format deposited by WH Smith. The purchase orders are subsequently printed and entered as sales orders into the Sage Line50 system. Discussions are underway with GE Global eXchange Services and Sage to find ways to eliminate the printing and re-entry of data, possibly once both products become XML enabled.

ODETTE

Odette is an EDI standard developed and used mainly but not exclusively in the European automotive industry. There are a number of specialised messages, subsets of EDIFACT messages, such as DELINS (Delivery Instructions) and despatch advice (AVIEXP). There is also growing co-operation with the American automotive industry for common standards, and developments for Web-based EDI.

OFTP (Odette File Transfer Protocol) has been developed by Odette for the exchange of data. It is similar in principle to FTP in the TCP/IP world, and has a standard set of four-letter commands to manage the file transfer process, such as SFID (Start File Identification), a request to send a file. Another useful facility is EERP (End to End Response), which is generated when a file reaches its ultimate destination. An EERP is sent back as confirmation to the sender. OFTP was designed originally to work over X.25 networks, but can also be used over TCP/IP and ISDN.

Operation of EDI

Within an existing trading community, EDI usually starts when the dominant player or 'hub' in the community decides for commercial reasons to implement EDI. This might be a retailer with several hundreds of suppliers, looking to reduce inventory by speeding up delivery times. An agreement needs to be reached within the community (usually a decision taken by the dominant player) on the EDI standard to be used, the information to be exchanged, the means and frequency of the information to be sent.

Sending EDI Data

The data can be sent through a direct connection (point-to-point), or through an EDI VAN (Value Added Network) service. A point-to-point connection may be as simple as a dial-up connection using a protocol such as Z-modem, like using a bulletin board, or these days a dial-up TCP/IP connection using FTP or SMTP. But such bulletin board dial-up connections are not robust enough for some large users, who refer to them disparagingly as 'dial, dump and pray' connections – you dial a service, dump the data and pray it has arrived. High-volume users require greater security, reliability and resilience. For that reason, volume users often have permanent leased lines or use ISDN, or for even better resilience, use leased lines with ISDN backup.

In addition, there is more to sending data than just dumping it on to another system. Some sort of audit trail is needed to show whether the data has arrived safely. In the case of VANs, where users have mailboxes, there is a need to manage the mailbox. For that reason, VANs may have proprietary connection protocols that provide additional services such as:

▷ Confirmation that the data has been delivered successfully to the VAN.

▷ Audit trail – confirmation that the data has been delivered to the trading partner's mailbox, and later that it has been extracted by the trading partner. This information may be stored in a postbox, and the whole facility works like registered mail in the traditional postal system.

▷ Facility to find out what messages have been received in a mailbox, and then to extract them selectively.

▷ Facility to delete extracted or unwanted messages.

▷ Facility to prevent the sending of duplicate messages. Sending the same order twice to a supplier can cause havoc in the supply chain, and such mistakes are often difficult and expensive to detect and rectify. Duplicates can be identified by the Sender's Reference.

▷ Facility to manage trading relationships – these are agreements between trading partners that define what kind of data is to be exchanged through the VAN. A typical pattern for a retailer is to set up trading relationships to send orders and receive invoices Similarly, a supplier would do the opposite - receive orders and send invoices.

These services are well beyond what can be supported by protocols such as Z-modem or FTP, though they are similar to the facilities in protocols such as POP or IMAP (see Chapter 16). Nevertheless, VANs users may need special software incorporating the services and commands needed to manage their mailboxes efficiently. Such software may use proprietary protocols, or other protocols developed by industry associations, such as OFTP – Odette File Transfer Protocol, used in the automotive industry and elsewhere.

Enterprise Application Integration

The ultimate goal of EDI is to automate as far as possible the whole process of getting data from internal systems, generating EDI messages and sending them out. Similarly, inbound messages from trading partners need to be retrieved, converted to in-house formats, and uploaded into the internal systems. The whole process is summed up in the phrase **Enterprise Application Integration** – EAI for short.

Once created, such EAI systems are very cost-effective, and can substantially reduce the cost of processing commercial documents such as orders and invoices, and thus can speed up and improve the whole supply chain. But the investment needed to achieve this is often beyond the reach of SMEs. Even in large organizations, there is often a need to hire people with special skills, or to bring in outside consultants.

The main issues involved in EAI are:

▷ Legacy systems

▷ Generating EDI messages and middleware

We shall look at these in more detail.

Legacy Systems

Most organizations have what are called 'legacy' systems – in-house computer systems developed years ago that are essential to the running of the business. Some large organizations, particularly in financial services like insurance, have literally thousands of programs developed over the years. In some cases, the programmers who wrote the original programs are no longer available, or the programs were written in languages no longer used, or perhaps using old-fashioned techniques or databases. It is often risky, and sometimes impossible, to upgrade these. Even if more modern facilities are used, such as ERP (Enterprise Resource Planning) systems, most organizations still have very large amounts of legacy data. The problem gets worse when companies grow by acquisition – buying other companies. It is then more than likely that the newly acquired companies will have different computer systems and different applications and different databases. The history of such commercial acquisitions is littered with the problems and occasional disasters of merged companies struggling with incompatible computer systems.

FunFigure 6.3 Problems with legacy systems

Generating EDI Interchanges and Middleware

Another problem facing every organization using EDI is how to generate an interchange. Because of the strict rules about syntax, creating an interchange manually is an error-prone business. In any case, the data needed for the interchange is probably already in some internal system or database. So it makes sense to use a program to extract the data and generate the interchange. This can either be a custom-built program, or one of the specialized data translation or mapping programs on the market. Mapping programs will take data from a file or database and reformat it according to the rules laid down in the EDI standard. These days they are often 'drag-and-drop' programs, which display the input file on the left, with all its data and attributes, and the same thing for the output file on the right. Using a mouse, you can then drag elements from the input file on the left to the location in the output file where you want them. You can also control aspects such as:

▷ Define whether data is mandatory or optional, and maximum occurrences

▷ Define loops, and loops within loops

▷ Do conversions (change date/time formats for different countries, etc.)

▷ Handle errors (e.g. missing data in input file)

▷ Do small amounts of processing on the data if required

153

EAI – Enterprise Application Integration

To see what is involved in EAI, we shall look at a typical example of what is required to achieve such end-to-end integration. We shall assume that there are two trading partners, retailer A and supplier B, and that they both have in-house systems. Trading Partner A has the widely used ERP software SAP. This handles many aspects of an organization's computing requirements, such as production planning, finance, human resources etc, but we will focus on the use of SAP by the retailer to generate orders. Trading Partner B has some other ERP brand. (Even if Trading Partner B also used SAP, it would not make that much difference, because ERP systems are usually highly customized to individual requirements, making direct data exchange impossible).

SAP provide a convenient method for the first stage of this process. The data required to generate an order can be extracted from the various parts of the SAP database and stored in a file called, in SAP terminology, an 'intermediate document', or Idoc for short. In computer jargon, this is described as a flat file, because it consists only of printable ASCII characters, in records and fields, with no metadata – information about the type and meaning of the fields. A SAP Idoc is too big to show on a printed page, but to give you an idea of what it looks like, here is a very shortened example:

```
EDI_DC   021120000000075723331H 30ORDERS021EDI      KI0010000171
E2EDK010027211200000000757233000001E2EDK01002000000010   FRF  1.00000      ZD01
```

As you can see, the data is in fixed positions, with spaces to fill out any text, and zeroes to fill out any numbers. To understand it, you need metadata, and that is supplied in SAP documentation.

The next stage is to convert this flat file into an EDI interchange (or XML file). This can be done either by a custom-built program, or more often by special translation or 'mapping' software or toolkits specially designed to convert data formats. The resulting data can then be sent to the trading partner, and there the whole process is repeated in reverse. Figure 6.4 summarizes this process end-to-end.

In this diagram, data goes from the SAP system at trading partner A, through mapping and translation, then via data communications to a clearing centre or VAN. Routing, tracking and audit information is available to tell trading partner A what is happening to the data.

Trading partner B then connects to the clearing centre or VAN, fetches the data, sends it through mapping and translation to generate a file that is understood by their own ERP system (in this example, not SAP). All in all, this is a very complex procedure, but it does achieve the overriding EAI objective of the end-to-end transmission of data between the incompatible computer systems without human intervention – the foundation of e-Business.

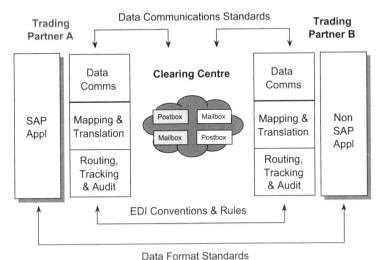

Figure 6.4 Components of an EDI solution

Much work is going into trying to improve and streamline the process, but EAI remains a complex and difficult area, and one very popular among management consultants because it is a lucrative specialist area, requiring a number of skills, particularly when an EAI system is being developed, installed and tested.

EDI over the Internet

The Internet would seem an obvious way to deliver EDI data, particularly as it is already so successfully delivering E-mail and XML. However, it also has disadvantages. First, the advantages:

▷ The Internet is mostly cheaper than traditional VANs.

▷ The Internet has proved to be robust and scaleable.

▷ The Internet has world-wide coverage and a huge population of users.

▷ TCP/IP is stable and mature.

However, there are still several concerns about using the Internet for e-Business, compared to VANs:

▷ The Internet is perceived as being insecure and liable to hacking.

▷ No performance or delivery guarantees.

▷ No central authority to take responsibility.

▷ Limited message tracking and audit trails.

▷ Limited authentication of senders.

There are a number of Internet standards and recommendations for making the Internet a better place for not just EDI, but for all kinds of B2B data, including XML. We'll look first at how the Web can benefit SMEs.

The Internet and SMEs

The Internet provides an opportunity for smaller businesses to become EDI enabled and to realize the benefits only afforded to larger organizations in the past. In part, this is made possible by lower costs of getting started, as well as lower on-going running costs when compared to traditional EDI that involves the use of EDI VAN services. In addition, the Internet provides access to an online global marketplace which operates on a 24 hour basis, with millions of customers and thousands of products and services.

In simple terms EDI transactions may be sent over the Internet using the same transport mechanism used for E-mail but with extensions to cover the rather special requirements of EDI described above. A variant on this may be to simply send an EDI Interchange (envelope with a number of EDI transactions contained within it) as a file using FTP (the Internet service for file transfer) over a 'secure' link. Or lastly to use Internet Web browser technology to display a form that can be completed by the sender and in due course be translated into an EDI standard for onward transmission to the recipient. Again, at this stage it is important to focus upon the principles, as further details can be found later in the book.

EDI Web Forms

For an SME with scarce resources, EDI requires the purchase of particular software packages, as well as developing an understanding of EDI standards. It is primarily these technical complexities and associated costs that have deterred SMEs from using EDI and it is estimated that less than 1% of all businesses in Europe use EDI. Even for large retail organizations with their developed EDI supplier communities, there are frequently smaller companies that fall into the SME category that still request paper or fax-based business transactions.

e-Commerce offers an opportunity for SMEs to participate in EDI, using a Web forms capability, without the complexities mentioned above. This is achieved by using the Web browser to present the end user with forms that closely resemble their paper-based equivalents of a purchase order, invoice etc. The necessary information is submitted to the Web server where it is processed to create a file that is input directly into an EDI mapper/translator. The translation process creates an EDI transaction in the required EDI standard for onward transmission to the trading partner. This EDI Web forms capability is offered by most of the valued added network service providers as a low priced option that is integrated with their EDI VAN service. Work has also started to agree standard layouts for the EDI Web forms, since a supplier participating in several supply chains does not wish to be working with completely different forms for each retailer.

Several other Web related initiatives are underway focused on considerably simplifying the EDI process for SMEs, particularly the mapping effort, where the use of the XML language (richer functionality than SGML) appears to be a natural fit for EDI and is receiving a good deal of attention. The objective being for smaller organizations to use Web technology to openly exchange structured business transactions in a secure and meaningful manner, but with reduced emphasis upon a separate EDI mapper/translation function.

Security

Naturally, conducting e-Business over the Internet has to be completely secure and, this above all else has represented one fundamental reason that has kept both business customer and home consumers away, a perception of a non-secure environment. Much has been achieved to address this issue which is described in detail within Chapter 12. However, in respect of EDI, CommerceNet, a non-profit industry association that has evolved into a consortium of business, government, technology, and academic organizations to promote e-Commerce, successfully completed a number of formal interoperability tests with software vendors that demonstrated the secure exchange of EDI transactions over the Internet. These interoperability tests were based upon recommendations for secure EDI over the Internet prepared by Electronic Data Interchange Internet Integration (EDIINT), an Internet Engineering Task Force (IETF) work group. Some 14 tests included successful exchange of digital certificates, signed messages, encrypted messages and signed receipts (non-repudiation of receipts) for EDI and general e-Commerce data over the Internet.

As we have seen Electronic Data Interchange (EDI) is a set of protocols for conducting highly structured inter-organization exchanges, such as for making purchases or requests for payments. The initial RFC1767 defined the method for packaging the X12 and EDIFACT transactions sets in a MIME envelope. However, several additional requirements for obtaining multi-vendor, inter-operable service, over and above how the EDI transactions are packaged, have come to light since the effort concluded. These currently revolve around security issues such as EDI transaction integrity, privacy and non-repudiation in various forms. Additional requirements for the heading fields are also needed to support exchanges by point-to-point, FTP and SMTP protocols. Many believe these heading fields are best described in XML. Standards in these and other areas are necessary to ensure inter-operability between EDI packages over the Internet. Various technologies already exist for these additional features and the primary requirement has moved to select a common set of components for use by the EDI community when it sends EDI over the Internet. This has resulted in a project to provide EDI over the Internet Informational and Applicability Statement Documents.

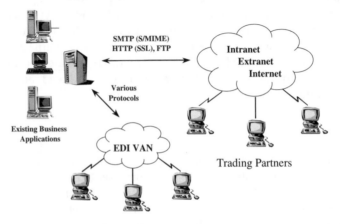

Figure 6.5 EDI over the Internet

Currently IETF AS2 (Applicability Statement 2) represents the second round of testing. AS2 is a draft specification standard (RFC Standards Track) by which vendor applications communicate EDI (EDIFACT or X12), binary or XML data over the Internet. AS2 is an expansion of the AS1 specification (which specifies EDI data transmission over SMTP) to provide for EDI data transmission over HTTP. The purpose of the testing is to provide a venue for vendors to test and correct their software systems in a non-competitive environment.

To sum up, the aims are to achieve a 'secure transmission loop' for EDI (EDIFACT or X12), binary or XML data over the Internet, to enable an organization to:

▷ Send a signed and encrypted EDI interchange to another

▷ Request a signed receipt

▷ Later receive the signed receipt

EDI over SMTP

The main focus for EDI has been on using SMTP to send messages to a trading partner, and using MIME or S/MIME to hold the data. Much has been achieved in recent years by the Internet Engineering Task Force (IETF) through its Electronic Data Interchange Internet Integration (EDIINT) Work Group to address the very real and serious concerns of transaction security across the Internet.

There are various RFCs devoted to this, including:

RFC 821	SMTP
RFC 822	Text Message Formats
RFC 1767	EDI Content Type
RFC 1847	Security Multiparts for MIME
RFC 1892	Multipart/Report
RFC 2015, 2156, 2440	MIME/PGP
RFC 2045 to 2049	MIME RFCs
RFC 2298	Message Disposition Notification
RFC 2630, 2633	S/MIME v3 Specification

The diagram below summarizes some of the proposals that have been put forward:

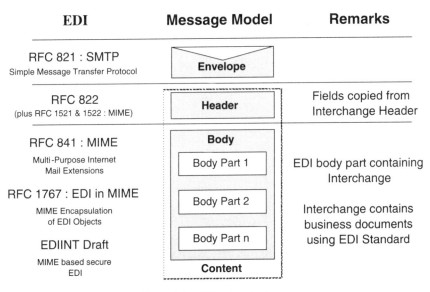

Figure 6.6 EDI using the Internet

There are a number of competing possibilities, but the favoured IETF standard for E-mail security is Secure MIME (S/MIME), based upon technology from RSA Data Security Inc. to transport digitally signed and encrypted information in MIME. S/MIME is based on Public-Key Cryptography Standards (PKCS) and in particular one such specification PKCS #7 which defines how to protect a MIME body part, creating a new data structure, which itself becomes a new MIME content type, called 'application/x-pkcs7-mime'. Further details in Chapter 12.

But it is sufficient to understand at this stage that through these security standards, 'easy-to-use' products are available that employ certificates, encryption, authentication and digital signatures to guarantee data integrity and security of sensitive business transactions.

Web-based EDI and Internet

Will the Web replace EDI? While the Web clearly has attractions for SMEs, it is not the same for large organizations with large existing investment in EDI. They are more likely to go for a hybrid solution, retaining EDI for existing trading partners, and using Web-based EDI for newer or smaller ones. In that way, SMEs can use just a browser to send and receive business documents through their ISP, at much lower cost than with traditional EDI.

---

[1]   Quoted by kind permission from *K.I.S.S. - Keep It Simple, Standard, Speedy and Certain - the Principles of Value Chain Management and Electronic Business* - pub. e.centre 1999

Evolving B2B
– Electronic
Business XML

Introduction

This chapter examines XML (eXtensible Mark-up Language) – what it is, what it offers, and why it is important. From an e-Business perspective, the main attraction is that XML promises to provide an internationally agreed standard for the exchange of structured business data based upon defined business processes. That is of course very similar to what EDI is designed to do, so that EDI and XML can be viewed as complementary approaches. As previously discussed in Chapter 6, EDI is based upon EDI standards, such as UN/EDIFACT and ANSI ASC X12 that are viewed by many users as difficult syntaxes to learn. XML has the ability to replace an EDI standard and perform exactly the same function of uniquely defining the data being exchanged. But XML can be used for far more than just business data, as we shall see. Another major advantage of XML is that it is designed for use in today's Internet environment, and is a logical development from existing facilities such as HTML (HyperText Mark-up Language).

Therefore XML is the latest approach to a perennial problem in business of how to exchange electronic business data between separate companies often with differing computer systems. As explained in Chapter 15, there are many technical hurdles in the way of an easy exchange of data, ranging from simple low-level ones such as the character set, the definition of a 'line', whether a computer is 'big-endian' or 'little-endian' and from there, right up the scale to the application level, where different databases, programs and integrated systems have their own requirements for access and control. Even the same program implemented differently on different machines, or simply different versions of the same program, can cause integration problems.

XML and the Web

Although not designed only for the Web, that is a significant part of its use. XML also provides a standard way of adding intelligence to HTML pages. It makes Web pages smarter, and opens up the possibilities not just to view information, as with HTML, but also to process it, even analyze it locally. With only HTML, current browsers are not that different from old-fashioned dumb terminals – it is easy to browse information with them, but still very hard to make use of it locally. There is nothing in an HTML page to tell your browser what the data means, only how to present it on the screen.

But it is important to appreciate that XML is not a programming language, like for instance JavaScript, nor a database management system – it is only about structured data, and in particular, how to process it, not just display it. In a nutshell: HTML provides Web pages, XML provides Web services.

Origins of XML

XML is fairly new – the first release came in 1998, when W3C (World Wide Web Consortium – see glossary) announced version 1. This was a few years after XML's close relation, HTML. As we will see later in this chapter, both XML and HTML are derived from another standard, SGML, published as an ISO standard in 1986.

Three different uses of XML

XML can usefully be divided up into three different levels of usage:

1. Core XML technology – the basic elements, as defined by W3C, covering three main elements:

    ▷ XML syntax rules – how an XML document is structured

    ▷ XML metadata – what the data means, defined in DTDs and Schemas

    ▷ How XML is presented – stylesheets and styling languages

2. XML initiatives and XML-based messages – proposed standard ways of exchanging data (ebXML, RosettaNet, OASIS, OAGIS etc.)

3. XML terminologies – specialized versions of XML for specific industries, such as finance, health services etc.

We shall look at these in more detail in this chapter, but first, a look at XML itself.

Core Technology – Syntax Rules

Central to all this is how to convey both data, and what the data means, to a remote computer system. One of the key aspects of XML is that it includes 'metadata' or data about data, along with the actual data that you want to send. In that way, one file contains both the data and an explanation of what it means. Bear in mind ISO's definition of metatada – "the information and documentation which makes data sets (files etc.) understandable and shareable for users" (see glossary).

In XML, the metadata is placed in 'tags' identified by the < and > signs, and the data is placed in between them. Thus a typical bit of XML might look like this:

```
<Name>John Smith</Name>
```

This immediately tells you two things – there is a type of data called Name, and its value in this instance is John Smith. This simple principle is at the heart of XML, and provides the foundation for an effective way of exchanging data between different computer systems. If the remote system has an XML parser (software that understands XML) then it can separate out the data and metadata, and make sense of both. Another advantage is that it is also easy for humans to read and understand.

Another way to understand metadata is to think in terms of paper documents. If you work for an organization and you need to send a paper invoice to another organization, the chances are you will simply pull out a pre-printed form, fill it in and send it. That form will contain various boxes, with labels like Name, Address, Item and suchlike for you to fill in. The labels tell you what the information means, and you just add the relevant data for this particular invoice in the right boxes. Effectively, the labels are the metadata, and what you add is the data. There might also be a separate help guide to show you how to fill in an invoice. That too counts as metadata. Each type by itself is of little use. But bring data and metadata together – and you have information. That is the key.

XML and HTML

If you are familiar with HTML, you will immediately notice the similarity. That is no coincidence. Both XML and HTML are based on an older standard called SGML (Standard Generalized Markup Language), in turn derived for an earlier one called just Generalized Markup Language – GML). SGML has been used for many years, above all for complex technical documentation. But to cater for that sort of use, for example, describing mathematical equations, SGML is inevitably very detailed and demanding. Both HTML and XML are simpler variants, but with different objectives. HTML is all about the presentation of data, so in HTML you will see tags to define for example bold, or italic, and all the different facilities needed to display data effectively and attractively. When you are looking at an attractive Web page, you can see how it is done by viewing the source – that shows the HTML that has generated the output in your browser.

But HTML suffers from various limitations:

▷ Concerned only with presentation of data

▷ Must be viewed on a browser

▷ Hard to process page contents, e.g. to write contents to a database

This last point is vital – for true e-Business, it is essential to link Web pages to an organization's back office systems – summed up in the word 'integration' or more formally – Enterprise Application Integration. HTML is designed to present an attractive display to human beings, and that is as far as it goes.

XML is more ambitious, because it is designed to convey the meaning of the data, and thus enable integration. To put it another way – unlike HTML, XML is about more than just the presentation. It is also about the content and the structure of the data. As a result, XML can be employed in much more useful ways, in particular these three:

▷ Users – provides a more powerful display method on browsers

▷ Data – can be used to exchange data between computer systems

▷ Messages – can be used to exchange messages (for example, requests and commands) between separate computer systems for true distributed computing

These three features are what XML is all about.

Core Technology – XML Metadata

Document Type Definitions

Returning to our small XML example, how does an XML parser know what the metadata 'Name' actually means? In HTML, tags all have fixed names such as <BOLD> or <ITALIC>, whereas in XML, these are user-defined (and, incidentally, case-sensitive). The answer is what is called a 'Document Type Definition', or DTD. This is a formal description that defines the structure of a particular document type – in other words, more metadata. Actually, HTML also has a DTD, but it is fixed in advance in the browser – and that is why your browser understands what <BOLD>

means – it is defined in the built-in DTD for HTML. In contrast, in XML, you can define your own DTD. In there, you specify the elements to be used, and various attributes of those elements – for example, not just the name of the element, but also whether it is required or optional, how often it can occur, and the values if any it must match. You can also specify the language to be used. Tags do not have to be in English.

Why XML is 'eXtensible'

So a key difference between HTML and XML is that HTML has a fixed set of tags, while XML tags are user-defined – and therefore unlimited. That is why XML is called 'eXtensible' – because, unlike HTML, you can extend it by defining your own tags, like the <Name> example above, not valid in HTML.

This in turn leads on to another important aspect in XML – XML data must be both well-formed and valid:

▷ Well-formed – in other words, syntactically correct, with proper opening and closing tags, as in the Name example above. The rules are similar to those in HTML, but stricter.

▷ Valid – if a DTD is being used, the values must match those defined in the DTD. (Strictly speaking, a DTD is optional – but not using a DTD defeats the purpose of XML).

Let's look in more detail at a fragment of an XML file:

XML file

```
<?xml version="1.0"?>
<USER>
    <Name>John Smith</Name>
    <Telephone>+44 123 456 789</Telephone>
</USER>
```

The first line is an XML Processing Instruction – it tells the browser to use the built-in XML parser to analyze the text. Then follow the XML user-defined tags, here Name and Telephone, nested inside a top-level or 'root' tag, here called USER. This is how this file is displayed in a browser that understands XML – for example Microsoft's Internet Explorer 5 (and the same in IE6):

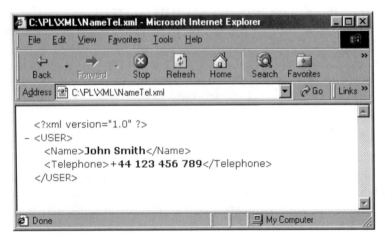

Figure 7.1 Display of XML data

At this stage, there is nothing but the XML data, so IE6 just displays the contents of the file (using, of course, a special DTD inside IE6 that tells it how to display raw XML). The fact that the file has been displayed at all proves that it is well-formed – all the opening and closing tags match. However, we have no idea if it is valid or not. For that we need a DTD to define the elements, either contained within the XML data, as in the example below, or in a separate DTD file, held either locally, or remotely on a Web server:

```
<?xml version="1.0" encoding="UTF-8"?>
<!DOCTYPE USER [
   <!ELEMENT USER (Name, Telephone) >
   <!ELEMENT Name (#PCDATA) >
   <!ELEMENT Telephone (#PCDATA) >
  ]>
<USER>
   <Name>John Smith</Name>
   <Telephone>+44 123 456 789</Telephone>
</USER>
```

The first line now also tells the browser to use the character set UTF-8. The XML specification mandates that "all XML processors must accept the UTF-8 and UTF-16 encodings of ISO 10646" – in effect consisting of Unicode, and also ASCII-compatible.

DOCTYPE

The next line <!DOCTYPE is the start of the DTD itself. It defines a root item USER, and then inside the square brackets [ ] spread over several lines it defines the !ELEMENTs – namely USER, which in turn contains two nested items, Name and Telephone. The plus sign after each item in

the first !ELEMENT line means they can occur one or more times. That also means they are mandatory, not optional – they must occur at least once. Other options in DTDs are Name* (can occur zero or more times), and Name? (zero or once). If they can occur zero times that means of course that they are optional.

The word #PCDATA stands for 'Parsed Character Data', and means that the data must consist of valid characters only. For example, it cannot include the characters < or > because they have a special meaning in XML (reserved for tags, as in HTML). If you really want to use the < character in data, then you can do so, but you must use a special HTML expression > (greater-than sign). Microsoft Internet Explorer v.6 (IE6) does not show the full DTD, but tells you how to see it – by viewing the source.

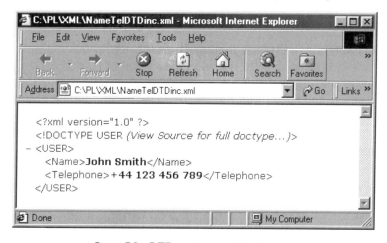

Figure 7.2 DTD and Internet Explorer

It is well worth browsing the Web, and looking at the source data – these days, if you have an XML-compatible browser, you are likely to come across live XML.

Advantage of DTDs

The IE6 display above gives little idea of the advantages of using DTDs. But consider for a moment what is required to exchange data like that with another system. Suppose, for example, you belong to an organization with a members' database, and it is important to keep that database updated. If you used the same DTD as the organization, then you could send this information to the organization, and it would be easy for them to automatically update their database, because they know what the data means. Of course, in a trivial example like this, it would probably be easier to do the job manually. But you can see that for larger amounts of data, it makes more sense to automate the process.

The key point here is that by sharing DTDs, organizations, and communities of organizations in a supply chain, can have a standard way of exchanging data – they both know what the data means. Creating standard DTDs for specific purposes is thus a fundamental requirement for e-Business, and many have already been developed. What is even better is that DTDs come originally from SGML, which has been around for years, so there are already many thousands of DTDs. But new ones are always needed, and that is the focus of a great deal of the current effort in developing XML for e-Commerce. One of the main objectives is to create so-called 'repositories' of DTDs, available over the Web, so that many organizations can download the same DTDs. However, that creates its own problems, as we shall see further on.

XML Schemas

One limitation of DTDs is that they do not cater for the 'typing' of values – for example, to specify if a particular element is a date, or a numeric value or a string of characters; also if there are any size limitations such as minimum and maximum values, or patterns to validate values. These factors become very important when data is to be transferred to another system, such as a database, or to be processed in some way by a program. These generally store numbers, dates or words (strings) in quite different ways, and will cause errors if the values are not defined correctly.

The answer is a proposal by the W3C for Schemas, which do allow such 'typing' of data. They also cater for many other useful features, such as minimum and maximum values, and for patterns to be matched against input values – for example; you might want to ensure that a particular value is in a special format, like a date, or an ISBN book number. A pattern in a Schema like this: [A-C]{1}d{1} means that the value must consist of a single letter A-C, followed by a single digit. So A1 is acceptable, D1 is invalid. Nothing like that is possible in DTDs.

Another advantage of Schemas is that they are written in XML syntax, unlike DTDs. There is an example below. However, the full details of Schemas are fairly complex, and beyond the scope of this book. They are an approved 'recommendation' and almost all new XML work is being undertaken using Schemas. There are many books and Web sites about all aspects of XML. The key point is that Schemas are better than DTDs, and important for e-Business.

XML Example Order

To illustrate the use of XML in a more realistic scenario, below is an example of an XML order, matching the EDI order shown in Chapter 6. It is deliberately kept short – a real XML order would be bigger, usually quite a lot bigger. Also, to keep it short, this example does not follow the various XML standards and initiatives now available and described later in this chapter:

```
<?xml version="1.0" encoding="UTF-8"?>
<!DOCTYPE  OrderMessage SYSTEM "OrderMsg.dtd">
<OrderMessage>
   <Order OrderDate="2001-02-03" CustomerRef="SNRF01" >
      <ShipTo>ABC / HIGH STREET 123 / ANYTOWN / XX1 1YY / GB</ShipTo>
      <LineItems>
         <Item>1</Item>
         <Part>BF01</Part>
         <Quantity>21</Quantity>
         <Description>BRASS FITTING</Description>
         <Price>1.75</Price>
      </LineItems>
      <LineItems>
         <Item>2</Item>
         <Part>PF02</Part>
         <Quantity>4</Quantity>
         <Description>PLASTIC FITTING</Description>
         <Price>0.50</Price>
      </LineItems>
   </Order>
</OrderMessage>
```

The <!DOCTYPE line shows that the DTD is held as a separate file, and below is an example of such a DTD. Note how each item is identified as an ELEMENT, using the * + ? characters to identify the number of times each item may occur, and therefore also whether the items are optional or mandatory:

```
<?xml version="1.0" ?>
<!- OrderMessage with DTD ->
  <!ELEMENT OrderMessage (Order*)>
  <!ELEMENT Order (ShipTo?, LineItems+)>
  <!ATTLIST Order OrderDate CDATA #REQUIRED>
  <!ATTLIST Order CustomerRef CDATA #REQUIRED>
  <!ELEMENT ShipTo (#PCDATA)>
  <!ELEMENT LineItems (Item, Part, Quantity, Description?, Price)>
  <!ELEMENT Item (#PCDATA)>
  <!ELEMENT Part (#PCDATA)>
  <!ELEMENT Quantity (#PCDATA)>
  <!ELEMENT Description (#PCDATA)>
  <!ELEMENT Price (#PCDATA)>
```

As a comparison, the next illustration is a shortened and simplified example of what a schema for the same order might look like. You can see straight away that it is more verbose than the DTD, and it is in normal XML format, not the special format in DTDs (derived from SGML). Note also one significant advantage – schemas allow 'typing' of data. Some values are defined as strings (of characters), while for example Quantity is defined as a positive integer in the range 1 – 9999. This may seem small and restrictive, but it is common practice to keep such values short, to prevent people from ordering ridiculous quantities of for example washing machines.

```
<?xml version="1.0" ?>
<xsd:schema xmlns:xsd="http://www.w3.org/2001/XMLSchema">
<xsd:element name="OrderMessage" />
<xsd:element name="ShipTo" type = "xsd:string"/>
<xsd:element name="LineItems">
   <xsd:complexType>
      <xsd:sequence>
         <xsd:element name="Item" type="xsd:string"/>
         <xsd:element name="Part" type="xsd:string"/>"
         <xsd:element name="Quantity">
            <xsd:simpleType>
               <xsd:restriction base="xsd:positiveInteger">
                  <xsd:minInclusive value="1"/>
                  <xsd:maxInclusive value="9999"/>
               </xsd:restriction>
            </xsd:simpleType>
         </xsd:element>
         <xsd:element name="Description" type="xsd:string"/>"
         <xsd:element name="Price" type="xsd:string"/>"
      </xsd:sequence>
   </xsd:complexType>
</xsd:element>
</xsd:schema>
```

This is what the OrderMsg (with DTD) looks like in IE6:

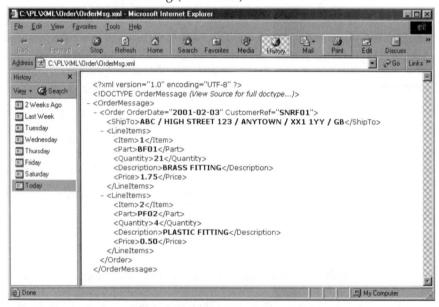

Figure 7.3 Orders message example

XML Tools

There are various software tools available these days that are very useful for viewing and also constructing XML data. For example, Microsoft have a product called XML Notepad, designed as a test bed for building and prototyping XML files. It will also validate the XML data against the DTD.

Below is what the OrderMsg above (with DTD) looks like in XML Notepad, and you can see straight away that it is a more useful version than Internet Explorer. It gives a much more useful display, and you can shrink or expand groups of items as required:

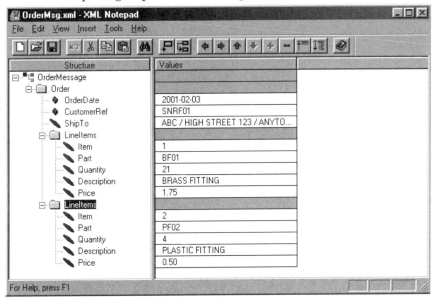

Figure 7.4 MS XML Notepad

There is more information about XML Notepad on:
msdn.microsoft.com/xml/notepad/intro.asp

Core Technology – Presentation of XML

So far, we have seen only rather plain text-based displays of XML – nothing like as interesting as most HTML pages. The reason is simple – XML is about the exchange of data, preferably automatic without human intervention. Nevertheless, there are times when you want a display suitable for humans, and as you might expect, there are various ways of improving the presentation of XML data. This is also where we start to get deeper into the jungle of TLAs (Three-Letter Acronyms), in which XML is particularly rich. (There can only be 17,576 TLAs, so some people now talk about FLAPs – Four-Letter Acronym Proliferation).

Presentation Techniques

The main ways of improving the appearance on screen of XML data are by using CSS or XSL or XQL (Cascading Style Sheets or eXtensible Stylesheet Language or XML Query Language – we did warn you about the TLAs). Cascading Style Sheets are not new to XML. But they are simple and effective. Here is the data file shown earlier, this time identifying a separate CSS file called, in this example, NameTel.css:

```
<?xml version="1.0"?>
<?xml:stylesheet type="text/css" href="NameTel.css"?>
<!DOCTYPE USER [
    <!ELEMENT USER (Name+, Telephone+) >
    <!ELEMENT Name (#PCDATA) >
    <!ELEMENT Telephone (#PCDATA) >
  ]>
<USER>
    <Name>John Smith</Name>
    <Telephone>+44 123 456 789</Telephone>
</USER>
```

And this is the CSS file NameTel.css, specifying how each value is to appear – in this case, using the 'Broadway' font :

```
Name           { display:inline;
                 font-family:Broadway,sans-serif;
                 font-size:24pt;
                 font-weight:bold }

Telephone      { display:inline;
                 font-family:Broadway,sans-serif;
                 color:red;
                 font-size:16pt;
```

The display in IE6 now looks like this:

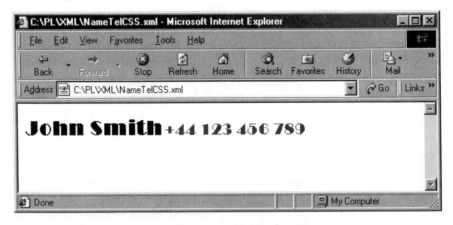

Figure 7.5   Cascading style sheets

Note that we no longer get the default display from IE6 – instead, it is now controlled by the style sheet. The same effect can of course be achieved using HTML. This example illustrates that XML with a CSS stylesheet like the one above can do anything that HTML can do, but XML can also do many more things, particularly when DTDs and Schemas and some of the other advanced facilities are used. We have achieved one of the chief aims of XML – to separate out the presentation of the data from the actual data contents and structure.

XSL – Presentation via Transformation

Though better than nothing, CSS is really just a way of painting XML data with styles. A more powerful facility is XSL, the eXtensible Stylesheet Language. This does much more than paint. XSL enables you to selectively transform the XML data, for example into HTML. You can define templates that put the data through a sort of filter, using a variety of programming functions. That way you get the best of both worlds – XML data, but in an attractive HTML presentation. The details are a good deal more complex than CSS, and there are again plenty of books and Web sites.

The diagram below summarizes the various techniques discussed. When received, all XML data must be processed by a parser that understands XML – and preferably assisted by a DTD (Document Type Definition). If the data is destined for an application, then it can be sent directly there. But if it is to be shown on a browser, or printed out, then it is much better to put it through some process such as XSL to improve the presentation for human beings:

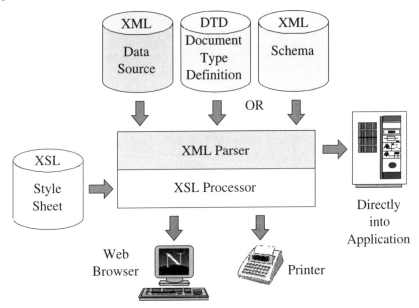

Figure 7.6 Interaction of XML components

Processing of XML

Data Islands

One common requirement on a Web site, particularly for e-Commerce, is to extract data from a database, and display it to the user. That means that data, such as a list of books for sale, can be dynamic – changing, depending on sales and stock levels – rather than static, as in conventional HTML. There are many solutions to this problem, ranging from CGI (Common Gateway Interface) through Perl, ASP (Active Server Pages), and Java, described in Chapter 17. But they all have one disadvantage in common – they all process the data on the server, and then create a dynamic HTML page to be displayed on the client's browser. This is fine for small searches, and small quantities of data. But large quantities will overload the server. It would be better to send the data to the client, and let the client process the data locally – particularly if the client needs to reorganize the data, for example, to sort it by date rather than by alphabetical order, or to search it for particular values. This is where XML comes in. It provides a universally accepted standard for data, and using XML, we can download data from the server to the browser, and store it there for local processing. What's more, this can be achieved by including XML in an HTML page, in what is called an XML Data Island.

Document Object Model (DOM)

The DOM is another way of providing more powerful processing. It is defined by W3C:

> "The DOM is a programming API for HTML and XML documents. It defines the logical structure of documents and the way a document is accessed and manipulated. With the Document Object Model, programmers can create and build documents, navigate their structure, and add, modify, or delete elements and content."

Going back to our earlier XML example file, we can see that it has a nested structure:

```
<USER>
    <Name>John Smith</Name>
    <Telephone>+44 123 456 789</Telephone>
</USER>
```

This could be described as a 'parent-child' relationship – USER is a parent with two children – Name and Telephone, and they in turn are siblings of each other, and also children of the parent User. Alternatively, it could be described as a tree, with User as the trunk and Name and Telephone as the branches. In both cases, this analogy could be expanded to include grandchildren, or using a tree with multiple branches and leaves. The key point is that there is a clear structure, and that means that a program on the browser (perhaps downloaded from the server) can traverse this structure and, as it were, feel its way through the data, find and understand the data and process it. Once again, the details rapidly become complicated, and mainly for programmers, but that gives the broad idea. To sum up, with XML and DOM a program can traverse or navigate the data, and thus manipulate it locally.

Exchanging XML Data

A vital requirement in e-Commerce is to exchange data between trading partners, and one way of achieving this, as mentioned earlier, is to share specifications. For XML, this means using the same DTDs or Schemas. For that reason, several industry bodies are preparing standard DTDs or schemas that can be distributed in advance, so that those taking part can simply define which DTD or schemas they are using without sending it, and be certain that the trading partner will understand the data.

XML and Firewalls

Another and perhaps unexpected advantage of XML lies in the area of security. Many corporate firewalls place strict controls over data flows in and out of an organization. This is often done by blocking all port numbers apart from a few well-known ones for specific purposes. One such port is port 80, the default port for HTTP (HyperText Transfer Protocol). There is more about this in Chapters 16 and 17, but the basic principle is that when you type a URL into your browser, by default it will connect to the Web site on port 80. Any organization wanting to offer a Web service must therefore leave port 80 open – otherwise browsers could not get in. This also means that XML can get through because it is transmitted, using HTTP, through port 80 in the same way as HTML.

XML Issues

While XML is an attractive technical solution for many integration problems, at the end of the day it must meet business requirements in order to be accepted and used. There are several issues that need to be resolved, such as:

▷ Legal issues. For example, are electronic invoices using XML accepted by trading partners, and more importantly, by the country's tax authorities?

▷ Language. Although some implementations of XML support multiple languages (for example, ebXML – see below) it seems generally assumed that English will be used. If you are sending an XML file to a foreign country, should you translate the tags? If you receive an XML file from a foreign country, what happens if you do not understand the tags? Or if a foreign trading partner sends you a DTD with foreign names for the elements? (Traditional data exchange formats, notably EDI, have an advantage here – they are much less language-specific).

▷ XML proliferation. As we'll see at the end of this chapter, there are now a remarkable number of different implementations of XML-based standards for different purposes and industries. What's worse, there are a proliferating number of DTDs (Document Type Definitions). Proliferation is the enemy of standardization. While it may be convenient to have an XML implementation tailored for a particular industry, some organizations will be involved in several industries, and therefore potentially have to use several different implementations of XML and DTDs of different designs even for similar purposes, such as invoicing. All this proliferation defeats the purposes of a common standard.

▷ For some purposes, particularly A2A (application-to-application integration, also known as EAI), XML offers no particular advantages over other traditional methods of exchanging data. If XML continues to proliferate, such integration becomes more complex, not less. The fact that XML is readable by humans is no advantage here.

▷ Verbosity. In some industries, notably finance, the sheer volume of data to be transferred (such as thousands of constantly changing share prices) means that even with today's high-speed networks there is a need to send as little data as possible. Although XML's verbosity can be viewed as a disadvantage, in reality it lends itself to compression techniques. When comparing the compression of an EDIFACT message with its equivalent XML message, much greater compression is achieved with the XML message.

▷ While standard XML is pretty straightforward, the growing number of facilities around XML such as style sheets, XSL, XSLT, XPath, Xpointer, XHTML etc., as well as the growing variety of XML facilities and varieties make for an increasingly steep learning curve, and a requirement for specialist expertise.

▷ XML is not compatible with existing EDI systems. It requires new skills, training and investment. This is made worse by XML proliferation.

On the other hand, we should also note XML's advantages.

XML Advantages

▷ Other methods of exchanging data, particularly EDI, have proved to be relatively complex and expensive, and beyond the reach of many SMEs. One reason is that standards may not always match organizations' requirements exactly, and therefore time and effort has to be spent on reconciling the business needs with the standards. The hope is that XML will provide greater flexibility.

▷ EDI focuses on the exchange of commercial data, and does not provide the broader range of facilities, such as the 'discovery' facilities in XML approaches offered in ebXML and RosettaNet. These XML approaches therefore provide a broader range of services, and greater opportunity to automate processes between trading partners, and also to find new trading partners. There is no equivalent discovery mechanism in EDI.

▷ Despite attempts to enforce standards in EDI, there are a number of variants and special cases, and in some cases larger organizations or 'hubs' introduce their own variants, and force their spokes (suppliers etc.) to adapt to these.

▷ Language. Despite the disadvantages referred to earlier, a real strength of XML is that it supports almost any language, including tags. Only the DTD/Schema must be in English.

▷ Application developers never really 'built in' EDI. On the other hand, as the examples later in this chapter illustrate, XML is fast becoming a mainstream IS technique.

▷ The growth of the Internet, and the number of people with browsers, means that it is now easier to order goods interactively on the Internet using forms. This is much easier with XML than with EDI. This is particularly true for the vast quantity of non-strategic supplies required by many larger organizations – day-to-day products like stationery. XML is well suited to such business-to-business purchasing, often called 'procurement' or 'catalogue' systems.

Summary

For many organizations, particularly large ones, the Holy Grail of e-Business is to achieve end-to-end integration between buyers and sellers, or to put it another way, to improve the effectiveness of the supply chain.

This implies a range of integration requirements as illustrated in Figure 7.7 below:

▷ Tight integration of independent applications owned by trading partners using EDI or EDI/XML

▷ Sharing and transfer of data between internal applications (EAI)

▷ Capture of data to be used by collaborative applications for planning and forecasting purposes using XML

▷ Online integration of Web users for small volume buying and selling activities using HTML, XML and XML/XSL

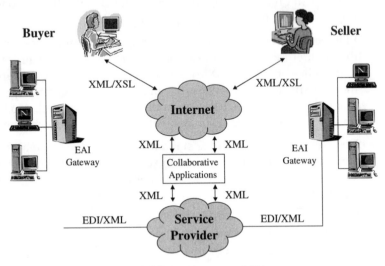

Figure 7.7 XML integration posibilities

XML Initiatives

Introduction

Although XML is relatively new, the power and flexibility that it provides has already sparked off a number of initiatives and standards. (But, as an IT cynic put it: "The nice thing about standards is that there are so many to choose from, and if you don't like one, another will be along in a moment".)

The basic aim of these initiatives is to standardize messages (using DTDs or Schemas) and to develop the whole framework or infrastructure for e-Business. Below is a selection of current initiatives:

ebXML

ebXML is an initiative sponsored by the United Nations CEFACT body and another industry body, OASIS, and is the most international and broad-ranging of all the initiatives. The aim is to create an environment in which anyone can do business with anyone else. It is basically a set of specifications that provide a framework for e-Business, based on widely used and well understood principles of business workflow. While leveraging existing technologies and standards, it allows business processes and technologies to evolve independently.

One significant aspect of ebXML is to try to overcome the technical and financial hurdles that have deterred SMEs (Small and Medium Enterprises) from doing business electronically, and also to enable the developing countries to trade more easily with the developed world. Most existing e-Business systems assume that trading partners have existing contractual arrangements and connections. In contrast, ebXML is designed to enable companies anywhere in the world to discover each other electronically over the Internet. This is clearly in a significant step beyond what earlier e-Business systems, particularly EDI systems, were designed to do, and opens up some interesting and exciting opportunities.

The ebXML mission is:

"To provide an open XML-based infrastructure enabling the global use of electronic business information in an interoperable, secure and consistent manner by all parties." **www.ebxml.org**

In outline, the aim of ebXML is far wider than previous approaches, such as traditional EDI. The main ones are:

▷ Discovery	Find out about products and services on offer
▷ Business processes	Agree on the processes and documents needed to obtain products and services
▷ Contacts and contracts	Who to contact, in order to agree contract terms

To achieve this, business transactions are analyzed from two points of view:

▷ Business Operational View (BOV)	Business processes defined using a graphic modelling language UML
▷ Functional Services View (FSV)	Describes the technical framework for exchanging information (protocols etc.)

There is a registry set up by each trading partner that holds, among other things, two vital items of information:

▷ Collaboration Protocol Profile (CPP) lists a trading partner's technical capabilities

▷ Collaboration Protocol Agreement (CPA) defines agreements between two partners on their common profile, based on the CPP.

Once the CPP is agreed, the trading partners can start to exchange business messages, called in ebXML 'the payload'. The payload is exchanged as defined in ebXML Messaging Services, which includes standard TCP/IP protocols such as SMTP, FTP, HTTP, and optionally supports security methods such as HTTPS and digital signatures.

To summarise with reference to Figure 7.8, this is how the business workflow is visualized:

▷ Company A uses the ebXML specification as the basis for defining business processes and business semantics and then uses it for building an electronic trading system (steps 1, 2 and 3).

▷ Company A then creates a CPP (Collaboration Protocol Profile) that describes its products and services, and uploads the CPP to the industry-wide electronic registry (steps 4, 5 and 6).

▷ Company B searches the registry for information on companies providing particular products and/or services. Having found details about Company A from the registry Company B downloads the details (step 7).

▷ Companies A and B agree trading arrangements, messages etc. (steps 8 and 9).

▷ Companies A and B agree technical details including network protocols (step 10).

▷ Companies A and B start trading electronically (step 11) and optionally agree on network security measures (step 12).

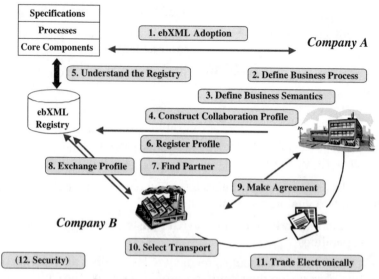

Figure 7.8   ebXML business workflow

RosettaNet

RosettaNet is named after the Rosetta Stone, found in Egypt in 1799, and now in the British Museum. This stone shows the same text in three ancient languages, and thus enabled scholars for the first time to decrypt and understand the ancient Egyptian hieroglyphics. It is an apt symbol for mutual understanding among incompatible systems – just like XML.

RosettaNet is a consortium of several hundred electronics companies aiming to establish standard processes, particularly XML Schemas, for the electronic exchange of business information.

Like ebXML, RosettaNet aims to cover much more than previous methods. It publishes guidelines for e-commerce, with a specification for what is called a Partner Interface Process (PIP), which defines:

▷ A flow diagram for the business interface process (showing information to be exchanged)

▷ Analysis of business impact, and benefits

▷ Messages to be exchanged

▷ Implementation plan

In summary, a PIP is an XML-based dialogue that defines business processes between trading partners.

PIPs are developed in two stages – first an 'as is' version, showing the existing partner interfaces, then a 'to be' version, showing the desired future interfaces, and the partner roles (buyers, sellers etc.) who will do this. This version also provides metrics to assess the business benefits.

The current PIP implementations are based on XML, and the World Wide Web, using HTTP or HTTP with SSL (Secure Sockets Layer) for added security. See **www.rosettanet.org**

Open Applications Group OAG

The Open Applications Group, Inc. (OAGI) is a consortium of ERP (Enterprise Resource Planning) software developers. They develop the Open Applications Group Integration Specification (OAGIS), for business messages and for integrating business applications.

BizTalk

Microsoft's BizTalk is designed to encourage the use of XML for Enterprise Application Integration (EAI) and business-to-business (B2B). Microsoft have created a 'BizTalk Framework', which is a set of guidelines for implementing XML for exchanging messages between applications.

Microsoft encourage users to create Schemas, and to register and store them on the BizTalk Web site. Anyone else can then download and freely use any of the published Schemas from this repository.

The BizTalk architecture is based on messages. One system prepares and sends an XML message to another system, using HTTP, though other protocols like SMTP can also be used.

Microsoft expect that over time many applications, particularly ERP ones, will be enhanced to support XML. However, until then, many messages will need to be transferred or translated into XML, and then at the receiving end be translated back into the application's native format. See **www.BizTalk.org**

ARIBA

Founded in 1996, Ariba's software products are designed to manage the multitude of transactions taking place within and across businesses, and provide 'connectors' to integrate its products with several popular ERP systems. The basis for these 'connectors' is cXML, a freely available protocol intended for the communication of business documents between procurement applications, e-Business hubs and suppliers. Since the initial release of cXML, Ariba has driven most of the changes to the protocol and retains control over the standard.

See **www.ariba.com and www.cXML.org**

XML/EDI

According to the XML/EDI group's Web site, the aim of the XML/EDI group is to deliver business transactions via electronic means, not by creating new standards but by defining how companies can use current standards. See **www.xmledi-group.org/xmledigroup/guide.htm**

XML/EDI brings together various aspects of XML to provide a standard framework to exchange data:

▷ XML for data interchange
▷ XSL for presentation
▷ Can be used with HTTP, FTP and SMTP
▷ Can be integrated with EDI
▷ Uses tools like Java and ActiveX to share data

OBI – Open Buying on the Internet

The Open Buying on the Internet (OBI) Consortium is an independent non-profit organization that develops open standards for B2B commerce, aimed mainly at business-to-business purchasing or so-called 'requisitioning' of indirect materials.

OBI provides a framework that contains detailed technical specifications and guidelines, compliance and implementation information. Copies of the standard are available from the OBI Web site **www.openbuy.org**

BASDA

Based in the UK, the Business Application Software Developers Association (BASDA) is an international organization with members mainly drawn from software developers within the business and accounting software market. BASDA has championed the development of eBIS-XML, which is an open e-Business messaging standard developed by the software industry and is available free to users.

See **www.basda.org**

Collaborative Planning Forecasting and Replenishment (CPFR)

CPFR is a US initiative to use XML to share information within the retail industry to improve the efficiency of the supply chain – specifically by better planning, forecasting and replenishing. It is being developed by a committee within a larger e-Commerce community already active in EDI and supply chain improvements, the Voluntary Interindustry Commerce Standards Association (VICS).

The objective is to develop a communication infrastructure to enable collaboration among the partners in the supply chain. This infrastructure has three components:

▷ Data content and format of the data that will be shared/ communicated

▷ Communication vehicle to support the sharing of the data

▷ Security measures to ensure the data is secure

Trading partners agree on a plan for what is to be sold, how it will be merchandized and promoted, in what marketplace, and during what time frame. XML schemas are being developed for use in the retail industry. See www.cpfr.org for further information.

Summary

Within e-Business then, XML has an important role to play in the exchange of structured business data between buyers and sellers. The ultimate aim is to simplify and speed up the supply chain between buyers and sellers, and to automate it as much as possible.

XML Terminologies

Another important development is the use of specialized terminologies and vocabularies based on XML. These range from obvious uses through to some less obvious and even surprising ones:

▷ XML for financial products and services

▷ Scientific, technical

▷ Oil and gas operations

▷ Advertizing

▷ Human resources

▷ Languages

▷ Archives

▷ Education and training

▷ XML versions of Shakespeare's plays

Below is a selection of such specialized use of XML:

XML for Financial Products and Services

The finance industry deals in vast amounts of information every day, and has actively adopted XML for this purpose. There are already a number of different standards and proposals. Among them are:

FIX www.fixprotocol.org

> The Financial Information eXchange (FIX) Protocol defines electronic messages for communicating securities transactions between two parties. FIX defines the message format and the session-level protocol between applications.

OFX www.ofx.net

> Open Financial Exchange defines the electronic exchange of financial data between financial institutions, businesses and consumers via the Internet. It supports various financial services such as banking, bill payment, bill presentment, and investment tracking.

Specialized Financial XML

There are also a variety of specialized markup languages, among them:

FinXML Financial XML **www.finxml.org**

> XML for a range of financial products in capital markets.

FpML Financial Products Markup Language **www.fpml.org**

For transactions of financial instruments, such as derivatives between financial institutions.

MDDL Market Data Definition Language

A financial information specification for equity prices, financial indices, and mutual fund data.

swiftML SWIFT Society for Worldwide Interbank Financial Telecommunication)

SWIFT is an existing electronic messaging system used by major banks. The messages are being converted to XML. swiftML is close to ISO 15022.

XBRL Extensible Business Reporting Language

For company filings and reports.

XFRML Extensible Financial Reporting Markup Language **www.xfrml.org**

For company filings and reports.

XML for Computer-based Learning

An education organization called IMS Global Learning Consortium is developing XML-based standards for computer-based learning. For example, a very common device in such learning is a multiple-choice question, consisting of a question followed by several radio buttons offering alternative answers, plus the chance for feedback. Currently, organizations developing computer-based learning are likely to develop their own techniques for doing this. However, once such devices are coded in XML, in a standard way, then they can be made available (or sold) to other educational organizations – not only colleges and universities, but also publishers, government agencies, universities, schools and training organizations. In that way, they can rapidly assemble material for training courses, perhaps from a variety of sources, all based on the same standards. It would create an open marketplace in educational resources, something that is currently barely possible, and enable these organizations to work together much better – in other words, to achieve interoperability.

Other examples of XML

PetroXML   Oil and gas field operations **www.petroxml.org**

HR-XM Consortium Human Resources **www.hr-xml.org**

XML for Advertising	Advertising **www.adxml.org**
Visa Invoice	Business expenses **www.visa.com/xml**
TpaML	Electronic B2B contracts **www.xml.org**

XML and Shakespeare

Finally, an example of what may seem at first to be a very unlikely use of XML – in Shakespeare's plays. Yet if you look at the example below, you can see that an XML version gives a useful structure and coherence to the text. Each act, each scene, each famous speech is tagged. Clearly, you would not want to use this version during rehearsals for the play, but you can perhaps see that adding tags makes the play easier for a computer to search. So, for someone doing research on Shakespeare, it can be very useful.

Here is part of the start of the XML version of 'Hamlet', developed by an XML pioneer, John Bosak

```
<?xml version="1.0"?>
<!DOCTYPE play PUBLIC "-//Free Text Project//DTD Play//EN">
<PLAY>
<TITLE>The Tragedy of Hamlet, Prince of Denmark</TITLE>
<fm>
<p>Text placed in the public domain by Moby Lexical Tools, 1992.</p>
<p>SGML markup by Jon Bosak, 1992-1994.</p>
<p>XML version by Jon Bosak, 1996-1997.</p>
<p>This work may be freely copied and distributed worldwide.</p>
</fm>

<PERSONAE>
<TITLE>Dramatis Personae</TITLE>

<PERSONA>CLAUDIUS, king of Denmark. </PERSONA>
<PERSONA>HAMLET, son to the late, and nephew to the present king.</PERSONA>
<PERSONA>POLONIUS, lord chamberlain. </PERSONA>
<PERSONA>Ghost of Hamlet's Father. </PERSONA>
</PERSONAE>

<SCNDESCR>SCENE  Denmark.</SCNDESCR>
<PLAYSUBT>HAMLET</PLAYSUBT>
<ACT><TITLE>ACT I</TITLE>
<SCENE><TITLE>SCENE I.  Elsinore. A platform before the castle.</TITLE>
<STAGEDIR>FRANCISCO at his post. Enter to him BERNARDO</STAGEDIR>
<SPEECH>
<SPEAKER>BERNARDO</SPEAKER>
<LINE>Who's there?</LINE>
</SPEECH>
<SPEECH>
<SPEAKER>FRANCISCO</SPEAKER>
<LINE>Nay, answer me: stand, and unfold yourself.</LINE>
</SPEECH>

<SPEECH>
<SPEAKER>BERNARDO</SPEAKER>
<LINE>Long live the king!</LINE>
</SPEECH>
</SCENE>
</ACT>
</PLAY>
```

B2B Electronic Marketplaces

The Advent of the e-Marketplace

We are in a time where one of the oldest of business activities is being reinvented using new technology, and as discussed briefly in Chapter 5 (where e-Marketplaces were introduced) the concept of a marketplace has been around for many years. There are many examples, with one of the more interesting being the numerous waterways intersecting various parts of Bangkok in Thailand. These have facilitated commerce since ancient times, and continue to do so successfully today. Thailand boasts many floating markets, where merchants ply their trade along the various klongs, or canals in long, open ruilla pai (boats). From what seems like precarious perches to the untrained eye, merchants load produce and provide freshly cooked dishes, amongst other items, to barter and exchange. The marketplace has excellent liquidity, in that merchants are plentiful and a buyer can easily choose the best deal available on the day, providing for an efficient pricing mechanism.

At the other end of the spectrum one can visualize the more prevalent marketplace today - one being transformed by sophisticated advances in technology. The ancient waterways described above are replaced with high tech Internet-based tributaries, carrying vast amounts of data around the globe in a matter of seconds, and information flows continue to expand in this growing global market. The financial markets are excellent examples of these types of marketplace, with technology continuing to play an ever important role in their operation.

E-marketplaces appeared with much fanfare in 1998, providing a compelling vision to transform commerce forever, leveraging technology and uniting thousands of buyers and sellers in an efficient and global manner. This in turn would provide significant cost savings for those participating and open up large new markets and buyers previously unavailable to sellers. At their heyday e-Marketplaces were showcasing the inevitable shift to a global e-Marketplace and their growth and success seemed inevitable.

While the concept of trading exchanges appears to be a great idea and before getting too carried away with enthusiasm, it must be noted that their extension beyond the financial markets has had a rather rocky start. The facts show that many electronic marketplaces having declared themselves as 'open for business' never handled even a single transaction or progressed any further. This assertion is supported in a study conducted by Morgan Stanley that suggested that 90% of the 225 B2B trading exchanges it examined in the sample had yet to process a transaction. In addition to an industry consortium approach, individual companies have also been looking to automate their procurement process using the Internet. To make this possible, new intermediaries have emerged primarily offering a technology infrastructure in an attempt to 'kick-start' these new marketplaces into operation and transform the way in which buyer and seller conduct their business negotiations. Whilst there are some notable successes for trading exchanges, IDC has forecast that trading exchanges would decrease over a three-year period from the initial 1,500 to around 200. Those trading exchanges that have been most successful to date are those where dominant players within the industry have been willing to make the initial investment to get it started and then support the marketplace with their active participation.

e-Marketplace Evolution

Most e-Marketplaces began as a model for sharing pertinent information, usually static, providing rich content for a community with common interests. This soon developed into facilitating the buying and selling of goods and services, connecting disparate buyers, sellers and other trading partners. This was a logical evolution from the successful B2C models who had provided online catalogues and relatively simple shopping facilities. A number of e-Marketplaces emerged, with some focusing on one particular industry segment, referred to as vertical markets and others that spanned numerous industries, termed horizontal. Verticals concentrated on one industry supply chain and provided value added services specific to that industry, such as news, information services and discussion forums. In contrast, horizontals crossed numerous industries focusing on specific links within supply chains common to many industries. Terminology for these entities also included trade exchanges, and in the context of this chapter, we use both terms interchangeably.

Table 8.1 outlines some of the characteristics of different types of e-Marketplaces.

Type	Characteristics
Public e-Marketplace	A marketplace that brings together buyers and sellers with the purpose of facilitating commerce. These entities can be vertically aligned against specific industries (i.e. Chemicals) or specific geographies (i.e. Sesami in Asia). These are usually owned by a group of investors.
Private e-Marketplace	A marketplace that has built interconnections to its own trading partners. These are closed marketplaces with integration between many partners to one operator.
Consortium Backed e-Marketplace	A marketplace created by large organizations in a particular industry or vertical market to provide commerce and collaboration services. The marketplace is owned and operated by the backing organizations (i.e. Covisint – automotive, e2open – electronics)

Table 8.1 Type of e-Marketplace

Early B2B capabilities were centred around the dissemination and sharing of relatively static data to potential clients for most organizations. As capabilities were enhanced, this matured to a two way interaction with clients and trading partners (amongst a larger potential community) through more elaborate applications. As the sell side application and functionality bloomed, organizations began to focus on the e-based possibilities opening up for their own purchases, or procurement, especially for non-strategic purchases. A common example was maintenance, repair and operation (MRO) supplies in the manufacturing industries. This fuelled a further growth in the number of e-Procurement based solutions being provided by vendors for an organization's own operations, or those offered by e-marketplaces. As applications were sourced and utilized, organizations and e-Marketplaces quickly realised that one of the major challenges was the integration of information flows between this emerging channel and existing legacy technologies, such as enterprise resource planning (ERP) systems or other platforms underpinning an organization's operations. Web-based order processing was efficient, but real time processing of orders was not simple. Typically, client interaction was re-entered manually, or manipulated in a manual manner to enable information flow throughout an organization's various back-end systems. Web-based interactions were not easily integrated with order processing and logistics applications which in turn made it difficult for organizations, and e-Marketplaces, to allow dynamic collaborative process flows between disparate platforms.

Collaboration between partners was the elusive goal, allowing organizations to interact and interchange commerce transactions providing Web-based inter-enterprise activities. This evolution to a newer supply chain model using e-Marketplaces enabled organizations to achieve greater efficiencies in many areas, such as lowering procurement costs, lowering inventory levels through access to better information and reaching a much larger pool of suppliers and distributors as geographic constraints vanished. Key to this shift was the efficient access to information networks which fuelled transparency in the supply chain, radically changing buyer and seller relationships. The very nature of e-Marketplaces were introducing transparent information channels along all of the supply chain, allowing greater efficiencies to reduce participant costs. The advantages were not limited to just costs though – potential process improvements meant lower inventories and better monitoring of internal and external events, and improved co-ordination resulted in less costly mistakes being made.

Putting it rather simply, the Internet and e-Marketplaces possess the potential to significantly enhance supply chain performance, supporting intricate co-ordination between partners. It is this capability that provides the ability to meet the continual demands of clients, in terms of mass customization, scalability and ever faster fulfillment cycles. Given this, process improvements were beginning to promise dramatic increases in productivity growth and innovation. This would result in sustained economic growth for organizations, and resulting increases in shareholder wealth. It was partly for these reasons that stock prices for organizations involved in these initiatives began to soar.

With a seemingly winning vision from their conception, numerous companies were persuaded to establish e-Marketplaces, and thousands were proposed. Organizations that were building numerous exchanges grew in prominence. An excellent example was VerticalNet, one of the first that started providing industry exchanges with an initial focus on information hubs in the mid 1990s. These then evolved into transactional hubs looking to provide additional value added services and at one point, VerticalNet had launched almost 60 such industry specific exchanges that had their roots in providing community expertize.

Understandably large organizations were anxious about these beasts and what they meant for competitive advantage to each organization – the response was a huge interest in the creation of industry specific vertical exchanges which were wholly owned and operated by a consortia of backers; essentially companies in that industry. Some organizations decided to go it alone, worried that competitive advantages would be compromised, and created private exchanges, which were individually operated or together with a few partners – Volkswagen Group was a good example of this. The consortium backed exchanges were the most prominent, with large amounts of capital funding and the potential to consolidate billions of dollars of commerce amongst the largest organizations in the world. Although, in the early days, these e-Marketplaces were not leading in numbers of transactions, they certainly gained in terms of mind-share. The examples were numerous.

Covisint – Founded in February 2000 by General Motors, Ford and Daimler-Chrysler. The exchange touted its combined founders' $300 billion in annual spend.

e2open – In June 2000, e2open was founded by Acer, Hitachi, IBM, LG Electronics, Lucent Technologies, Matsushita Electric (Panasonic), Nortel Networks, Seagate Technology, Solectron and Toshiba, and backed by Crosspoint Venture Partners and Morgan Stanley. Initial capital funding was $200 million.

Transora – Approximately 50 companies committed $250 million when this consumer goods exchange was launched in June 2000. The name originated from the prefix "trans" meaning crossing or movement and "ora" derived from Greek origins, indicating boundary or entrance.

Exostar – Aerospace exchange, backed by leading companies BAE Systems, Boeing, Lockheed Martin, Raytheon and Rolls-Royce.

Since the late 1990s, the number of e-Marketplaces has been shrinking, with numerous going out of business, others merging and the number of new entrants decreasing in number. At the turn of the century, given the slow delivery of the promised benefits of consortia-based exchanges, the private exchanges were taking on more prominence and delivering solid benefits with substantial volume flow. Despite this, the value proposition of the public and consortium-based exchange was still sound and the expectations were that these entities would gain the critical mass over the next few years as additional services were bought to market and consolidation between leading vertical players provided a defacto choice for that industry.

Strategic e-Sourcing

The purchasing and selling of materials has historically been riddled with inefficiencies. Buyers of products and services would typically have to produce detailed and often complex Request for Quotes (RFQs) describing in detail what they required. This was then followed by a distribution of the RFQ to a limited number of known suppliers. Typically product catalogues did not exist, or where they did were often not up to date. A response from the prospective supplier together with a quotation was then anticipated, usually taking many weeks before it arrived. Comparisons between suppliers were usually difficult. In many cases, bids were sealed, and potential suppliers did not have an opportunity to revisit their initial pricing resulting in the organization ending up with a quote that was not necessarily the most competitive. To exacerbate the issue, buyers had a tendency to stick with the incumbent supplier, since the incumbent already knew what the buyer required, and as long as their pricing was 'in-line', they would keep the business.

With strategic sourcing topping $20 trillion globally every year, it is not surprising that this was an area that technology could play a role, providing a dynamic pricing mechanism which closely suits the majority of purchases that make up indirect non-strategic materials. Commodities themselves have enjoyed a highly efficient market already, in the form of the futures markets, but direct materials had not. In many industries, this efficiency simply did not exist.

As discussed earlier, one of the popular applications e-Marketplaces offered was strategic sourcing and many e-Marketplaces provided as a fundamental aspect of their offering, an ability to direct source (typically e-Procurement on MRO type products). Perhaps one of the best examples of this is exemplified by FreeMarkets, the auction (seller initiated) and reverse auction (buyer initiated) strategic sourcing e-Marketplace which arguably commercialized the concept of the reverse auction – they focused on e-sourcing capabilities as their core service (see Case Study). There are other providers, such as eBreviate (wholly owned subsidiary of EDS), B2eMarkets and MOAI to mention a few. Essentially the process is similar – that of electronically aggregating suppliers in a dynamic environment to bid for contracts where suppliers can lower their prices until the auction is concluded and closed. Buyers could tap larger markets, and suppliers could conduct trade with existing or new clients allowing greater efficiencies to be realized in the sourcing process. Additionally, traditional auctions can also be conducted (i.e. perhaps for surplus inventory), again online. Not surprisingly, the buyer nearly always wins in this process, although suppliers are also able to potentially break into new clients where historical relationships have kept them out. Suppliers can also act anonymously if they wish.

Service providers (acting as an intermediary) operating the e-Marketplace also offer numerous services and approaches, ranging in functionality. The full functionality approach would typically include services to manage the market operations (the auction), provide the technology platforms and support to make the market (auction) as well as extensive consulting and supplier intelligence services. Not surprisingly, these approaches attracted a much higher fee and hence were better suited for large value strategic purchases (as opposed to MRO) where savings are significant in absolute value.

Case Study – FreeMarkets Inc

FreeMarkets was founded in March 1995 – its history unfolding in an interesting turn of events.

Glen Maekam, a MBA graduate from Harvard, become knowledgeable about electronic markets during his stint at General Electric (GE), working on GE Global eXchange Services' electronic network established for internal GE businesses – later to evolve into a commercial network known as the GE Trading Process Network (TPN).

Maekam had a bold vision in late 1994. He bought to his senior executives an idea that would potentially save organizations millions of dollars, whilst at the same time build the foundation for 'transforming the global economy'. Like most successful ideas, his was simple – suppliers should be made to compete for orders in a live open electronic marketplace. Unfortunately the estimated $10 million required to get the initiative going was deemed too risky at the time, although GE did allow Maekam a small laboratory to operate, experimenting with online auctions. The initiative was not allowed to be developed into a full blown business.

With the lack of support, he approached an old ex-colleague, Sam E. Kinney, working for McKinsey in Pittsburgh at the time, who successfully persuaded Maekam to establish FreeMarkets. They had both met before Maekam had joined GE, at McKinsey, where he claimed to have learnt the importance of possessing superior information to make money. With a few hundred thousand dollars seed capital from friends and family, FreeMarkets was born.

FreeMarkets pioneered approaches that were not allowing other online exchanges to succeed. Maekam had recognized the need to not only have a technology solution, but to also have the ability to standardize the RFQ process and ensure that suppliers had been thoroughly vetted and identified to ensure a successful auction process. He recognized that parts were not necessarily the most expensive elements to buy, but usually the most inefficient. A number of initiatives underscored the FreeMarkets proposition:

▷ Two models existed. QuickSource for basic e-sourcing services, RFQs and auctions. Full Source, which was a full-service sourcing package consisting of hosted software, hosted auctions, market making and supplier intelligence.

▷ The RFQ process was scrutinized to ensure all important elements were clearly identified. All elements, where possible, were standardized.

▷ Suppliers not only had to provide the specified goods, but within the same schedules, payment terms, and associated conditions to ensure standardization – all non-price terms are standard.

▷ Suppliers were thoroughly vetted through extensive questionnaires, examining financial metrics and quality initiatives amongst a number of other areas scrutinized. This also encompassed areas such as machine capabilities and cycle times.

▷ FreeMarkets acted as a consultant – advising new clients on the RFQ process; some of which can become exceptionally complex and detailed. This facilitated the platform to handle custom manufactured parts that may be required, allowing for specialized components to also be bid out.

▷ FreeMarket's technology platform provided data-management capabilities, housing thousands of client part numbers, as an example, to allow customers to easily build RFQs.

FreeMarkets continued to build on its early successes, attracting heavy weight Fortune 500 organizations such as H. J. Heinz, Siemens, Caterpillar and United Technologies just to name a few. With just over 1,000 employees, by 2002, the firm had processed more than $30 billion in volume boasting over 120 buying companies, supported in 30 languages. Over 150,000 suppliers were connected to the online process. Savings varied, but generally anywhere between 5% to 30% savings were being achieved. By their own statistics, FreeMarkets claimed to have saved their clients in excess of $6 billion in their first seven years of operation.

From Transactions to e-Collaboration

Much of the early e-Marketplace attention and efficiencies were focused on transactional elements of Web-based procurement approaches. Through the use of reverse auctions, buyers and sellers could participate in larger communities and buyers could benefit from lower prices, and this activity represented the majority of the more recent transactions on e-Marketplaces. Ideally, product catalogues were provided by suppliers, and the trading exchange could present these in a consistent and structured manner. E-Marketplaces brought together many trading

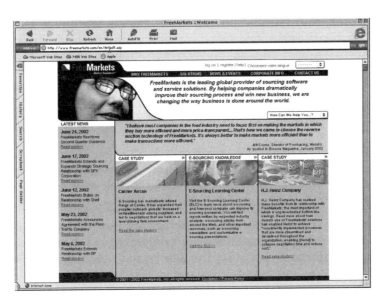

Figure 8.1 FreeMarkets

partners bypassing the need for an organization to create numerous bilateral relationships with different partners. Indeed, some of the providers of e-Procurement software, such as Ariba, evolved from a provider of e-Procurement software, to selling software to create and run marketplaces, and then realized that they could operate their own e-Marketplace. Especially as their clients were already linked to a large number of trading partners in a consistent manner, enabling a many to many relationship.

Historically, this was sorely missing for most e-Marketplaces, with a distinct lack of standards, and as a consequence electronic-based documents (such as purchase orders) were not structured in a consistent manner between trading partners. Where EDI had historically provided a basic format for the interchange of business documents and data flows between organizations, this was now beginning to be superseded by new standards. The emergence of XML compliant platforms promised to alleviate some of these issues, but this was still in its nascent and emerging stages. XML was not alone, with others such as cXML from Ariba, xCBL from Commerce One and Rosettanet just being some of the more popular examples. Back-office and trading partner integration was key, especially given the enormous investments organizations had made in ERP and MRP systems.

Despite the success of e-sourcing applications, e-Marketplaces were continually challenged to provide business models that provided enough value to attract and retain participants. This fuelled the growth of collaborative services that provided added value over and above initial e-Procurement based services, and started to fulfill the complex interaction between partners and an organization's supply chain. The business environment has continued to ensure only the fittest survive and this Darwinian aspect on competing in the global markets has put a lot of focus on areas such as cost, time to market and efficient processes to ensure competitive advantage. Organizations that were viewed as competitors in a previous age, were now partners in alliances or outsourcing arrangements, with collaborative efforts driving complex solutions for potential clients. Product development was also taking on new directions, and in some cases the whole development cycle being outsourced.

Historically organizations have approached the product development conundrum using internal resources, and perhaps in some cases enlisting the support and input of a number of key suppliers. Collaborative approaches are not new, but the use of Internet-based technologies has opened new ways of working. Past approaches used mainframe client access technologies which were not flexible, and expensive. This led to client server based approaches and simple collaboration tools such as Lotus Notes, or other popular technology platforms. Numerous exchanges had realized that offering e-Collaborative services would enhance the customer experience and also provide value added services, whilst opening new revenue streams. The focus was to provide advanced tools to allow for complex interaction between trading partners, whilst linking numerous back end systems in the process.

The ability to conduct collaborative design processes provided a compelling competitive advantage. Typically profit margins in the early part of the product cycle are the greatest – technologies that can allow faster product design linked together with manufacturers and other associated parties allowed customized iterative designs to be bought to market in ever shorter cycles, maximizing revenue opportunities. Continual innovation to ensure the products remain ahead of the market also became easier with tighter linkages with appropriate stakeholders.

These services were quickly offered by a number of B2B exchanges such as e2open, Exostar, Covisint and WorldWide Retail Exchange just to mention a few (see Figure 8.2). Industry verticals could also specialize their services by industry. For example, high values and low volumes are characteristics of industries such as aerospace and defence. The supply chain is not focused on finished goods as a key aspect, in stark contrast to retail-based industries (such as consumer goods), where this is key.

Figure 8.2 e2open product collaboration

A number of technology providers have been working on electronic collaborative software packages, and solutions have been available in the market for several aspects of the supply chain. Complex products that need to be bought to market quickly are increasingly requiring multi-disciplinary teams, usually located in diverse geographies and timezones. These technologies are increasingly helping to bridge the complexities and challenges that this way of working imposes. As an example, Covisint 'the automotive exchange' uses a number of providers for various collaborative services, such as:

▷ Virtual project workspaces can be established using a software technology from NexPrise.

▷ Engineering Automation provides visual access to technical drawings and specifications over the Covisint platform.

▷ Mercator – a popular data exchange engine, facilitates exchange between different standards and formats.

▷ Supply chains between different partners can be linked through SupplySolution's application, allowing disparate ERP and associated systems to interact.

Collaborative Planning, Forecasting and Replenishment

It seems that most of the early transaction volumes going through the big exchanges involved the auction purchases of indirect goods such as office supplies and equipment including computers. Whilst this can be a route to substantial savings, another approach considered as more important is collaborative planning, forecasting, and replenishment (CPFR)[1], an EDI like a retail industry initiative to improve the partnership between manufacturers/distributors and distributors/retailers through shared information and processes. Stated simply it aims to achieve minimum inventories throughout the supply chain and maximum in-stock positions at all times. Therefore, while full customer satisfaction is assured by the customer finding the required product on the shelf, significant costs can be removed throughout the supply chain by reducing inventories.

Most auction activity involving goods to be sold through retail outlets concern store-brand products because they can be sourced from multiple suppliers. Whereas, when dealing with national brands that are not interchangeable or substitutable with products from other manufacturers, retailers focus on supply chain costs when looking to save money. It appears that national brands, although very suitable for applying CPRF principles, are less likely to be suitable for auctions.

Example   Transora

Transora, a data exchange formed in June 2000 by 49 food and drink suppliers in the US, believe that individual companies do not want to built their own infrastructure, and would prefer a third party to provide the infrastructure, at a reasonable cost. Transora offers a CPFR service to its members that can not only generate direct savings from working collaboratively with suppliers, but also savings that come from reduced overheads, improved business processes and reduced inventory levels.

A Question of Integration

Marketplaces have arguably achieved excellent successes in managing and Web enabling the procurement process, with auctioning capabilities (and reverse auctions) effectively driving down costs for the buyer, whilst at the same time utilizing the Internet's capabilities to reach a vast global community of suppliers. Success of organizations such as Freemarkets discussed earlier, as well as others is clear evidence of the effectiveness of this model.

Despite the promise of XML-based, as well as other, technologies beginning to help alleviate integration issues, the broader sceptre of integration within complex supply chains still evades most B2B e-Marketplaces, as opposed to B2C and C2C propositions, as outlined in Figure 8.3. Although the emergence of approaches using specific standards such as Rosettanet and XML have made some impact, this has been minimal, and today most exchanges can provide little integration capabilities for its member community, and many have been criticized for this shortfall. For some, attempts to solve this conundrum have centred on using intermediary technology such as that provided by vendors like Mercator whose products can translate formats. Although this can ease some processes, it's a far cry from the truly integrated processes most participants seek.

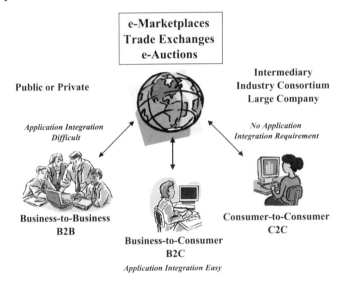

Figure 8.3   e-Marketplace integration

Given this situation, some of the most startling early successes have been from private exchanges, driven by large global organizations already experienced in electronic trading using established EDI networks with their suppliers. Organizations such as General Electric (see GE Lighting case study) and Volkswagen are excellent examples. As standards mature and adoption reaches critical mass, however, one can see e-Marketplaces augmenting their value propositions with increased supply chain interoperability, which in turn will drive increased standard process adoption across industries.

Case Study – GE Lighting

GE Lighting, one of General Electric's (US) 12 businesses, has its corporate headquarters in Ohio, USA, where the global sourcing team is responsible for co-ordinating the centralized sourcing for GE Lighting's 45 plants worldwide. By mid-1995 GE Lighting had over 25,000 global suppliers and whilst the sourcing system had been re-developed in recent years, the system was still too labour and cost intensive to support the demands of the business, particularly the evolving global operations.

GE Lighting classified its purchases into five discrete segments consisting of: finished products, raw materials, packaging, MRO (maintenance, repair and operation) and indirect/machine parts, the latter representing high volume purchases of low value products and the most troublesome of the five sourcing segments. The buying characteristics of the indirect/machine parts had remained the same: low value products purchased in high volumes. The 300-500 requisitions received each day represented over £26 million in annual purchases. The buying process was entirely manual, involving the accompanying blueprints to be requested from storage, transported, photographed, etc. before being sent out to suppliers with a request for quotation (RFQ). Because the process was so time consuming, sourcing were unable to send out RFQs to more than two to three suppliers at a time. By the time the suppliers' RFQ responses were received, bids evaluated and business awarded some 18 to 23 total days had elapsed leaving sourcing with less opportunity to focus upon cost-cutting activities.

During the early 1990s as GE Lighting moved to consolidate its purchasing in Ohio, USA, several process improvements were made, including, the implementation of a Purchasing Management System (PMS) for electronic purchase order generation. While this eased the purchasing process, it still relied heavily upon manual intervention for the preparation and shipment of blueprints. Because of the high cost associated with purchasing of indirect/machine parts, it was decided that further process improvements were necessary. This resulted in an automated purchase order capability being added to PMS, that covered requisitions for MRO parts that met certain purchasing criteria and sourced from the same qualified supplier. This had the effect of reducing requisition processing by approximately 60%. The next step occurred in 1994 when a quote module was added to PMS.

By 1994, GE Lighting had also implemented EDI for the electronic exchange of purchase orders and material releases with suppliers and had decided to outsource some of its more manual tasks. At this same time a company was retained to manage and begin the task of electronically scanning each blueprint to focus upon the very costly bottleneck that remained. In 1995, GE Lighting started to experiment with an electronic bidding solution and whilst not a success, the experience convinced them that the principle was right and important for future growth.

Having seen progressive enhancements to its PMS system, use of purchase order to Fax, automated purchase orders, EDI, quote system using Fax and a chance to see suppliers fight in an electronic bidding marketplace, the time was right to make a significant process change in search of productivity gains. GE Lighting decided to proceed with the implementation of a fully automated sourcing system based upon Internet technologies. Having reviewed the option of implementing such a capability themselves, GE Lighting decided that it would be too costly and joined forces with GE Global eXchange Services to base its future vision on TPNPost, an Internet-based electronic RFQ distribution and bid receipt system, part of the GE Trading Process Network.

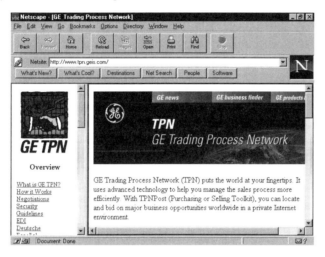

Figure 8.4 GE Trading Process Network

GE Lighting decided to start with the purchasing of indirect/machine parts on a pilot basis, before implementation of TPNPost across all categories. Implementation started in 1996 and soon demonstrated many of the expected improvements. Initially working off-line, GE Lighting simply selected the requisition system on their desktop PC, created a customized requisition project and chose the suppliers from the community supplier database to receive the RFQ. They then connected to a Web server that hosted the Trading Partner Network and posted the bid package to the selected suppliers around the world. The system automatically retrieved the electronic blueprints and attached them to the electronic requisition form. All data was encrypted and entirely secure. The RFQ process that used to take more than seven days was reduced to less than two hours. Suppliers were automatically notified of incoming RFQs by either E-mail or Fax and used a Web browser to access the RFQ information and responded within 7 days. GE Lighting then retrieved the bids, evaluated them and awarded the business the same day. The entire requisition process that used to take between 18-23 days (and sometimes a lot longer) was now reduced by well over 50% and combined with overall cost savings of between 5-20%, made this a highly successful project for GE Lighting.

There were similar experiences in other GE divisions including GE Transportation that made $80 million of purchases and saved $18 million and GE

Medical Systems achieving a 11% reduction on a $660,000 purchase of electrical cabling. This led to an article in The Economist[2] stating that "GE now does 1 billion dollars worth of business a year with 1,400 of its suppliers, single-handedly exceeding all consumer electronic commerce over the Internet." Trading Partner Network evolved in 1999 into Global Supplier Network covering over 36,000 suppliers using the GE Extranet with greater collaborative working that resulted in over 27,000 electronic auctions and an average saving of 8% to GE. GE now operates one of the world's largest private trading exchanges for the sourcing of supplies.

Global Commerce Initiative

This lack of standards is beginning to change, and efforts by the Global Commerce Initiative (GCI) are indicative[3]. Formed in October 1999, GCI's purpose was to create the very standards that would facilitate electronic collaborative inter-business process interoperability, primarily in the retail industry. Comprising of approximately 50 retail and manufacturing companies, GCI was also sponsored by industry trade groups such as the Food Marketing Institute and the Grocery Manufacturers Association. Standards bodies in America and Europe, such as the Uniform Code Council (UCC) and EAN International also lent their support providing a broad platform to push GCI standards within the industry.

The retail industry, like many others, has seen numerous standards build up over time – today's EAN/UCC standards evolved in specific country isolation, hence different standards exist for each country. As a consequence, most large organizations had to support as many as 10 to 20 different EDI standards. Participating in industry exchanges such as Transora exacerbated the issues, and although XML-based approaches were beginning to take hold, the migration from EDI to XML was anything but mature. Given this, in April 2000 the GCI directors established a working group, the Global Commerce Internet Protocols (GCIP), to recommend a global set of XML-based standards. The resulting standards, one of the first global recommendations for management of standardized data across B2B communications, appeared in March 2001.

The core components of the GCI architecture consist of a local registry, data pools and exchanges, which together drive data synchronization. The registry is simply a series of entities where basic information on an item is housed and checked for compliance with definitions that are pre-stored and updated as necessary, much like a global directory. Data pools house components of the registry data on specific items, but also include relationship oriented data. In turn exchanges can interact with standardized data pools and registries (and in many cases housing their own data pools). Of course organizations that do not wish to interact via exchanges can also inter-operate directly, complying with the GCI standards and architecture.

Given many of the participants of GCI were also prominent members of retail e-Marketplaces, it was no surprise to see both the WorldWide Retail Exchange (WWRE) and GlobalNetXchange (GNX) both announcing that they would comply with the GCI standards by the second quarter of 2003.

Platform Providers

The intense focus on e-Marketplaces allowed a number of new organizations to appear which grew to monolithic sizes in terms of market capitalization, as the interest in these approaches continued to gain significant momentum in the late 1990s. These organizations were promising to build the very platforms of future commerce, and gained much attention.

The players were numerous and included established as well as new names, including Ariba, Commerce One, VerticalNet, Ventro, Oracle, i2 and SAP. Some institutions had simply focused on providing certain aspects of the platform, with others starting with more specialist integration services. Not surprisingly, as the market matured and consolidated, a number of alliances, partnerships and acquisitions provided a core nexus. IBM, i2 and Ariba joined forces in an alliance and Commerce One and SAP came together. We examine two of the most prominent players in the following sections.

Ariba

This California-based company was arguably at the forefront of the B2B exchange movement when in 1997, it launched an e-Procurement package called Operating Resource Management System (ORMS). June 1999 saw Ariba going public and expanding its software proposition to build a platform for building and running Internet-based e-Marketplaces. With the changing focus on e-Marketplaces in general, in late 2001 Ariba decided to re-direct its focus on licensed e-based solutions (what it termed as 'enterprise spend management') as opposed to its historical direction, effectively pulling back from e-Marketplaces. Some of Ariba's key clients included major consortia players such as e2open and WorldWideRetailExchange. Ariba's three main product streams were:

▷ Ariba Buyer – the flagship e-Procurement application

▷ Ariba Sourcing – an application that supported the development of Request for Quotes (RFQs) and associated processes relating to the purchase of direct materials

▷ Ariba Commerce Services Network – a web-based platform that provided a conduit to product catalogues and related information

Commerce One (C1)

Much like Ariba, Commerce One's rise to fame focused on the provision of e-Procurement applications as well as Internet-based e-Marketplace solutions. In June 2000, SAP injected $225 million as an equity investment into Commerce One, as well as forming a strategic alliance between Commerce One's e-Marketplace infrastructure and SAPMarkets's e-business supply chain management applications. This transaction solidified Commerce One's strategy to continue to aggressively pursue e-Marketplaces and exchanges. With its acquisition of AppNet in September 2000, C1 gained the ability to provide e-Marketplace consulting services, which were deriving a substantial element of its revenues.

Key clients included players such as Covisint, Quadrem, Pantellos and Exostar. Its product suite included:

▷ Commerce One MarketSet – the C1/SAPMarkets collaborative platform

▷ Commerce One MarketSite – C1's legacy technology platform

Figure 8.5 Commerce One

The Bubble Bursts

With the almost evangelical focus on the B2B e-Marketplace rise, zealots were investing in institutions within this space with religious fervour. The capital markets were in turn pushing up stock prices to astronomical levels, with tried and tested financial ratios being thrown out of the window overnight as investors and venture capitalists continued to invest millions. The value of these organizations only seemed to be going in one direction, with capitalization values exceeding those of institutions that had been in business for over a century. This was despite the fact that these institutions were losing money (see Table 8.2). Amazingly, in early 2000, Ariba had a market capitalization of over $33 billion, despite losing $19 million on revenues of $62 million the year earlier. At its intra-day peak, Ariba stock had hit $662.

In early 2000, a worrying trend began to emerge. The number of new e-Marketplaces were dwindling. Furthermore, those in existence were either going out of business, or not achieving anywhere near the projected transactional flows that promised large revenues. Licensing fees for the major e-Marketplace players were dropping, and consequently the financial markets began to reflect this. Not surprisingly, a shake-out in the business continued, and stock prices plummeted as consolidation continued.

Company	Stock Price (May 2002)*	Peak Price (early March 2000)	Market Cap at Peak (billions)	1999 Revenue (millions)	1999 Profit (millions)
Ariba	$4	$367	$33	$62	$(19.1)
Commerce One	$1.20	$331	$23	$33.6	$(63)

* Not adjusted for stock splits.

Table 8.2 Market prices of leading firms

---

[1] See www.vics.org Voluntary Inter-Industry Commerce Standards

[2] The Economist 10 May 1997

[3] See www.globalcommerceinitiative.org

Business to Consumer (B2C)

Introduction

Aside from the Internet's technical progress over the last three decades, its sociological progress has been phenomenal, becoming a prominent feature of business life as well as creating a whole new sales channel to reach consumers. As suggested in earlier chapters, the business-to-consumer market is probably the most widely reported and hyped field of e-Business. Since business-to-consumer uses the Internet together with other information and communications technologies to market, buy and sell products and services, this activity is interpreted as being electronic (or Internet) commerce. In essence this book supports the growing consensus that e-Commerce is really a subset of e-Business and describes the emergence of online retailing or 'e-Tailing'. Business customers, as opposed to home consumers, often use similar technologies and are also included under the banner of e-Commerce when operating in this way.

Online retailing using electronic shop-fronts permits the purchase of a very wide range of products including books, music CDs, flowers, computers, clothing, and even cars. Similarly e-Tailing provides the means to purchase services, many of which are based around reservation and booking systems, for flights, trains, cinemas, theatres, holidays, etc. In a later chapter the strategic choices open to companies embarking upon the e-Business journey is examined. However, growing numbers of retail companies in their efforts find new ways to reach consumers see the Internet as a complementary sales strategy to their traditional network of 'bricks and mortar' stores.

Contrasting B2B and B2C

As discussed in earlier chapters business-to-business usually consists of trading between existing and known trading partners and often typified by pre-negotiated commercial conditions such as pricing, discounts and delivery terms. While this has been the case in the past, the emergence of e-Marketplaces is causing new trading relationships to be established based upon highly competitive commercial terms. Nonetheless, for trading to commence some prior negotiations need to be undertaken between the business partners. Aside from commercial conditions, there are other matters of product quality and delivery that need to be addressed. Equally the process is driven by recognized business transactions and the supplier will most certainly demand a purchase order from the buyer to initiate the supply of goods.

In business-to-consumer markets the retailer is expected to handle many thousands of spontaneous purchasing transactions from equal numbers of anonymous consumers for which no prior commercial relationship necessarily existed. In other words, a consumer may never have purchased from the retailer previously, and certainly no preconditions existed prior to the consumer committing to the transaction by selecting the 'submit key' on their Web browser. Since no prior commercial arrangements exist, sellers are naturally concerned to authenticate the buyer or limit their commercial risk. A fraudulent order from a non-exiting customer could result in significant business resources being consumed or diverted from a genuine customer. For this reason e-Tailers normally insist upon payment with order, typically by credit card, as a condition of doing business over the Internet. Figure 9.1 illustrates the positioning of business-to-consumer as compared to the other categories of business-to-business and business-to-employee.

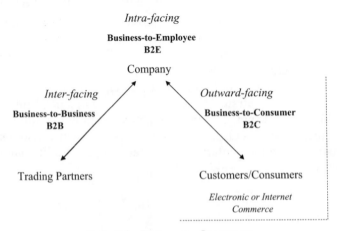

Figure 9.1 Business-to-Consumers

E-Tailer Benefits

In terms of the e-Tailer there are many attractions in using the Internet as an alternative sales channel, including the lower cost of sales. In a recent study into the future of Internet banking the cost of a typical banking transaction using different methods was examined. A telephone call, involving a banking staff member to field and handle a simple transaction, amounted to 100 units, while a similar ATM transaction reduced the cost to 19 units. For customers using telephone banking the cost of the transaction reduced still further to 14 units, and finally for an Internet transaction the cost was calculated as 6 units. This low level of Internet transactional cost applies to an e-Tailer also and it suggests that the reduced barriers to entry are likely to attract greater competition.

In consequence, retailers face a dilemma. To what extent can they reduce their traditional 'bricks and mortar' businesses with its high associated cost of sales in relation to Internet shop-fronts with their much lower associated cost of sales, and still be sure of taking the order? On the surface the Internet seems a highly attractive proposition for the consumer, since it eliminates geographic boundaries offering global accessibility on a 24 hour seven-day a week basis. Through well-designed ordering processes greater efficiencies are possible benefiting not only the seller, but resulting in greater customer service for the consumer, because of automated order confirmation and delivery information. In addition, intermediaries in the selling process may not market a product as extensively as the manufacturer and therefore are usually unable to communicate the same passion and interest in the product. Well-structured Web sites can communicate this passion and back it up with strong customer service support by offering telephone call-back or immediate online chat (see the Lands' End case study later in this chapter) significantly enhancing the customer's buying experience. Such enhanced customer service can include personalization of the Web homepage and the opportunity to directly market new product and services further increasing customer loyalty.

Creating Positive Customer Experience

Atler (2002) supports a commonly held view that positive customer experiences of Internet purchases are crucial to the success of e-Commerce. The initial aim of the e-Tailer must be to assist the consumer define their requirements or help create a need awareness. Thereafter, encouraging them to identify the product or service that best fits this need and where feasible, offer customization which provides an even closer match to their requirements. When finalizing the purchase it is important that the process is simple and that the consumer understands both product availability and pricing. Studies stress the importance of timely delivery or updated delivery status as being of high importance to the consumer heavily influencing their overall satisfaction with the buying experience. For some products and services, the Web represents an ideal medium to deliver supplementary information or training materials to enhance use of the product purchased. During the life of a product information may be required on consumables and simple maintenance tasks to extend the product life cycle. Finally, retiring or disposal of the product once its useful life is exhausted can enhance the attitude of the consumer to the e-Tailer and affect repeat business.

Case Study – Hewlett-Packard

As an example, Hewlett-Packard (HP) have a strong presence in the computer printer marketplace and offer a wide range of associated information on their Web site. Normally, online purchases of printers and replacement laser cartridges are made through an e-Tailer selling a range of computer supplies, rather than by HP directly, although this exists as an option. Irrespective of the online purchasing channel, HP provide software utilities on their Web site which can be downloaded to clean the printer when a new cartridge is fitted, thus satisfying the maintenance need. Included with the new laser printer cartridge are instructions on the disposal of the old cartridge, which should be returned to HP for recycling using a prepaid address label and the packaging the new cartridge came in.

Factors Impacting Growth

Not surprisingly, one significant obstacle frustrating the early growth of the business-to-consumer market was the lack of a critical mass of consumers having Internet access from the home. In recent years, both in North America and across Europe, the position has changed dramatically and growing numbers of the population now have access. In North America the figure is as high as 60%, and whilst it varies greatly across Europe, the UK enjoys the highest consumer acceptance with over 35% of households having Internet access. Aside from home consumers, many business employees have Internet access as part of their job and many employers take a relaxed view of the personal usage by their employees as long as the privilege is not abused. Indeed, some organizations offer their employees online access to food retailers via the corporate Intranet, which is particularly appreciated by working women, reluctant to let their partners loose with a trolley in either a physical or virtual supermarket! Even with the growing numbers of consumers having home Internet access, the typical profile appears to be at the lower end of the age spectrum, typically 35 years or less. Unfortunately many older people, as well as disadvantaged members of society, often feel excluded from these developments and this has to be a concern for governments.

Many e-Tailers have found their efforts to establish an online sales presence also frustrated by a realization that they have too few employees with the required expertize of dealing in this new environment, both from a technical and business perspective. Other prospective e-Tailers have discovered that simply adding an online sales presence without paying adequate attention to the existing back-office systems can cause major headaches. Being able to take an order in an instant using an Internet shop-front is one thing, but integrating this Web application with a legacy order service system can be more of a challenge. Equally, it is quite likely that the physical distribution network, while adequate for the 'bricks and mortar' business, is unsuited to home delivery, requiring some radical re-thinking of the company's logistics operation.

The comparative ease by which an online sales presence can be created, suggests that there are reduced barriers for entry, and is another reason why this sales channel is likely to attract greater competition. Because of the nature of the Internet this increased competition may not necessarily be the traditional competitor down the road, but may well be companies from other parts of the world. If indeed the e-Tailer is trading on a global basis then legal issues can become quite complex because of the different legal systems applying when crossing geographic boundaries (see Chapter 13).

One other factor that figures highly in the list of consumers' worries with electronic retailing is the perceived insecurity of the Internet. While this is a natural concern, the submission of a credit card number over an encrypted (secure sockets layer) session between Web browser and Web server is far more robust than handing a credit card to a waiter in a restaurant. However, while much has already been achieved to improve Internet security, the longer-term move to implement a public key infrastructure (PKI) will greatly improve consumer confidence and bring greater security to other forms of information exchange, notably E-mail.

What Sells Best

At the beginning of this chapter examples of products and services which can be purchased by consumers over the Internet were listed. However, the real question is whether those listed products and services are the most suited to marketing in this way and, if this is the case, what makes them so? It is important for companies to have this information. Indeed, it may well influence whether or not they proceed to set-up an additional Web presence to their existing 'bricks and mortar' businesses; or, for companies entering the market for the first time to set-up new economy dot.com venture without a physical presence.

A simple grid has been constructed that plots the product and services on the vertical axis, whether these are traditional or electronic, against delivery on the horizontal axis whether physical or electronic. A non-exhaustive list of products and services has been placed in the four boxes making up the grid as a point of reference, see Figure 9.2.

New *Electronic* *Products/* *Services*	① Specialized Travel, Leisure & Holidays	④ Banking Insurance Customer Service
Traditional *Products/* *Services*	② Books Wine Music CDs Grocery Products Cars Computer Supplies	③ Computer Software Music (MP3) Newspapers & Magazines Greetings Cards Research Reports Training (e-Learning)
	Electronic Ordering/ *Physical Delivery*	*Electronic* *Delivery*

Figure 9.2 The e-Tailing grid

In Grids 2 and 3, most of the products and services listed are those where the consumer is likely to have identified a specific need and already has good knowledge or prior experience of these products and services. For example, stationery and computer supplies, e.g. envelopes, marker pens, printer cartridges, CD-ROMS, even standard software, are very specific and the consumer would generally know exactly what it is they wish to purchase. Grocery products, music CDs and even a research report also fall into this category, where some but not extensive additional information or advice is required before purchase can proceed. However, some products listed in Grid 3 such as newspapers, magazines, greeting cards, music (MP3), and online training require a change of culture on the part of the consumer to accept electronic delivery and previous knowledge or experience cannot be presumed.

Example Slate e-Magazine

While other ventures such as *Feed*, *Word* and *The Industry Standard* have floundered, *Slate* the electronic magazine started by Microsoft, but operated at 'arms-length', still continues to persevere in the uncertain market for electronic Web journalism. Launched in June 1996, *Slate* built up a steady readership under the editorship of Michael Kingsley on a subscription free basis, although its longer-term plans were to introduce subscription charges (which were announced twice then cancelled). Yet despite previous indecision, in Spring 1998 *Slate* became available to subscribers only ($19.95 per year) for similar services given away free elsewhere on the Web. It was heralded as signalling a milestone in electronic publishing history as the industry moved from an environment where digital media had until then been made available free, to a new age of 'click and pay'. However, almost immediately *Slate's* readership fell dramatically from the 400,000 visitors on the free incentive trial to some 30,000 paying subscribers. By the beginning of 1999 the number of paying subscribers had fallen to 20,000 and a decision was made to drop the standard subscription charge and focus upon revenue generation from the sale of online advertizements. Whilst *Slate* became free again, a subscription option still existed for the readership that wanted access to past editions and other services. The result was dramatic with Microsoft reporting 446,000 unique visitors to *Slate* in February 1999.

The publishing of e-Books is not considered very different from publishing online magazines, although so far all companies have been unsuccessful in making either pay. The publishers of *Esquire* having given 7,000 copies of an e-Book away free, found that the follow-up fee paying 'Love and Murder' e-Book only sold a small fraction of the copies of that number. *Slate* secured an impressive 28,000 downloads for the republishing of Lemann's *New Yorker* essays on the presidential race in e-Book form, but again the downloads were free. Despite the apparent ability to attract greater readership when the offer is free, the fundamental problem facing electronic journalists and authors is that reading a Web site or even a file download is a very different customer experience from reading a hard-copy newspaper, magazine or book. Indeed, palmtop devices are now being introduced offering the reader a very similar 'look and feel' to hard-copy publication, but with much greater capacity and flexibility.

Many market research organizations (e.g. Gartner and Forrester Research) primarily targeting business customers, already have mechanisms in place to charge for reports accessible by subscribing to their services and, in this sector, appear to be quite successful. However, the future success of magazines such as *Slate* as well as e-Books, ultimately depends upon a culture change for the consumer both in accepting digital publications (perhaps delivered by purpose built palmtop readers) in place of their hard-copy equivalents and a willingness to pay. This aspect of a willingness to pay by consumers is similar to the issue faced by the music industry following the exploits of Napster and MP3.com in providing Web sites for the free exchange of music recordings (See Chapter 13).

Therefore, Grid 2, offering the convenience of electronic ordering for the physical delivery of traditional products and services, appears to be the least risky option, but is likely to attract a good deal of competition.

For some products and services varying degrees of information are required to support the purchasing decision, e.g. books, holidays, travel, etc., which with thought and creativity can be incorporated into the design of the Web site. A consumer wishing to travel from London to Paris via Eurostar will need to consult the train times and having found the desired time of travel will need to have an option for immediate ticket purchase. Similarly, a consumer wishing to purchase a book is likely to want to read an abstract of the book and see any published reviews, perhaps by other readers, together with a list of alternative books from the same author. Again, having chosen the book, there needs to be an option to purchase.

The danger for retailers is that consumers may visit a 'bricks and mortar' shop, obtain the information they require then order the product or service over the Web using a competitor offering better terms and conditions. Indeed there is evidence to suggest that consumers also use the Internet to obtain information from various Web sites before making their purchasing decision in a 'bricks and mortar' shop. For the consumer there is real merit in being able to use a search capability (operating in a similar manner to the traditional search engine) that identifies Web sites with the best pricing and conditions. This characterizes a commodity market and presents a real challenge for the seller. E-Tailers need to recognize that Web presence implies transparency of pricing between different Web sites, allowing the enthusiastic cyber shopper to readily make price comparisons. Abandoned shopping carts where the consumer browses the site, selects goods but fails to complete the purchase is every e-Tailer's nightmare. Having attracted the consumer to their Web site it is crucial that the site content helps re-enforce the buyer's instinct to follow through with the purchase. For this to happen there has to be perceived added value for the consumer in the total buying experience on offer from the e-Tailer, rather than price considerations alone. An approach adopted by some e-Tailers to enhance the buying experience is to provide an opportunity for consumers to speak directly with their customer service representative, either using online chat or a returned telephone call (see Lands' End later in this chapter).

Specialist travel, leisure breaks and holidays figure prominently in Grid 1, where the Internet offers a very convenient way to gather the necessary information, come to a decision and make the purchase. Travel operators spend considerable sums of money in promotional materials and advertizing, and the delivery of these materials using Adobe acrobat .pdf files over the Internet can achieve significant savings for these companies.

Example   Airtours

> Airtours, (the UK charter carrier and packaged holiday company) spend £50 million annually on brochures, £350 million on agent commission and £125 million on marketing. Its strategy is to reach customers in a variety of different ways including, high street shops, television, Internet, mobile phones, etc. Airtours believe that its increasing use of the Internet as a marketing and sales channel will make a significant contribution to cutting costs and growing sales revenues.

Finally in Grid 4, banking, insurance and other financial services are grouped together with customer services. The former having grown out of traditional products and services in the financial services marketplace, precipitated by the crisis faced by retail banking and the resultant radical re-design of products and services, offer full electronic delivery of a very different nature to their physical counter-parts. Call centres, the fastest growing area of employment in many of the developed countries, typifies the strong support for electronic customer service delivery.

Products and services with the following characteristics do not appear on the grid and seem less suited for marketing over the Internet at present:

▷ Complex products and services requiring a high level of pre-sales support and advice in order to understand the consumer's exact requirements

▷ Products that frequently pass through several iterations, before the consumer feels confident to proceed with the purchase

▷ More complex financial service products or the sale of medicines/drugs, both of which require a higher level of technical competence and knowledge

▷ Products and services where face-to-face advice is considered as an important and integral part of the purchase

▷ Where the nature of business transaction between buyer and seller requires the establishment of an on-going business or personal relationship, possibly requiring unlimited or unrestricted contact

Brand Presence

Establishing a brand presence in the mind of the consumer is absolutely vital to the success of an online business, as it is to the traditional 'bricks and mortar' business. Speaking shortly after the successful flotation of Lastminute.com, Martha Lane-Fox (one of its founders) made several key points, including the necessity for the e-Tailer to really get to know their customers and develop a proactive rather than reactive posture. Having identified a customer profile with likes, dislikes, key life events and interests, respond with helpful suggestions and alternatives, e.g. "tell me when you have a flight to San Francisco for less than £250." In addition with a limited marketing budget of £5 million Lastminute.com was able to achieve very significant brand recognition across Europe, that from a survey conducted on their behalf showed a staggering 50%.

For many traditional 'bricks and mortar' businesses seeking to establish an online Web presence, the brand recognition built up over many years is a great asset in gaining acceptance and building a solid base of online consumers. Equally, this intangible asset contributes greatly to the worth of a business and needs to be protected, as adverse publicity can damage the brand image and impact on business results. For this reason, companies are concerned with the worrying emergence of anti-Web sites (so called suck sites) used by disaffected customers, employees, or even competitors, to publish grievances or spread malicious gossip. The following most highly valued brands such as Coca-Cola, Microsoft, IBM, General Electric, Mercedes-Benz, Nokia, British Airways and Toyota have been the subject of attacks in this way. Companies need to guard against a number of activities in protecting their brand within the new economy for the prevention of:

▷ Unauthorized use of images or logos

▷ Use of images or logos in anti-social context including pornography

▷ Abuse of domain names purporting to be what they are not

▷ Unauthorized Web sites and malicious news group postings

Dis-intermediation

An important factor in the B2C sector is the ability of the manufacturer to bypass or eliminate retailers and distributors and deal directly with the customer. This process of eliminating functions within the supply chain/selling process is known as dis-intermediation. This is occurring in a range of industries and impacts on both home consumers and business customers engaged in e-Commerce. The real issue for companies which have traditionally used intermediaries is to understand the implications of removing them from the supply chain. Clearly, if the new venture is successful then there is no issue, but if it fails the company may have seriously damaged its business relationship with its trading partners, who may not wish to re-establish the status quo. Examples of dis-intermediation in the marketing and selling of products and services over the Internet are numerous and include insurance, clothing, computer supplies and books.

In international trade, an exporter who has dealt traditionally with a freight forwarder, such as GKN Freight Services, may decide instead to go directly to an international carrier, such as P&O Nedlloyd. Usually, the freight forwarder will undertake a range of services including road haulage and document preparation, which now has to be arranged by the international carrier or be automated. Freight forwarders are facing up to the challenge and are now demonstrating to their customers the value they contribute to the business cycle. What is becoming obvious is that intermediaries affected in this way must re-define their business and change the services they offer, or risk not surviving.

Internet Shopping Therapy

Consumer interest in e-Commerce is driven by a belief that existing goods are available at lower prices, there is greater choice, new products and services add greater convenience, and customer service is improved via the 'self-service' model. The Web's interactive capabilities, availability, and abundance of 'live' information are all unique. Indeed, a consumer has extraordinary access to a wide range of sales materials, giving the buyer an unprecedented level of control in a sales situation where there is virtually no pressure to purchase. As with most successful sales, it is necessary to reduce the consumer's perception of risk and uncertainty. In this respect Web-based sales are no different from any other type of sales but, the novelty of the Internet for first time users can only add to the underlying doubt that occurs to any buyer in a strange context. Removing this concern is a major part of the Internet shopping experience in order for it to become an enjoyable therapy, in much the same way as shopping in the high street.

It is worth stressing that e-Commerce in the B2C context is very much about self-service where the customer is doing the buying and the e-Tailer can only sell in a passive sense, through the design and creativity of their Web site. Having connected to the Internet the customer can:

▷ Use a search engine to locate suitable Web sites

▷ Enter a Web portal that acts like a shopping mall and gives access to a number of virtual shops

▷ Go directly to a specific 'book-marked' Web site

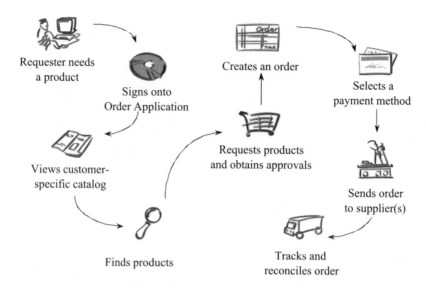

Figure 9.3 Internet shopping therapy

Once the required product has been chosen, it is placed in the virtual shopping basket and, if no further purchases are required, the customer proceeds to the 'checkout' process (see Figure 9.3). With the purchase of a product completed the customer would then await delivery, possibly within a few days or less.

The following case study involving Lands' End provides a practical example of many of the points discussed in this chapter and hopefully serves as a stimulus for those consumers who have not yet ventured into the world of Internet shopping therapy to try it.

Case Study – Lands' End

Introduction

Lands' End Inc. was founded in 1963 in Chicago, USA selling sailboat hardware and equipment by catalogue. In 1975, it published its first full-colour catalogue with 30 pages of sailing equipment and two pages of clothing and from that point the proportion of clothing sold grew steadily year-by-year. The company went public in 1986, and in 1988 reported sales revenues of $486 million. In 1995 it established an Internet presence by launching **www.landsend.com** and in 1999 announced that the previous year's Internet sales grew threefold. Lands' End describes itself as a leading direct merchant of traditionally styled casual clothing for men and women, as well as soft luggage and products for the home. The company's products are offered through regular mailings of its catalogues and via the Internet. Customers shop directly (from home or office) by phone or mail, by fax or the Web. Products are then shipped from warehouses in North America and Europe direct to customers, wherever in the world they may live.

Purchasing an Attache Case

Step 1

The customer completes the login to Lands' End at **www.landsend.co.uk/** and is presented with the Lands' End home page, an uncomplicated but appealing screen. Various options exist including browsing the Women's or Men's part of the Web site, or searching for a product.

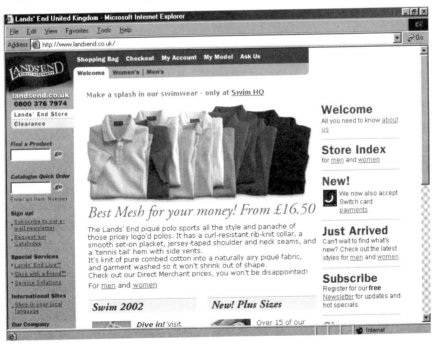

Figure 9.4   Lands' End home page

Step 2

After two unsuccessful attempts at searching in the 'Find a Product' search box using <briefcase> and <document case> the following screen is displayed, offering the customer the option to seek assistance from a customer service representative.

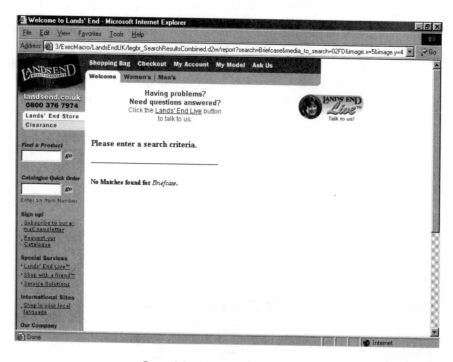

Figure 9.5 Failed keyword search

Step 3

The customer can then decide whether they want the customer service representative to ring them or to have a live chat there and then. In either case they need to enter their first and last names in the boxes provided and the telephone number if requesting a call, and select 'Connect'.

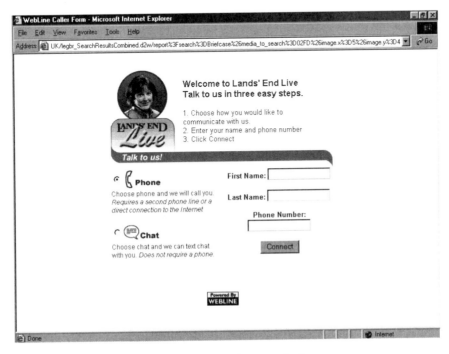

Figure 9.6   Conact via phone or chat?

Step 4

In this case having entered their details, the customer selects a live chat session, initiating the setting-up of the link. The following set-up screen tracks the progress, with a reassuring comment that 'A customer service representative will be with you in a moment'.

Figure 9.7 Establish a chat session

Step 5

It only takes a few seconds before the live chat screen appears and a dialog is established between the customer service representative (Alison P) and the customer (Mike Chesher). The customer simply types in the message in the window at the top, then selects the 'Post Message' button.

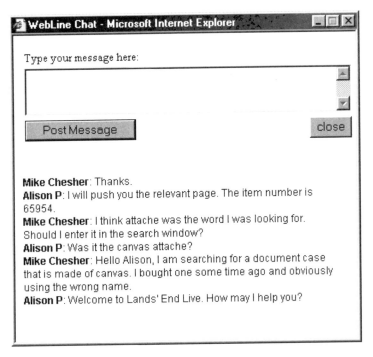

Figure 9.8 Representative and customer conversation

Step 6

The customer service representative causes the customer's Web browser to be refreshed with the product identified in the live chat session, permitting the customer to examine product details and decide whether or not to proceed with the purchase.

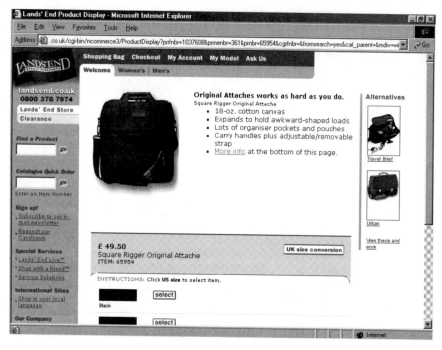

Figure 9.9   Representatives forces display of required product

Step 7

The live chat session can now be terminated by selecting the 'close' button to allow the customer to proceed with their purchase.

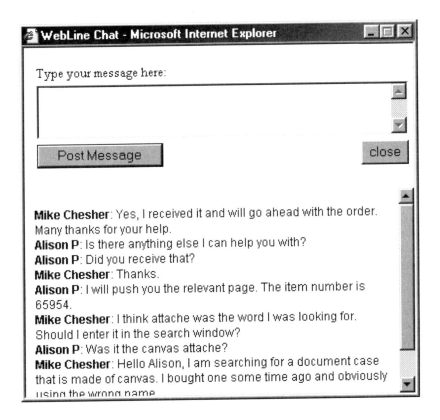

Figure 9.10 Terminating the conversation

Step 8

Having selected a black Square Rigger Original Attache the order screen now appears from which it appears there is a monogram option for an additional £3.50. Once decided, the item is added to the 'Shopping Bag' by selecting the button.

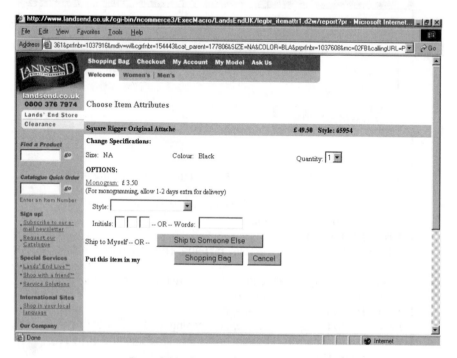

Figure 9.11 Display of order form

Step 9

The Web browser now displays the shopping bag. If the customer had ordered other items then these would be listed together with the Square Rigger Original Attache. The option now exists to 'Keep Shopping' or 'Checkout using the Secure Server'. The secure server means that at this phase of the transaction the communications between the Web browser and Web server are encrypted to ensure that if the data (perhaps containing a credit card number) were intercepted by an interloper they could not read the information. For more details of the encryption process, see Secure Sockets Layer (SSL) in Chapter 12. The customer knows that security has been invoked as a picture of a 'lock' appears on the display bar at the foot of the Web browser screen.

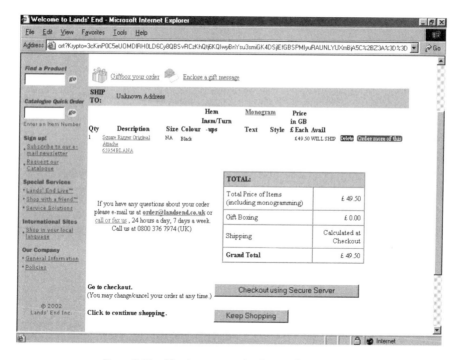

Figure 9.12 Checkout using the Secure Server

Step 10

Billing and shipping address information is then entered using the boxes presented on the Web browser including the customer's E-mail address if they possess one. This information is then presented to the customer for checking and amendment if necessary, together with the total cost of the order.

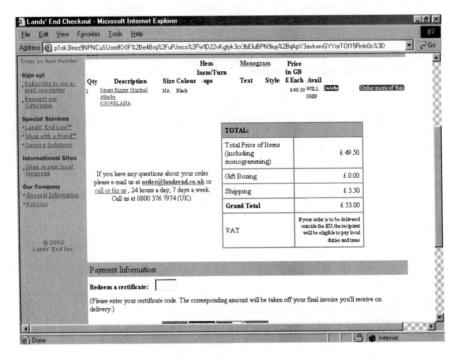

Figure 9.13   Billing and shipment address details

Step 11

The customer now needs to decide upon the method of payment and enters their credit card details into the boxes provided. Upon selecting the 'Process my order' button, this information is then checked by the Web server using a remote electronic database application containing details of credit card numbers, together with credit ratings and stolen cards.

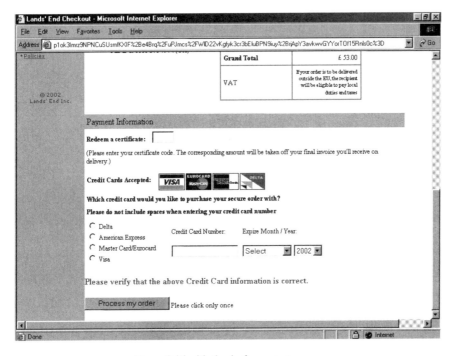

Figure 9.14 Method of payment

Step 12

After a few seconds a screen is displayed on the Web browser thanking the customer for their order and very shortly afterwards an E-mail will be received by the customer:

Figure 9.14 Thank you for shopping with Land's End

——-E-mail Message——-

From: order@landsend.co.uk [SMTP:order@landsend.co.uk]
Sent: 26 February 2002 23:00
To: mike@chesherassociates.co.uk
Subject: Lands' End Order Confirmation

Thank you for shopping at Lands' End.

Your order #099065139 is being processed.

If you have questions about your order, please call us free from the UK at 0800 0969 869. (Freephone from The Republic of Ireland, France, The Netherlands and Germany: 00800 00 220 106. From all other countries: + 44 1572 758070; please leave your number, we'll call you back immediately.)

Thank you for shopping at landsend.co.uk.

——-End of E-mail Message——-

Two days later the Square Rigger Original Attache is delivered by a courier service, which successfully completes the purchase.

Purchasing Clothing

Step 1

Lands' End use an interesting concept to help customers obtain a better feel for how their products will look on them by the allowing the customer to create of a virtual model of themselves. This can be used to 'try on' clothing and examine different colour combinations from different angles. The first part of the process involves creating the virtual model and it is possible to choose from four simple criteria to create the model using body, features, face and hair. An example Web browser display for the body and hair options is shown below:

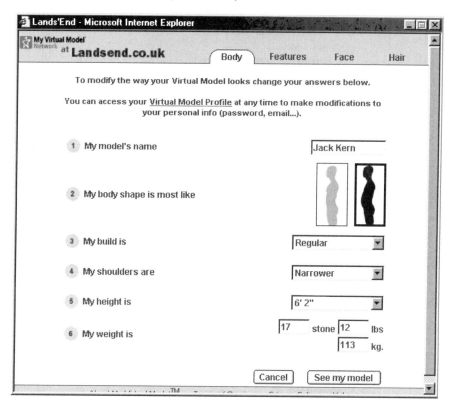

Figure 9.16(3) Virtal model body features

Step 2

Once the initial selections have been made the customer can select the 'See my model' button to view their virtual model, although the virtual model may be viewed progressively after each criteria has been modified.

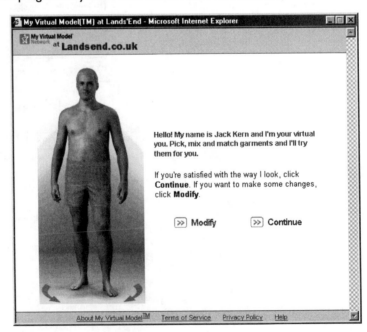

Step 3

Once the customer is happy with their virtual model, they can proceed to browse the clothing on the Web site and try it on their model. This process is a one-time activity and the customer's virtual model can be saved for subsequent re-use.

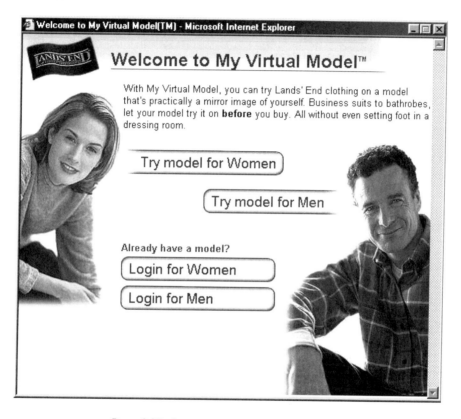

Figure 9.17 Retrieving your virtual model

Step 4

Having completed the login as appropriate to retrieve their virtual model, the customer now is at a point where they can select clothing that can be tried out on their model.

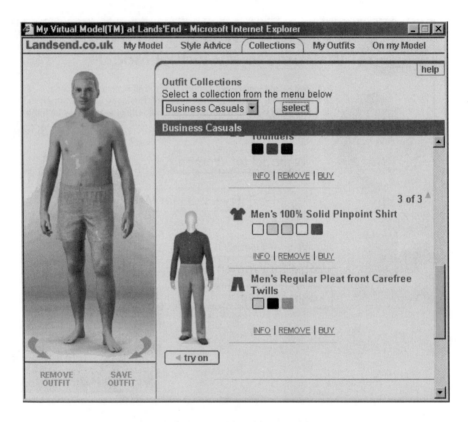

Figure 9.18 Selecting clothing to view on your virtual model

Step 5

Once clothing has been selected by the customer it can be 'tried on' their virtual model. Colour combinations can be altered and different views be seen by rotating the virtual model.

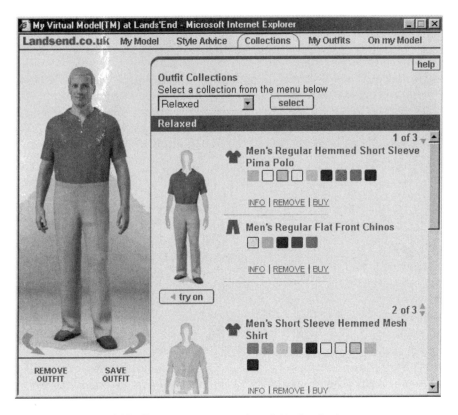

Figure 9.19 Examining your virtual model before buying

Once the customer is satisfied with their choice they can then proceed with the 'buy' option, which brings up very similar screens from Step 9 onwards in the Square Rigger Original Attache purchase.

Wireless Commerce

Nomads of the Future

The possibility of becoming a corporate nomadic wanderer, geographically far removed from the organization's web of networks and computers, yet still able to link into this fixed topology via a plethora of small portable devices offers many advantages and promises new ways of working and balancing one's working life. Wireless computing heralds a new way of working which has profound implications for the psychology of workers and the future organizational structures of our companies. We are beginning to see the evolution of a society where networks of workers, possessing a wide portfolio of skills, are supported by emerging technologies which help facilitate a new way of working. These mobile devices can also provide the gateway into a new world of rich information and entertainment, linking into the ever prevalent online services markets. The vision is especially appealing to vendors attempting to reach those that have not accepted the personal computer paradigm.

Newer technologies are allowing mobile units to become more human-friendly. As many of the new units being offered are aiming to have broad market appeal, they have to be. Human habits can be generally described as analogue, so it not without surprise that adapting to the digital changes that these devices have introduced to our daily lives, not only during working hours, but increasingly during our social hours has been a challenge for vendors and users alike. Are we humanizing new technology, or digitizing the consumer? It is a combination of both – the trend is clear with the latter.

The emerging convergence of the traditionally different spheres of technology, communications and global networks are hinting at promising something elusive and exciting – the prospect of reaching the two thirds of the population that have not embraced PC technology, in its variety of forms. These consumers have accepted the fax machine, purchased advanced games consoles for their children, and are perhaps awaiting for the functionally rich, mobile devices to make their lives more productive – whether in a professional or social capacity.

A key aspect of the looming new paradigm is the synthesis of existing and new hardware technologies, creating new challenges for organizations hoping to benefit, and derive advantage. These themes are explored further in this chapter.

The Next Generation of Hardware

Earlier, when examining the desktop environment (Chapter 4), we looked at the phenomenal changes that have taken place in the personal computer arena, with respect to the hardware and software advances achieved in the past 20 years. The birth of a portable computer soon moved on to the first notebook, and then sub-notebook – the emphasis was on faster performance in a smaller box. The consumer was eager to use this tool while on the move. Newer, smaller units known as Personal Digital Assistants (PDA) were enthusiastically received, and sales far exceeded initial expectations. Furthermore, consumers expressed their appetite for this product by paying a premium and were willing to sacrifice performance in order to obtain this added portability – the trend continues today, with these small units converged with cellular telephone technology.

The units have become widespread, and are widely used by workers connecting to corporate or personal networks whilst on the move around the globe, or squeezing an extra few hours out of the working day while at, or travelling from/to the home. Users have had to accept a relatively poor quality of mobile communication technology available to them – publicly connected computing via the PSTN is slow and of poor quality, yet widely accepted due to the lack of cheap alternatives. Even with the use of cellular technology, the bandwidth is only now becoming more acceptable and coverage is almost widespread enough for reliable national services. This situation continues to improve, as demand for mobile computing continues to grow at a phenomenal pace. Much has been achieved in a relatively short time – one only has to think about how long the telephone system has been in place, and how long it took before achieving broad coverage. In developing countries, cellular phone networks have totally leapfrogged fixed telephone line infrastructure (places like the developing Eastern European and African countries provide excellent examples).

This scenario of several portable personal digital devices (typically a laptop computer or PDA together with a cellular phone) and worker epitomizes the popular concept of mobile computing today. The Information Age is providing new toys for us to play with though, with early versions maturing in the marketplace – they are getting progressively closer to delivering what we hope, are the productivity tools we always dreamed about having. The concept of wireless computing is changing but not without challenges.

Perhaps one of the greatest challenges mobile computing faces concerns a simple aspect of the portable box – the battery. Energy conservation is of paramount importance in existing, and the new generation of products, with manufacturers facing a paradox: add more powerful energy sources and the units become bigger and heavier; less and recharging frequency increases. Recharging is a nuisance, and all too often the unit will run out of juice just when you need it most. Simple solutions such as carrying an extra battery pack only exacerbates the portability conundrum. Despite the huge leaps in technology advances we have witnessed in other aspects of the computer's anatomy, the lifetime of a battery unit is only estimated to increase by 20% over the next 10 years! This has led to an emphasis on energy efficient CPUs and also power saving, energy efficient software.

Cutting the Umbilical Cord

Today we have a whole community of satellites of varying sizes orbiting our planet, together with radio and cellular technologies covering almost every aspect of our planet. Quietly and efficiently, amongst their many tasks, they facilitate communication around the globe and are just one of many ways of allowing corporate nomads, away from their home bases, to continue to work, communicate, learn and keep in touch with their personal domains. They are no longer attached to these domains by physical umbilical cords, whether a network or telephone cable, but rather virtual connections utilizing the technologies that have been developed over the past years, and are now being deployed on a broader scale. The coming of the wireless network is upon us.

These nomads will use portable computers, whether the new generation of powerful notebooks or smaller Personal Assistants, to connect to information networks using wireless connections. This combination of mobility and portability creates not only a variety of new markets, some of which we are already seeing, but also a new way of interacting and working with colleagues and friends. Wireless networks are proving to be a large scale project for those providing them, and for corporations utilizing them or building their own. For large operations looking at wireless networks, the myriad of new potential IS challenges faced by managers are diverse and often all the answers are not yet available. Nevertheless, the mobile wireless network connectivity model of the future needs to be robust and transparent to the user. Progress is being made towards this vision, and one can examine today's technologies that are being used for wireless networks, discussed later.

These technologies more or less all face some core challenges, such as coping with a user connected while travelling over different coverage areas – this exchange of coverage, termed 'handoff', needs to be handled in a manner that does not interrupt data flow. The sheer magnitude of the scale will also require new approaches. Imagine a communications network that has to support thousands of wandering users, with machines of varying capabilities all around the world.

Wireless computing necessitates diverse accessibility to the network – the user could be connecting from anywhere in the world. This poses some very difficult questions regarding security issues, such as access fraud, intentional jamming, eavesdropping and so on. The potential for abuse increases exponentially as mobile computing becomes a regular service for a corporate network, if security aspects are not considered. Security can be achieved by effectively utilizing technologies such as encryption and challenge and response, where the network will issue a challenge (i.e. prompt for a password from a smart card issued to the user), and the user has to respond within a set period of time. Often there is a belief that wireless computing communication cannot be kept private, due to its broadcast nature. This is not the case, and with effective processes in place wireless networks can be as secure as their terrestrial counterparts. As usage increases across different sectors, and lessons are learnt, these and other challenges are being addressed.

Wireless Networks – Why?

Why the big fuss over wireless connectivity? The key aspect is access to information, in its variety of formats, including E-mail, fax, voice, image or video. The past few years have been characterized by the increasing need for information and has led to a new class of worker, termed 'the knowledge worker'. Information, and the timely delivery of it, is key to these workers and with increasing requirements to be away from a fixed work location, mobile access becomes of paramount importance.

Knowledge workers, and the information that they use are beginning to define today's organizations. Look back to an earlier era during the industrial revolution, and one could clearly value a company by its assets – typically these were the large industrial machines that were helping fuel growth around the world. Today, when examining the value of a company, we see its assets typically being information and workers – up to 10 or 20 times the value of physical and tangible assets. This information may include research, 'know-how', experience, and knowledge. One only has to look at companies as diverse as Microsoft, to companies such as the Wall Street investment firms. Today's environment has levied a large competitive premium on access to information, and the ability to communicate it to those that need to know.

Earlier we examined the archetypal mobile worker; the white collar professional using a portable computer while away from the office – whether this was while travelling on business or working at home. The users of mobile services are in reality somewhat more diverse, and in fact the greatest use of this technology in the past few years has been in other areas. A more realistic list would include:

▷ Mobile Office Workers – white collar professionals using services such as E-mail, file transfer and various desktop/LAN applications.

▷ Field Services – these include white collar workers such as sales/insurance representatives and blue collar workers in data collection, repair, customer service and distribution.

▷ Fixed Location – applications such as Point-of-Sale and electronic display and control.

▷ Personal Communication – private consumers using information services, messaging etc.

▷ Industrial Applications – where the technology is used to direct process flows (i.e. pallets in a warehouse).

Radio Frequency Identification (RFID)

Radio frequency identification (RFID) relies on memory chips equipped with tiny radio antennas – RFID tags (tags) – which can be attached to objects to transmit streams of data about them. The data can be highly informative or the tag can simply eliminate the need for barcode scanning. Tags are particularly suited to non-contact reading environments where bar code labels might not survive. In addition because no line of sight is necessary to read tags, items can be scanned much faster than with traditional barcode technology. Many e-Business professionals believe that RFID will in the future have a major impact upon the supply chain by creating an infrastructure capable of identifying and tracking individual objects such as pallets or products, all in real time.

Tags are generally of two types, either read only (RO) or read and write (RW). RO tags provide constant updated data about the attributes being monitored e.g. identification, temperature, time, movement, etc. while RW allows additional data to be written into the tag, such as status information and use of the tag as a data carrier. To put this data to the best use, the information needs to be quickly available up and down the supply chain to applications that can use it.

Generally tagging tends to be limited to high-value items, where the tag cost is small in comparison to the item cost, or where it is applied to a reusable item such as materials handling unit. Indeed as the price of RFID devices decrease, much greater use of 'smart' pallets is expected within the supply chain. There are already a number of trials underway that demonstrate the varied nature of the applications to which this technology can be applied. See **www.rfid.org** sponsored by AIM, the Association for Automatic Identification and Data Capture Technologies.

Example   Toyota (South Africa)

Toyota (South Africa) replaced a paper-based system in its manufacturing plant with a Radio Frequency Identification (RFID) solution from Escort Memory Systems to automatically track vehicles at any point during the painting process. Tags are mounted on the auto paint shop hangers (to which vehicles are suspended) allowing their position to be continually monitored by interrogation hardware (analogous to a barcode reader). A further phase will involve the tracking of vehicles from assembly departments.

Example   Edinburgh City Council (Scotland)

Edinburgh City Council (Scotland) use RFID technology from Texas Instruments to automatically give buses the green light to reduce traffic congestion and encourage the use of public transport. The priority system uses an individual RFID transponder attached to each bus. When a bus passes over a loop in the road, a roadside reader communicates the vehicle identity to the traffic light control system and triggers the lights to change depending on the priority attached to the vehicle. The RFID transponders mounted on the City Council's fleet of 800 vehicles controls the sequence of traffic lights at 57 approaches to the west of the city. The system can trigger green light 'wave-throughs' for buses and other public transport vehicles as well as emergency vehicles such as police, ambulance and fire appliances.

> Across Europe, crime involving stolen goods in transit is estimated at over 200,000 incidents per year and amounting to $10 billion of goods lost. Increasingly RFID devices are being fitted to trucks for electronic freight security (EFS) that can monitor halted vehicle, off-route, door open, movement and anti-tamper conditions that are relayed back to a control centre using triple mode communications (SAT/GSM/UHF). Nokia together with its logistics partner DHL have an RFID trial underway called CHIEFS (CHIpping and EFS) to monitor the delivery of phone shipments from the point of production to the customer's location. In addition the trial is aimed at gaining speedy confirmation of correct delivery or notification of incorrect delivery where intervention is required. A further objective is to reduce losses due to theft during transit, down to a trailer, pallet and case level. Identec i-Q tags are used in the trial supplied by TRI-MEX and are low cost (approximately $50 per tag) with a five year battery lifetime for long-term maintenance free operation. A similar trial involving Argos (UK market leader in catalogue retailing) together with its distribution partner Securicor covers a fully auditable track and trace system for vulnerable and attractive merchandise, initially covering jewellery products.

Mobile Workers

Certainly, by far the greatest use of wireless technology will be represented by the professional Mobile Workers segment, who collectively constituted almost a half of the potential market at the turn of the century. The other majority being Field Service workers, who have derived tangible benefits from the technology. Some of the inhibiting factors for the other segments have included cost, size of specialist modems (such as radio or cellular), complexity and unpredictable coverage and usage costs. For mobile workers, the major impediment has been the lack of wireless solutions operating on the corporate client/server LAN level.

Mobile workers, or telecommuters as they may be sometimes referred to, will clearly represent a large market, and the concept has been one that is favoured by employees and employers, as both win. Although the concepts of a mobile worker overlap with a telecommuter, the two possess some fundamental differences – the mobile worker is based full-time at an office and requires access while away from their home location. A telecommuter may spend a period of their working week based outside of their office (from one to several days of the week, every week). Both share the same challenge though – that of ad hoc access to corporate network resources from diverse geographical locations, and in the context of this chapter we view both in the same vein.

Telecommuting has promised much over the years, and there have been some very successful cases. These have typically involved workers spending extended periods away from the organization's central site allowing the organization to learn, and finally benefit. The concept is an appealing one, especially as the touted benefits include tangible financial savings, as well as the more desirable intangible benefits. Mobile computing addresses issues such as balancing family values, flexible schedules and commuting time frames as well as allowing organizations to achieve considerable savings in expensive office space when employees are located elsewhere. This latter concept was popularized as the SOHO (Small Office Home Office) model and differs from the principal requirements of the mobile worker who would dial-in where-ever they happen to be located; this does of course include the home and more often then not, mobile workers establish a semi-permanent set-up at home, including peripherals such as a printer.

The philosophy behind working away from the office has suffered some impediments, as the proponents of telecommuting know all too well. Although some were technological or cost benefit related, these reasons are less of a hindrance today. By far the largest reason remains cultural, and organizations have been wrestling with the new way of working that is inferred. The Orwellian nature of some management has restricted the concept of telecommuting as workers cannot be 'seen' to be working – in actual fact the ideology behind telecommuting can be viewed in the opposite sense: the technology allows more working hours in the day, suiting ambitious employees burning the midnight oil.

This new way of working has some significant implications in terms of an organizational cultural shift, and an adjustment of working patterns. The key aspect is perhaps a question of trust – without it advantages of working away from the office are diminished, as overtly or covertly, those against the philosophy try their best to oppose it. Organizations are experimenting with small user bases, and are realizing tangible results, especially with their sales teams. This shift is being accelerated by more mobile users requiring ad hoc access to corporate LAN resources, and consequently having the means to spend more time away from the office.

Mobile Commerce

We are already in the midst of an interesting and fast moving change in the manner we can interact between each other, and communicate with the outside world whose geography knows no limitations in the new order of things. The concept of portable computing continues to defy in terms of the functionality that can be squeezed into ever-smaller devices – whether these are communication devices such as cellular phones, or personal digital assistants. The ubiquity of these devices and their ability to be 'always connected' to a wireless network, coupled with the convergence of the devices into multi-functional units, is beginning to provide radical new business opportunities and models for us. The concept of mobile commerce (m-Commerce) is not a new one, but technologies such as WiFi, Bluetooth and GPRS (discussed later) are fuelling the possibility of e-based wallets and a form of interaction free of any umbilical cords connecting rich devices to each other. Some of these technologies are already achieving critical mass, although others are in an evolutionary stage which will become more widespread over time – either from a demographic segment (such as the young with SMS messaging) or from specific geographic regions (such as Japan for innovative services such as ÑTT DoCoMo i-mode).

Although the research varies a little, much is centring on a prediction that up to 35% to 45% of B2C e-business transactions will be initiated from a portable cellular-enabled device within five years. Almost 400 million mobile handsets were sold in the year 2000. The owning of a cellular phone was viewed as a luxury in the early 1990s and you can now see children below the age of ten comfortably using the technology in many countries – the UK, Scandinavia and technology driven countries such as Japan, Hong Kong and Singapore being excellent examples. In the following sections we look at wireless commerce, its applications and the underlying technologies that are driving this fundamental change in the manner we live.

The Wireless LAN

In recent times, it has become mainstream to be productive (whether for business reasons or personal leisure) while waiting in what used to be 'dead' time – waiting for a train, a plane or just catching a coffee in the numerous outlets that have proliferated around the world. Armed with functionally rich mobile devices, it was always possible to check voicemail but never that easy to surf the Internet, or connect to the corporate LAN and download E-mail with decent transmission rates. Imagine being able to be always connected in numerous public and private areas, ranging from airports to your local coffee shop, with access to high bandwidth connectivity allowing rich streaming of data. Or visiting another branch of your international organization and being able to connect to the LAN without having to hunt for a spare Ethernet connection port.

The proposition of being able to do that at the end of the 1990s was still uncertain, with a plethora of standards and no stable offering gaining critical mass. That was until the end of the 1990s and the turn of the century when two standards started changing this scene. Wireless LAN (WLAN) technology had grown up and was beginning to emerge from its roots in niche markets, principally manufacturing and warehousing. Essentially WLANs provide short range (metres to a few kilometres) connectivity using radio bands which vary by region. Data transmission rates can vary from a few Mbps (megabits per second) to a blistering 54 Mbps, using point to point linkages or connecting through central units referred to as Access Points. Applications already included approximately 400 hotels being equipped with these technologies in the US, as well as a large scale implementation by Starbucks to have some 3,000 of their outlets offer this type of technology.

Two particular approaches, Bluetooth and the IEEE 802.xx standards, began achieving critical mass at the turn of the new millennium, which are discussed in detail. Although the two are often confused (primarily due to the fact that they operated in the same radio bands), they serve different needs and applications and provide a glimpse of the direction wireless approaches are taking.

Bluetooth

The Bluetooth Consortium was officially launched in 1998 with principal sponsors IBM, Toshiba, Nokia, Ericcson and Intel. The group built a specification for a small-form factor, low-cost radio solution providing links between mobile computers, mobile phones and other portable handheld devices, and connectivity to the Internet, which was published in 1999. Essentially devices enabled with Bluetooth wireless technology will be able to:

▷ Free electronic accessories and peripherals from wired connections

▷ Exchange files, business cards, and calendar appointments

▷ Transfer and synchronize data wirelessly

▷ Take advantage of localized content services in public areas

▷ Function as remote controls, keys, tickets and e-cash wallets

Bluetooth benefited from excellent industry support, with over 2,000 organizations being members of The Bluetooth Special Interest Group (SIG), comprised of companies in the telecommunications, data networking and computing industries. Primary promoters of the standards include 3Com, Agere, Ericsson, IBM Corporation, Intel Corporation, Microsoft, Motorola, Nokia and Toshiba Corporation.

Bluetooth networking technologies have transmission rates of approx. 1 Mbps within a range of about 10 metres. This functionality positioned it well for cable replacement applications, which was the focus of the technology in its early years. The concept of eliminating the spaghetti like proliferation of wires between a desktop, laptop, mouse, keyboard, printer, PDA, mobile phone etc. holds an alluring proposition. Indeed early products received a healthy press, with Ericcson achieving much publicity with its launch of a futuristic looking wireless headset for its cellular phones using Bluetooth technology.

Although this application itself holds a rich and varied market, the focus has been to evaluate new applications that will allow this hardware and software based solution (each Bluetooth enabled device requires a Bluetooth chip) to be used in newer and more innovative ways. An excellent example of this is illustrated well in the concept of an e-cash wallet – a popular application well publicized in Scandinavia being able to pay for a drink dispensed from a vending machine using your cellular phone. Extrapolating this potential holds an interesting future for this type of technology. Other applications are varied and innovative in their manifestation, and major organizations are beginning to use the technology – the Chrysler Group is looked to launch its first Bluetooth application in 2002 providing hands free applications for Bluetooth enabled devices.

Despite this, take up of Bluetooth in the early years has not achieved expected results. The technology suffered from many of the usual factors that hound new approaches, with market perception preventing high adoption rates coupled with high costs of the chips – although these continue to drop as demand grows. There was also initial confusion between Bluetooth and the IEEE standards for Wireless LANs. Both standards used the same radio bandwidth although this will diminish as an issue as the more powerful IEEE 802.11a standard becomes more prevalent, operating in the 5 GHz band.

IEEE 802.11x (Wireless Fidelity – WiFi)

The WLAN market took a major step forward in October 1999, when the Institute of Electrical and Electronics Engineers (IEEE) approved a family of standards for high speed wireless connectivity between various mobile devices – essentially for wireless, Ethernet local area networks in 2.4 gigahertz bandwidth space.

The 802.1x standards are categorized within three major working groups, namely:

▷ **802.11**   Wireless standards that specify an "over-the-air" interface between a wireless client and a base station or access point, as well as among wireless clients.

▷ **802.15**   Working Group for Wireless Personal Area Network (WPAN) consensus standards for short distance wireless networks.

▷ **802.16**   Broadband Wireless Access Standards, with a goal to define physical standards for broadband access.

Within the 802.11 standard, a number of variants exist, with the best known being the 802.11b standard (Higher Rate Wireless Ethernet Standard). A number of the more popular categories are listed below in Table 10.1, and the full list of specifications are available on the IEEE Web site.

Standard	Description
802.11a	Successor to 802.11b – an ironic terminology. Both 'a' and 'b' standards were approved at the same time, but 'b' became more popular due to a lower level of technical difficulty in implementation. Operates in the 5GHz frequency range providing less interference and a much greater throughput.
802.11b	The earliest adoption of the standards providing throughput of up to 11Mbps in the 2.4Ghz band. Widely accepted and gained a fast critical user base.
802.11e	Project scope is to enhance the 802.11 Medium Access Control (MAC) to improve and manage Quality of Service, provide classes of service, and enhanced security and authentication mechanisms.
802.11g	A standard for 2.4Ghz wireless LANs providing an increase in transmission rates to 20+ Mbps.
802.11 WEP	Security standards incorporating encryption systems under the Wired Equivalent Privacy (WEP) standards.

Table 10.1   Popular 802.11 standards

The 802.11b standard (rather more interestingly also known as the WiFi standard) is promoted by an industry group called the Wireless Ethernet Compatibility Alliance (WECA), whose mission is to certify interoperability of Wi-Fi (IEEE 802.11) products and to promote Wi-Fi as the global wireless LAN standard across all market segments.

The WiFi standard has gained a good mass of support, and is expected to be a standard that is widely adopted and utilized. Although some other competing standards do exist, principally in specific geographies (such as Europe), expectations are that WiFi will succeed. The various working groups have already started on the next generation of standards and issues surrounding security using WEP approaches are also being addressed. As WiFi gains additional critical mass, without a strong contender, it may provide a robust defacto standard for wireless commerce.

Remote Access

Today, despite the increasing proliferation of wireless networks based on newer technologies, by far the greatest number of mobile users connecting to disparate networks, corporate or public information service providers, utilize the existing infrastructure of the PSTN. Corporations are utilizing available software solutions to provide remote access services to mobile users of their network, and using sophisticated security solutions in an attempt to ensure confidentiality.

Users demanding remote access to corporate LAN resources are also growing in number – armed with the required hardware; typically a notebook with modem, they are discovering the productivity advantages and convenience that remote access can provide. As a greater number of notebook configurations, in conjunction with or replacing a desktop solution, are introduced into organizations, so the challenge to provide what is becoming a necessary function on a LAN increases. The notebooks can provide local access to application software residing on the machine's hard disk unit, but users still demand access to LAN-based corporate databases, schedules and E-mail facilities. Users are also fuelling the supply for remote access products, as technological functionality overrides price, encouraging vendors to bring to market newer more powerful solutions to this growing requirement. Currently, typical access speeds range from 33.6 Kbps (kilobits per second) to increasingly prevalent 56 Kbps implementations, with the two most popular approaches to providing remote access to the LAN being remote control and remote client.

Remote Control

Remote access in the early 1980s was characterized by the PC technology of the day. This typically translated into a 286/386 processor-based machine, or one with similar processing characteristics, coupled with a modem operating up to 9600 bps, but usually at 2400 bps. This led to remote access solutions being built around the limitations of this technology; namely slow modem speeds and a need to limit processing on the dial-in machine.

Remote Control is a remote access technique that allows the dial-in machine to essentially assume control over a dedicated LAN-based PC. This can either be a one-to-one relationship, where there is a PC for every dial-in user, or a virtual PC in a multi-user operating system running on a server. Usually the latter is implemented via a rack of PCs, with processing clustered and shared amongst dial-in machines. With a one-to-one relationship, dial-in PCs A and B would communicate with different dial-in slave PCs. In a multi-user configuration, the processing would be shared between all the slave PCs.

When using a remote control solution, the dial-in PC is effectively a dumb terminal – all processing is performed at the LAN level on the slave PC, with screen updates and keyboard/mouse interaction sent over the dial-up connection. As the central suite of software is used, additional software licenses are not required for the dial-in machine. As a result, the dial-in PC capabilities are not important and a relatively low performance machine will suffice, although this does have an impact when using applications which support high levels of graphics – such as Windows-based software.

Although sometimes perceived as dated technology, remote control access has several benefits and can be an excellent solution depending upon the particular needs of an organization. For instance:

▷ For text-based services, the solution is fast.

▷ When interrogating databases, as the slave PC's capabilities are used, performance is excellent as only screen updates are transmitted through the connection. As the dial-in PC's processing capabilities are not an issue, older machines can be used for remote access.

▷ Depending on software licensing deals, there is no requirement for additional licenses on the dial-in machine, which can represent a significant saving.

The increasing use of Windows-based applications has put a strain on this type of access model, and although popular remote control products have been improved to work with Windows, access is still slow. Furthermore, there are confusions when using this model as simple tasks such as file transfer can be convoluted. Take for instance the example of copying a file from a network drive to a local drive – the result will be files copied to the slave PC's local drive rather than the dial-in machine. Hence, users need to be aware of the distinction between the slave and their dial-in PC. Although there a few manifestations of this approach still being used, it is essentially now outdated.

Remote Client (RC)

The Remote Client solution makes the most of inexpensive technologies, such as PCs (usually notebooks) with faster processing speeds, used in conjunction with high speed modems. As opposed to connecting to a slave PC on the LAN, and having all processing performed by that machine, RC software allows the dial-in machine to be essentially viewed as a client on the LAN, by the software emulating a network interface card. The software operating on the Remote LAN Server then receives data as if being sent to an interface card and sends the data over the modem link as opposed to the LAN. The dial-in PC would connect directly to the LAN, usually through a pool of modems, hence benefiting from the same software environment as users local to the LAN, including higher-layer functionality.

Unlike remote control, remote client does make full use of the dial-in PC's processing capability, and uses application software running on the dial-in machine. Consequently this solution is relatively more expensive in terms of hardware and software; especially if an un-limited software license is not in place. The higher functionality afforded by this approach does result in degraded response time, as the modem link is not as fast as the network speed. Despite this, the remote client approach is becoming the first choice for organizations implementing a remote access solution, especially as this model works best with Graphical User Interfaces (GUIs), such as Microsoft Windows, Apple System OS, Unix Windows – the most popular operating systems in use today.

Virtual Private Network (VPN)

The use of a VPN is becoming ever more popular and in most cases, the underlying technology network is outsourced to one of the numerous providers of these services (examples such as AT&T and UUNet are popular). This approach provides a complimentary aspect to the remote client configuration by ensuring the access speeds into the corporate network are maintained at the upper end of the spectrum, and local access numbers around the world are accessible enhancing the user experience and cost. Typically challenge and response security approaches are also utilized in conjunction with this approach (see Chapter 12).

Increasingly, organizations are evaluating the use of the Internet, or IP-based remote access solutions. Although this provides numerous benefits, key areas of concern, such as security, response times etc. continue to hamper its adoption. As the technology matures, a hybrid approach will become more prevalent with different classes of users being provided solutions that better fit their requirements.

Satellite Technology

Satellite services received a lot of hype in the 1990s and significant expenditure was utilized to build the networks promising high bandwidth and extensive coverage (up to 1000s of miles as opposed to up to 50 miles with Packet Data Radio), allowing for true WAN wireless networks. The systems that were being built relied on a network of Low Earth Orbit (LEO) satellites, and were held up as the next new approach to take us to a rich multimedia exchange of information all over the globe. Unfortunately, the networks never achieved the critical mass they were seeking, and high profile projects such as the Iridium Project with 66 LEO satellites and Qualcomm's Globalstar with 48 LEO satellites, never reached the subscriber bases initially anticipated. The Iridium initiative was named after the element Iridium, as the original project called for 77 LEO satellites orbiting the Earth; the element has 77 electrons rotating around its nucleus. The name was kept after the project was scaled down to 66 satellites as Dysprosium, the element with 66 electrons, was not deemed as catchy.

Although this technology continues to have its niche market, the mass continue to rely on the different generations of cellular technology.

Cellular Technology – Proliferation of the G's

When asked, most people would immediately identify the Internet as one of the most profound new technologies in recent times – which it is. What is perhaps not so well recognized, is the sheer impact of the cellular phone. At the turn of the century, approx 65 million people used the Internet once a week or more. In contrast, 110 million used cellular phones. In Western Europe the numbers were even more startling, with cellular penetration rates typically exceeding 50% of the population. Yet, less than one-third of this number qualified as active Internet users.

Cellular technology has impacted our lives in a profound way via the use of cellular phones and the spectacular growth continues at a pace, with increasingly sophisticated services being delivered to the market. Advanced services began to appear in the late 1990s, and extensive investments were made in a rush to offer sophisticated, media rich streaming services which would hopefully garner extensive new revenues to the providers of the services – predominantly the mobile network operators. Despite much noise and hype, technologies such as Wireless Application Protocol (launched in 1997) did not ignite the imagination of consumers and usage was lower then initial expectations. However there were pockets of notable exception with services in Japan gaining huge critical mass and a large generation, predominantly in their early teens to mid thirties, actively using one of the most sophisticated offerings. In Europe and Asia, a simple messaging capability, SMS (Short Message Service) became incredibly popular and an estimated 240 billion SMS messages were transmitted globally in 2001, with rudimentary multiplayer games becoming available using this technology. In addition, the UK Government had announced a project to test electronic voting in local elections using text messaging from mobile phones – there was a particular focus on capturing that elusive younger segment of the demographic spectrum aged between eighteen to the mid twenties. By end of 2001 it was estimated that there were more mobile phone users in China than in the US – ironic when over half the world's population had never made a phone call yet.

The turn of the new millennium bought additional excitement as the advent of the new next generation of advanced technology arrived, and the markets experienced a sense of maturity as subscriber bases swelled around the world and services became more user friendly. The evolution of mobile communications was progressing to the next stage of its lifecycle, and platforms were becoming more robust. Some 75% of all the digital cellular phones in the world use a standard that was conceived in Europe throughout the 1980s and commercialized in 1991, known as the Global System for Mobile Communications (GSM). This has continued its growth and maturity to provide newer capabilities (see Figure 10.1: Evolution of GSM networks) and by 2001, there were over 400 GSM networks operating in 162 countries across the world. In the US, the preferred standard was a time-based air interface (TDMA) and CDMA which used a coding mechanism.

Not surprisingly, all this growth had taken its toll on the bandwidths of existing technologies.

The end of the last century saw a proliferation of handsets leveraging technology that were poised to be advanced to new platforms, with their associated terminologies – we briefly contrast between the different generations (Gs) of technology rollout:

▷ **First Generation – 1G:** Analogue cellular phone services.

▷ **Second Generation – 2G:** These communications are broadly based on digital cellular technologies that operate over the popular standards of Global System for Mobile Communications (GSM), Time Division Multiple Access (TDMA) and Code Division Multiple Access (CDMA), with data transfer rates of around 9.6 Kbps (varies on service between 7 – 14.4 Kbps).

▷ **2.5 G:** 2.5G technologies required additional hardware over and above 2G, providing significant improvements in bandwidth providing the ability to carry richer applications with data rates of up to 115 Kbps using General Packet Radio Service (GPRS) technology. Essentially information is divided into packets and re-assembled at the other end, allowing concurrent sharing between users and provides an "always on" feature for users. With the addition of Enhanced Data Rates for GSM Environments (EDGE) or High Data Rates (HDR), rates are further increased up to 384 Kbps. Data compression on one or more time slots has previously been the approach to develop higher speeds. With High Speed Circuit Switched data (HSCSD), more than one time slot is used to provide extra capacity up to a maximum of eight slots. Typically, GPRS is well suited for bursty data traffic and HSCSD is suitable for large file transfers and multimedia.

▷ **Third Generation – 3G:** 3G technologies allow data rates up to a theoretical 2 Mbps. The specifications under this terminology include Universal Mobile Telecommunications System (UMTS) and EDGE. The former was essentially one of the first 3G networks with the latter being a technology that is enhancing GSM and TDMA networks.

▷ **Fourth Generation – 4G:** Although still very much in their infancy, these technologies provide transmission rates approaching 20 Mbit/sec.

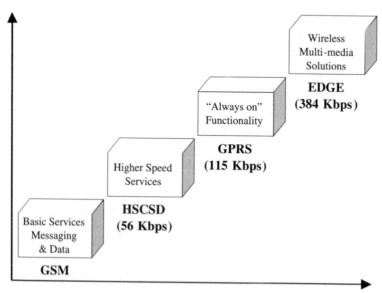

Figure 10.1 Evolution of GSM networks

Licenses for 3G services were offered to the various markets around the world at an astonishing price – either via an open auction, or offered directly to a short-list of companies considered best equipped by the authorities to fulfil the terms of the licence. In Europe alone, approximately US$100 billion was spent to acquire 3G licenses with Germany ($45 billion) and the UK ($35 billion) leading the pack via open auction. Other countries took a slightly different approach of offering a lower cost to entry with an associated cut of revenues. As an example, in Sweden a license cost an operator just over $10,000 with 0.15% of revenues being shared. Some operators in Asia also took a similar approach, but in contrast with significantly higher revenue shares (India levied a 15% share).

The fact that the auctioning of these licenses attracted such phenomenal prices was an indication of the projected revenues that these technology platforms could return, although there was literally no evidence at the time outside of the successes in Japan, with NTT DoCoMo's i-mode service (see case study).

WAP

The Wireless Application Protocol (WAP) specification initiative began in June 1997 and the WAP Forum was founded in December 1997, established by Ericsson, Motorola, Nokia and Unwired Planet and was established with the goal of enabling sophisticated telephony and information services on hand-held wireless devices such as mobile telephones, pagers, personal digital assistants (PDAs) and other wireless terminals.

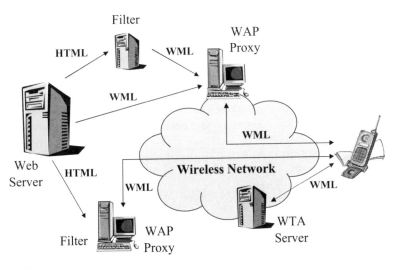

WML Wireless Markup Language
HTML Hypertext Markup Language
WTA Wireless Telephony Application

Adapted from http://www. wapforum .org

Figure 10.2 WAP infrastructure

WAP also leveraged the use of XML (discussed earlier) via a core mark-up language developed for WAP applications known as Wireless Mark-up Language (WML), used to create pages that can be displayed in WAP compliant browsers. WAP's proposed infrastructure model is outlined in Figure 10.2.

WAP promised much and provided a greatly needed standard in the industry. Despite this, its success in the market was disappointing in terms of adoption and success. This was down to many reasons, but some of the more significant could be categorized as:

▷ The promotion of WAP was somewhat un-coordinated and coupled with a shortage of handsets made adoption limited.

▷ Despite vendors promoting the infrastructure, the deployment was slow and consequently few applications were developed.

▷ The services were slow due to the circuit switching nature of the technology. Essentially, a user had to 'dial' and wait before services became usable. Until GPRS packet switching becomes more prevalent, this remains a core element of dissatisfaction.

Case Study – NTT DoCoMo i-mode Service

In February 1999 NTT DoCoMo, a subsidiary of Japan's telephone operator NTT, launched what was to become the most successful mobile portal in the world at the dawn of the new millennium when it launched its iMode services – a mobile Internet access system. A huge achievement given that iMode was proprietary in nature.

In early 2002, iMode boasted a subscriber base of over 30 million users (see figure below) with approx 40,000 to 50,000 new subscribers signing up a day in mid 2001. In fact this substantial increase in new users caught DoCoMo unprepared in the days of its infancy, and network failures were common under the weight of an increasing base of users. The startling subscription rates allowed iMode to attain critical mass in a short period of time.

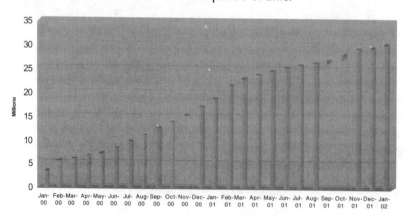

From a technical perspective iMode was simply an overlay to DoCoMo's ordinary mobile system, with the added functionality of being packet switched which allowed users to be connected at all times if a signal could be received. This was in stark contrast to WAP configurations (predominantly in Europe) which were circuit switched – i.e. a dial up approach with its inherent delays. iMode also leveraged cHTML, a compact version of ordinary HTML which made it simple for developers and encouraged an explosion of content. Additionally, un-official sites were welcomed and users allowed to roam at will between the approved ones. In early 2001, there were approx 40,000 voluntary sites in contrast to around 1,500 official sites. This rich content provided a virtuous circle attracting new sites which provided additional m-Commerce opportunities.

iMode's lead in the global market and success was apparent by the turn of the century and NTT DoCoMo is actively attempting to widen its base outside of the Japanese market. The success of this strategy is still unclear, and many would point to the rather specialist elements of the Japanese market that helped iMode's success. The major reasons touted included:

▷ A strong cultural acceptance for the service (the Japanese love gadgets) and handsets were as much a fashion accessory as a technology tool. DoCoMo very successfully marketed this aspect in conjunction with the benefits of the service.

▷ Relatively low prices for the service.

▷ A strong collaboration and partnership with domestic handset technology providers.

▷ A low penetration of PC usage at home, and access to Internet-based services were less expensive via cellular handsets than PCs.

▷ A technology that was "always on".

▷ More then 70% of Japanese workers have an hour commute, providing extensive time to be using their iMode services.

▷ Efficient micro-billing options. The technology allows the measurement of packets of information that an user sends/receives. Additionally DoCoMo established the billing process which lowered the barrier to entry for content providers facilitating growth.

DoCoMo continued its market leadership to be the first operator to launch a 3G mobile service under the brand name FOMA, which started test phases in Spring 2001 and launched later that year. Japan was the first country to introduce a commercial 3G service and plans were already afoot to evaluate fourth generation (4G) services expected to be launched in 2006, with theoretical transmission rates approaching 20 Mbit/sec, potentially promising high quality smooth video transmissions.

Personal Digital Assistants

Classification of the new emerging hand held devices, seems almost as difficult a challenge as that faced by Darwin, when he was classifying his beetles many years ago. Since sophisticated portable products, such as advanced calculators, storage devices and schedulers, appeared in the early 1980s, we have seen a proliferation of products produced by manufacturers obsessed with miniaturization. The early products, such as Psions', had limited functionality, complicated connectivity and the added restrictions of a small keyboard. Technology has inevitably advanced, and it is now possible to move away from the archetypal keyboard format to a more intuitive form of interaction – hand-written input augmented by icons and voice. We begin the process of further humanizing the technology available to us, so that the tools we use everyday more closely reflect the way we naturally think and work.

The new products are ever smaller, functionally rich, offer immense communication capabilities and are known collectively as Personal Assistants. The shift towards this type of product, and mobile computing, is being fuelled further by the advent of the flexible worker, whose only future link with the office will be an invisible electronic umbilical cord. This symbiotic relationship between computing devices and comm-unication technologies is exemplified by the emerging market of Personal Digital Assistants (PDAs). The best known early example being Apple's Newton MessagePad, followed by the Palmpilot from Palm Computing, and Blackberry's wireless devices. Additional units were the product of the early fertilization of the digital technologies of silicon and wireless telecommunications converging – essentially a cross between a personal organizer and the mobile phone.

The current PDAs on offer in the marketplace support varying functionalities, depending upon price and size. Well known offerings include Palm Computing's products which operate on Palm's OS, although the significant early market share continues to be eroded from competition with Microsoft's Windows CE (Compact Edition) platform. Both platforms have grown and been adapted, reflecting early criticisms and continue to increase their user bases. Others manufacturers are following at their heels, hoping to carve out a share of a market reported to be worth tens of billions of dollars, as sales of PDA units continue to grow sharply.

The estimates are not surprising, given the exponential numbers of units being sold against a backdrop of an increasingly mobile workforce, most of whom are spending increasing amounts of time outside their offices. That trend is exacerbated with the fact that millions of workers now have jobs that necessitate being on the road at least 20% of their time as well as a potential 45 million business users in vehicles. As the units are becoming more flexible, users are beginning to evaluate their potential use for simple applications such as text information retrieval, scheduling updates and E-mail. Currently, a large user base of laptop computers are lugged around simply for these uses – the PDA offers a much more compact solution.

Despite the high growth potential, there are some inhibiting factors though: the technology is still not totally effective at handling cursive (joined-up) handwriting, and the cost of the units, although dropping, are still relatively expensive to reach broad market appeal – the more 'intelligent' units with connectivity extras cost around $400 upwards. There has also been criticism about synchronization between desktop applications, although this continues to improve with additional utilities (the latest popular operating systems support synchronization tools). There is still dispute over the 'standard' operating system to be used, with two major camps – those who support the Windows technology Microsoft have developed for pen-based and other providers who follow Palm's software platform.

The Future of Wireless Networks

In the first decade of the new century, mobile knowledge workers are enjoying the luxury of not having to worry about how their communication to diversely located information is being handled. One access point will allow them to communicate, receive and peruse through information repositories at their will, often situated all around the world. The segregation of existing communication systems and technologies are merging into an intricate wireless solution, providing the ubiquitous service that mobile workers continue to demand. When examining the trends of wider geographical coverage and higher bandwidths required to support throughput hungry multi-media applications, it is not surprising to see wireless technologies appearing not only in our organizations, but our homes, our hotels, airports as well as our coffee shops.

Clearly the availability of wide scale wireless connectivity, at a cheap price is an appealing prospect not only to commercial interests, but also to the wide population of everyday users of the new mobile technologies being developed and coming to market. This availability will herald a new type of mobile commerce and the prospect of handling more information which is immediately available. Digital communication already allows incoming calls to be identified, and soon, perhaps your personal electronic agent can handle the call and make some rudimentary follow up. This has many social implications – we only have look at what E-mail is doing to the art of letter writing.

The increasing use of cellular technologies will have a profound impact on what we call 'my office' or 'home'. No longer will people be tied to one location by virtue of a telephone number – that person could be anywhere, and often is. As with most new technology, it has a tendency to creep up on us, and before we know it, it becomes widespread within our lives. The potential changes are numerous, and those that will benefit the most will be the ones that understand the implications of the new technology and how it can provide benefit from a personal perspective and competitive advantage within a business environment.

Despite all this progress, perhaps one of the most fundamental improvements will be the good old battery – a theme we started the chapter on. No matter how advanced the wireless commerce potential, without any juice each functionally rich device yields no productivity gain!

Dot.Com Economy

The New Economy

In the past, economists have used the term 'new economy' to differentiate an emerging period of economic reform. However, over the last three decades this term has taken on new meaning with a rapid growth in the adoption of information technology and the impact that this has had in reshaping the business world. Over this period the developed countries of the world have seen a very dramatic redistribution of employment from manufacturing into the service sector, fuelled by the use of new technology. In addition, technology has assisted manufacturing operations to become far more efficient with the advent of robotics and other computer controlled materials handling equipment. The labour burden has been reduced and, even for those industries that still depend upon a high labour content in their products, the developing economies around the world have only been too willing to provide cheap labour resources.

Further, the widespread deployment of information technology has resulted in new business opportunities, where information and knowledge are the primary commodities in opening up new employment possibilities for those displaced from manufacturing. Clearly, it is not quite so simple, as many of the employees displaced from the manufacturing sector do not possess the necessary skills to take full advantage of the new business opportunities information technology has created in the service sector, without re-training.

Over the last decade, the concept of the new economy has gained greater credence by the emergence of the Internet as a dynamic new force to reach both business customers and domestic consumers more directly. New Internet start-up companies have received much of the publicity and hype over this period which has given rise to the term the 'Dot.Com Economy', regarded by many as synonymous with the term 'new economy'. Others argue that the new economy encompasses more traditional 'bricks and mortar' businesses that have successfully made the transition by integrating the Internet into their operations.

This evolution is best illustrated by looking at the Forbes 400 in the US and the FTSE Euro 250 in Europe which list the top companies based upon market capitalization. Two decades ago, the Forbes 400 was dominated by manufacturing companies, followed by oil and real estate, the three industries making up some 60% of the total list. Today, the same industries account for less than 15% of the list and the three different industries now dominating the list are technology, finance and media/entertainment. It is also interesting to note that the richest American is the founder of Microsoft, Bill Gates, who represents the technology swing heralded by the new economy. In addition, the Forbes 400 list is also very much more volatile today than in the past, with companies entering and departing at a much greater rate, approaching a 20% turnover. This seems to indicate that the new economy is much more dynamic and moving at a much faster rate than the old economy ever did.

Using the FTSE Euro 250 in Europe, the same analysis over the last two decades does not show quite such a marked swing, but the trend is unmistakable. Manufacturing, energy and real estate companies have moved from 52% to 29% of the total list, while technology, finance and media/entertainment have moved from 28% to 47% of the total list over the same period.

The Chairman of the US Federal Reserve, Alan Greenspan, also refers to the concept of the 'new economy', but appears to have difficulty in updating the economic yardsticks, which have served him so well in the past, with new measurements required to satisfactorily monitor the new economic environment.

In response to the question 'what characterises the new economy?', the former IBM chairman and chief executive officer, Louis Gerstner, indicated that he resisted the idea that there was a new economy – something that was separate and distinct from some other economy. However, he concluded that the Internet and the investment being made by companies in information technology was indeed driving a period of sustained economic expansion in the developed economies. Gerstner also felt that in time the Internet would be best remembered, a little like the electric motor today, first used in heavy industry then eventually adopted across all industries.

However, whichever way you look at this phenomenon, these new ways of reaching customers with the help of the Web are the essence of what identifies the new or Dot.Com economy. The Web is viewed as a completely new sales channel in addition to more traditional face-to-face, telephone and mail.

Dot.Com Frenzy

Some writers in North America have likened the Dot.Com frenzy of recent years to the excitement accompanying the Californian gold rush of 1849. While many of the prospectors and speculators amassed great fortunes, inevitably the vast majority of the 'forty-niners' went home disappointed. So it seems that the same analogy applies to the Dot.Coms where, in this first rush to capitalize on the riches of the Internet, a relatively small number of ventures have proved to be successful. Clearly, there must be lessons to be learnt and indeed the second wave of Dot.Com ventures are starting to take full advantage of the mistakes made by the early pioneers, thereby increasing their chances of success.

Figure 11.1   Dot.Com frenzy

Over a brief period leading up to the turn of the millennium there was a scramble for new start-up companies to establish a Web presence based upon a creative idea developed by their founders. In many instances they offered new products and services not thought possible under the traditional business model. As the world's most developed economy it is not surprising that US consumers were the first to enjoy greater access to the Internet and, as a result, many of the early Dot.Com examples come from North America.

While the Internet is rightly credited with accelerating the growth in doing business electronically within the business-to-business sector, it has created a whole new market for trading electronically in the business-to-consumer sector, which largely never existed prior to the commercialization of the Internet. Many of the Dot.Com visionaries saw the Web as a new and competitive way to reach the consumer markets offering a very wide range of services including banking, selective retail markets such as books and fashion goods, music, travel, holidays, etc.

With the media hype predicting immediate success for these new ventures, many Dot.Coms found a willing number of investors. When several of these companies went public with stock market flotations, their share prices hit unprecedented levels, such that their market capitalization appeared to be quite unrealistic compared to their short-term profit earning potential. A good example is the flotation on the London stock exchange of Lastminute.com in Summer 2000, with an initial market capitalization of £820 million which compared favourably to a company such as WH Smith[1], with 20,000 employees and over 120 stores, and which had been trading for over a century.

End of the First Wave

Before greater realism entered the Dot.Com economy in the summer of 2000 some astounding Dot.Com results were seen both in North America and Europe. While Amazon.com continued to lose money, its stock valuation was some eight times that of Barnes & Noble the 'bricks and mortar' bookstore. A company called eBay went public in the summer of 1999 and by the end of the year had a market capitalization of $10 billion. America Online had a market capitalization that was even greater than General Motors.

The challenge faced by many traditional 'bricks and mortar' organizations has been how to make the successful transition from their current mode of operation to a new way of working which embraced information technology in order to conduct more of their business electronically. However, for many organizations this change in philosophy (described in Chapter 1) has allowed them to progressively reshape organizational culture and business processes. In the case of organizational culture, this requires the leadership team to develop an environment that accepts the need for change and encourages employees to view change as an opportunity rather than a threat. This then opens the way for continuous improvement programmes challenging the status quo and resulting in the evolution of new business processes with a much richer IT content.

Since these business developments are very much technology-enabled it is not surprising that some of the basic information technologies needed to be developed and extended further so that organizations can take the fullest advantage of them. This can be seen to be happening in several ways, including the provision of adequate bandwidth and accessibility to the Internet, initially for business customers and then for home consumers. Some of the difficulties faced by the early pioneers of the Dot.Com economy were due to the fact that the needed technology and its deployment was not in place. In particular new electronic businesses trying to open up the online consumer marketplaces initially found difficulties because of the relatively low Internet access that existed outside North America. However, supported by governments, much has changed in a very short period of time. Perhaps the most notable and key factor in the significant growth of e-Commerce has been the increasing availability of cost effective Internet access, bringing it well within the reach of the average person within the developed countries of the world.

One of the main differences between the industrial age and so called information age, heralded in during the 1970s, is the almost unbelievable exponential rate in which information technology capabilities have grown for the same or often lower costs. Therefore, the new Internet start-up companies are much more able to scale up to the increasing demands of business through the unprecedented advancement in chip technology and deployment of low-cost high bandwidth global networking infrastructures, when compared to a traditional 'bricks and mortar' business.

Many Dot.Com companies trade exclusively over the Internet with new products and services that hitherto could not be delivered by traditional means. However, several Dot.Coms have reinvented the way traditional products are sold. The classic example is Amazon.com (Amazon) and book purchasing. Amazon 'tore up' the traditional way people purchase books (normally associated with walking into a bookshop) and offered an online experience with many additional features including author searches, abstracts and peer book reviews. Many of the 'bricks and mortar' bookshops including Barnes & Noble (US) and Waterstones (UK), have tried to emulate Amazon, but with less success for some of the reasons discussed later in this chapter.

The term downsizing was popular during the 1980s to describe the phenomena of 'laying off' or 'shedding' of staff enabling organizations to meet the challenges of an increasingly competitive marketplace by the reduction in costs. This achieved a more dynamic organization by reducing levels within the hierarchy and speeding-up decision-making and communications. Another important by-product of downsizing was improved productivity from reduced labour costs. Many Internet start-up companies have faced the need to conserve cash if they were to continue trading. This has brought downsizing back into vogue and many Dot.Coms have had to dramatically restructure their organizations by shedding staff in an effort to re-focus their businesses.

Prompted by a general tightening of markets, the turn of the millennium saw greater realism emerge in the Dot.Com economy with a shake-up in companies that had failed to achieve their expected market potential. This resulted in a number of high-profile companies going out of business, both in Europe and in North America. Companies failing during this period included such names as Boo.com, Clickmango.com, Webvan.com, Urbanfetch.com, sportal.com, gameplay.com and govWorks.com. In total it is estimated that over 450 Dot.Com companies ceased training over a three-year period. Some of the reasons for Dot.Com failures include:

▷ The injection of venture capital came before many Dot.Coms were able to show that they were really ready for it.

▷ Some Dot.Coms did not observe sound financial management in the use of funding and spent excessively on technology and staff.

▷ A rather insular and arrogant view from the founders that whatever was created would attract customers, which frequently was not the case.

▷ Unrealistic estimates of sales revenues and market penetration meant that many DotComs had no clear path to profitability (P2P).

▷ A basic flaw in the original business plan that failed to identify the unsuitability of a chosen market niche for a Dot.Com company.

The downturn in the market and reduced scope for investment funding, exacerbated the already challenging task of succeeding in today's world markets with a new economy business. In some instances Dot.Com companies succeeded in the North American marketplace but failed when trying to establish a similar business model in Europe. It is a mistake to assume that what succeeds in North America will naturally translate to a successful operation in Europe, with its complexity of different cultures, languages, monetary and regulatory regimes and lower levels of Internet access.

In many instances European Dot.Com failures have simply lacked a coherent strategy, not just in reaching their target customers, but in not fully considering the logistics issues associated with their distribution networks once orders are taken. This is also a problem faced by some traditional companies that, in their haste to embrace Internet technology, particularly in the use of shop front software for order processing, have found that existing downstream processes for distribution have proved to be a bottleneck. Other companies have been very successful in thinking creatively around the problem, by outsourcing their stock management and distribution. Compaq has established such a centre in the Netherlands where orders taken by its customer service centres throughout Europe are able to access the central stock and fulfilment system to confirm availability, and arrange shipment using overnight couriers such as TNT. The Netherlands has become an important location for companies wishing to service the complete European marketplace, because of the quality of its distribution infrastructure, logistics service providers, and the efficiency of its distribution centres.

Despite some of the well-publicized disasters faced by the first generation of Dot.Com companies entering the new economy, it is interesting to note that in both North America and Europe many governments have established a cautious but successful presence on the Web. For example, UK government departments such as Customs and Excise, Inland Revenue, Department of Trade and Industry and the Houses of Parliament, as well as local government departments, are reachable via the Web. Their intention of improving their image by being less remote, to achieve productivity gains and to improve services to the citizen, has given rise to another new 'e' word, 'e-Government'.

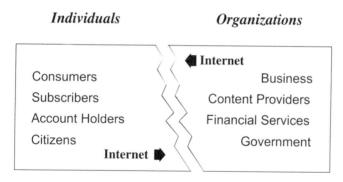

Figure 11.2   e-Government

Dot.Com Successes and Failures

Webvan, at onetime the largest Internet grocer in the US, spent some $1.2 billion in investment capital in just three years and became the biggest Dot.Com failure in July 2001 when it ceased trading. Some $350 million was spent on establishing a Web-enabled network of warehouse and distribution centres allowing consumers to purchase groceries online and have their orders delivered direct to their doors. While of no real comfort to Webvan, its competitors and other potential e-Businesses are looking hard at their experience in order to benefit from their mistakes. It would seem that some of the major problems experienced by Webvan centred on its somewhat complex ordering process, pointing to inadequate software design and development. In addition, frustration was voiced by consumers at slow Internet access speeds from home and problems with grocery deliveries to consumers at times when they were not at home. One lesson is that a single sales channel, namely the Internet, is not enough and that offering consumers multiple choices of how to buy is desirable. Since online shopping represents a culture change for the consumer with all the attendant risks, there is a distinct advantage in taking a more cautious approach, particularly for the established so called 'bricks and mortar' major food retailers. In the UK, 'bricks and mortar' major food retailers such as Tesco and Sainsburys are using a home delivery model focused on local stores rather than warehouses as the point of distribution for their Internet-based shopping service. This service is growing in popularity and both companies have announced major expansion plans.

Urbanfetch.com was another US Internet-based company offering the convenience of being able to order almost anything via the Web and be assured of direct home delivery. While the concept was good, it failed to meet its financial targets and, like Webvan, ceased to trade. During the year 2000, *Fortune Magazine* tracked and reported the failure of 124 Dot.Com companies.

Many of the failed Dot-Com start-up companies had incomplete business plans that failed to demonstrate clearly where and in what numbers the paying customers/consumers were likely to come from. These companies emerged because of the innovative ideas and enthusiasm of the founder but very few have been able to make the transition from start-up to established business. In many instances cash has become a major need in order to fuel the initial growth and establish a market presence. Often income alone has been insufficient to cover this early start-up period and external funding through venture capital or apparently friendly strategic investment has been necessary.

Lastminute.com, which is in the image of Amazon, illustrates an innovative company seeking to exploit a market niche that only information technology could enable. The two founders of the company recognized the need for ongoing investment if the company was to grow and to reach profitability, often referred to by the market as 'path to profitability' (P2P). This involved raising funds through a stock market flotation and the strengthening of its management team by bringing on board the former chief executive of ASDA (a large UK food retail supermarket chain).

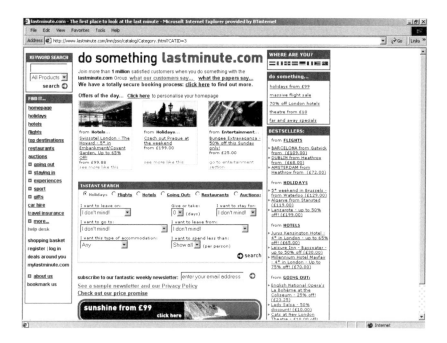

Figure 11.3 Lastminute.com

GE (General Electric company) describes itself as an integrated diverse organization present in many different sectors from manufacturing to financial services. While GE portrays a somewhat conservative image, it adopts a highly innovative and consistent approach to the management of its different businesses, driven for many years by the energy of its legendary chairman Jack Welch. GE has integrated the use of e-Commerce into the way it runs its businesses and has a separate Global Information eXchange division offering outsourced e-Commerce services to companies on a global basis. In realizing the potential that the Internet was bringing to the marketplace, Jack Welch sponsored a GE-wide program entitled 'destroyourbusiness.com' to examine ways in which the Web could reduce costs, increase responsiveness and eliminate bureaucracy. After the initial urgency to ensure that GE was not being left behind by competitors exploiting the Internet, GE has moderated its strategy. It recognizes that the Internet will not totally replace all that has gone before, but build upon its existing established and successful businesses to provide fresh opportunities to reach customers.

Lessons Learnt

To complement the concept of 'bricks and mortar' companies representing the traditional ways of selling based on physical locations visited by consumers, is the virtual store navigated by the 'click' of a mouse on the computer. Much of the analysis of Dot.Com failures focuses upon the need to achieve a better balance between the traditional 'bricks and mortar' and Internet start-up 'point and click' companies. One clear message emerging concerns the real dangers in trying to separate Internet initiatives from the traditional business. The most successful and innovative Internet players are looking to integrate their physical and virtual operations. Indeed, it would seem that the level of success is largely determined by how well the integration of physical and virtual operations is achieved.

The following case studies bring together a number UK-based companies that have emerged to form part of the Dot.Com economy and complement the US examples used elsewhere within the book. They illustrate the diversity of products and services now encompassed within the new economy.

Case Study – Egg

Egg, the UK telephone/Internet bank, was launched in the late 1990s and sought to create a new sort of organization. The idea was to establish a bank which would act as the customers' agent in managing their financial affairs and in processing their transactions online quickly and securely, as well as keeping them fully informed of their account details. Ultimately, the idea was to create an environment that, from a customer perspective, felt less constraining than a conventional bank. Extensive market research prior to launch had revealed a strong level of customer dissatisfaction with traditional banking. Customers complained that they were not treated as individuals, but most were resigned to the situation.

Egg saw an opportunity with the new economy to reinvent financial services to more closely match customer expectations. Two key aspects were the way the new economy had freed information and knowledge from physical and organizational boundaries and made it available as a value-added component of commodity products. In addition, the lower cost of doing business on the Internet meant that suppliers could do much more for their customers at an affordable cost. Customers using the Egg-branded transactional banking products are able to obtain assistance in choosing and purchasing recommended investments, insurance and mortgages from multiple suppliers. Online shopping services are also provided on the same basis by assisting those people who need to transact online. The service is held together by a personal balance sheet providing a fully integrated picture of a customer's financial affairs with multiple suppliers. Egg's understanding of the help customers really want with their financial affairs has brought immediate and resounding success. While its business plan was based upon 200,000 customers a year, it created 500,000 customers in its first six months of operation and its customer base now stands at more than 2 million customers.

Figure 11.4 Egg

Case Study – J Sainsbury

One aim of a new joint venture between supermarket J Sainsbury and Carlton, would allow viewers watching a TV chef working away in a kitchen and then have the ingredients of the dish being prepared delivered direct to their own home. This initiative links interactive digital TV to a publishing Web site and then to home shopping. The approach is viewed as being visionary in the sense that it is ultimately about entertainment in the same way that, traditionally, retailing has been about 'location, location, location'. Those involved consider that entertainment will play an ever-increasing role in people's shopping experience and there is a need to offer customers further convenience and entertainment value from shopping. This interactive TV and home shopping initiative is also driven by Sainsbury's belief that 20% of its future sales will occur outside its traditional 'bricks and mortar' stores.

A number of technologies have been identified such as interactive television, mobile phones, the Internet and cable television, that will form the basis of the 'new' shops for the future. Traditional retailers such as Sainsbury are not technologists, so ventures of this nature are creating companies that can build the 'new shops'. Clearly one of the biggest challenges faced by these joint ventures is the need to bring two very different organizational cultures and skills sets together.

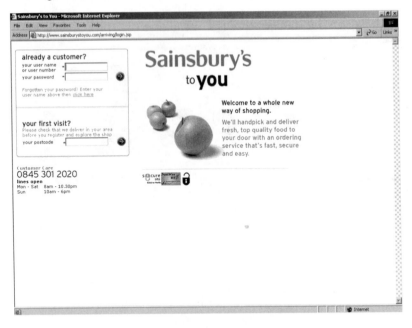

Figure 11.5   J Sainsbury

Case Study – Handbag.com

Women have been the fastest-growing group of Internet users, yet their needs and interests were not being well served by what was on offer. Not, that is, until the launch in October 1999 of handbag.com, a 50/50 joint venture between Boots plc and Hollinger Telegraph New Media.

Their Web site offers 18 categories of content, including careers, fashion and relationships. Users also have a range of opportunities to interact with each other through discussion groups chaired by well-known experts and moderated chat rooms. The popularity of community areas such as these has been one of the unexpected outcomes of the handbag.com story. The women who use the discussion boards have christened themselves 'handbaggers' and have also moved their meetings out of the Web space and into the real world.

The 300,000 visitors to the site every month provide valuable feedback that both drives site content and builds an impressive database of customers' preferences. Rather than insist on registration on the site, a 'give to get' principle rules, where handbag.com captures customer data in exchange for a useful service. For example, customers wanting a horoscope leave their date of birth, and for the

TV listings they leave their TV region. This is enriched by competition entries, which capture postcode and house number.

Figure 11.6 Handbag.com

Case Study – Peoplesound.com

Peoplesound.com is Europe's leading new music download site. In 1999 the company's four founders spotted an opportunity created by the changing structure of the music industry and Internet growth for a significant business, serving artists, consumers and record companies. Recent industry changes such as exploding marketing costs and less commercial success in launching acts have had a profound effect on record company economics. More than 11,000 artists are featured on the site and peoplesound.com receives 1.5 million visitors each month. Visitors to the site select the type of music they prefer and new navigation techniques direct them to music matching their taste. They can listen to selected tracks, using a technique called streaming, before downloading the track in MP3 format. Consumer preferences are tracked and opinions gathered. This market information is then sold to record companies so that, in addition to the detailed marketing data, they can also preview emerging talent and monitor how well new bands do on the peoplesound.com site before investing in a full launch. It is estimated that the industry writes off $5 billion a year in the cost of failed launches, so these services help the industry address the problem of decreasing margins and also become more efficient and responsive.

Figure 11.7 Peoplesound.com

Case Study – The Welding Institute

Experience has shown that structural failures of metal constructions, such as aeroplanes, bridges, motor vehicles etc., is often to do with welding and joining of materials. TWI founded in 1946 and formerly known as The Welding Institute, has developed a global network of expertize in welding and joining materials, and has spread this knowledge worldwide to ensure improved manufacturing environments and safer constructions.

TWI consists of individual fee paying members and associates ranging from specialist research organizations to large corporations and smaller engineering project teams, all of whom have access to 450 technology specialists based near Cambridge and a range of services. The Internet has allowed TWI to expand the scope of its services as well as its reach, previously constrained by the size of its staff. Activity is now reaching over 35,000 user sessions per month benefiting from the knowledge management environment established by TWI.

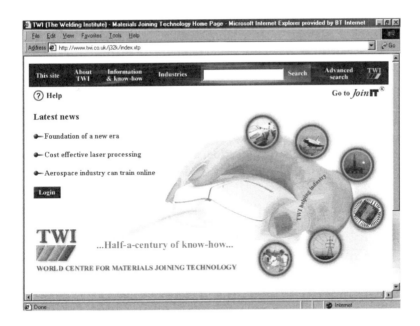

Figure 11.8   The Welding Institute

Case Study – Virgin Wines Online

Figure 11.9   Virgin Wines Online

With the ever-growing popularity for wine in the UK, several different marketing initiatives have emerged. Internet wine retailer Virgin Wines Online plans to make the purchase of wine less daunting and reach a greater marketplace of customers who are perhaps lacking in knowledge about wines.

Launched in June 2000, it is site where customers can find wines that they will like but might not have otherwise discovered. Emphasis is placed upon classifying wines by taste, rather then by region. Virgin Wines captures the knowledge of its customers by asking what they like, dislike and what they have never tried. With the help of this profile they develop an understanding of the customers' preferences so that customers can be guided to suitable choices from the 17,500 wines listed on the Web site.

Case Study – Generics Group

The Generics Group, established in 1986, was founded by Professor Gordon Edge to create wealth through technology in areas such as telecommunications, biotechnology and materials engineering. Today, this Cambridge (UK) based ideas factory has a global reputation, not only for technological consulting but also for turning brainwaves into businesses. It consists of approximately 250 employees, with research laboratories in Cambridge, Stockholm and Baltimore, and offices in Boston, Stockholm, Zurich and Tokyo. Generics was valued at more than £220 million when floated in December 2000.

Figure 11.10 The Generics Group

Employees are encouraged to invest personally in spin-off companies and the entrepreneurial are encouraged to develop their own ideas. The Innovation Exploitation Board (IEB), comprising a committee of employees drawn from across the company, discusses all the technology and business opportunities received by Generics, which ensures a rigorous but effective review process for any emerging opportunity.

Case Study – Ryanair and EasyJet

The de-regulation of the airline industry in Europe became fully effective in 1997 and brought significant advantages to European travellers. The increased competition resulted in the emergence of so-called 'low fare' carriers such Ryanair, EasyJet, Go, and Buzz that have brought about drastic price reductions and the availability of cheaper flights.

Ryanair and EasyJet are Europe's leading low-fare carriers. In the early 1990s Ryanair adopted a low fare model pioneered by Southwest Airlines in the US, and modified it for the European marketplace. The company flies a total of 55 routes across 12 different countries and carried in excess of 9 million passengers over the last year. Since its first flight in November 1995, EasyJet has grown from its Luton (north of London) base offering two routes from Luton to Glasgow and Edinburgh, served by two Boeing 737 aircraft, to an airline offering 44 routes from 17 European destinations and flying thirty 737 series aircraft.

With the introduction of their Internet sites both airlines have become huge success stories within the airline industry. Their Web strategy has allowed both companies to save over $30 million, by keeping marketing and distribution costs low and has revolutionized the way these airlines conduct their business. Ryanair recently announced that 84% (measured over a 12 month moving average) of its ticket sales were coming from its Web site (the most recent month being 91%). Indeed EasyJet is so confident in its Web strategy that it has moved away from telesales completely to ticket sales exclusively from its Web site www.EasyJet.com.

[1] UK high street newsagent and stationery products

Securing
e-Business

The Elusive Search for Security

The search for security is not a modern day phenomenon. Around 2000 B.C. the Egyptians developed what was perhaps the first key operated lock mechanism. This device consisted of a solid beam, carved from hardwood and hollowed from the end to create a slot. When locked, this beam was prevented from moving by the means of pegs in a staple, attached to the hollowed beam. Unlocking the lock required a key, typically a foot in length or more. This ancient design evolved into its modern day equivalent known as the tumbler lock, which still fundamentally uses the same technology. The only major difference is simply the size.

The centuries have gone by, with the same technology adequately serving the same purpose – offering an acceptable level of security for those that required it. In the last several decades, though, we have seen the need and demand for a new type of lock and key, one that cannot be physically discerned or touched, yet secures virtual connections and possessions that have significantly greater value than those protected by the old technology. Additionally, these new locks and keys transcend borders and geographies, providing added complexities. The advent of the digital information age requires sophisticated and multifaceted digital locks.

Introduction

This chapter explores the emerging security measures that are available to organizations wishing to make their electronic dealings more robust and secure. The increasing use of the Web and continued use of EDI, which embraces virtually all sectors, means that by the nature of the information exchanged, secure and impenetrable systems are of critical importance.

What then is the appropriate response from commerce, government agencies and standards bodies? Certainly the increasing fusion of different technologies has attracted much debate on the subject, as corporate and civil liberties are compromised and violated. Potential abuse through the use of computers and global networks is increasing daily, and new innovations in technology bring to bear novel new ways of abusing the system.

The debates have centred on a triad of thinking. Social scientists have advocated attempting to educate and reduce the imbalance between those that have a good grasp of the technology, and those that do not. A more ethical framework is re-enforced at different levels of education and a new culture is being implied. The lawyers see a need for the updating, and creation of new legislation, in order to address idiosyncrasies that are prevalent in the system which do not adequately cover new technology and work practices. Although in progress, the latter concerns have perhaps lagged more than they should. By far the greatest discourse has been from the technologists who see the way forward as the introduction of better systems and network security technologies.

Organizations face a paradox: the challenge is to implement and use 'friendly' systems, yet the user-friendliness and ease of access are two major factors that create a greater potential for misuse. As complex algorithms become more sophisticated and allow greater levels of security, users are subjected to increased processing time frames. We can never achieve total security, and will always find ourselves playing catch-up with those who can compromise the system. Even when we do have widespread access to futurist biometric security technologies, such as retina, fingerprint and voice recognition, methods to bypass and foil the systems will blossom in the same manner that these technologies have. Technologies to break the systems receive the same efforts as those trying to protect – the rewards of compromising a system can be substantial.

Successful operation in this environment is then derived from understanding the tools available, and to *get close* to total security, or at least closer than your competitor or potential cyber criminal. An optimization process is usually considered, where a balance between security and ease of use is achieved. The process and end result depends upon an assessment of the security risks faced by the organization. This implicitly implies the need for a strategy, usually requiring commitment from senior management, coupled with extensive IT audits to uncover improper use of the security tools available. All too often, it is not the underlying technology that compromises the system, but ill-trained personnel or errors in the installation and set-up process. Security of the system is only as secure as its weakest link and is as much about people as technology, if not more.

In the following sections, we explore some of the technologies and terms associated with security approaches that are being used to secure e-Business, their adoption in enterprise systems and the Internet, as well as examining technologies being developed for future applications. The processes possess a wide range of terminology and jargon, which are discussed, clarified and explained.

Cyber Crime

The image that computer security often conjures up, due largely to the popular press, is one associated with the teenage hacker, trespassing in critical and confidential system domains, leaving cryptic messages and sometimes causing damage. Whether this electronic trespassing is by those who are seeking an intellectual challenge, or those intent on more fraudulent purposes, it is a real and worrying threat, especially with global e-Business traffic ever increasing. This modern worry has attracted much media attention and alerted organizations, often of significant size with matching security systems, to the vulnerability of their set-ups. There are numerous examples:

▷ In 1994, a 24-year-old Russian programmer relieved a prominent US bank of $10 million.

▷ An estimated $550 million loss, suffered at the hands of hackers by a group of unnamed US and UK banks in 1996. The incident was reported in the London popular press, but no bank ever came forward and confirmed it.

▷ A hacker known as "Maxus" broke into a US online merchant database, allegedly acquiring as many as 350,000 customer credit card numbers. Another known as "Curador" stole 25,000 databases from 13 e-Commerce sites.

Perhaps less publicized, are threats that originate from more mundane sources than the hacker – often these are more serious and result in a larger monetary loss. Computer-based fraud is thought to cost many billions of dollars worldwide and most likely, this number is underestimated as most organizations are too embarrassed to admit to it. The key to protecting computer networks from unauthorized access lies in the effective utilization of modern data security technologies, such as encryption, authentication and effective firewalls, discussed in detail in this chapter. Not only does this protect against malicious intent, but also offers individuals data privacy that protects their electronic communication.

Cyber crime in its variety of forms (cyber terrorism, computer fraud, malicious intent etc.) is high profile and gains much attention, and consequently, traditional thinking and a first response by many when asked about security results in security being defined or discussed in terms of secrecy and confidentiality. This is only one aspect of a number of security aspects that are relevant to e-Business, with others being perhaps even more important in many respects. It is critical that information that needs to be accessed, can be at the relevant time and that accuracy is maintained. The availability of data ensures that information is accessible within set time frames, without extensive security algorithms making retrieval times unacceptable. Integrity of the data and information used to make decisions attracts many security implications – emphasis centres on threats of the data being inadvertently altered, or changed without authorization. The old adage of 'garbage in, garbage out' is apt in this case. These three aspects of security, *Confidentiality, Integrity* and *Availability*, have become to be known as the CIA model. The framework is a useful one for those thinking about security aspects within their organizations. All three aspects of the model are covered within the scope of this book, but this chapter mainly focuses on the confidentiality aspects of the CIA model.

Passwords and PINs

Newer encryption techniques are a vast improvement on the traditional password system, yet the associated cost and implementation issues of implementing crypto-graphical methods universally are slowing their take up, not to mention the impact that they have on high speed networks. Password security is simple, cheap and a very effective defence against computer crime, but only if used effectively. Despite all the new technologies coming to market in the next few years, the majority of security-based interaction will still consist of a password or PIN being utilized, perhaps in conjunction with another security device.

Unfortunately, something like 80% of all passwords are contained in a few hundred known names or words, making the choice of password of crucial importance. All too often uncomplicated guidelines to password choice are ignored, making the technology less effective. The repercussions of not adhering to security guidelines are all too clear in retrospect when vulnerable data is violated, especially within systems where passwords can be re-used, or users are not forced to change passwords within a set time period.

The increasing use of the Internet for computer crimes is a well known occurrence; the Federal Bureau of Investigations (FBI) claimed that in 80% of the FBI's computer crime investigations, the Internet was used to gain illegal access to systems in the mid 1990s. This had prompted emergency teams (such as the Computer Emergency Response Team on the Internet) to send alerts over the global network warning millions of users about illegal network monitoring – the act of installing 'sniffer' software to monitor network port activities, and to collect log-in information, most often passwords.

Although passwords can be viewed as a dated technology, if used sensibly they represent a very effective and cheap security solution. Unfortunately, it is the laxity of the users that usually result in passwords being compromised. Often, users will not change their passwords unless they are forced to. In an environment that allows re-useable passwords, and where general security is low profile, the potential risks are enormous. A survey[1] on the use of passwords outlined results utilized to substantiate the hypothesis that password usage did not follow simple known guidelines, such as the use of abstract words containing several characters, typically more than six. The results are outlined in Figure 12.1. Almost three quarters of the passwords used contained six letters or less. A computer will only take a few seconds to break a password that is a person's name, up to two minutes to break a password if the word is found in the dictionary but significantly longer if it is a combination of letters and numbers.

One of the challenges of many organizations, is one of ensuring that 'strong' passwords are used and maintained. This is not easy, given the numerous systems and access points most employees have today, resulting in many passwords being used, or a few being re-used. This has also led to an increased manifestation of the passwords being listed on a post-it, or pad situated close to a desktop computer providing serious compromises to network security. Much debate has centred on the continued education of the workforce on security concerns. All too often, one can walk around an office with many desktops leaving open access to secure and critical systems left unattended.

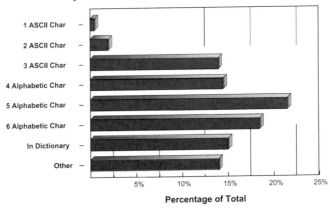

Figure 12.1 Password distribution

As Warman[2] states, assuming one checking process takes 1 millisecond, a system with a similar password distribution could have all of its passwords compromised within 89 hours.

Prevention of unauthorized access can be enhanced through the use of a challenge and response system, used in conjunction with the password system. This approach, which is relatively cheap and gaining wider acceptance and deployment, consists of an electronic device which is used to obtain a seemingly random code in response to a logon input. As codes are different each time, typically changing every few seconds, hackers can not use the same code to enter the system.

Viruses

Nobody likes a biological virus – especially a nasty one that can knock you out for many days. Unfortunately, we now have to deal with additional viral threats on our machines at work and home. These annoying and often malicious software programs, that on execution insert copies of themselves, continue to become more prevalent and damaging. Regrettably, the hackers and virus-writers are just about as smart as the virus detectives. It seems almost inevitable that the scary race against these cyber criminals continues to require more innovative methods to overcome them.

Contrary to popular belief, viruses are not only about the Internet and predate its commercial success. Early variants utilized floppy diskettes to propagate themselves once hard drives were infected. Managing these risks was relatively straightforward with antivirus software detecting a small population of known infections. The rise of the Internet allowed a much more sophisticated line of attack, freeing the virus from its floppy diskette constraints, and one of the early progenitors to the modern day virus was the 'Internet Worm', released in 1988. This was a program that replicated itself in order to infect connected computers (known as a Worm) and was written and let loose into the Internet community by Robert T. Morris Jr, a student at Cornell University. The worm possessed a list of over 400 passwords to bypass connected systems, and also utilized a complex algorithm to break unknown passwords. The small program infected 6,000 computer systems in a short period of time, replicating at an astonishing speed and hence not only causing havoc with systems being violated, but also extensive processing congestion on the systems that were infected.

It was then that the Computer Emergency Response Team (CERT), at Carnegie Mellon University, a federally funded organization, was instituted as a central clearing house of computer security information and technical advisor on incident response for companies and government agencies. At CERT's inception, only about 60,000 hosts were connected to the Internet. Today, there are more than 50 million hosts using the Internet, a number that continues to track upwards at an astonishing rate. Consequently, the number of security vulnerabilities and attackers has risen correspondingly and modern day viruses are sophisticated in their nature and can proliferate across the globe in a matter of minutes and hours. The examples and cases are numerous, with a few outlined below.

In March 2001, a worm known as Magistr augured a new era of vicious attacks on computers. Unlike earlier worms, which clogged E-mail servers, Magistr sat dormant for a month on the infected PC, after which the worm destroyed data files and attacked the CMOS (which boots up the PC).

On 18 September 2001, the Nimda Internet virus (a variant of the Code Red virus) attacked at least 100,000 computer systems nationwide in the US alone, crippling many business operations. Nimda was the first virus that could attack Internet-based systems in five different ways, including Web sites and E-mail messages. The Nimda worm was entry path for other malicious behaviour. It added an account called "guest" and gave it administrator privileges before opening the local hard drive to the public on the entire Internet. Nimda not only sent E-mails to everyone in personal address books, but also probed for vulnerable servers, and modified the Web pages of the infected server so that they included the virus. Computer industry analysts estimated that the damage it caused, far exceeded the approximate $3 billion cost of its summertime predecessor, the Code Red worm.

Driving by the Rear View Mirror

The security industry is a huge one, and anti-virus software products have become a multi-million dollar industry – Norton and Symantec have almost become household names. Products such as these are in use in virtually all organizations, and the majority are based against specific programs or viruses that have been identified (referred to as signature based detection). This however causes some issues such as the software is always lagging the most up-to-date virus which has been identified. This 'gap' before virus definitions are distributed continues to shrink with automatic updating once a user logs onto a network, as an example, however there are still numerous complications. An increasingly large community of users in an organization are working remotely, and it may potentially be anything between several days and weeks before they log into the corporate network forcing an update. Furthermore, variants of a virus continue to become widespread with an ever increasing frequency.

Clearly the signature-based method is important, but today's environment requires a more sophisticated multi-layered defence against the various threats against a numerous number of viruses. Signature-based detection is being increasingly used together with other approaches discussed later.

When examining what a virus is, one can essentially outline a number of different types of malicious code that are collectively referred to as viruses. A Worm is a script that the recipient does not have to run for it to become active. These are typically coded in Visual Basic for Applications (VBA) or Visual Basic Script (VBS) and are mostly hidden within macros of popular programs. Given most are transmitted through E-mail, and with the success of the Microsoft Office suite of programs, usually this approach leverages Microsoft applications. The situation is exacerbated as many toolkits are available, which allow relatively novice users (sometimes termed 'script kiddies') to easily assemble a malicious virus. Furthermore, with several modular design toolkits available, many variants of a virus can be created, allowing numerous permutations.

An increasingly popular mechanism is to embed VBS into an E-mail formatted in Hypertext Mark-up Language (HTML), which is almost the defacto standard for popular E-mail applications. The sinister aspect of this approach is that a program does not need to be run and the script is automatically executed as soon as the E-mail is previewed or opened. Infection occurs without pre-warning and deleting the E-mail does not make any difference.

Another approach, although rare, is using a spying tool which allows malicious code to propagate, and once installed into a host machine can allow the hacker to access the machine using remote control agents. Functionality can extend to any task a legitimate user would be able to perform. A key aspect of this approach is the dormant nature of the code, usually remaining on the infected system for months. Perhaps one of the most famous incidents of this was the Microsoft QAZ spy, which allowed hackers to access development PCs within Microsoft, although as with many of these cases the exact details were never disclosed.

Sandboxes and Heuristics

Clearly anti-virus software has a part to play, and this is being augmented by additional tools that provide a more proactive approach to security. The first of these is known as a Sandbox – essentially a software application that possesses specific rules that prevents certain actions within applications or the operating system. As an example, this could be barring external access to document folders that are typically local in nature (i.e. 'My Documents'), or preventing ActiveX applications accessing specific aspects of the PC. The sandbox prevents applications, such as Internet Explorer, to do something outside of predetermined normal operations. The maintenance and administration of sandboxes are relatively flexible and modern applications are robust enough to be customized to be genuinely useful, controlled either by a global administrator or locally for specific communities of users. The difficulties arise in the definition of what is normal behaviour, especially for increasingly complex users and applications.

The second approach, known as Heuristics, is one where a set of rules are applied to an application to determine whether the application may contain malicious commands or behaviours, especially for sequences of commands typically found in virus code. Once configured effectively (there is always a balance of how finely tuned the approach can be to minimize false alarms), detection rates can be as high as 80% to 90%. This approach is especially effective with potentially malicious code in script or macro languages such as VBS and VBA discussed earlier.

Organizations are also looking at using blocking techniques to prevent malicious code penetrating the organization. Breaches are prevented by restricting internal users from accessing questionable Web sites that may contain viruses. In essence, certain URLs are blocked from being accessed and users are limited in terms of where they can surf. Many companies are also not allowing customers to download executable files, or at least blocking certain code outside of the usual files (for example Microsoft applications) such as .xls, .vbs etc. Most software is sophisticated enough not to be fooled about a file type by the manual adjustment of the extension type.

A newer approach is one of having all executable software digitally signed, and PCs within the corporate network are configured to check this signature before execution. Signature only comes from a trusted party and hence controlled access can be achieved. This approach is robust, although presents many issues, not least of which is the sheer administrative burden it imposes, coupled with user inflexibility. Windows XP already supports the functionality, and it will be interesting to see if the approach matures.

Public Key Infrastructure

Public Key Infrastructure (PKI) refers to a set of tools, approaches and techniques that can be used to secure interaction between parties. PKI as a terminology began to be used in the mainstream in the mid 1990s, and gained popular press a few years later, although most of its underlying technology has been around since the late 1970s. PKI uses a number of tools such as cryptography, encryption, keys, digital signatures and certificates amongst others. These aspects are explored as well as the management of the process and tools such as certificates and keys.

What is Cryptography

Cryptography is the art of writing, or solving ciphers – disguised ways of writing or representing symbols. It has been increasingly utilized to protect communications, especially on networks in the past few decades, and the process of encrypting data has gained credence as a secure and robust mechanism. Encryption is the process of altering data (termed plaintext) into unintelligible data (termed cipher text). This transformation requires the use of keys to encrypt and decrypt the data, discussed in the next section. The process of hiding data behind a sequence of code words alone is not the answer to thorough security though, and is usually one element of a range of crypto graphical techniques to protect networks and users. Cryptography has been around for decades, and attracts large amounts of military funding, not only in the creation of new ciphers, but in cryptanalysis – the art of breaking them.

The Use of Keys

Everyone is familiar with the use of keys – two people wanting access to the same house, protected by a lock, would require the same key. Similarly users can transmit data through physical and virtual networks around the globe, but to ensure that their communications are not tampered with, or integrity violated, some form of protection is required. In Figure 12.2, the sender is using encryption to 'disguise' the data sent, by the use of an algorithm – mathematical algorithms are used to scramble the message and a message string is produced and appended to the original message. The recipient would then use the same algorithm to decode the string. The coding and decoding processes are controlled by a *key*.

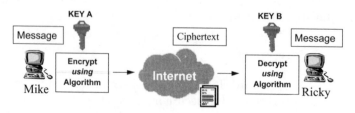

Figure 12.2 Symmetric keys

Simple encryption of text (referred to as cipher text) cannot be decrypted unless the receiver has access to an identical key. In situations where Key A and Key B are identical, the process is termed a *symmetric* (secret key) cipher. This process is outlined in Figure 12.2, where the encryption algorithms are usually public (discussed later) and the symmetric keys are private.

This is not the exclusive case though, and situations are possible where a pair of distinct, yet mathematically related, keys are utilized for cryptographic purposes – this process is known as an *asymmetric* (public key) cipher. One key is only known to its owner (the private key) which is used for decryption, while the other is publicly known, referred to as the public key, used for encryption. In Figure 12.3 the symmetric key is used in conjunction with an algorithm to encrypt the message and Ricky's (the recipient) public asymmetric key is used to encrypt the symmetric key. When used in conjunction with Internet Mail, once MIME attachments are received, then Ricky's private asymmetric key is used to decrypt the symmetric key that is then used to decrypt the message. If someone else intercepted the MIME attachments, it would be impossible to decrypt them without having access to Ricky's private asymmetric key, which he alone retains.

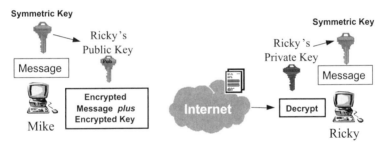

Figure 12.3 Asymmetric keys

In general, symmetric ciphers, or secret-key encryption, tend to be more popular due to the excellent levels of performance they can provide, when compared to asymmetric ciphers, or public key encryption. For instance, DES, a symmetric cipher, is about 100 times faster in software than RSA, an asymmetric cipher (DES and RSA are discussed in the next section). Consequently asymmetric ciphers are not often used to encipher data directly, but are instead used alongside symmetric ciphers.

Asymmetric ciphers (like RSA) can be used in conjunction with symmetric ciphers (like DES) – once a secure communication channel is established by two parties, a key to use for symmetric ciphers (e.g. DES) can be exchanged to decrypt all subsequent messages. The transmission of a secret key across a network is risky, and therefore an asymmetric cipher (e.g. RSA) is used to ensure that the exchange of keys is not compromised. This provides high performance coupled with increased security in the exchange of keys.

Public key cryptography was invented in 1976 by Diffie and Hellman[3] – the system provided two keys, one public and one private. All information communications utilized the public key, without the private key ever being shared.

Algorithms

Many different cryptographic algorithms are in use today, but by far the two most popular and established are RSA and DES, with the latter's successors, Triple DES and AES gaining more prominence. Other algorithms also gained popularity in the last decade, IDEA being the best known example. It is claimed that these methods are virtually unbreakable, and the proponents state that it would take supercomputers years to decode encrypted messages using these security methods. However with each new crypto graphical technology, advances in hardware continue to challenge these claims.

Rivest-Shamir-Adleman

The Rivest-Shamir-Adleman (RSA) method uses prime numbers and the use of keys – special numbers used to encode and decipher messages. The technique was developed in the late 1970s at MIT with public funding by three individuals who have given their names to the algorithm: Ronald Rivest, Adi Shamir and Leonard Adleman.

This method possesses the capability of utilizing a known and distributed public key, overcoming the problems associated with many other encryption methods (including DES). Private communication therefore does not require the secure exchange of encryption and decryption keys between sender and receiver prior to secure communication. RSA should not be viewed as an alternative to DES, but rather an enhancement – the technique is widely used in the exchange of symmetric keys. This provides added safety, without the performance issues that would be experienced if the whole message was encrypted using RSA. Furthermore, RSA provides the added feature of a digital signature capability. It is the latter functionality that had fuelled much of the growth of the technology, rather than encryption.

RSA is widely licensed and incorporated into many company products and platforms including products from all the major providers. The technology has also been incorporated into a number of formal standards and accepted by industry standard groups:

▷ RSA is utilized within the Internet Privacy Enhanced Mail (PEM) initiative.

▷ The Society for World-wide Interbank Financial Telecommunication (SWIFT) standard uses RSA.

▷ RSA is an element of the CCITT X.509 security standard for messaging.

▷ RSA algorithms are accepted by the International Standards Organization (ISO) 9796 guide-lines on security.

Data Encryption Standard

The Data Encryption Standard (DES) was adopted by the National Bureau of Standards in 1977 as an official standard. The standard was developed by IBM as a 64-bit key cryptosystem and implemented widely as a 56-bit system. In its early adoption, almost 17 man years were spent attempting to break the system in order to verify the technique's robustness. This provided a strong level of confidence in the system. However with the advances in technology continuing at a phenomenal pace a successor was recognized as necessary and Triple DES (3DES) was conceived – a 112-bit key system. DES has been studied widely and is perhaps the most well known and established system in the world.

As well as single user encryption, to safe-guard personal files for instance, DES supports symmetric cipher encryption, or secret key encryption – both sender and receiver must share the same key. As it was designed initially to operate on hardware, it is very fast – typically a thousand times faster than RSA, and up to a hundred times when implemented via software. Despite its wide take up, the standard's largest short coming is that it does not possess the capabilities to support public key encryption techniques.

DES and Triple DES continued to be successfully deployed until a National Council Research Report in 1996 (and subsequent changes to policy in 1998) recommended certain changes and updates. This was driven by continued criticism that the standard was out of date and also by an event in 1998, when a $250,000 special purpose machine built by the Electronic Frontier Foundation (a civil liberties organization) cracked a DES encrypted message in 56 hours. This was subsequently improved by enhancing the machine with an additional 100,000 networked PCs, bringing the time down to 22 hours.

Advanced Encryption Standard

Clearly a replacement for DES was overdue and in 1997, the National Institute of Standards and Technology (NIST) approved a competition (with a deadline of 15 June 1998) for the replacement of DES which would need to have a minimum key length of 128 bits. They termed this the Advanced Encryption Standard (AES) and by the deadline, 15 out of the 21 approaches submitted had met the minimum criteria established, with five finalists selected each with rather esoteric names:

▷ MARS – IBM designers

▷ RC6 – RSA Security backed

▷ Rijndael – two Belgian cryptographers

▷ Serpent – three cryptographers from the UK, Israel and Denmark

▷ Twofish – Counterpane Systems, a US consulting firm

In December 2001, "Rijndael" was announced as the winner, and all US federal departments were to begin using the standard by May 2002. Proponents also declared that AES would take up to 149 trillion years to crack a single 128-bit AES key using computers of the time. There is no doubt that AES is a strong standard although with advances in technology progressing – especially if it continues to follow Moore's Law – within a decade or two, AES will need to be further enhanced, not so differently to its predecessor DES.

International Data Encryption Algorithm (IDEA)

First published in 1991, this symmetric key algorithm has gained attention and favour with users. The key length of IDEA is over twice that of DES and patented both in and outside of the US.

IDEA became popular when it was incorporated in the widely used Pretty Good Privacy (PGP) electronic mail security programme, which was distributed freely on the Web (discussed later). As a result, it was probably one of the most widely used encryption algorithms for electronic mail in the 1990s.

Authentication

Usually associated with encryption is the authentication of messages, used by the recipient to ensure that the message has not been tampered with during transit. Confidentiality may not be an underlying requirement, but the receiver of the incoming message needs to be assured that the message was not modified in any way, prior to receiving it. Authentication verifies that the message has indeed originated from the sender unmolested – the two parties can be sure of each other's identity by the use of a protocol.

To ensure that the contents of a message have not been tampered with, an additional code is appended to the message which is a function of the message – this integrity check value is then regenerated by the recipient of the message. If the two values agree, the data has not been modified. A more robust mechanism is to utilize a secret key in the process of generating the integrity check value – one such mechanism, widely employed by the financial industry, is known as the Message Authentication Code (MAC).

If the protocol is supported by a public key scheme (as is the case when using RSA) it is important to ensure that users of other public keys do indeed own them. This is supported in the X series of standards (X.509) and is achieved through the use of certificates and authorities (see later).

Digital Signatures and Repudiation

Digital signatures provide an additional value over and above message authentication. The recipient of a signed message has *proof* that the message was from the sender. The electronic signature is therefore message dependent as well as signer dependent. The distinction is an important added value, especially in applications such as electronic funds transfer, as the signature cannot be attached to any message and cannot be forged by any recipients.

The signature is formed by computing a value (known as the hash function) representing a complex function of the data transmitted, effectively making a digital 'fingerprint' of the data (known as the message digest). This signature is then encrypted using a private key, as outlined in Figure 12.4. The received signature is subsequently validated using an algorithm (such as RSA) as an element of a multi-step process:

▷ The receiver computes the hash function using his or her own algorithm;

▷ The function is then transformed using a public or private key and compared to the computed function; and

▷ The results are compared – an identical match would signify a valid signature.

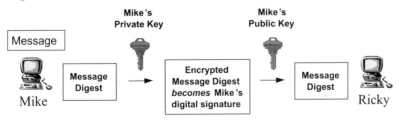

Figure 12.4   Digital signatures and repudiation

A certificate(s) may also accompany a digital signature, providing proof of the identity and public key of the signer – this is discussed in more detail later. Digital signatures utilize the strengths of public key encryption. As both sender and receiver can verify that the document did indeed originate from the person who 'signed' it, digital signatures cannot be repudiated. The term describes the act of a user denying receiving or originating a message. This feature allows digitally signed documents to be legally binding, and is referred to as *non-repudiation*.

Finding the Key – A Question of Management

By the very nature of public key cryptography, one must be able to publicly let others know of their own key, and have access to a mechanism to locate and verify others' keys. Without this, the system does not work. The management of keys is provided through Certification Authorities (CAs), facilitated via the use of Certificates and maintained by Certificate Revocation Lists (CRLs).

Certificates, Certification Authorities and Revocation Lists

A certificate is simply a digital data structure that is used for the purpose of mapping public keys to certain attributes, for example a name or entity. Certificates are issued by Certification Authorities, and verify that the person in question does in fact own the key in question. This certificate is signed by the authority's own private key, as outlined in Figure 12.5.

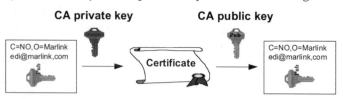

Figure 12.5 Certificates

For instance, there has to be some mechanism for other users to be able to identify the true owner of a public key – the digital certificate performs this function, much like a general item of identification such as a passport, or driving licence. The certificate itself is signed by a third party certifying its legitimacy – the role of the Certification Authority (CA). The role of the CA can be likened to a notary, or credit bureau.

Certificates hold a variety of information, such as a distinguished name, public keys, validity periods of the certificate (i.e. expiration date), serial numbers and so on. A distinguished name is a globally unique name, formed in a hierarchical structure, used with certificates to provide a name for identifying an individual (or entity) – for instance individuals, organizations, devices and so on. An example of a distinguished name may be:

Country = US

State = New York

Organization = ACME Co

Organization Unit = Sales

Common Name = Rukesh Kaura

In this case, the entity is an individual, located in the Sales department of ACME Co, based in the US. Certificates attest to the legitimacy of a public key. Importantly, certificates are also used to ensure the authenticity of digital signatures, with secure authentication involving the enclosure of the certificate(s) with the message sent. For anyone to be able to check on the validity of a certificate, or to get access to the public element of a key, the certificate needs to be stored in a publicly accessible database. Most implementations advocate the use of structures outlined in the CCITT X.509 directory standard, allowing an accepted format for the reading and writing of certificates. The standard, originally developed by ISO and the ITU in 1988, has since been updated and was adopted in various Internet standards, such as S/MIME, appearing in applications such as Netscape Navigator and the Visa and MasterCard SET standards. The newer version removed the requirements to use X.400 style addressing, allowing domain name system style addressing, as used on the Internet (i.e. name@domain).

A certification authority (CA) provides a reference point to vouch for the binding between a user's distinguished name and public keys within an organization – an authority trusted by users to create and assign certificates. The CA will publicise its public key, which must be trustworthy and accepted for users to gain confidence. Each CA is free to set its own identification criteria prior to issuing certificates. Typically, this may mean a driving licence, to more stringent identification methods, such as fingerprints. Each CA should publicize their own criteria, which in turn dictates the level of confidence each user has in that authority.

A number of organizations already provide CA services, and several on the Internet itself (such as Verisign amongst others). Often, a CA may provide a certificate from a higher level CA, vouching for the legitimacy of its key – for instance this may be a University who has obtained a certificate from a Value Added Network (VAN) provider for instance. This structure provides hierarchies of CAs. This hierarchy is also well illustrated by the Internet domain, through the use of Policy Certification

Authorities (PCAs). The CA system was actually developed by the Internet Society, as an element of its PEM (Privacy Enhanced Mail) environment where PCAs are utilized. The role of PCAs are to issue public-key certificates to CAs and certify CAs. Guidelines are drawn up by PCAs, under the supervision and guidance of the Internet society, to be implemented and used by CAs. In general, PCAs carry responsibility for its sub-domains, and are accountable to their higher domain. In the case of the Internet, this would be the Internet Policy Registration Authority (IPRA).

What would happen if you lost your key, or suspected a key to have been violated in some manner? These administrative type questions are handled through the use of Certificate Revocation Lists (CRLs). CRLs are simply lists of keys that should not be accepted. They are necessary for the identification of certificates that are no longer valid for various reasons (i.e. the validity dates have expired, distinguished names have changed, the key has been lost, or the private element of the key has been compromised). CRLs are maintained by the CA, who is responsible for these administrative tasks for certificates issued by that CA. Checks against CRLs are usually performed automatically by software, typically a User Agent which may house several CRLs from different CAs.

Some Legal Consequences

The increasing use of digital signatures and certificates has highlighted many 'grey' areas where the legal implications of the technology are concerned. These are discussed in more detail within Chapter 13 on the legal aspects of e-Business.

Governmental Initiatives

With the increasing digitization of our assets and other personal information, it is no surprise that governmental agencies are looking to implement appropriate measures, including legislation, to ensure that they are ahead of the game. This has not always been straightforward, as illustrated by the efforts of the US, and indeed the US is not alone in this situation. Digital signature laws passed in Germany and Italy in 1997 were exceptionally strict and technology rigid, which made the use of them very difficult. In fact the European Union has some of the strictest data protection legislation compared to anywhere in the world.

The Capstone Project

Following the Computer Security Act of 1987, the US Government's initiative to establish standards for public cryptography, known as

Capstone, was launched under the auspices of NIST (National Institute of Standards and Technology) and NSA (National Security Agency). NIST, formerly the National Bureau of Standards, issues standards – the Computer Security Act of 1987 authorized NIST to develop standards for ensuring security of unclassified material in Government systems. It was NIST that promoted DES as the official standard in 1977, followed by AES (discussed earlier). The NSA's mandate is to protect the country's secrets, intercepting and decoding communications since its inception in 1952 and it holds some of the most advanced crypto graphical technologies, as well as having access to huge financial and computer resources. The Capstone initiative called for the establishment of four major standards for:

▷ A bulk data encryption algorithm

▷ A hash function

▷ A digital signature algorithm

▷ A key exchange protocol

The data encryption algorithm was developed and named Skipjack, coded on hardware known as the Clipper Chip. The hash function that was defined was named the Secure Hash Standard (SHS). The digital signature was known as the Digital Signature Standard (DSS). Of the four standards, only SHS had been officially adopted as a Government standard, with Clipper and DSS attracting much controversy that had delayed their official acceptance. The reasons are interesting and representative of the issues that agencies face when attempting to introduce new technologies such as these.

The 'Clipper' (Skipjack) Chip

The US Government had been aware of the need for an effective encryption method that could be widely deployed within the US, being an element of the US administration's telecommunications initiative. The result had been the birth of the Clipper Chip, a microcircuit that provided privacy through encryption developed by the National Security Agency (NSA). Clipper was also sometimes referred to as Skipjack, named after its underlying algorithm due to potential trademark conflicts with the name 'Clipper'. The driving force behind the development of Clipper had undoubtedly been the frustrated efforts of national security agencies having to combat encrypting technologies that were not under government control. The wide-scale use of Clipper, through the endorsement of the government, was to allow access to information encrypted with Clipper by federal agencies, facilitated through specified government agencies having access to one of the keys provided with each chip, in what is termed a *key escrow* system. The keys would be kept by one or more third parties, known as escrow agencies.

The chip itself contained a 64-bit algorithm, called 'Skipjack' which used 80-bit keys (as opposed to 56 for DES) and had 32 rounds for scrambling (compared with 16 for DES). The chip had been developed so that the algorithm could not be read from the hardware – in other words, it could not be reverse engineered.

There were concerns that there may be un-documented 'trapdoors', deliberately included to allow government agencies back-door access, and the International Chamber of Commerce and the European Union had declared that it would not accept a system that was kept secret by the US Government, especially a system for which the keys are potentially held by government. This is far from surprising, as foreign customers certainly did not want US Government officials listening in on their communications. Added to this was the fact that the US Government wanted to make the use of the technology law, meaning users in the States would have to ensure that recipients of messages around the globe would also have to use the chip. The initiative never gained critical mass, and was illustrative of a technology push approach.

The Digital Signature Standard

It was in the early 1990s, that the National Institute of Standards and Technology (NIST) was instructed to advocate a single digital signature algorithm as an US standard, between several contenders. The result was the Digital Signature Standard (DSS) which provided a standard authentication technology using the Digital Signature Algorithm (DSA), available without any licensing or royalty fees.

Again, the introduction of DSS caused some issues with the security marketplace, primarily as most organizations were already widely using RSA for their algorithms, but NIST had developed its own digital signatures (SHS – Secure Hash Standard). This caused some potential inconvenience for hardware and software vendors, as RSA had become the defacto standard in the industry. In addition to this, there were some real concerns about the secure aspects of the technology, with NIST revising its original 512-bit key size, up to 1024-bits after much public criticism. In contrast, some of the newer initiatives such as Identrus use keys up to 2048-bits.

Secure Hash Standard (SHS)

This hash function, proposed by NIST and the NSA, had been accepted as an official government standard, and was designed to be used in conjunction with the Digital Signature Standard (DSS). A hash function is used to generate a string, known as the *message digest*, that is representative of the original message (a longer string of text). For performance reasons the message digest is used for digital signatures, as they can be computed in a shorter time using the shorter string.

SHS can, from a variable input size, generate a 160-bit hash function. This was a little slower than popular industry wide used hash functions, such as MD4 and MD5 (which stand for Message Digest 4 and 5 respectively).

US Initiatives – The Next Generation

In February 1998, the Department of Justice and the FBI created the National Infrastructure Protection Center (NIPC) at FBI Headquarters in Washington. The center was a joint government and private sector partnership that includes representatives from the relevant agencies of federal, state, and local government. The concept for the NIPC grew out of recommendations of the President's Commission on Critical Infrastructure Protection and from the government's experiences in dealing with illegal intrusions into government and private sector computer systems over the years.

In May 1998, President Clinton announced two new directives; Presidential Decision Directives (PDD) 62 and 63 which highlighted the growing range of unconventional threats that the US faced such as cyber terrorism. PDD-63 specifically focused on protection from both physical and cyber attack. The NIPC was part of a broader framework and served as the national focal point for threat assessment, warning, investigation, and response to attacks on the critical infrastructures. A significant part of its mission involved establishing mechanisms to increase the sharing of vulnerability and threat information between the government and private industry.

Secure Messaging

Since its humble beginnings in 1969 as an experimental US Defense Department network called ARPANET, the Internet has grown. This growth continues at an amazing pace, transforming it into a global metropolis, and like all large cities it is having to face the ugly face of crime. This has led to the need for, and introduction of, several Internet-based security standards – somewhat of a turnaround, as the Internet was never intended to be a secure network, rather one that advocated the free spirit of open communication of its various governmental and academic research communities. As the use of e-Business increases on the Internet, privacy issues have also become increasingly paramount.

Many organizations have not fully considered the impact of adequately securing their e-Business communications – encryption is certainly not as expensive and is now provided as a standard functionality with a large range of applications. This is fine with traffic internal to the organization, as the software automatically encrypts/decrypts messages without the user being tacitly aware of the fact, but it causes problems when users are attempting to communicate with other vendor's products – the techniques are sometimes proprietary. The standards issue is once again key and the problem is being alleviated with public key encryption being more widely available and employed.

We examine some of the standards that established the foundation of today's popular approaches and those being widely adopted to re-address the lack of security on the Internet, which in turn is helping to further fuel the growth in the use of the Web for commerce.

Internet Privacy Enhanced Mail

The primary focus of the initiative for Privacy Enhanced Mail (PEM), started in 1985, was to provide a level of security for E-mail users in the enormous Internet community. Although PEM was oriented towards the Internet mail environment, the technology could be usefully employed in a wider range of environments. Essentially the technology supported authentication, message integrity and confidentiality via encryption, using RSA's algorithms for public keys and DES for the encryption of the actual messages. PEM provided a variety of services, including an optional confidentiality service, which if elected protects messages while stored in a user's mailbox, whether this was a desktop machine, or remote mailbox maintained on Message Transfer Agents (MTAs). Additionally it provided message integrity checking and originator authentication.

Most E-mail systems at the time did not support facilities to verify messages that had been forwarded – the message may well be different to the one sent by the originator. This has serious implications for electronic business, especially when E-mail was used for transmission of purchase orders and delivery confirmations, for instance. PEM provided for non-repudiation – i.e. it allowed the verification of messages forwarded to other parties. Not only was the message content then verified, but also the identity of the originator. Cryptography was supported in the PEM environment allowing flexibility to use either secret-key or private-key algorithms, although public-key cryptography was advocated due to its ability to support very large user communities.

PEM was an interim step before the availability and proliferation in business of OSI messaging and directory services, but with the take up of X.400 and X.500 being very slow in the market, it had gained attention for only a short time. PEM was an important evolution of the Internet as a viable business service and although work was underway to link PEM with MIME (providing secure multi-media E-mail capability, as PEM cannot handle binary data), the approach had stagnated and is not utilized widely now.

Secure MIME (S/MIME)

Secure Multipurpose Internet Messaging Extension (S/MIME) was an extension of the existing MIME standards, already in wide use in the industry, that was developed in parallel to the MOSS specifications by a private group led by RSA Data Security.

To ensure wide compatibility, S/MIME was developed using the Public Key Cryptography Standards (PKCS), created in 1991 by a consortium of major computer vendors, and in particular one specification denoted PKCS #7. Utilizing these de facto standards ensured multi-vendor interoperability, which had been a major factor in the wider adoption of S/MIME in a large number of applications, despite the fact that the underlying MIME technology is relatively inefficient. In addition, by ensuring PKCS compatibility, S/MIME was interoperable with PEM.

S/MIME used the X.509 certificate standard, utilizing the Version 3 format, introduced in 1996, which supported the "name@domain" convention, used within the Internet. Essentially, S/MIME relied on RSA's public key cryptography to underpin the digital signature and envelope – the latter being used to ensure privacy. The message itself was not encrypted using RSA's algorithms, but rather the DES cipher, with the key encrypted using RSA's public key. The encrypted message and encrypted key were then inserted into a digital envelope and sent together.

In a move to make S/MIME the industry standard for E-mail encryption, RSA had applied to the Internet Engineering Task Force (IETF) – who had previously worked on the development of Multipurpose Internet Mail Extensions Object Security Services (MOSS) – to establish S/MIME as a security standard for electronic messaging.

Pretty Good Privacy

Philip Zimmerman gained worldwide notoriety in the Internet community when he developed an encryption program called 'Pretty Good Privacy' (PGP) based on the RSA encryption algorithm. Components for PGP were developed through the late 1980s, and in 1991 he released the software as freeware, propelling its adoption, and it has since been freely distributed on worldwide networks. During a time when encryption was tightly controlled by the US Administration and not easily obtained, PGP became an international standard for cryptography used by businesses and millions of individuals. Strong cryptography was available to pretty much anyone who cared to learn how to use it.

Zimmerman, a self confessed peace activist, was investigated by federal authorities as they attempted to crack down on the distribution of such technologies, claiming that they are utilized by criminals. Zimmerman was also investigated for exporting full-strength encryption, which was an illegal act in the US. Strong encryption was classified as munitions, an outdated remnant of World War II – ironic in a country where guns are so freely available. However, the government dropped its case in early 1996, the year in which Zimmermann and Jonathan Seybold founded PGP Inc. Network Associates acquired PGP in December 1997, and continued to market the product until late 2001, when they announced plans to dissolve its PGP Security division.

PGP is available for a number of different platforms, including DEC VAX VMS, UNIX, Microsoft Windows and also DOS. Advocates of the technology praise its near flawless capabilities and it is rumoured that federal government experts have been unable to crack PGP.

Technically, PGP is similar to S/MIME, as well as PEM, supporting digital signature and encryption functionalities, although PGP does define its own public key management system with corresponding certificates. For this reason it has not been widely adopted in electronic business, but does enjoy a huge installed base of casual E-mail users. PGP has also been used with MIME.

The case of PGP made Zimmerman an Internet folk hero, and even today, PGP is used widely in numerous countries around the world.

Securing the Internet

The e-Business supply chain requires the interconnection of numerous users (suppliers, customers, partners) across the Internet to a host of different back-office systems and relationship management oriented systems. This interaction needs to function with as little obstruction as possible. This poses a challenge for today's Internet-based security technologies, be it the firewall or a variety of the numerous technologies available, to allow a fluid flow of information that businesses place on modern networks. Competitive business advantage is gained from opening up the network to these various partners, and securing the exchange becomes of paramount importance.

The Web continues to impress and dazzle us with its startling growth statistics, akin to a virus growing and propagating around the globe. With this tremendous commerce opportunity comes a gargantuan challenge to those wishing to exploit the potential – an overriding concern about security and privacy from those interacting in this digital universe. In response to immense demand, security protocols continue to be developed and deployed in this fast developing arena. In the following sections, we examine some of those that grew prevalent since the mid 1990s and those gaining critical mass in the new century.

Secure Sockets Layer (SSL)

Secure Sockets Layer technology was developed by Netscape Communications in 1994 and the SSL protocol has reached widespread acceptance and is in wide use on the Web today, and fully supported by popular client applications such as Internet Explorer and Netscape Navigator. SSL is essentially used to provide a level of communication protection on the Internet, for applications such as Hypertext Transfer Protocol (HTTP), File Transfer Protocol (FTP) and Telnet. By utilizing many of the encryption techniques already discussed, the technology ensures confidentiality, authenticity and integrity of data being exchanged.

It is most widely recognized, and used, to secure HTTP communications on Web pages, and Network News Transfer Protocol (NNTP). Security services provided include authentication, integrity checks and encryption. The use of a SSL session can be noted by a URL commencing with **https://**, as illustrated below.

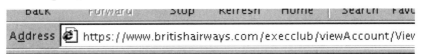

Figure 12.6 Secure HTTP session

The process flow between the user (usually a client) and the bilateral party (typically a merchant) is relatively straight forward and relies on the techniques of public and private key encryption.

(i) The client's browser requests the merchant certificate, verifying it by comparing the signature with that of the Certificate Authority (in the merchant's certificate) to the public key of the Certificate Authority available in the browser.

(ii) If it matches, the certificate is valid.

(iii) The merchant may request a valid certificate from the client (this step is typically omitted with retail transactions over the Internet).

(iv) The merchant would then compare the certificate in the same manner as step (i). In addition, the client would provide a message digest that the merchant recalculates. Once these steps have been completed successfully, messages between the client and merchant are encrypted and session keys are exchanged and decrypted using private keys.

(v) The client encrypts their message to the merchant under the session key which upon receipt, the merchant can decrypt using the shared session key.

Secured HTTP (S-HTTP)

The purpose of Secured Hypertext Transfer Protocol (S-HTTP) is somewhat similar to SSL, in terms of the security objectives, but presents a slightly different solution to the problem – the difference being the level at which the protocol operates at, with S-HTTP operating at the Application Layer, marking individual documents as private, or signed.

As with SSL, the security services provided by S-HTTP encompass authentication, integrity checks and encryption. In addition, S-HTTP also offers the support for digital signatures. S-HTTP was designed by Enterprise Integration Technologies, and supports a wide array of hash-functions, as well as digital signature systems. The protocol is relatively flexible, in terms of the key management formats – PEM, PKCS, RSA as well as others. The use of a Secured HTTP session can be noted by a URL commencing with **shttp://**

The Firewall

Castles of yesteryear were majestic fortifications, allowing a community to thrive while offering an acceptable level of protection through a variety of ways – archers, high walls, boiling pitch, and the first level of defence – the moat. This perimeter defence was certainly not impenetrable, but did inconvenience those attempting to enter with malicious intent, as well as providing a means of preventing those who wanted to leave. In latter day security, the moat can be likened to a firewall – a means of protecting a private network from the outside world. To extend the analogy, the entry/exit point of the firewall is akin to the drawbridge, and therefore allows for a single point for tracing and audit purposes. A few basic forms exist (although specific implementations vary widely); the wall that exists to block network traffic coming in, and the one that explicitly permits traffic in.

The adoption of firewalls has increased dramatically since their introduction in the 1990s, especially as connections to external communities and business partners continue to grow. An excellent example is the Internet, with organizations keen to use the infrastructure, but wary of what security issues this can cause. One of the first lines of defence is the use of a firewall, with implementations varying in design and complexity – in each case the relevant choice is dependent upon the nature of the information being protected, and its respective value to the organization. As with all security measures, much is dependent on a cost-benefit-analysis of having the data violated or compromized. Some of the more popular topologies are outlined below, and a typical configuration is illustrated in Figure 12.7.

Screening Router

A screening router performs packet filtering on IP addresses and protocols (using TCP port numbers) to nodes within a private network. The extent of the risk with this set-up can easily be controlled, with services being defined as acceptable or not. Although not the most secure solution, routers are popular due to their high level of flexibility and relatively low cost.

Gateway

A gateway (sometimes referred to as the Bastion Host), segregating the outside network and private network, is perhaps the most appealing topology, as not only is this easy and quick to implement but also requires very little hardware. No traffic is directly transferred between networks, rendering the private network effectively "invisible" to the outside world. The gateway provides a high level of control over dialogue between networks.

Screened Host Gateway

By far the most popular firewall implementation consists of a screening router and/or Web server together with a Bastion Host, with the latter residing on the private network. The screening router directs traffic directly to the Bastion Host allowing access to a protected domain, termed a demilitarized zone (DMZ). In turn, this zone is the buffer between an internal network.

Firewalls have been used for protecting various e-based services, and are an effective precaution when used in conjunction with other security measures. One cannot fully rely on the wall itself as adequate protection, as it is not effective for all applications, with a good example being computer viruses. However as commerce increases, their use has become more mainstream.

The trend of organizations conducting increasingly different types of commerce with business partners has created fresh requirements including a demand for higher bandwidth. As a result firewalls are evolving into more virtual entities, dynamically expanding to include other domains as necessary, by the means of using encryption and strong authentication technologies between the partners. By using key management with outside organizations, commerce with other organizations is being facilitated without having to pass through gateways or routers.

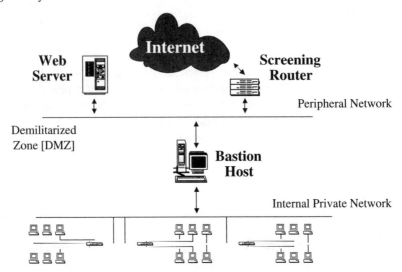

Figure 12.7 Firewall configuration

Additionally, the continued expansion of the remote access community within an organization, whether these are ad hoc remote users or users within a Small Office/Home Office (SoHo) environment places additional needs on the firewall technology. This has led to the introduction of additional configurations that can provide personal firewall security – essentially access routers that can establish Virtual Private Network connectivity for multiple devices accessing corporate networks through numerous high bandwidth access approaches.

Firewall technology is relatively mature and recent advances continue to focus on increased speeds and bandwidths being offered, while continually focusing on a reduction in cost.

Security in a Wireless World

Our environment continues to spawn technologies to liberate us from numerous umbilical cords attaching a host of devices to each other in order to work together. Not surprisingly, all these trillions of bytes of data being exchanged around us necessitate a new type of security to ensure data is not compromised. Wireless communications represent additional challenges that add to the security conundrum. With limited bandwidths, resources on CPU and memory as well as battery concerns, this adds additional issues to contend with. We examine some of the most prevalent approaches in this fast growing market, with the landscape still evolving as the technologies continue to mature and gain critical mass.

Wired Equivalent Privacy (WEP)

The WEP algorithm was conceived together with the IEEE 802.11 standards (see Chapter 10 on Wireless Commerce) and was predominantly used to protect wireless networks based on these standards. Using either a 40-bit or a 128-bit RC4 encryption mechanism, WEP was typically implemented via a hardware approach to minimize performance degradation. Despite its association with one of the most popular wireless LAN standards, WEP did not gather much support, rather a lot of criticism about its limitations. WEP only offered Layer 1 and Layer 2 encryption and was based on an outdated protocol stack, critics highlighted, further emphasizing that the encryption built into 802.11 was completed at the last minute, and was the level of encryption the US Government allowed for export back in 1997.

Most acknowledged WEP's shortcomings and recommendations were made for users to supplement their installations with additional security methods, such as session keys, MAC address filtering and the use of secure Virtual Private Networks. Most anticipate a successor to WEP to become more mainstream.

WAP and Wireless Transport Layer Security (WTLS)

WTLS is a protocol describing channel-level encryption and authentication that uses public/private keys and digital certificates, and was modelled on Transport Layer Security (TLS), a revised form of Secure Sockets Layer (SSL).

The majority of Wireless Access Protocol (WAP – see Chapter 10) implementations are similar to the way SSL technology operates on the Web (i.e. the client does not exchange a certificate, but rather has a pre-installed self signed root key from a trusted Certification Authority), and refer to Class 1 and 2 implementations. WTLS encrypts transmissions from the device to the gateway, just as TLS/SSL encrypts from the browser to the secure Web server.

WTLS Class 3 requires the user to be issued a client public/private key, analogous to SSL v.3. Typically these keys are stored on a Subscriber Identity Module (SIM) or a WAP Identity Module (WIM).

Privacy Please

Security concerns have hampered e-Business for numerous years, and many technologies have been deployed to provide ever increasing levels of technology to counter balance the fear and apprehension that privacy is being compromized. Arguably this has received less interest or focus than the attention on security concerns.

While security problems continue to be addressed, little has been done to ease users' privacy concerns and many are still uncomfortable with the prospect of sharing their private information on Web sites – especially as technologies such as 'Cookies' gain notoriety within the public press. While many sites have extensive online privacy policies, these are often expressed in legalese that is often difficult for users to understand. This is changing with initiatives that employ XML-based language approaches. These initiatives, such as P3P, encourage sites to express their privacy policies with precision and specify exactly what they'll do with private information. We examine some of these trends and technologies in the following sections.

Cookies

'Cookies' are essentially records of data that are stored on a client machine by the Web server that can be retrieved at a later time, and have been used widely to identify visitors to sites since their introduction in the 1990s. Their use allows the automatic storing of various elements such as preferences for content, layout, username and password, as examples and cookies can remain stored for a variety of timeframes, ranging from the time of the session to many years. Clearly this can provide numerous benefits for the user, in terms of reducing the amount of information that may need to be keyed in repeatedly. Additionally, an online experience can be somewhat personalized facilitating an enhanced level of service.

Essentially the use of cookies in themselves does not pose a serious security concern, as Web servers only have access to information provided by the user or via the local browser's own configurations (E-mail addresses, systems used etc.). Importantly, it can also track the last URL visited and the manner in which the user navigated through those URLs. Given that cookies can then also be used to anonymously track the viewing habits of customers, this provides a more sinister aspect to the technology and many concerns have been raised about the social aspects and invasion of privacy that this use of the technology allows. The fact that cookies are almost always added to the user's machine with no notification has been sometimes viewed as suspicious.

There have been many high profile examples and cases where organizations have collected rich data using cookie technology (usually in the form of third party cookies coming from Web sites other than the site being browsed) – in many early cases with users not being aware of the process – and utilizing this for market competitiveness or financial gain. Perhaps one of the most prominent examples, DoubleClick Inc. gained much publicity as the public debate on cookies intensified. The organization has many approaches of capturing information and maintaining user profiles, which can then be utilized for highly targeted advertizements – DoubleClick has more than 100 million user profiles in its systems.

Given the attention the approach has garnered, it was not surprising to see governmental agencies being attracted to how the technology is being used, and indeed the European Commission is looking at mandating rules to ensure enterprises seek from consumers explicit prior consent, each time a cookie is served.

Platform for Privacy Preferences

Under the auspices of the World Wide Web Consortium (W3C), a standard was passed known as the Platform for Privacy Preferences (P3P) in the late 1990s, with initial work starting in 1997. It allowed Web sites to display their privacy policies so that users can decide how much personal data they would like to reveal to the site. There are two essential components of P3P. Web sites had to have machine readable privacy policies in place, and Web browsers had be able to support the protocol. At its most basic level, P3P is a standardized set of multiple-choice questions, covering all the major aspects of a Web site's privacy policies.

This standard was already being deployed within popular software applications such as Internet Explorer in 2001 – Microsoft Explorer v6.0 provided default settings to block all third-party cookies, usually manifested in the form of advertizement banners. Warning boxes are displayed when non-compliant P3P sites are accessed, where third party cookies are attempting to store themselves on users machines. The browser also warns users when Web sites don't live up to privacy parameters established by the user. This provided individuals with more knowledge about and control over how their data was being collected, stored, and used.

Smart Card Technologies

Smart Card technology has been around for a few decades, but it was only in the mid to late 1990s when the technology began to see tremendous growth. Historically this technology was predominantly used in specific sectors such as the financial and telecommunication industries, but its appeal continues to straddle other segments. Smart cards vary in terms of their capabilities, typically being 32-bit architectures with approx 32,000 bytes of memory.

There are numerous examples in use today, including the American Express "Blue" Card, or Visa's Fusion Card – indeed Visa plans to smart card enable all of its point of sale (POS) terminals accessing its networks by 2004. The futuristic looking American Express "Blue" card was released in September 1999 and combined conventional magnetic stripe card functionality with a smart chip, which holds a digital certificate that authenticates cardholders. A smart card reader is required to use the card's chip function. Electronic wallets store the Blue card number and other data used to shop.

The Subscriber Identity Module (SIM) card used in Global System for Mobile Communications (GSM) cellular phones has also significantly driven up demand. SIM Cards have been in use for some time, and in essence represent one of the simplest wireless security platforms. The SIM card has been a major influence on the rapid growth of the GSM network, which personalizes the telephone to its owner, holding secure data such as the subscriber's account information, phone list and Short Message Service (SMS) messages. The detachable SIM card identifies the subscriber to GSM networks and can be used in a number of manufacturer's handsets. SIM cards are evolving from simply being identity devices on the network (perhaps supporting one or two discrete services) to becoming the basis of a multi-application terminal offering subscribers their own customized set of additional services.

The leading standards in the US, TDMA and CDMA, are also evaluating similar technology in the form of removable identity modules (see Wireless Commerce – Chapter 10). Additional uses include the WAP Forum supporting a wireless identity module to the SIM, which could provide public and private keys beginning the process of providing Public Key Infrastructure (PKI) approaches.

Two primary impediments to the take up of smart cards have always been cost and the compatibility and support within major applications. As growth progresses, the costs continue to drop and we may begin to see standard readers in desktop and laptop configurations. On the software side, Windows 2000 already supports integrated smart card services.

Smartcards have been touted as an effective solution to enable m-Commerce, and indeed hold the promise to provide a workable solution to many of the issues. When we begin to see the financial institutions, who arguably hold the most appropriate seat of trust in consumers minds, working together with the telecommunication providers who own the networks, critical mass could be achieved.

National ID Smart Cards

The use of National ID cards has been long established in many jurisdictions, and this provides an excellent application to use smart card technology. Numerous countries have examined the application with a few early examples already in place.

The Hong Kong Special Administrative Region (SAR) first introduced National ID cards in 1987 and at the turn of the century, the government examined the case of introducing a new smart ID card, and the resulting Smart Identity Card System (SMARTICS) project was launched. The card promises much – as well as replacing existing national identity cards it will include additional applications such as a driver's licence, library card and even an electronic purse, as examples. The card will also provide free digital IDs for use in secure online transactions when the new smart card is introduced in mid-2003 for all of Hong Kong's 6.8 million residents. Hong Kong residents were familiar with the concept of having an ID card, so the new introduction did not pose the 'Big Brother' related issues many other countries face, although the introduction did cause controversy from the raised privacy concerns additional applications opened.

Despite this the project proceeded as the government felt the benefits to e-Business and adoption of online government services in Hong Kong, through the introduction of additional features on the ID card, outweighed the security and data privacy risks. Naturally, the government assured legislation for the protection of the data privacy of ID card holders, including new offences for the unauthorized access, use, storage and disclosure of personal information held on the card. Security is provided in the form of biometric fingerprint technology consisting of both thumbprints, which provides a form of human redundancy. In the event that one thumb is damaged, the other can still be used to check identity.

The offer of a free digital certificate with each ID card was an integral part of the government's e-Business and e-Government drive. An e-certificate issued by the Hong Kong Post Certification Authority was embedded into the card's memory chip. The underlying technology used a SHA-1 hash function, 1024-bit RSA with the digital certificates conforming to the X.509 standards. These digital certificates allow the holder to transact securely with government Web sites, e-Commerce merchants and banks through a unique digital signature.

One of the key beneficiaries of the new card is undoubtedly the immigration department, which can check validity and update temporary residents' conditions of stay electronically. It is also being touted as a way to introduce an automated passenger clearance system in the future. The new ID card is set to be introduced in phases from mid-2003 until 2007.

Hong Kong is not alone, with many governments paying close attention to this technology. Another example is China, which starts a similar rollout of smart-card based ID cards in 2002 – their project is somewhat larger with almost 1.3 billion citizens to contend with. The approach being taken is very similar to that of Kong Kong, with biometric data being utilized to provide identity validation. This card will also provide the individual's social security number.

Securing Financial Services

Online e-Commerce is seriously hampered by security concerns, and today one of the most used financial instruments to conduct B2C commerce on the Web is via credit cards, representing up to 90% of all transactions in the US. Despite this, online fraud continues to grow and initiatives introduced by various financial and technology organizations by them in the mid 1990s have had little take up. The sheer scale of the situation is illustrated by research from Gartner Group[4]:

▷ Internet fraud is 12 to 18 times higher than in-store fraud.

▷ $700 million was lost in online fraud in 2001.

▷ Fraud attempt rates can be as high as 1 in 20 transactions.

▷ 16% of online US adults have experienced credit card fraud, rising to 37.5% for those earning more than $100,000 a year.

Clearly this issue is a large one, and many initiatives were started in the mid 1990s to try and combat this. These included:

▷ **Secure Electronic Payment Protocol (SEPP)** – designed by MasterCard, together with IBM, Netscape Communications, GTE and Cybercash.

▷ **Secure Transaction Technology (STT)** – a protocol specified by Visa International and Microsoft chiefly, in conjunction with some other companies.

▷ **Secure Electronic Transactions (SET)** – MasterCard, Visa International and Microsoft have agreed to co-operate in providing secure credit card transactions over the Internet. Supported X.509 certificates for Public Key Infrastructure (PKI) approaches.

None managed to gain critical mass, although the latter initiative (SET) did gain some prominence. Essentially the resistance to PKI by consumers, in terms of the additional steps that needed to take place, constrained demand. SET was criticized for being too complicated to implement, as it required new infrastructure from merchants, processors and consumers. The high costs associated with this and its design prevented growth and the approach was barely adopted and overtaken by other technologies. These are categorized below:

▷ Visa's 'Verified by Visa' – a password related scheme which will take affect once the Visa rule changes are activated in 2003. Cardholders will use passwords which will provide merchants with specific benefits that are more akin to those when a consumer signs a paper receipt.

▷ MasterCard's Universal Cardholder Authentication Field (UCAF)

Furthermore, the merchants involved with the initiative had little incentive to make the change, given the interchange fees that were levied to SET-based transactions were not reduced. Despite the lessons learnt from this important aspect, it continues to be the case today, although both Visa and MasterCard have indicated that they will evaluate lower fees by 2005.

Disposable Numbers

These approaches began appearing in 2000, and although each manifestation was a little different a generic process flow could be mapped. Essentially these approaches relied on a one-off substitute number to be used in place of a credit card. The process flow is outlined below:

(i) Consumers obtain a one-off number (that conforms to card association number conventions) and use this in place of their usual credit card number.

(ii) This can be obtained directly from a financial services' provider site prior to the transaction being completed. The number is then manually entered (or copied and pasted) into the credit card field.

(iii) For compatible sites, a software program can be downloaded to the PC, which is activated automatically when a payment page is opened at a compliant Web site and the number automatically populated the site field.

(iv) Once the card issuer receives the authorization from the merchant, the one-off number is matched to the actual card number for authorization and posting. The cardholder's actual number is never revealed and does not travel on the Internet.

One of the first to launch this service was Allied Irish Bank, which launched its Transactonline service in July 2000. It was shortly followed in September 2000 by American Express, who launched Private Payments and although it had experienced a reasonable adoption, consumers had found the approach to be cumbersome. Although merchants would benefit, the added headaches over reconciliation (no consistent credit card number) made follow up service difficult and administratively unwieldy. Other providers also experimented with this approach, including Discover with its service termed Deskjob.

Security of the Future

In 1996, the modern day remake of the film Mission Impossible bought to our screens a crack spy team outsmarting a series of CIA headquartered biometric security devices – these top secret computer-machines read palm prints, eye shapes and voice patterns. The adventure was fiction, but the technology it depicted real, and has been in use by some federal agencies to restrict access to information or to secure the US borders for many years. Hollywood has been very successful in bringing to our screens numerous visions of the future, where highly sophisticated and advanced machines can provide un-imagined levels of security – you rarely see anyone on Star Trek having to deal with forgotten passwords!

Several trends in the technology available to us, and the way in which we interact with it, are precipitating new aspects of concern for those responsible for security. For instance, computers are no longer bulky boxes that sit on desktops, but have evolved into small highly functional units that can fit into a small pocket and interact in a wireless manner. These highly portable machines can be taken anywhere, and hence the information stored on the machine compromized anywhere.

The trend towards open and distributed systems is evident, and increasingly systems are linking various facilities offered by different organizations. These systems pose many security issues, and are often 'hacked' into to obtain proprietary information.

As security technology continues to develop, new innovative solutions are being introduced. One of the most promising and perhaps exciting, is in the field of Biometrics, essentially a measurement of a biological characteristic or trait. This measurement can then be used to verify or determine the identity of the person.

Biometric Security

The nature of security methods are changing and advancing as the needs of organizations become increasingly more complex, and the technology offered evolves further. Imagine not needing to remember easily forgotten PIN numbers, abstract codes or often changed passwords to gain access to our bank accounts, computers or voice mailboxes. Instead access may be achieved via retinal scans, finger prints, hand geometry patterns and voiceprints – somewhat more difficult to forget. A new symbiosis of technologies may be used, such as fingerprint analysis and the use of smart cards. In fact this vision is already reality. As error rates become lower, and diffusion becomes more widespread, we may see the death of the 'old' technologies such as passwords within the next decade. This is certainly not going to be a panacea, as criminal experts will also find more diverse ways of fooling the system. One thing is for sure – breaking the system will certainly become significantly more difficult.

Some of the biometric techniques that have been bought to market are outlined below:

Fingerprint or Hand Analysis

A high resolution image is captured of the fingerprint or hand, and converted into a mathematical representation. This is then compared to a stored representation, with differing thresholds that can be set by the administrator of the system. This technology boasts high levels of accuracy, and is perhaps one of the least intrusive in terms of user acceptability. In fact fingerprint data can already be held on a 79-character conventional magnetic stripe card, making applications such as ATM transactions feasible. Fingerprint analysis is the most mature of the biometric technologies and initial concerns about using latex fingers are diminishing by the use of fingerprint sensors that incorporate technologies that can detect pulse.

Retina Scan Analysis

Distinguishing features can be discerned by scanning the blood vessels on the eye's retina using infra-red light. This is perhaps one of the most accurate of the biometric technologies, but also one of the least accepted by users, due to their health and safety concerns (even if unfounded). The use of this approach is usually expensive and requires user training and co-operation which makes user resistance to the technology high.

Voice Analysis

Voice verification systems are trained by repeating a password, or name, which is used as an access code. Of the three most popular biometric systems, voice recognition has the lowest level of accuracy. Despite this, due to the fact that the necessary hardware (a telephone or PC based microphone) is already installed in a huge subscriber base, attention and investment in this technology continues. Users are also very accepting of this approach although several constraints make it unstable, such as changes in voice over time or illness. Additionally, different microphones provide different samples and hence thresholds may have to be lowered more than an ideal amount to provide acceptable usage parameters.

Face Analysis

This approach leverages closed circuit television cameras to capture an image of a face which is then compared to a database of known persons.

The field of biometric security uses human characteristics or behavioural idiosyncrasies to distinguish individuals, and has mostly been used in high security implementations to date, such as the military and government installations, although as the technology advances and costs drop, this profile is changing fast. There are numerous examples:

▷ In Sweden, the city of Stockholm is home to 85,000 elementary school students accessing servers in the city LAN to access various learning resources. The school district embarked on an interesting project in October 2001 to implement an advanced authentication system using fingerprint biometric technology. The student and teachers no longer need to contend with forgotten passwords.

▷ The INPASS programme allows frequent travellers to the US to skip immigration queues at larger airports by swiping a card and placing their hand on a scanner. The technology relies on hand geometry verification, which examines certain characteristics such as shape, size, finger length etc.

▷ By using existing networks of closed-circuit television (CCTV) camera, advanced biometric systems can employ facial recognition techniques by comparing the image of an individual against a database of suspects – all performed passively without the user being aware. This technology is being closely scrutinized in terms of its value in airports and is already employed in Britain to spot criminals and football hooligans.

The Future

There is little doubt that some form of biometric technology will touch our lives sooner rather than later. The question is when? The two major issues faced by the techniques, that of cost and accuracy, are falling for the former and increasing for the latter. The finance community continues to pay close attention to the technologies being developed, especially as costs associated with fraud and theft continue to increase. For many applications, the cost to benefit ratios continue to become increasingly attractive. The use of biometric technologies is fast making a broader presence felt in our lives but other more innovative projects are providing a glimpse of the future. The research being conducted by IBM is illustrative – IBM researchers are hard at work making operating systems more scalable. It is extending Linux, an open source operating system, to control a computer with 65,000 processors. As part of its $100 million Blue Gene research project, IBM plans to build a computer operating at 1 quadrillion floating-point operations per second to attack problems such as protein folding. Blue Gene is the ultimate test for many of the principles unfolding in IBM's Autonomic Computing initiative. The program aims to make operating systems self-optimizing, self-configuring, self-healing and self-protecting, much like the human body's autonomic nervous system.

1   R Morris, K Thompson, Password Security: A Case History, Communications of the ACM, Vol. 22, 11, 1979

2   A Warman, Computer Security Within Organizations, 1993

3   W. Diffie and ME Hellman, New Directions in Cryptography, IEEE Transactions on Information Theory, IT-22;644-654, 1976

4   Kenneth Kerr, Avivah Litan, Online Transaction Fraud and Prevention Get More Sophisticated, Gartner G2, January 2002

Legal Aspects of e-Business

Introduction

In the context of e-Business, bilateral trading partner agreements (TPA) have been in use for some years between companies wishing to exchange business documents using electronic data interchange. Such agreements have bound the parties to the legality of undertaking paperless trading and eased corporate concerns should disagreements subsequently occur. However, this chapter reviews the main legal issues that arise when conducting e-Commerce for the marketing, buying and selling of products and services over the Web. It does not pretend to provide an exhaustive treatment of the subject, but rather raise awareness of the issues and accompanying legislation so that these may be pursued with experts to address company specific situations.

Enabling Infrastructure

Earlier chapters have explored the evolution of e-Business since its inception in the 1970s by the banking community for inter-bank funds transfers and, shortly afterwards, by tightly controlled trading communities for the electronic exchange of business documents. The acceptance of the Internet by the business community in the mid 1990s has resulted in a period of unprecedented growth in global electronic communications. However, to ensure the longer-term success of e-Business there have been calls for an adequate enabling framework to be put in place, particularly of a legislative nature. Stakeholders are demanding less of the 'wild frontier' that typified some of the initial Internet initiatives and a more stable environment in which to conduct routine business and consumer transactions.

Figure 13.1 illustrates the changing situation as technology, and in particular telecommunications, very much dominated the agenda during the early days of e-Business in the 1980s. During this period the European Commission issued several notable directives, including the 1987 Telecommunications Green Paper aimed at creating the necessary commercial environment to stimulate the emergence of a global electronic marketplace. As indicated above, with the growth of the Internet, more specifically the Web, the situation has changed yet again. It is now common practice for companies to use the Web to advertize and promote their products and services, often including copies of product brochures, other promotional materials, and contact details. With a sound technology base and commercial infrastructure, e-Business is in the middle of a further transition involving greater concerns for legislative actions to safeguard the interests of all stakeholders.

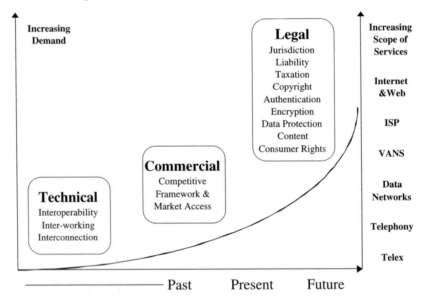

Figure 13.1 Enabling framework for the global electronic marketplace
(adapted from EC Communication (COM/1998/50)

When considering the distinction between e-Business and e-Commerce made in this book, it would seem that legal issues are of far more concern for those engaged in online commercial transactions over the Web than the more traditional Business-to-Business (B2B) e-Business, possibly involving electronic data interchange. This is because in the case of traditional B2B interactions usually some prior negotiations have established a relationship between the trading parties, whereas online customers appear as spontaneous users usually with no such prior relationship having been established between buyer and seller.

Indirect and Direct Transactions

E-Commerce transactions concluded over the Web between buyer and seller fall into one of two categories, namely indirect or direct transactions. Indirect e-Commerce transactions arise when tangible products or services are involved such as music, CD-ROMs, books, cases of wine, tickets (train, theatre or airline) etc. While the buyer and seller conclude e-Commerce contact via the Web, their obligations arising from the resultant contract are handled 'offline' through the physical delivery of the product or service purchased and, in some instances, the payment for such purchases.

On the other hand, direct e-Commerce transactions are where the contract and the obligations performed under the contract are fulfilled totally via the Web. This type of transaction only arises when the nature of the products and services are intangible or capable of being totally fulfilled 'online' through the web or other electronic means, e.g. computer software, electronic magazine/newspaper, music, etc.

The split between products and services grouped under indirect and direct e-Commerce transactions is continuing to change as a result of the rapid technological developments. Broadband data transmission services are dramatically reducing times for downloading electronic images and making possible the electronic delivery of products and services hitherto thought not feasible. With the continued emphasis on customer service and global nature of the markets now served, technological developments are likely to improve levels of support services and introduce new ranges of direct e-Commerce services, e.g. voice over IP, remote support, etc.

Governmental Action

Consider a consumer using their home computer to purchase a product from a Web site established by a company on the other side of the world. To what extent should governments involve themselves in safeguarding the interests of their citizens in this new era of Internet shopping?

For the continuing development of the global electronic marketplace, a suitable technical, commercial, and legal infrastructure is required. With the broad acceptance of open Internet standards by the business community much progress has been made in establishing the thick technical infrastructure required to support e-Business. Not only is global telecommunications a growth business in its own right, it is underpinning a global economic revolution in the way in which products and services are marketed, bought and sold over the Web. Excellent progress has been made by government action to break down many of the monopolistic and anti-competitive obstacles preventing intermediaries such as service providers from entering the market. Service providers are important since they create the necessary commercial environment needed to conduct e-Business. However, work still remains to bring about the necessary changes to the legal infrastructure that by the global nature of e-Business requires worldwide agreements to be put in place by governments covering a whole raft of issues. These include jurisdiction, liability, taxation, copyrights, authentication, encryption, data protection, content, and consumer rights.

Electronic Commerce Legislation

This first grouping covers the legislation that addresses the rather special needs of conducting business over the Internet/Web and is therefore relatively new and only now beginning to have a significant impact on business and consumers.

Distance Selling Directive 1997/7/EC

The Distance Selling Directive was one of the first pieces of legislation to address the concerns of online buyers and was intended to supplement existing country sale of goods legislation, rather than replace it. At first sight this appears a little strange, as shopping today is very different to shopping 10 or more years ago. Indeed most existing consumer law was established at a time when online shopping over the Web was an unknown phenomenon. However, it would seem that while the principles of consumer protection have not really changed, they clearly need aligning to this new mode of shopping.

This directive was incorporated into the UK Consumer Protection (Distance Selling) Act that came into force on 31 October 2000 and applies to the business-to-consumer sector. The Distance Selling Directive requires suppliers to ensure that their Web sites provide a minimum amount of information to potential buyers including:

▷ Prices, terms and conditions (including delivery costs)

▷ Supplier's name and address

▷ Details of the terms for the return of goods

▷ Duration for which prices and terms are valid

These requirements represent important criteria for Web designers to ensure that they include all the necessary information covered by this legislation. Many Web sites provide basic supplier information and contact details, but often fail to provide details of refund and exchange policies. In addition Web sites do not always state how they will handle the customer's personal details entered onto the Web site as part of the buying process including, name, address and credit card details. Some of the better Web sites clearly state that the contact details are required solely for the transaction in hand. They also provide the buyer with a 'tick-box' to indicate if they do not wish the address details to be retained for future mailings by the seller or passed to other companies.

A further provision of the Directive requires member-states to enable consumers to register objections to receiving unsolicited E-mails sent for the purpose of selling, and to demonstrate that their objections have been respected. Article 6 of the Directive also gives rights to consumers to cancel contracts without penalty and without giving any reasons for their withdrawal within a period of at least seven working days for purchases entered into either via E-mail or Web sites. Article 7 of the Directive gives sellers 30 days following the conclusion of the contract to perform their contractual obligations, beyond which the buyer is entitled to a full refund.

The Organization for Economic Co-operation and Development (OECD) have been active in a wide range of initiatives related to privacy and consumer protection and have made recommendations on possible actions by governments. The OECD *Guidelines for Consumer Protection in Electronic Commerce* appear to be consistent with the nature of the EU Distance Selling Directive and cover issues such, fair business, advertizing and marketing practices, as well as payment, dispute resolution and redress.

Electronic Signatures Directive 1999/93/EC

This European Union Directive sets out the general framework for the use of electronic signatures for reliable and legally valid electronic communication. Therefore, it is a very important piece of legislation for the development of e-Commerce in general, and an essential element for concluding contracts through e-Commerce transactions. The Electronic Signatures Directive was to be implemented into the national laws of the EU Member States by 19 July 2001 and in the case of the UK was enacted within the Electronic Communications Act 2000.

The directive has several main features:

▷ It creates an open European market for electronic signature-related products and services. For instance it prohibits national licensing schemes for certification service providers or the presumption that signature-creation devices which meet certain standards, have to be considered compliant with the requirements of the directive in all EU Member States.

▷ It provides for a European-wide acceptance of 'qualified' electronic signatures as a valid legal equivalent to hand-written signatures. In addition legislation is likely to be altered to allow the use of electronic communications in place of hard copy in a wide range of situations, e.g. house conveyance, insurance claims, etc.

▷ It promotes trust in 'qualified' electronic signatures with a requirement for the EU Member States to establish adequate supervision, liability provisions for certificate issuers, etc.

▷ Finally the directive contains a number of provisions, including the fact that users of encryption are under no obligation to deposit copies of their encryption keys with third parties (use of trusted third parties and key escrow).

Other main features of the Electronic Signatures Directive include its wide applicability for all kinds of electronic signatures, covering digital signatures, scanned manuscript signatures, the typing of a name and clicking on a Web site tab. Certification Services providers are subject to the laws concerning electronic signatures of the EU Member State in which they are established (similar to the 'country of origin rule' under the Electronic Commerce Directive – see below). The functions of electronic signatures are to identify a person, to provide certainty as to their involvement in the signing of the document and finally to associate the person with the contents of the document. The directive is established upon the principle of legal equality between electronic and hand-written signatures. By contrast, the directive does not define in which cases the national laws may stipulate hand-written and electronic signatures as a legal requirement for legally binding acts, should there be differences.

Electronic Commerce Directive 2000/31/EC

The purpose of this Directive is primarily to bolster consumer confidence in e-Commerce. Although an important directive it supplements other earlier Directives forming the European legal framework related to 'information society services'. The term 'information society services' is a European Union expression to describe the new way of 'doing business electronically'. It sets out a series of principles aimed at removing barriers for the availability of information society services within the European Union. In addition the directive recognizes that European consumer protection legislation already exists and seeks to supplement it rather than replace it.

The Electronic Commerce Directive covers five main areas:

▷ *Electronic Contracts:* EU member states are expected to remove any obstacles preventing the preparation and concluding of electronic contracts.

▷ *Transparency:* Suppliers are expected to make their business terms and conditions readily available to customers and the relevant authorities.

▷ *Commercial Communications:* Consumers must have the ability to opt-out of receiving electronic communications of an advertizing nature. In addition such communications must be clearly identified as advertizing as well as identifying the company concerned.

▷ *Codes of conduct:* This part of the directive sets out the principles for the handling of disputes between buyer and seller, and recommends that they resolve arguments outside the jurisdiction of the courts.

▷ *Intermediary liability:* The information society services provider will not be liable for the contents of third-party information that it transmits when simply acting as a conduit for such information.

A further important principle outlined in this Directive relates to the country of origin in which the service provider is 'established' and the legality of its activities. The directive states that if the service provider is established in an EU member state and what it does is legal in that state, then it need not worry if it is legal abroad. The presence and use of technical means and technologies required to provide the service do not in themselves necessarily constitute the establishment of the service provider. An established service provider is one that effectively pursues an economic activity using a fixed establishment for an indefinite period of time.

The Directive (Article 3 Internal Market para 2) mentions the 'co-ordinated field' and specifically prohibits member states from restricting the freedom to provide information society services from another member state. However, there is derogation to the above principle, where it can be established that the activity is outside the 'co-ordinated field' such that insufficient harmonization exists across the EU, and includes areas such as taxation, copyright and use of electronic money.

Data Protection

This next major heading provides a brief explanation of the issues surrounding data protection and how it relates to e-Commerce applications. While data protection has been the subject of harmonization across the European Union, there are still outstanding issues and inconsistencies between the EU, other parts of Europe and North America, which naturally affects companies present in these markets, particularly when personal data passes across country borders.

UK Computer Misuse Act 1990

This Act was created following a great deal of controversy during the 1980s arising from several highly publicized incidents when hackers had successfully gained unauthorized access to computer systems. At the time hacking was not itself an offence and the hacker was relatively free to attempt to break into computer systems. One particular group of hackers based in Germany specialized in breaking into Digital Equipment Corporation (now part of Compaq) computers, which were extensively used by military and research networks notably by ARPANET, MILNET and National Aeronautics & Space Administration (NASA). Other incidents in the UK included unauthorized access to an electronic mailbox belonging to a member of the Royal Family, which the more cynical would argue acted as the stimulus for action in the UK. In some instances damage to data was being caused and there was an understandable concern that hacking could develop into something far more serious. Prior to the Computer Misuse Act 1990, efforts were made to prosecute hackers under the Criminal Damage Act 1971. The main difficulty in applying CDA 1971 was that it required that property must be destroyed or damaged. In the case of computer programs (not tangible) on magnetic media such as computer disks, the data was erased rather than any physical damage to the actual disks, which resulted in several failed prosecutions.

The Computer Misuse Act 1990 was a serious attempt to address the problems of hackers and to deter criminals from computer crime. With the global nature of e-Business, the CMA 1990 is one of the laws that has significant international implications, since the hacker and the computer system being hacked, do not necessarily have to be co-resident in the UK for prosecution under the Act. There are three offences under the Act, which all relate to the unauthorized use of computers, or access to data on a computer, with maximum sentences of 5 years imprisonment and an unlimited fine:

▷ Unauthorized access

▷ Unauthorized access with intent

▷ Unauthorized modification of computer material

Case Study – Computer Hacking

In March 2000 two teenagers were arrested in Wales following an investigation involving United Kingdom detectives, United States FBI and Royal Canadian Mounted Police. The teenagers allegedly hacked into e-Commerce computer sites in the US and stole information from more than 26,000 credit card accounts across the US, UK, Japan, Canada and Thailand and published details on the Internet. The cost of closing the compromised accounts, issuing new cards, repairing sites, and any losses reported by cardholders was forecast as amounting to £2 million. Specialists believed that a security loophole in Microsoft's Internet Information Server (Web server) enabled the hackers to gain unauthorized access to the computer accounts. This incident illustrates how unlawful access into a number of business computers and the theft of credit card information outside the UK can lead to prosecution under the Computer Misuse Act 1990, as well as possible prosecution in the other countries concerned.

UK Data Protection Act 1984 & 1998

During the 1970s with the increasing collection, processing and storage of personal data on computer systems, several countries including the United States, Germany and Sweden became concerned with privacy issues that these developments posed for their citizens and introduced legislation. In 1981 the UK signed the Council of Europe's Convention on Data Protection, and work commenced to incorporate into UK legislation the principles outlined in the convention. The resultant legislation was known as the Data Protection Bill, which became law in 1984.

In July 1995 the European Parliament adopted the Data Protection Directive 1995/46/EC which further extended earlier work on the protection and processing of personal data. This Directive was incorporated into UK legislation as the Data Protection Act 1998 and contained several notable extensions to the 1984 Act. The scope of data protection was extended to include not only personal data held in computer files, but also personal data held in manual records, as well as the need to obtain consent for the processing of data in some situations. Companies are required to register (now termed notify) under the Data Protection Act 1998 with the supervisory authority, namely the Data Protection Commissioner. The registration process includes details of personal data held by a company and the way it is used.

The practical result of this legislation means that those responsible for marketing initiatives, such as launching a store loyalty card, need to be far more attentive to the nature of the customer data collected. This implies that customers must be informed about any additional uses to which the store intends to use the data collected, e.g. promotional mailings, and be given the opportunity to agree or decline. For companies engaged in e-Commerce, it is quite likely that personal data including names and addresses of customers are collected, not just when placing an order, but also when completing a registration form required for product guarantees and warranty. It is good practice for Web sites to contain a statement describing their data protection policy and indeed examples of privacy policies can be found on the UK Data Protection Web site **www.dataprotection.gov.uk**

UK Regulation of Investigatory Powers 2000

In a world increasingly dominated by electronic communications there are two conflicting viewpoints, namely the freedom and privacy of the individual, and rights of governments to monitor electronic communications which it believes may constitute criminal activity or a threat to the state. The European Convention for the Protection of Human Rights and Fundamental Freedoms enacted in the UK as part of the Human Rights Act 1998 makes provision for the right to 'respect for privacy'. This would seem to suggest that the monitoring of E-mails by a company without employee knowledge and consent maybe a breach of human rights and data protection legislation.

Also relevant in this area is the UK's *Regulation of Investigatory Powers Act 2000*. The UK was one the first countries to introduce such legislation giving the government wide ranging powers to introduce regulations for access to business information by the monitoring of E-mail and Internet traffic. The associated regulations issued under the RIPA 2000 make it clear that companies retain the right to monitor E-mail and telephone use in the workplace without the employee's specific consent. However the regulations make it clear that companies should introduce acceptable use policies that details what is permitted when using company communications (telephone, E-mail and Internet) and to inform employees that their communications might be intercepted.

RIPA 2000 is of concern to UK Internet Service Providers that may be required to install interception 'black box' devices as part of the UK's government interception framework. There is a suggestion that UK ISPs will be required to route all data traffic passing across their networks through the Government Technical Assistance Centre (GTAC) of the UK's security service MI5. RIPA 2000 also covers the surrendering by companies of encryption keys or the printed text of an intercepted encrypted communication. This parallels with government surveillance of electronic communications in the US by the FBI using a system called Carnivore that is legal under US wiretap laws. The FBI have implemented numerous installations of Carnivore with ISP and telecommunications companies which enables the device to detect IP packets having a specific IP address under investigation.

Internet/Web Content

Defamation

The UK Defamation Act 1996 covers untrue statements that damage a person's reputation. While traditionally prosecution under the Act has been brought following libellous statements contained within the newspapers and other publications, cases are now arising due to such statements appearing on Web sites. The EU Electronic Commerce Directive 2000/31/EC indicates that providers of information society services are not liable for the content of information when simply acting as a conduit. If a customer publishes libellous information on a Web site hosted by an Internet Service Provider (ISP), then the ISP is not in breach of the legislation if they are unaware of the situation. However, once they become aware of the situation they must remedy it by removal of the offending material within a reasonable time or be in breach of the legislation.

Copyright

Copyright protects the rights of the creator to control the copying of their work by other people, without the permission of the creator. Even if permission to make copies is granted this does not alter the rightful ownership of the copyright, which still rests with the creator. However, provision is made for the creator to legally transfer ownership of the copyright to a third party, usually for a consideration, such as a payment of money. Frequently the work of the original author or creator relates to a book, magazine article, poem, play, song, painting, etc. which the copyright laws are intended to protect. Users of the Web need to remember that much of this wealth of information now available on a global basis is protected by copyright, and copying is restricted unless there is an explicit statement on the Web site to the contrary.

In addition Web site designers need to be aware that if they intend using copyright material on their Web site then they need the permission of the copyright owner. If it is a photograph then it is quite likely that the original photographer that took the picture will hold the copyright and needs to be approached to obtain permission for its usage. With growing media interest in retro-characters from previous eras, including the early days of television, many owners of such properties are finding a second wave of income arising from royalty payments for the use of their characters on a range of products including electronic greetings cards.

Another area of consideration for the Web site designer concerns the creation of 'hyperlinks' to other Web sites, without the approval of the site owner. The issue of whether such action constitutes a Copyright infringement on the rights of the destination Web site is still unresolved by the courts. However, some Web sites are starting to include a statement under their terms and conditions of usage that only permits the linking of other Web sites to their home page, while others contain no restrictions whatsoever. It is a little difficult to understand the basis of their objection, since the Web site is freely accessible by anyone knowing the Uniform

Resource Locator (URL) e.g. **http://www.ibm.com** and including a hyperlink in a Web site merely substitutes for the user's need to type in the URL. However, this is a contentious area likely to receive more attention in the future.

A major issue facing many academic institutions is the 'cut and paste' use made by students of material found both on the Web and in electronic databases to answer course assignments, and is known as 'plagiarism'. Plagiarism (to take and use another person's thoughts, writings, computer programs, inventions etc., as one's own) is theft. All institutions take a serious view of plagiarism, which can lead to punishment of the offending student including failure to bestow their academic award. Students are told that reports/essays must be written in their own words without cutting/pasting from books or the Web. However, it is permissible to quote others' work, provided it is cited as a reference and included in the bibliography of the report/essay.

Case Study – Napster and MP3.COM

The arrival of the .mp3 file format for recording music and subsequently playing it using suitable PC software (or portable players) has given rise to one of the most popular applications on the Web, namely the downloading of MP3 files of song titles that may be subsequently copied onto CD-ROM. Napster.com and MP3.com are two of the most well known MP3 sites and indeed Napster's original operation was closed down in July 2001 following a court case in the US. Napster provided a Web site for the exchange of .mp3 recordings of songs amongst users. The court upheld that copyright materials required a specific license with the copyright owners for the songs to be exchanged by users in this way. Since this ruling, Napster and other similar Web sites have been seeking legitimacy by negotiating deals with the recording companies to offer subscription-based services. In the case of MP3.com it was bought out by Universal/Vivendi, one of the five largest music recording companies that earlier had contested MP3.com in court. This has heralded a new era in which many of the music recording companies have started to view the evolution of Internet online music as a business opportunity rather than a threat. Indeed Napster is reported to have received a significant investment from Bertelsmann, a company that it originally faced on the opposite side during its court case. It is estimated that sales of conventional music CDs is down by 10% over the last year and this has put several of the big five in the music recording business under extreme financial pressure. However, it is unclear whether consumers will have the same level of enthusiasm for the new fee paying music downloads as they did for the original free services and the longer-term impact this will have on the music business is uncertain.

Trademarks and Domain Names

A trademark or mark is primarily used to ensure that consumers are not confused by the origin of a product or service. Companies are particularly concerned about protecting their trademarks, which can take a considerable amount of time and money to establish positive recognition in the minds of the consumer. Often consumer recognition and comfort with a trademark influence their choice at the point of purchase.

In the world of e-Commerce using the Web to market, buy and sell products and services, having a suitable domain name is crucial e.g. amazon.com or lastminute.com. Many smaller organizations now entering e-Commerce for the first time are regretting not having secured suitable domain names much earlier, as many of the popular names, perhaps even including their own company name, have already been registered. In many senses the domain name has a very profound impact from a marketing perspective and is similar to the brand recognition associated with a traditional product or service.

Not surprisingly both registered trademarks and companies are in a strong position to contest the ownership of domain names registered using their names, particularly if a third party registered them for sale. Equally, it is prudent to check on trademarks and company registration before finalizing a domain name, as this can reduce problems at a later stage if ownership of the domain name is contested. In the domain name space there are several popular extensions including .com meaning company, without any country qualifier, so by implications global in character; and the country equivalent such as .co.uk that means a company within the UK.

Every Web server has a unique number known as an IP (Internet Protocol) address. These numbers, similar to telephone numbers, act as addresses, enabling browsers to locate the network segment and specific host computer of the Web site requested by a user. However, unlike computers, people find long strings of numbers difficult to remember and work with, which is why domain names are used. A domain name is an easy to remember alphabetic name that represents one or more IP addresses. In the following address, for example, **www.lightweightdesigns.com/index.htm**, the domain name is **lightweightdesigns.com**

When a customer or supplier tries to access a Web site using a domain name, an Internet service called a Domain Name System (DNS) translates it into the corresponding IP number. The last part of a domain name, for example in lightweightdesigns.com, the .com is referred to as a Top-Level Domain (TLD). There are a variety of TLDs to choose from, depending on availability and the type of organization the domain name is intended for and these are discussed more fully in Chapter 16.

e-Business Strategies

Introduction

A clear message that should emerge from this book is that, irrespective of size, all organizations need to develop an e-Business strategy, which is business driven and places them in the best possible position to maximize the use of the Internet and other information and communications technologies. This is simply because the Internet, coupled with other factors discussed in Chapter 1, has changed for ever the way business is performed both internally with employees, and externally with business partners and customers. e-Business is rapidly becoming business as usual and the accepted norm. For many market sectors, the decision to conduct business electronically is no longer a choice or because it offers competitive advantage, just the chance of survival. However, if the strategy is well thought through and successfully executed, the prospects for business profitability look good.

The task of developing e-Business strategies presents a rather conventional corporate image for what many people regard as a dynamic and very creative period of business development. There is no doubt that the birth of the new economy and the resultant Dot.Com companies that initially emerged were in many instances the result of creativity on the part of the founders and less the result of systematic business research and planning. Aside from marketing creativity, it is evident that the founders of those companies surviving the 'first wave' of the new economy possessed the necessary business skills to develop the strategic direction in which to take their fledgling businesses. Indeed, Chapter 11 'Dot.Com Economy' already contains a treatment of the strategic choices that companies need to address when pursuing e-Commerce initiatives.

Porter (2001)[1] makes the point that organizations need to move on from a preoccupation with Dot.Com companies and the new economy to ask themselves some fundamental questions. Who is in line to gain the economic benefits that the Internet will bring? Will the customer derive all the benefits, or will the value be shared between the customer and the supplier? Is the Internet likely to improve opportunities for sustainable competitive advantage, or will it make the task far more difficult? Whatever the case, organizations have little choice but to deploy the technology and think through how it can enable them to establish distinctive strategic positioning within their chosen markets.

Not only is e-Business increasingly enabling internal business processes to support the design, manufacturer and marketing of products, but also critical electronic links are being forged with the business processes of suppliers and other business partners. For these types of activities, and the development of e-Commerce initiatives using the Web for the marketing, buying and selling of products to customers, appropriate e-Business strategies need to be developed. Often in the evolving collaborative environment being established between business partners within the supply chain, the specific objectives and actions flowing from these strategies *need* to be shared with business partners, if they are to realize their full potential.

The following sections consider some of the organizational processes that assist in strategy development, their impact in prioritizing the strategic applications portfolio, and methods of integrating business and IT strategies towards the evolution of a winning e-Business strategy.

Corporate Transformation

The reasons for growth of e-Business are complex but, in addition to the Internet, another key factor is the highly competitive environment that has evolved over the last decade and the resultant search for new forms of market differentiation. This has engendered a new style of organizational leadership, capable of facilitating the necessary corporate transformation these new business opportunities demand. It is this determined search for new innovative ways in which to drive the organization forward, towards the achievement of new levels of performance, that brings about the identification of process improvements. For those organizations competing in growing and enlarged marketplaces, getting it right means significant and worthwhile rewards. However, for some organizations there is an added urgency for change when competing against new entrants naturally drawn into growing marketplaces. This is because many of the new entrants are not constrained with the 'baggage' carried by traditional players, such as legacy computer systems, over staffing, and inappropriate business models.

Strategic Management and Information Technology

Ultimately, corporate business strategy captures the vision of the chief executive and his top management team to provide the overall direction for the organization to follow, and also hopefully satisfy the various interests of its stakeholders. The desired corporate direction will usually be set down in some form of mission statement from which a series of specific objectives can be derived, for communication throughout the organization. Finally, each manager, assigned the responsibility for specific objectives, is tasked with developing action plans, which describe the activities necessary for their attainment. For some organizations, the dynamics of the marketplace, coupled with short-term pressures, frustrate attempts to develop business strategy. However, information technology (IT) strategies and, more specifically, the development of strategies for e-Business, need to be business led if the outcome for the organization is to be successful.

Having created a business strategy (the process is outside the scope of this book), it is important to appreciate the key contribution that IT can make in the achievement of the specific objectives set out in the strategy. Indeed IT's contribution to adding value to a product or service can be such that new opportunities to broaden or change the scope of business activities may emerge. IT applications having the ability to impact the business in this way are termed 'strategic computer-based applications' or simply 'strategic applications'. Naturally, every organization would like to believe that included in their application development portfolio are applications of this nature, not just contributing to improved efficiency and productivity, but really capable of making a significant competitive difference. However, in most cases few organizations formally evaluate the potential business outcome of IT applications in these terms, and certainly do not go back after the implementation to measure whether the stated goals were in fact achieved.

For a small business, the ability to interface EDI purchase orders received from a customer over an EDI VAN service directly into their sales order processing package could release precious human resources which could be applied to more value adding activities for the company. Equally, to judge whether this is the best use of IT development resources usually means some planning needs to take place. For a larger business the establishment of a Web presence as an alternative sales channel to reach customers, complementing its existing physical 'bricks and mortar' stores, is likely to require thorough research and planning which will ultimately be guided by its business strategy. The next section considers the thinking that is available to assist organizations align business and IT strategies in order to identify those strategic e-Business applications which should be given the greatest level of support and priority by top management.

Integrating Business and IT Strategies

Information Systems Development Framework

How do organizations integrate business and IT strategies? What is the process used to identify and develop strategic computer-based applications? While considerable attention needs to be given to the manner in which change is successfully introduced within organizations, as far as the IT contribution is concerned, experience shows that there are generally four main stages in the information systems development framework.

Macro Planning
Preliminary Analysis
Corporate IT Strategy & Plan

Micro Planning
Feasibility Analysis
Project Plan

Information Analysis
Information Analysis (Techniques)
Top-Down (Decision Analysis)
Bottom-Up (Process Analysis)
Inside-Out (Output Analysis)
Systems (Soft Systems Methodology)

System Development Process
System Analysis
System Design
Prototyping
Program Development
Procedure Development
Integration Testing
Quality Assurance

Conversion
Operation
Maintenance

Post-Implementation Review

Figure 14.1 Information systems development framework

Macro Planning

This stage ensures that a good understanding of the business requirement exists, including the outcomes required. Together with the close involvement of the management team, it sets out to define the likely application development portfolio to support the achievement of the business strategy. Since many of the internal stakeholders carry organizational baggage and are not viewed as being impartial, external business consultants are frequently used during the initial stages of macro planning. If the situation is not so well defined, information analysis techniques can be used to gain clarity about what is required. These techniques include: top-down (decision analysis), bottom-up (process analysis), inside-out (output analysis) and systems (soft systems methodology) approaches. This initial information gathering exercise is frequently referred to as a 'preliminary analysis'.

As described earlier, strategic applications are those few IT projects forming part of the portfolio critical to the organization in achieving its business objectives. Ultimately, the corporate IT strategy should be a direct by-product of this process, bringing together those resources required over time to meet the business requirements. Any actions arising from specific e-Business initiatives are complex, since these initiatives tend to serve both the needs of the organization and its extended organization (used here to describe suppliers, customers, freight forwarders, manufacturers, etc.). While information technology serves to blur organizational boundaries, great care has to be given to ways in which the extended organization can be influenced to co-operate in the process of change. Achieving successful change within the same organization can be tough, but between different organizations it can present greater challenges. The ultimate success of an e-Business project will be heavily dependent upon how well this co-operation has been established, as well as ensuring a realistic level of resourcing by the parties involved. The organization and its extended organization create what is also referred to as the 'virtual' organization, which may include the outsourcing of some functions not considered to be part of the core business.

Micro Planning

This step involves moving into the individual feasibility and planning phase for each specific project forming part of the application development portfolio. If the outcome of the feasibility study is successful, then a deliverable from this phase will be an outline project plan, which becomes the basis for allocating resources, namely money and people. It is quite likely that at this stage, sufficient information about the project which will become available in order to start classifying the project in terms of its strategic contribution to the business and, in consequence, its relative priority. A later section examines the potential tools available to assist in this prioritization relative to other projects competing for resources (also known as the 'rack and stack' process).

FunFigure 14.2   Importance of project planning

Information Analysis

The information analysis phase is important in defining the information requirements the computer-based application needs to satisfy and starts to re-shape the associated business processes. A number of techniques exist which can help increase the successful outcome of a project, and business process re-engineering (BPR) as a change initiative uses many of these same techniques.

A *top-down* (decision analysis) approach is best used for those organizations where a clear direction has been established by top management, and a reasonable level of stability in the business environment exists. In the context of the specific business process identified for improvement, an exercise involving successive managerial layers of organization seeks to understand the tasks/goals to be achieved and the supporting information requirements. Indeed, there are many similar methodologies developed by the major management consultancies based upon this analytical approach.

Bottom-up (process analysis) exercises tend to be used by those organizations where management leadership or communication is lacking and no clear top level business objectives appear to exist. This could be due to rapid changes taking place in the business environment making a formal goal setting process exceedingly difficult. However, a bottom-up approach can be used to test out whether similar information requirements to those already derived from a top-down approach, result from working upwards through the organization. It typically involves the evaluation of information obtained via surveys and audits. While very effective for specific departments/functions, there is a tendency with this approach to achieve sub-optimal solutions of a localized nature, since the information gathering exercise does not fully recognize that processes run across an organization.

The *inside-out* (output analysis) is really taking a very innovative and creative approach, 'thinking out-side the box' and testing ideas through prototyping or small scale trials. Many of the new economy Dot.Com companies fall into this category.

Finally, *soft systems methodology* is used to simplify a complex environment to gain a better understanding of the relationships between the people involved and their interaction with the various business processes that form a human activity system. When used in its own right, such an approach rarely defines information requirements. 'Soft' systems methodologies are sometimes used as a front-end exercise for one of the 'harder' methodologies described above.

Some of these techniques can be used in a slightly modified manner to assist when undertaking a preliminary analysis, conducted during the macro planning phase.

System Development Process

This final activity concerns the execution phase where functional users and IT professionals are formed into project teams working closely together on the detailed design, development and implementation of the computer-based applications. If the functional requirement is best satisfied by an enterprise resource planning (ERP) system such as SAP, Oracle Applications or Baan, then the development effort is better described as customization, but still regarded as a large project. Successful implementation not only requires applications to meet the original specifications, but also that they readily form an integral part of the new business processes.

For smaller businesses, Internet technologies enable rapid development of Web applications to meet marketing and order service requirements. Coupled with the rapid growth of low cost software packages, many of which are e-Business enabled, means that SMEs are now able to enjoy the benefits previously reserved for larger organizations with their greater depth of resources.

Approaches to the Integration of Business and IT Strategies

Ideally, the outcome of a business led approach to the determination of IT strategy ensures that the focus of business process improvement is directly related to the establishment of an IT infrastructure that makes the achievement of business goals possible. With the continuing pressure on containing costs and a finite budget for IT spend, it is crucial that funding goes to those projects that will really make a major difference to the organization's ability to achieve competitive advantage. As described earlier, projects classified in this way usually form part of the 'strategic applications portfolio'. For the reasons discussed in earlier chapters, such projects enable organizations to conduct their commercial business activities in new ways, through the use of e-Business concepts.

From the author's experience, few organizations follow formal approaches/methodologies to assist in identifying and prioritizing projects in this way, but those that do feel the process is beneficial in aligning resources to key projects. This process is frequently substituted by a member of the top management team who acts as a project champion and feels intuitively that a particular project is right for the company. The following summary is not exhaustive, but should serve as an overview and basis for further reading on approaches for assessing the potential strategic contribution projects can make, and their resultant prioritization within the application development portfolio.

Value Chain – This approach developed by Porter (1985)[2] has already been described in Chapter 5 and examines the activities performed within an organization to establish how they interact, and where improvements could be a source of competitive advantage. The value chain model helps identify those areas where IT can make an additional contribution, by adding value to products/services, and eliminating those activities that add cost, but no value. The value chain approach is an important concept, which has been successfully applied within the supply chain to make significant cost savings by the reduction and, in some instances, the elimination of inventories.

Multiple Methodology – This approach by Earl (1989)[3] is based upon the supposition that no single methodology to determine the strategic application portfolio will work and therefore several need to be applied in parallel to serve as counterchecks to each other. Earl suggests that such a complex approach is necessary because of the inherent complexity of organizations. In practice it is necessary for an organization to perform:

▷ Top-down analysis (decision analysis) to clarify business needs in IT terms

▷ Bottom-up analysis (process analysis) by evaluating current IT systems

▷ Inside-out analysis (output analysis) to apply innovative thinking to identify new strategic opportunities made possible by IT

The resultant areas identified for process improvement form candidates for the strategic applications portfolio.

Strategic Grid – Developed by McFarlan (1984), the strategic grid considers the contribution made by IT to the business now and into the future by reference to four categories of IT development, in which candidates for the strategic application portfolio are allocated. Ideally, those applications located in the strategic segment of the grid and critical for future success should receive the highest priority for funding. A simple but effective model to assist management in the integration of its business and IT strategies.

Strategic Thrusts – Originally described by Rackoff (1985)[4], and extended by Wiseman (1985)[5] this approach is based upon the belief that organizations determine a focus or target for their strategic intentions, such as suppliers, customers or competitors. Having decided the target, it is necessary to decide upon the alternative strategic thrusts, either offensive or defensive, that can be used by the organization to achieve its business goals. Wiseman identifies five alternative thrusts, including differentiation, cost, innovation, growth and alliance to form a matrix. This will result in an evaluation of current business processes supporting the strategic thrust to be adopted by the organization, and identify new areas of process improvement to be supported by IT.

IT induced Business Reconfiguration – Work by Nolan (1974, revised 1979) provided the first framework to track the stages through which organizations pass, as they apply IT in support of the business. A major assertion of his work was the simple, but obvious fact, that these stages represent an evolution for an organization, and to proceed implied having successfully completed the previous stage. Ten years later, following the personal computer revolution that heralded increased IT innovation and still greater organizational dependence upon IT, Venkatraman (1990)[6] identified new stages in order for the organization to proceed. Venkatraman suggests that the focus for organizations in the 1990s is upon the recognition and exploitation of IT, and his model recognizes the importance of business process re-design, the virtual or networked organization and potential for organizations to redefine the scope of their business. Above all, to proceed through these stages implies major organizational transformation, and many organizations have not yet started on this path. In practical terms, this model provides a checklist and challenge for management to assess whether they are taking the fullest advantage of IT, and poses the question whether or not the necessary organizational changes are in hand to make this possible. Some researchers have taken Venkatraman's model as a basis for defining 'strategic applications', as being 'those systems that have the potential to make a significant impact on the organization's business strategy by enabling change in the nature and/or conduct of the organization's business'.

Integration Summary – Alignment of the business and IT strategies of an organization is a complex issue and the above section represents just some of the thinking behind it. However, it is an important issue to grasp if the fullest benefits of e-Business are to be realized, not only in contributing to survival in a turbulent business environment, but also establishing the foundations for long-term growth through competitive differentiation. The very nature of e-Business and its implied close working relationship within a trading community means that many different organizations need to share the same vision of how their business can be re-shaped using IT.

e-Business Strategy Development

There are a number of key factors an organization needs to consider when developing a strategy towards e-Business, and these are identified below.

Business Driven

e-Business initiatives are 'business' led activities, with an implicit acceptance of process change and often involving the use of high-energy change initiatives, such as business process re-design (BPR). It is important to be able to describe project outcomes in terms that can attract the commitment of top management to results such as: the reduction of order to remittance time from 40 days to 7 days, stocks and work-in-progress slashed by 50%, customer service improvement up 5 points on the index, etc. e-Business initiatives cannot succeed by themselves, and are usually accompanied by fundamental changes in the way the business is run. Management must set the agenda, determine the goals, ensure they are aggressive but realistic, and navigate the organization through the resultant turmoil of change.

Customer Focus

Will the resultant new e-Business ways of working make it easier for the organization to target its potential customers, so they know more about its products and services? While the need exists to provide more and more information to customers, the real urgency is to make it easier for buyers to do business with the chosen seller/supplier. Customers can easily be lost, despite satisfaction with the product or service supplied, due to inaccurate or cumbersome administration of the relationship between buyer and seller, such as inaccurate invoicing. Telephone companies, traditionally bad in providing meaningful usage details to support their invoices, have been exploiting this inadequacy to achieve competitive advantage and improve customer satisfaction. The Web provides the foundation for e-Commerce initiatives and, together with E-mail and Chat, the means to develop innovative customer focused applications that strengthen buyer and seller relationships. However, the key to winning and retaining customers remains the development of a superior value proposition built around the products and services being sold. This should be tailored to the organization's target customers and be superior to competitors in the same market segment.

The Extended Organization

When looking to establish an e-Business environment, organizations should seek to be in a position to exert influence over their business/trading partners making up the extended organization. However, to be successful, this needs to be undertaken in a supportive and collaborative manner such that an open boundaryless culture is created where the mutual inter-dependence of all parties is seen as a benefit, rather than a disadvantage. Traditionally, most large/medium sized organizations and their trading partners are clustered in electronic trading communities of common interest, based upon the extended enterprise concept. However, already dramatic changes are underway within the supply chain with the growing use of private trade exchanges by major retailers to award contracts to suppliers and movement towards a form of open electronic trading.

Remaining Flexible

The old maxim, 'the only constant thing in life is change', seems more relevant today than at any time in corporate history. The key to future success is not only creating a culture that accepts and relishes change, but also in developing e-Business strategies that ensure the organization is not 'locked-in' to specific information technologies or software products. One way to remain flexible is to adopt an open systems strategy for the acquisition of software or when deciding upon corporate IT standards. Failure to retain such future flexibility in being able to rapidly respond to new business requirements will be damaging.

Enterprise Application Integration

Most organizations already have a heavy investment in legacy IT applications which cannot immediately be replaced and often have to exist alongside new business processes for some years. Care should be taken to integrate, as far as possible, legacy applications within new e-Business projects. After some years of neglect, management is now realizing the real benefits of enterprise application integration (EAI) in removing obstacles causing internal inefficiency and indifferent customer response. This has become particularly evident as new Web-based e-Commerce initiatives have been introduced which significantly improve customer order processing, but which are not integrated with legacy back-office applications. EAI coupled with the acceptance of XML as an interface standard is streamlining back-office processes to improve this situation. EAI is however resource intensive, and is best organized using cross functional teams who have the detailed knowledge of existing processes and have been empowered by management to make it happen.

Information and Knowledge

While data has a cost, information has a value, providing the incentive to develop an information resource/warehouse culture within the organization. It is important to establish ways in which information can be made available freely to those that can make the optimum use of it, in decision making and improving customer service. Will new e-Business initiatives create important new information sources that can be exploited for business benefit? Knowledge is the most enduring asset of any organization, and the scarce and precious knowledge held by employees needs to be incorporated into new applications. With the conflicting demands for improved customer service while at the same time reducing costs, organizations are deploying more knowledge databases to provide customers with the assistance they seek. Web technology is particularly suited to this type of application, helping customers by means of problem resolution and providing access to frequently asked questions.

Contrasting e-Business and e-Commerce

e-Business is interpreted in this book as the all-embracing term to describe the use of information technology by an organization for all facets of its business both internal and external. It is perhaps best to consider e-Business as extending across the supply chain, incorporating its internal business operations, as well as its interaction with trading partners. In this respect most of the initiatives are very much geared to continuous process improvements that make optimum use of information technology for the running of the business and its extended enterprise. Invariably, such initiatives bring benefits which can be expressed in terms of lower costs, competitive edge, improved customer service, extended products and services, higher sales revenues, improved profitability, greater market share, etc. e-Business certainly changes the way a company operates, but the transformation can be far more dramatic by opening up new ways of reaching out to communicate with customers via the Web. E-Commerce is viewed as this sub-set of e-Business that relates to the marketing, buying and selling of products and services over the Web.

Electronic Business	Electronic Commerce
Internal Applications (engineering, manufacture, logistics, marketing & sales, administration & finance) Enterprise Application Integration Business-to-Employee Business-to-Business PLUS **Electronic Commerce**	External Applications (Web-based customer order entry, order tracking & customer service). Primarily Business-to-Consumer or Consumer-to-Consumer (but also Business-to-Business)
Business-to-Business: Many line items per purchase order Many purchase orders per interchange	Business-to-Consumer & Business-to-Business: Fewer line items per purchase order Usually fewer purchase orders
Very specific delivery requirements	Delivery as soon as possible
Purchase orders and invoices sent via EDI	Credit card purchasing over a secure Web site
Usually application-to-application with little human interaction except for B2E	Customer/consumer driven with Web server application
Specialized application software with full-featured functionality	Geared to customer/consumer's ease of use and delivering positive customer experience
Business-to-Employee: Internal employee uses corporate Intranet for self-service access to required information	Business-to-Consumer: Home consumers browse Web sites for product, service or general information
Business-to-Business: Electronic marketplaces, trade exchanges or online auctions that bring business buyers and sellers together usually within a vertical market. Private rather public exchanges are more popular	Consumer-to-Consumer: Public trade exchanges provided by third parties to bring consumers together to buy and sell Business-to-Consumer: Public marketplace operated by a business to sell directly to consumers

Table 14.1 Contrasting e-Business and e-Commerce

In practice it is not always so easy to make such a clear distinction between e-Business and e-Commerce. Consider for example the following situations:

▷ A business customer calls a free-phone number and orders office supplies using the seller's interactive telephone system linked to its order entry system.

▷ A major food retailer orders grocery products using an EDI VAN Service.

▷ A home improvement store chain orders paints via a direct connection to their paint supplier, via the store chain's Extranet.

▷ A manufacturing plant orders electronic components for assembly into its products from another plant within the same company using the corporate Intranet.

▷ A business customer purchases computer equipment online or through an electronic auction.

▷ A home consumer purchases a book and several music CDs from their favourite Web site.

▷ A government employee books a hotel room and EuroStar train ticket over the Internet.

These are all examples of e-Business at work, but the last three are also considered as being examples of e-Commerce with their online Web-based orientation.

Business Models for e-Commerce

The traditional model of a business views raw materials entering the company and being transformed in some way such that value is added during the manufacturing processes. This then permits the selling of the products (transformed raw materials) at a premium reflecting the extent to which value has been added. The principle is much the same for marketing and selling of services where the intermediary adds value as perceived by the end customer. This is shown diagrammatically in Figure 14.3 where a customer ultimately enters a traditional store or shop to make their purchases. The different trading parties in the process form the supply chain ensuring that required products are available for the customer to purchase. In e-Business terminology, the outlet is often referred to as a 'bricks and mortar' business to differentiate it from 'virtual' stores existing in cyberspace.

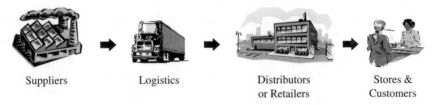

| Suppliers | Logistics | Distributors or Retailers | Stores & Customers |

Figure 14.3 Traditional 'bricks and mortar' business

The traditional bricks and mortar business represents the foundation on which products and services are sold today. This supply chain driven business model is increasingly adopting e-Business practices such as EDI and collaborative applications to reduce inventories, cut costs and improve customer service. It is based upon the premise that its customers find it acceptable, even enjoyable to visit the store for the purchase of products and services. Information technology is very important to the company in support of its back-office systems, links to trading partners and for the efficient operation of its stores through electronic point of sale checkouts. Some companies have used an alternative channel to reach customers through the use of sales catalogues, sometimes combined with physical bricks and mortar stores which customers use to shop in the traditional way. In all cases, catalogue companies have some form of order taking using either the post or telephone, as well as a distribution network which despatches goods against the orders received. In many respects it is just the manner in which they interface with their customers that is different to the traditional business.

As described in Chapters 10 and 12, new business models have emerged in the 1990s enabled by the Internet and, more specifically, Web technology. The so called Dot.Com companies exploited the potential of the Web to offer business customers and home consumers a number of new products and services delivered electronically, including software, research reports, games, music, financial and insurance products, etc. Figure 14.4 illustrates the 'point and click' business model where the customer selects the seller's Web site and then proceeds to navigate the site in order to make their purchase. In most cases the seller is only present through their Web application, which is reachable at any time of day or night and considerably reduces the seller's cost of sales. Recent developments allow the customer to initiate contact with a customer service representative, either using an electronic chat dialogue or via the telephone. More frequently, the tangible nature of the product or service being sold over the Web such as books, music CDs, computers and supplies, groceries, etc. means that the customer effectively places an order for subsequent physical delivery.

Earlier chapters have discussed the trials and tribulations of the Dot.Com companies forming part of the new economy. However, following the first wave of Dot.Com failures, a decision to establish an Internet start-up company now would require a considerable amount of planning for it to be successful, or to have a chance of gaining the necessary venture funding to get it off the ground. Many of the Internet pioneers who have become household names have yet to return a profit, so this business model is not for the faint hearted.

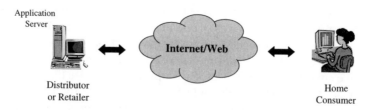

Figure 14.4   Dot.Com 'point and click' business

An interesting question being asked by many traditional businesses is whether or not they should extend their current marketing Web presence in order for it to become a sales channel. This poses some challenges as, frequently, the understanding and knowledge of using Web technologies in this way is lacking within the company. For a retail chain there are natural concerns that by adding the Web as an alternative sales channel it will cannibalize their existing business without the equivalent level of sales revenue. However, companies no longer have a choice in whether or not to deploy Internet technology as they simply have to do it to remain competitive. The issue is more about *how* to deploy it. One possible scenario involves establishing a strategic alliance with a Dot.Com company that already has a Web presence and, therefore, brings its experience of this new sales channel to the venture.

Case Study – Waterstone's

Waterstone's, a traditional bricks and mortar chain of bookshops in the UK originally launched Waterstones.co.uk to establish a Web presence for book purchases. Lacking the electronic retailer expertize, the venture was not wholly successful with a high level of customer complaints, including lengthy order fulfilment times as well as a costly support infrastructure. When Waterstone's came to re-launch the Web site it announced that it had joined forces with Amazon. While apparent competitors in the book marketplace, it conceded that this strategic alliance with Amazon would ensure a more cost effective online presence being established, without affecting its traditional bookshop business. The re-launched Waterstone's Web site offers a distinctive look and features outstanding book knowledge, events news, branch information and exclusive articles that consumers have come to expect, delivered using the same e-Commerce platform as Amazon.co.uk.

Case Study – John Lewis Partnership

John Lewis is a major UK department store chain, which decided to be a follower and to learn from the mistakes of other UK retailers, who established Web sales channels at an earlier point in time. One key observation made by John Lewis which shaped their entry strategy was that, frequently, retailers tried to do too much in-house, often without the right level of expertize or simply that the existing infrastructure failed to match the requirement of the new sales channel. As a result, John Lewis took a considered and balanced approach to the project by deciding to outsource the fulfilment of orders and customer contact to two companies experienced in the field. In addition, when looking to establish the e-Commerce platform, it was able to acquire proven technology and expertise by purchasing the UK division of buy.com at the beginning of 2001.

Finally, while operating the new venture separately from its stores, it is sufficiently integrated with the core business to allow customers to return faulty goods to the stores. It also uses the same customer database.

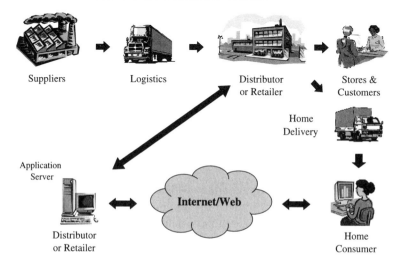

Figure 14.5   Integrated 'bricks and clicks'

Clearly there are many other variations that can be envisaged, but in e-Business jargon the resultant business model is characterized as an integrated 'bricks and clicks' operation (see Figure 14.5). The exact nature of implementation requires careful thought and planning to get it right in the context of each business and, in this respect, there is no easy formula of what is right and what is wrong. In the main, this discussion equally applies to companies developing business-to-business or business-to-consumer business models as the final distinction is between a business customer and home consumer. As an example the Dell Computer Corporation Web site receives visits from both categories of buyers.

Strategic Choices

Gulati and Garino (2000)[7] reflect upon the experiences of several successful bricks and mortar retail businesses in the US that have faced the decision of how to enter the market as electronic retailers [e-Tailers].

As an example they comment upon the strategy adopted by Barnes and Noble, with an established network of bookstores, which established a completely separate entity Barnesandnoble.com to compete against Amazon.com. Their general conclusion is that Barnes and Noble may have sacrificed a great deal more than they gained by failing to integrate and promote Barnesandnoble.com within their bookstores.

Separation Spin-Off Strategic Partnership Joint Venture In-House Division Integration

- Greater focus
- More flexibility
- Access to venture funding

- Established brand
- Shared information
- Purchasing leverage
- Distribution efficiencies

Figure 14.6 The 'clicks and mortar' spectrum

Staples (UK) is a chain store selling office products that offers customers the choice of in-store or mail order catalogue purchases. Benefiting from the experiences of similar companies in the US, Staples is adopting a strategy of tight integration between its e-Commerce Web presence and its physical stores, where the Web is considered as just another sales channel. In addition, they are able to benefit from the experience/ knowledge of their mail order catalogue business in moving to a Web presence. Indeed, they are not very concerned if the Internet channel cannibalizes their catalogue business, since the cost of an order over the Web is significantly cheaper than via the catalogue.

Other examples include bricks and mortar businesses with established brand presence within a specific retail sector that have established strategic relationships with e-Commerce Internet-based retailers moving into the market-space. These e-Tailers bring to the venture the knowledge of the Internet as a sales channel that many of the established bricks and mortar businesses do not possess. In contrast, the e-Tailer is able to take full advantage of the established bricks and mortar retail business either through brand recognition, purchasing economies and customer satisfaction and from the ability to use the physical store for the return of goods. To formalize the strategic relationship, it is common practice for an established retail business to take equity holding in the Internet-based retailer present in their market-space. However, in most instances their business operations continue to be managed quite separately, although leverage of purchasing power may cause procurement to be more closely coupled. Developing the right integration strategy involves making choices relative to brand, management, operations and equity on the degree of separation and integration for each factor (see Figure 14.6).

Retaining Customers through Loyalty

All organizations are aware of the high cost of winning new business, yet many still do not apply an adequate level of effort to retaining their existing customers. In both the business-to-business and business-to-consumer categories of e-Commerce, it was originally imagined that the dynamic nature of the Web, coupled with software agent technology, would mean that customers would be more fickle and less loyal to suppliers. In consequence, customers would abandon any loyalty created with a supplier when presented with a more advantageous offer from another supplier. However, practical experience suggests that Web customers are less fickle and more loyal than first thought. This important observation implies that where companies have established loyalty with their online customers, they would be well advised to devote additional efforts to retain and build the loyalty of their customer base. The Internet is ideal for this purpose and once a business customer or home consumer has been through a positive online shopping experience referral to other colleagues or friends, possibly using E-mail to point them to a recommended Web site, can generate additional business.

In many ways this is an extension of the customer service focus, which dominated so many companies during the 1990s by recognizing customer service as a key factor in securing competitive advantage and building customer loyalty. It is hardly surprising that the call centre sector devoted to customer care continues to grow, implementing new customer relationship management initiatives often coupled with Web presence, e.g. electronic chat, request for a telephone call, etc. (see Lands' End case study in Chapter 10).

Summary

Much has been written about the changing world of business as it became transformed into e-Business. However, with the increasing pervasiveness and adoption of information technology by companies, many regard the way e-Business operates today as nothing unusual and the 'e' is ceasing to have the meaning that it originally had. However, this should not be interpreted that the process is complete. While good progress has been made, the challenge remains for many organizations to fully embrace e-

Business into their strategic thinking and develop appropriate strategies to exploit its potential. This means that appropriate planning processes need to be put in place to ensure strategic e-Business projects can surface and receive management support and resourcing. In addition, e-Business requires a number of key considerations when companies look to strategic development to counteract the uncertain turbulent environment of the new millennium and continuing rapid developments in information technology. Lastly, the shaping of the business to embrace the Web as a new sales channel for both business customers and home consumers needs careful research, planning and execution if the venture is to be successful.

[1] Porter ME (2001) *Strategy and the Internet*, Harvard Business Review, March 2001, P.63

[2] Porter ME (1985) *Competitive Advantage – Creating and Sustaining Superior Performance*, The Free Press

[3] Earl MJ (1989) *Management Strategies for Information Technologies*, Prentice Hall

[4] Rackoff N, Wiseman C & Ullrick W (1985) *Information Systems for Competitive Advantage: Implementation of a Planning Process*, MIS Quarterly

[5] Wiseman C (1985) *Strategy and Computers: Information Systems as Competitive Weapons*, Dow Jones-Irwin

[6] Venkatraman N & Leghorn R (1989) *IT Induced Business Reconfiguration: The New Strategic Challenge*, MIT – Sloan School of Management

[7] Gulati R & Garino J (2000) *Get the Right Mix of Bricks & Clicks*, Harvard Business Review, May-June 2000, P.107

Communications Fundamentals

Introduction

Reliable computer communications are a relatively new development. Long after computers evolved from the primitive early machines in the middle of the 20th century, computer communications were often restricted to slow and error-prone telephone lines, using expensive and cumbersome modems. It was not until the 1980s and 1990s that improving technology and other changes such as the deregulation and privatization of many national telephone corporations opened the floodgates to faster and better communications, followed by the explosive growth of the Internet and the World Wide Web. But communications remain something of a black art. Partly for that reason, there have been many proprietary solutions. In the days when there were numerous computer companies, mostly with their own operating systems and computer architectures, the networking systems had to be designed to fit in with those individual environments. And perhaps the computer companies realized that proprietary networking was another way to lock in customers. But there has been increasing emphasis on open systems, and the growth of the Internet, based on TCP/IP, has reinforced that trend. These days most computer companies actively support open standards, because it is to their commercial advantage to do so. There is also a convergence between different types of equipment such as mobile telephones, small and hand-held or palmtop computers, PDAs (Personal Digital Assistants), digital cameras, etc. In the future, you may want to communicate with your central heating system or hi-fi setup.

LANs and WANs

Broadly speaking, communications can be divided up into two major categories:

> ▷ Local Area Networks   (LAN)

> ▷ Wide Area Networks   (WAN)

LANs are designed to provide high-speed convenient access within a small geographic area – typically an office building. The extent of a LAN is limited because electrical signals degrade as they travel along wires. However, within this limit, communications are fast and reliable.

In contrast, WANs operate over long distances, and are generally slower than LANs. The problem of signal degradation is greater, requiring more regeneration of the signal. Even though these days parts of a WAN may run over very high-speed optical cables, the speed of the connection ultimately depends on the slowest part of it. Very often for domestic users this is what is called the 'local loop' – the final mile or so between the nearest telephone exchange and your house.

These days, though, the distinction between LANs and WANs is often blurred and even invisible to the user. For example, in a large international corporation LANs are often interconnected over a WAN, and computers in another country are just as accessible as local ones. There are also in-between categories, such as MANs (Metropolitan Area Networks). For domestic users, more and more countries are offering faster broadband access using cable modems or ADSL.

In short, communications are evolving at a rapid rate, giving faster and more reliable access at lower cost. In this chapter, we will focus mainly on computer communications, and in particular these aspects:

> ▷ Exchanging data between computers

> ▷ Communications technologies

Exchanging Data between Computers

The drive towards open systems arises because of a fundamental issue that has been around since the dawn of computing, and has still not been completely resolved – in fact, developments like XML are yet another attempt to solve this problem, The problem is an apparently trivial one – how to exchange data between different computers. It may sound simple, but is in fact remarkably complicated. It is not unusual for such 'interoperability' problems to affect e-Business. For e-Business though it is a fundamental requirement – the ability for different computer systems to co-operate.

At first sight, this might seem a non-problem. If one computer has a file of data containing, for example, just the letters ABC, then it seems simple enough to send that to another computer system, and expect it to understand those three simple letters. To see why this is not necessarily the case, we need to look at the technical fundamentals, and how, over the years, computer system designers have tried to solve this problem. There are many aspects to it, with different solutions and different standards. It starts with the most fundamental aspect of all – how computers work.

Bits and Bytes

At its most basic, a computer is made of transistors, which can only switch on or off (or to be precise, they can switch between a low and a high voltage). Hence, any single transistor can be in one of two electrical states, which by convention we call '0' or '1', in binary arithmetic. This number we call a 'bit' – short for 'binary integer'. So in mathematical terms, one transistor can represent 2^1 (2 to the power of one) = 2 possibilities = on or off. Inside a computer, everything must ultimately be reduced to this simple level – both data and programs ultimately consist of nothing but these electrical states or bits. But by combining transistors into electronic circuits, we can combine several bits, thus giving us enough possibilities to represent numbers, and we can also encode characters as numbers. That's an important point – a computer has no concept of letters of the alphabet. All it knows is binary arithmetic. So here we come across the first problem – how many bits are needed to represent a character? In the days not so long ago when computer memory was expensive, there was a need to use as few bits as possible. Hence the 5-bit Baudot code used in telex and some early computers, giving $2^5 = 32$ possibilities, enough for the letters of the alphabet (capitals only) for each character or 'byte'. Other later systems used 6 bits, giving $2^6 = 64$ possibilities per byte. These days, a byte is pretty well universally 8 bits, giving $2^8 = 256$ possibilities – enough for all the letters of the alphabet, plus the digits 0-9, various punctuation marks, control characters etc. (Incidentally, people sometimes talk about 4 bits (half a byte) being a 'nibble', and 4 bytes being a 'dinner').

Character Sets

Bytes however lead to the next problem – how to encode characters as numbers, in other words, what numbers to use. This can only be an arbitrary decision by a computer designer or authoritative body. In the Baudot code, originally used for telegrams and telex, the letter 'A' is represented by the number 1, B by 2 etc. The main standards these days for computers are ASCII, EBCDIC and Unicode, though each has variants and derivatives.

ASCII

ASCII (see glossary), strictly speaking, uses only 7 of the 8 bits in an octet, thus giving $2^7 = 128$ possibilities. (For the difference between octet and byte, see glossary). This provides space for all English characters (upper and lower case), numbers and punctuation marks, and is fine for the English language, and a few others such as Swahili and Hawaiian which happen to use the same characters. It is also the basis of IA5 (International Alphabet 5) standardized as ISO646 (which allows a few national variants) and specified for some systems, notably X.400. IA5 becomes important when data is exchanged between countries that have different accented or special characters. If a message is sent from one country using its accented or special characters to another country with different characters, problems and misinterpretations are likely. IA5 means that characters like æ have to be sent as two separate characters – ae.

Standard ASCII is no use for other languages with additional characters, or accented characters. Hence there is what is commonly (but somewhat incorrectly) called 'Extended ASCII' which uses all 8 bits, allowing 256 possibilities, and therefore room for a range of European special characters. But there are many variations, and, strictly speaking, it is not part of the ASCII standard, and leaves out many non-Latin languages. For some, such as Chinese and Japanese, there are special conventions using 'double byte' characters – two characters to represent an ideogram.

EDI Character Sets

EDI standards also need to specify what character sets they are using. The EDIFACT standard, for example, specifies the use of a range of 7-bit codes, a subset of ISO 646 (though other codes can be used by specific mutual agreement between trading partners). One EDIFACT subset, called Level A, allows only upper case letters A-Z, numerals and a few punctuation characters. EDIFACT Level B has a wider range, including lowercase letters and more punctuation signs.

ISO Standards

To cater for the various extra characters needed, ISO developed a new standard, often called 'ISO Latin1' and more formally ISO 8859-1 which includes ASCII as a sub-set (but with some variations, such as the currency sign), and also uses the extended range of codes 160-255 to include many accented characters. The remaining range, 128-159, was reserved for control characters. Microsoft Windows uses ANSI, a variant of Latin1, in which some of the extended range is used for certain special printable characters, such as the copyright symbol ©. Later versions of Windows, such as NT, use Unicode (see below).

By now you are perhaps getting the impression that character codes are not as straightforward as they might seem. But there's more.

EBCDIC

EBCDIC (see glossary) uses 8-bit bytes, and was designed in the days of punched cards to be reasonably human-readable. It is still widely used on mainframe systems, particularly on IBM machines. The result is that a letter 'A' in EBCDIC has an entirely different binary value than an ASCII or ISO 'A'. If a file of data is passed from an ASCII-based computer to an EBCDIC, or the other way around, it has to go through a conversion process.

Being based on single bytes, both ASCII and EBCDIC are well suited to communications protocols, because they are very efficient in terms of computer processing and storing data in files. But the disadvantages and possible ambiguities of these character sets are too great in a world where accuracy is vital, and where localization (adapting software to suit individual countries) is more and more important.

Unicode

Unicode, also called UCS (Universal Character Set), is the latest attempt to standardize character sets, and it does so by using 2 bytes (16 bits) for each character – thus giving 2^{16} = 65,536 possibilities. This allows for a huge range of characters, not only for languages based on the Latin alphabet, but also for many other non-Latin languages, including Chinese, Japanese, etc, plus a great variety of special punctuation marks. However, Unicode is still evolving, and there are already several variants. In any case, Unicode is only supported on specific operating systems, such as Microsoft Windows NT and some Unix variants. Fortunately, at the bottom end, ASCII and Unicode overlap, so 'A' has the same binary value in both. In ASCII, it is the decimal number 65, or in hexadecimal 41. In Unicode notation, 'A' is more fully defined as U+0041 LATIN CAPITAL LETTER A ('A') – the first byte is hex 00, the second is hex 41. Unicode is also the basis of an ISO standard, ISO 10646, which is recommended for all new Internet protocols, including XML. In fact, ISO 10646 goes a stage further than Unicode and specifies a four-byte character set. However the top two bytes are not yet used, and the bottom two are the same as Unicode. The full name of ISO 10646 is Universal Multiple-Octet Coded Character Set, or UCS for short.

However, even Unicode does not solve all character set problems, because even two bytes, with 65,536 possibilities, are not enough for all the characters and symbols in the world, and from time to time new ones are added, such as the recent Euro symbol . There are various solutions which extend Unicode's range, notably UTF-8, which uses a variable number of bytes to encode characters, and is compatible with ASCII. It is one of a series of character sets called UTF (Unicode Transformation Format). In UTF-8, 1-byte characters are the same as ASCII; 2 bytes are used for non-Latin such as Greek or Arabic; and other special characters (symbols etc.) use 3 or more bytes. The details are complex, and mostly of interest to programmers. But it is worth having a broad understanding of the remarkably complicated issue of characters and character sets, and the potential effects on e-Business. It is not unusual to come across such character set problems, particularly when exchanging data between different countries as well as different computer systems.

Unicode and XML

For flexibility, XML supports these Unicode transformation formats (UTFs):

▷ UTF-8 with single 8-bit byte for ASCII characters, and additional bytes if required for Unicode characters

▷ UTF-7 is like UTF-8, but uses 7-bit bytes

▷ UTF-16 allows transformation between Unicode and ISO 10646

XML also allows other encodings, as long as they are specified. In addition, regardless of the encoding, a value like this A in XML always means U+0041 LATIN CAPITAL LETTER A ('A').

Dealing with Numbers

There is a similar problem for numbers. Once again, a computer has no concept of a 'number', particularly a decimal number that we are so familiar with. Take a number like '12345'. In binary, this is 0011000000111001 – two bytes. But there are two ways that a computer can store a number – either in the sequence shown, or with the second byte first. Some computer systems and computer file formats are designed to store the big value in the first byte as 00110000 followed by the second byte 00111001. For that reason, they are called MSB (Most Significant Byte) or 'big-endian'. But other processors, notably the Intel family, and other file formats store the smaller value first, for performance reasons. Naturally they are LSB (Least Significant Byte) or 'little-endian'. In some cases and programming languages the values are stored as 4 bytes or other more complex structures but the same principles apply. Within the computer itself, this design decision makes no difference. But if you are exchanging a file containing numerical values between two such computers with different architectures, then the resulting number will be quite different, and it is easy to imagine situations in which such arithmetic discrepancies can cause severe and potentially expensive problems. So once again you need a conversion routine to handle this. Many communications systems do this automatically. TCP/IP (and therefore the Internet) requires data to be sent in 'Network Byte Order', which is 'big-endian'. Fortunately, a TCP program designed to run on a 'little-endian' machine will convert automatically. Similarly, the OSI 7-layer Reference Model handles these issues in layer 6 – the Presentation Layer. This problem also affects characters in multi-byte systems, so Unicode, for example, specifies that data must be sent 'big-endian', though it also has a special character that can be used to distinguish which end comes first.

Incidentally, the terms 'big-endian' and 'little-endian' show that the computer business does have a sense of humour. The terms come from the book Gulliver's Travels by Jonathan Swift, where the Lilliputians have violent political disagreements about an apparently trivial matter – whether eggs should be cut open at the big end or the little end.

Defining a Line

Another problem when exchanging data between computer systems is what is meant by a 'line' of text. Many computer systems define a 'line' as being a row of characters such as ABC, followed by one or more invisible control characters that enable the operating system to recognize the end of the line. On PCs, a line generally ends with two invisible so-called 'control' characters – Carriage Return and Line Feed. But on a Macintosh, it is just Carriage Return, and on Unix systems, it is just Line Feed. On mainframe systems, it is quite common to use a 'fixed-length record' - a line of data of a fixed length, often 80 characters, with no terminator. All these different ways of handling data present problems when exchanging data.

System	Definition of line/record
PC/Windows	A B C cr + lf
Macintosh	A B C cr
Unix systems	A B C lf
Mainframe systems	A B C (no terminator)

Table 15.1 Defining a line of text

Defining Date and Time

A further problem when exchanging data is how to specify dates and times. For example, a date of '010203' can mean very different things in different countries – 1 February 2003 in most of Europe, 2 January 2003 in other countries, notably the US, and in yet other countries it is 3 February 2001. Times are generally simpler, but some countries use a 24-hour clock, others use a.m. and p.m. Finally, there is also the question of time zones, and related issues like summer and winter time. In addition, time zones may vary by different amounts. India is $5\frac{1}{2}$ hours ahead of GMT, and Nepal is $5\frac{3}{4}$ hours ahead.

Data and Metadata

Once we get beyond these technical issues, we get to a higher level where we are trying not just to deliver data, but also to deliver meaningful data – one that can be understood by the people at the far end of the communications link. It is no good sending a file unless that file is meaningful at the far end.

One obvious example of such a problem is an E-mail written in a foreign language. That assumes that you have information available to you about the message, and how to make sense of it (a dictionary). This highlights a fundamental issue in the exchange of data between systems – very often, information by itself is no use – you need information about the information you have received. This is often called 'metadata' from the Greek 'meta' meaning 'after' or 'beyond'. Metadata is information that enables you to make sense of the original information. In some cases, you may have that already to hand, for example a dictionary or other documentation. In other cases, it may be included in the file – for example, a spreadsheet may have headings and other text to explain the meaning of the figures in the columns.

Metadata is defined by ISO as 'the information and documentation which makes data sets (files) understandable and shareable for users'.

Metadata and e-Business

All this becomes much more important when we look at e-Business. If you want to place an order for a quantity of sand for a building project, do you specify the weight in pounds or kilos? Tons or tonnes? In other words, do you include the metadata in the data you are sending, or do you assume that the receiving party already has the metadata to work out which you mean? The first approach will be more verbose, but will also be much more human-readable. The second will be more efficient, but less readable. This apparently minor decision about including metadata or not will in turn have a significant effect on information systems.

This distinction is basically a design issue; some might even say a difference of philosophy. It is, for example, one of the most striking differences between traditional EDI and the more recent XML standard. One of the prime design requirements for EDI was to send data in a condensed form, making extensive use of short code values to replace longer words or descriptions. One good reason for this is that EDI developed at a time when communications links were much slower than today. Another reason is that codes are language-independent, so you can send a code to a foreign country without risk of misinterpretation. So EDI data by itself is generally cryptic and even meaningless by itself – until you look at the metadata. In contrast, XML has gone down the opposite route, taking advantage of faster communications. It includes metadata in the file along with the data, but placed within tags so that you can easily tell what is data and what is metadata. For some purposes, this readability is a big advantage. But if all you want to do is to transfer data automatically between systems, readability is no advantage.

To sum up, there are therefore two approaches:

▷ Send just the data in a file, on the assumption that the recipient already has the metadata needed to make sense of the file

▷ Include the metadata in the file itself

In practice, these distinctions are often not so clear-cut. In XML, the metadata may also exist as a separate file, on your system or elsewhere on the Web. But the broad principle still applies: to understand structured data, you need metadata. EDI separates them totally; XML always contains at least some metadata.

Other Formats

There are some other existing standards for exchanging data:

▷ ASCII   Printable characters in ASCII standard

▷ CSV   Comma-Separated Values

ASCII is still widely used as a data exchange standard for text – every computer system in the world can handle ASCII, whether natively, as with PCs and Unix systems, or after conversion, for machines using EBCDIC. However, that still leaves many issues unresolved, such as date and time, format, and the meaning of the data – ASCII has no concept of metadata.

CSV (Comma-Separated Values) is another popular way of exchanging data, for example between spreadsheets. It is plain ASCII text, with the values separated by commas, like this:

Smith, John, 5 High Street, Midtown, UK,

Many databases and spreadsheets can accept values in this format, and CSV uses the commas as delimiters – not part of the data. However, if you need the comma then you have a problem – for example some European countries use the comma as the decimal separator. Usually you have to put the whole value in quotes: "12,5%". However, again there is no metadata.

There are other widely used proprietary formats that are unofficial so-called 'de facto' standards, such as Microsoft Word, used for word-processed documents.

Integration

One of the reasons why this exchange of data is so important can be summed up in the word 'integration', in other words, how to combine data from different systems. Suppose you are preparing a spreadsheet and want a contribution from someone else. You cannot just ask for the data – you also have to specify what kind of spreadsheet you are using, and the format of the file to be imported. You also need to know what the date means, and exactly where in the spreadsheet it needs to be imported. In short, you need to know how to integrate the data.

For a large organization, the problem is many times bigger. That organization may have a large number of different programs, developed over many years by different people, often in different ways and based on different standards. In some cases, they may have taken advantage of various methods of standardizing, such as CORBA or RPC. But many organizations have what are called 'legacy applications' – custom-built programs, often with a particular format, and often quite old. The costs and risks of upgrading old systems can be too great, so the old ones continue to be used, sometimes for decades. In such cases, they may have to write special conversion software. Integration can be a real headache, particularly when it comes to making changes in old programs.

Communications Technologies

Having looked at the problems of communicating data between computers, we can now turn to the problems of sending data over communications links. The fundamental problem is that as soon as data is sent out from a computer, it enters a hostile environment of telephone lines, cables, plugs, sockets, electrical interference, all outside its control.

However, the advantages and benefits of communications are so great that much time, money and effort has gone into developing a worldwide communications infrastructure. The explosive growth of the Internet and the World Wide Web has shown how important telecommunications have become for information technology. Already this is having a major impact not only on large organizations, but also the home consumer, by providing a range of new services such as home banking, leisure services including videos on demand, computer games, video phones, home shopping, directory services, tele-working, etc. All over the world, a new infrastructure is being built to support much greater telecommunications traffic volumes than at present. This involves the re-cabling of whole countries using fibre optic technology, as well as developing techniques that allow greater traffic volumes to be sent over the existing copper cable still in extensive use between switching centres and the consumer – that last mile or so of wire often referred to as the 'local loop'. Even with twisted pair copper cable, high speeds can be achieved between 10/100 Mbps (megabits per second). Agreement is needed upon the basic services that will be offered over this infrastructure providing the containers within which information can be transported and finally the information content itself based upon the nature of the application services to be offered. For organizations, the decision to use electronic business communications is becoming no longer a choice but mandated by the business community in which they operate as the means of conducting business, in much the same way that the telephone and facsimile has become.

Physical Connection

For computers to connect, there must be an electrical or electronic path between them – which may include optical fibre or radio connections via satellite. The important point is that the path must be able to deliver the zeros and the ones being sent out by one computer to another. A network is created when two or more computers are connected together and configured in such a way that communications can take place between them. This could be at one geographic location such as an office where a number of PCs are connected together to form a local area network (LAN), or the linking of several host computers or servers within or across country boundaries to form a wide area network (WAN).

Two Phases

Such networking always has two phases:

▷ Make a connection at the electrical level

▷ Start communicating, or in IT jargon, interworking

All this can only happen if both sides co-operate, and use a well understood set of rules and procedures – summed up by the word 'protocol'.

Protocols

We use protocols a great deal in ordinary life, often without thinking about it. For example, when you telephone someone, you go through a set series of steps – first you look up the telephone number, then dial it. When the connection is established, communication can begin. You first identify yourself, and so does the person at the other end. In doing that, you also implicitly indicate what language you are going to use, for example by saying 'Hello'. If you say 'Bonjour', that indicates you wish to speak in French. Then you talk – in computer terms, you exchange information. Finally you say 'Goodbye' to indicate the call is at an end. If you don't follow the protocol, errors or misunderstandings occur. Exactly the same sorts of rules are required for computers to communicate and manage a connection.

Network and Session Protocols

Another useful distinction is between network and session protocols. If we return to our telephone analogy, we can see that there is a high-level or session level layer where you are formulating words and phrases, and a low or network level layer where the telephone is sending electrical signals to the telephone at the other end. The same applies to computer communications.

Protocol Layers

This concept of protocol layers is a very good way of analyzing and understanding communications. A useful analogy here is with sending a parcel to somebody. You want to be able to hand over the parcel to a transport company that will deliver your parcel quickly, safely and reliably. You are not interested in the details of lorries, motorway routes, times, whether the lorry uses petrol or diesel engines etc. All that you leave to the transport company.

Similarly with computer communications, you want to be able to hand over some data to a transport function that will deliver the data quickly, safely and reliably. How the transport layer achieves it is just low-level detail to you. You could represent the requirement like this:

Application level	You have data to deliver
Transport level	Takes responsibility for delivery

Network level	Details of network connections, electrical standards, topology, etc.

We can elaborate this simple structure a bit by relating it to the earlier points about connection, communication and co-operation:

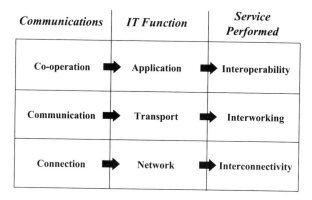

Figure 15.1 Networks, computers and applications

This three-layer structure provides a simple basic structure for understanding communications. However, in reality, computer communications are a good deal more complex, and a more detailed model gives a better understanding of what is going on such as the OSI Reference Model.

OSI Reference Model

One of the most widely used such models is the OSI model from the International Organization for Standardization (called ISO, not IOS). This has seven layers, but is basically just an elaboration of the three-layer model above:

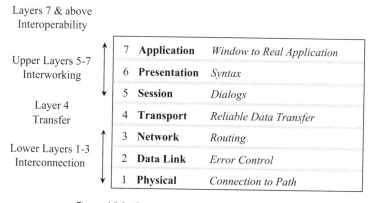

Figure 15.2 Open system interconnection model

The bottom three layers of the OSI model are concerned with the movement of the bits and bytes, and it is the job of the transport layer to manage all this. The top three layers are concerned with the actual application data (for example a file):

▷ Layer 7   Application – provides the interface or window into the application

▷ Layer 6   Presentation – formats and converts data

▷ Layer 5   Session – establishes and terminates dialogs/sessions

▷ Layer 4   Transport – manages the reliable end-to-end movement of data

▷ Layer 3   Network – concerns the routing of data to the correct destination

▷ Layer 2   Datalink – transmits and controls data to and from each node on the network

▷ Layer 1   Physical – connects nodes electronically forming a path

While each of the layers is important for the functioning of a network, the layers of most interest in understanding the process are still the three basic ones:

▷ Layers 5–7   Application level   Prepare the data

▷ Layer 4   Transport level   Responsible for end-to-end connection

▷ Layers 1-3   Network level   Deliver the data across the network

While this OSI model is useful for understanding communications, and is in fact the basis for OSI software, it is not always easy to fit other communications protocols exactly into this model. This applies to the other main worldwide networking architecture, TCP/IP. However, TCP/IP still fits in well with the basic three-layer model.

Internet TCP/IP Network Architecture

The growth of the Internet has also established TCP/IP as the protocol of choice for e-Business. Though other protocols such as X.25 can be used, and indeed are being used, TCP/IP is the dominant one, and worth studying for that reason.

TCP/IP started in the late 1960s as a set of military standards for computer communications. Later it was delivered as standard on computers running the Unix operating system. That made it popular for academic and research communities, who needed to connect up their own networks. It also proved to be an excellent vehicle for the World Wide Web and the Internet. It is also very suitable for Local Area Networks. Recognizing this, Microsoft have bundled it with Windows.

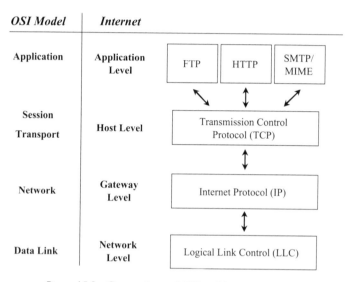

Figure 15.3   Comparison of OSI and Internet models

Technical Overview of TCP/IP

TCP/IP was developed as a way of exchanging data between computer systems, and to do so robustly – to keep going even in wartime, when communications links are vulnerable. Until then, the normal way to connect computers was over a telephone line. Any break in the line, whether caused by too much line noise, a bulldozer cutting through a cable, or a bomb would terminate the connection. What was needed was a network connection that could change dynamically, and re-route data by a different path if the first one stopped working.

Another important requirement was to optimize the use of the network. In an old-fashioned telephone system, there is a direct electrical connection or 'circuit' between you and the person you are speaking to, and while you are using the line, no-one else can – the line is engaged. This is called 'circuit-switched', and is simple and robust, but very inefficient, because a line can carry far more data than is required for voice communications. TCP/IP therefore is 'packet-switched' which means that the information is broken down into blocks of data, called 'packets' with an IP address at the front of each packet. In that way, a packet can be sent out over the network, and at the various switching centres, special devices called routers look at the address, work out the best available route, and forward the packet. If one route is congested or blocked, for whatever reason, the router tries another path from a list it holds in memory. In addition, this means that many different packets from different users to different destinations can all use the same line, only milliseconds apart because each packet is individually addressed. The traditional analogy is that circuit-switched is like sending a whole book in a continuous stream, while packet-switched is like sending lots of postcards, each with a section of the book, to be reassembled at the destination.

This means of course that packets do not necessarily arrive at their destination in the same order they were sent, and might not arrive at all. One route might simply fail in the middle of transmission. More likely, one route might be congested, to the point where a router in the path does not have enough physical memory to store the flood of packets arriving, and simply has to throw them away.

To cope with this, there needs to be a program at the receiving end to accept all the packets, and reassemble them into the correct order – and if necessary, request re-transmission of any packets that had not been delivered. This is the main role of TCP – explained below.

IP – Internet Protocol

Let's start with the second part of TCP/IP – IP (Internet Protocol now at version 4, defined in RFC 791). This operates at the network level, and defines the rules for sending a packet of data to another computer over a network. To do this, it must know the address of the remote computer. IP specifies that the address of a computer is a 32-bit number, which therefore allows $2^{32} = 4,294,967,296$ addresses.

In fact, this address identifies two things – both the computer itself, and the domain of which the computer is a member. Thus if you are connected to an ISP (Internet Service Provider), the ISP has a range of addresses, one of which is allocated (often just temporarily) to you. So the IP address identifies both the ISP and your particular computer, in much the same way that a telephone number identifies both the local telephone exchange and your telephone.

By convention, an IP address is not shown the way the computer sees it – which is of course in binary, for example 11000000 10101000 01001001 01111010. In decimal this is 3232254330, not easy to remember so, for the convenience of humans, this is broken up into a format easier to read – the familiar decimal 4-dotted-number or 4-byte format, in this case 192.168.73.122 which really means $(192 * 256^3 + 168 * 256^2 + 73 * 256^1 + 122 * 256^0) = 3232254330$. When sending data, this destination address is placed at the start or 'header' of the packet of data, together with the address of the sending system, and various other details, and is launched on to the Internet. This works rather like the telephone system, which routes your message, if local, within the local exchange; else if not local, it routes your message to another telephone exchange, and so on, until you reach the number you want. Similarly, an IP network has routers, which are programmed with routing tables with the details needed to route each IP packet to its destination, often through a series of such routers.

Incidentally, it is sometimes claimed that the Internet will soon run out of IP addresses. Some years ago that seemed possible, but new techniques have been developed, such as NAT (Network Address Translation – see glossary) and a recent facility called CIDR (Classless Inter-Domain Routing) that makes more efficient use of available addresses, and also simplifies the routing tables needed by routers to manage the huge flow of information. CIDR is explained in RFCs 1517-20. Neither of these provide a permanent solution to the addressing problem, but they give a breathing space while other longer-term solutions are developed – such as the next generation of IP protocols, called IPng (Internet Protocol Next Generation) or more correctly IPv6 (version 6 – see glossary; and before you ask, IPv5 exists but has not been implemented).

As discussed earlier, IP merely delivers data, and does not guarantee delivery, nor that the packets will be in the correct sequence. There is no retransmission of faulty packets in IP, and no flow control. In short, it is unreliable. This may sound at first like a disadvantage, but it also has big advantages. It avoids the need for continuous error-checking and return of status codes, thus reducing the volume of traffic and speeding up delivery – there is no need to wait for acknowledgements. Some way is therefore needed to make this process reliable – and that is the job of TCP.

TCP – Transmission Control Protocol

This supervision is done by the other part of the protocol – TCP, at the transport layer (defined in RFC 793). On the sending side, TCP breaks a file or stream of data into packets of a suitable size for IP (maximum allowed 65,536 bytes, but usually much less – usually just under 1500 bytes). It also generates a sequence number, adds the IP addresses, and passes this to the IP layer for delivery.

At the receiving end, TCP accepts each packet, checks the sequence number, and rebuilds the stream of data so that what is received is exactly what was sent. It also sends back an acknowledgement, not for each sequence number, but usually for a batch of such numbers – it sends the last sequence number successfully received in a batch of packets, a technique called the 'sliding window'. In that way, the sending TCP can work out what needs to be resent, if at all. There are also mechanisms to reduce congestion, by slowing down the rate of sending data, and to prevent packets going round the network forever. The routers in the network can also work out alternative routes in case of failure, and that is how a TCP/IP network can survive damage, even severe wartime damage.

UDP – User Datagram Protocol

UDP is an alternative to TCP, but provides an unreliable service. That may seem bizarre – who wants an unreliable service at the transport level? The answer is that UDP is useful in particular circumstances, because it is very quick and efficient, and does not need a reply from the destination system. That makes UDP ideal for some purposes – for example the high-speed distribution of frequently changing data, such as share prices. If a packet gets lost, no problem – another one will be along in a moment.

Types of Connection

The characteristics of the connection have an effect on what interworking can be achieved over it. Standards for computer connections have been around longer than for communication, so it is much better understood.

Terminal Connections

Originally, most connections were simply terminal to the host computer and the connection was relatively easy to achieve, by connecting a cable between the two.

In this scenario as terminal usage grows, so the number of cable connections grows. Aside from the heavy cost of additional cabling, in most cases the capacity of the existing cable is able to support more than one terminal. The obvious approach is to connect a concentrator or cluster controller at both ends of the cable, which allows multiple users to run their terminal sessions concurrently down the same cable or line. The ability to handle multiple sessions down the same cable is known as multiplexing: the cable effectively gets divided into a series of virtual cables or channels each capable of handling a proportion of the traffic.

Modem Connection

At some point the distance between the terminal concentrator and the host computer concentrator or communications controller becomes too great, resulting in loss of signal. At this stage modems may be introduced at each end of the cable and connected to the concentrator devices. This provides the scope for connecting terminals that are large distances away from the host computer to which they are to be connected. This type of connection is termed 'dial-up' and can apply to single terminals or concentrators, connecting to a host computer via modems over the telephone network.

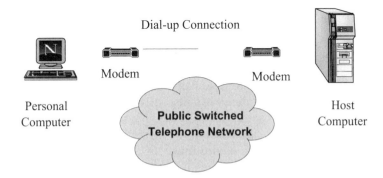

Figure 15.4   PC dial-up connection

Analogue versus Digital

From a computing point of view, the disadvantage of telephone lines is that they are designed to carry speech, and speech is basically analogue, not digital. So a normal telephone has a small microphone that converts the analogue sound waves produced from your mouth into equivalent analogue electrical signals, and at the receiving end that process is reversed through the tiny loudspeaker in the phone handset. But computers deal only in binary digits. Therefore modems are needed to convert or 'modulate' the digits into electrical signals that can be sent over the phone system, and to 'demodulate' them at the other end – hence the name 'modulator-demodulator' or 'modem' for short, and the sounds they make, often described as "like a demented bumble-bee". The modem is using different frequencies within the telephone's narrow audio range to represent the digital ones and zeros:

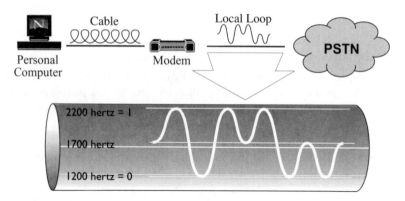

Figure 15.5 Analogue to digital

Popular Modem Standards

As the quality of phone lines has increased over the years, the speed and sophistication of modems has also increased. However, there is still the possibility of unwanted noise on the line, resulting in transmission errors occurring. Error detection and correction techniques are therefore important. Below is a summary of some popular current modem standards:

Standard	Details
V.34	28,800 bps. Formerly known as V.Fast or V.FC.
V.34bis	Up to 33,600 bps.
MNP	Microcom Network Protocol. An error-correction de facto standard. V.42 includes MNP as an alternate method of error correction. There are 10 different classes of MNP. MNP Class 4 provides error control; MNP Class 5 provides data compression.
V.42	Standard for error correction that supports MNP4 and LAP-M.
V.42bis	Standard for data compression with compression ratios up to 4:1.
V.44	Additional compression standard, faster than V.42.
V.90	Up to 56K bits per second (but in practice somewhat less) by using directly connected digital servers.
V.92	Enhancements to V.90 – faster connect times, faster upload etc.

Table 15.2 Popular modem standards

For the business traveller, access to a telephone point in hotel rooms is more and more important, allowing business communications away from the office. Growing use of wireless communications using a portable phone connected to the PC even removes this dependency. Bear in mind, however, that if you are connecting via an ISP, your modem speed is limited to what the ISP supports. Like the weakest link in a chain, a network connection is only as fast as the slowest part of it.

Asynchronous Transmission

Most such connections are described as 'asynchronous'. This means that the data does not come into a single continuous stream at precisely timed intervals, but in fits and starts. This is exactly what happens if you are typing commands or some text at the command line — there are short irregular pauses between the characters, perhaps only fractions of a second, but however fast you type, from the computer's point of view you are fantastically slow. It can handle data far faster than you can ever type. The same applies to data coming through your modem from another computer. Although more regular and faster, it is still no match for the computer's internal processing. So therefore each character is processed as and when it arrives, and the computer does other things in the intervals (for example, the computer has to react immediately to any movements of your mouse, and also has to update its clock several times a second).

Asynchronous or Synchronous

There are in fact two methods used by terminals and hosts to separate the ones and zeros into their individual characters:

▷ Asynchronous (character by character)

▷ Synchronous (block by block)

Asynchronous Communications Protocol

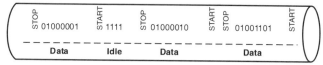

Synchronous Communications Protocol

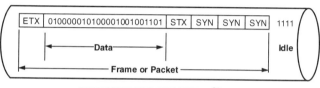

Direction of Data Transmission

Figure 15.6 Asynchronous and synchronous communications

Asynchronous transmission is typically used for low-speed, character by character, human to host communications. Synchronous transmission is used for high speed, computer to computer communications. Blocks of characters called packets or frames are transmitted between the sending and receiving devices. With synchronous transmission, the sending and receiving devices are re-synchronized for each block of data and therefore no start and stop bits are required. This enables continuous streams of data to be sent efficiently in large blocks, since the amount of control information accompanying the data is less than in asynchronous transmission.

Other Communications Technologies

ISDN – Integrated Services Digital Network

ISDN is a step up from modem connections, because it operates entirely digitally over telephone lines. Special ISDN adapters are needed for this, but the result is a quicker and more robust connection than over a normal telephone line, with speeds of 64 kilobits per second or optionally 128 kbps (plus a slower control and signalling channel). However, this is not that much faster than the latest generation of V.90 modems, and is more expensive. But one attraction of ISDN is the speed of connection to a service – normally just a few seconds to make a connection, much faster than a modem dial-up connection. That makes it suitable for a variety of uses – it can be used to link together geographically separate LANs, and can also be used instead of, or as backup for, permanent leased lines. ISPs are often connected to the phone system via ISDN. Another interesting but very different use of ISDN in the U.K. is to update the information panels at bus stops, telling you how many minutes until the next bus.

Leased Line

For organizations sending or receiving large volumes of data, particularly in e-Business, a permanent so-called 'leased line' connection provides higher speeds and superior quality than a dial-up connection. Such point-to-point connections are supplied by telecommunication companies. Payment is usually by a fixed monthly charge (based on the capacity of the line) regardless of volumes. However, these days DSL, and in particular ADSL, (see below) is a serious alternative to leased lines.

DSL

While modems are the commonest and easiest way to connect over a telephone line, they are severely handicapped by the fact that the telephone system was designed for speech, and therefore has limited bandwidth. Historically, there was no need to provide more capacity than needed to carry the human voice. The Internet has changed all that. Fortunately, the copper wire connection between your telephone and the local exchange can carry much more data, and that is something that the new technique called DSL (Digital Subscriber Line) takes advantage of. Provided the distance is no more than a few kilometres, and the quality of the line is good enough, data can be pushed to and from your telephone in digital format, not analogue, much faster than is possible with a modem or even ISDN. What's more, because this data is sent down the wire at different frequencies from normal telephone conversations, you can use the phone at the same time – a technique known as 'broadband' because different connections use different frequency bands or channels in the same medium, in much the same way that many radio stations can use the same radio waveband by using different frequencies. (The opposite of broadband is 'narrowband' or 'baseband', with just one channel). Another useful analogy is with roads – broadband is like a three-lane motorway, and narrowband like a single-track road.

Special equipment is needed in the exchanges to provide this DSL broadband access, and you will need a special DSL modem on your PC, but many countries are now introducing these new facilities.

ADSL

DSL comes in various different versions and configurations. The best known is ADSL – Asymmetric DSL, which means that the data going from the telephone exchange comes more quickly than data going to it. For some purposes, such as Web browsing, ADSL is a good option, because you generally receive more data downstream (as Web pages) than you send upstream (as short URLs). ADSL is currently the most widely used form of DSL.

One significant attraction of ADSL is that it is 'always on' – there is no need to dial in to make a connection every time. It is more like a permanently connected LAN. However, that raises security issues, and you will need some sort of firewall software to protect yourself against unauthorized hacker access.

Local Area Networks

LANs now form an important part of the IT strategy for both large and small organizations; and have created a whole new software industry geared towards team working (known as 'groupware'). At the connection level, the most popular LAN standards are 'Ethernet' ISO 8802.3 and

Token Ring ISO 8802.5 which cover the bottom two layers of the OSI Model. There is also growing interest in a new wireless standard 802.11 that enables computers to be connected to a LAN without the rat's nests of cables needed for traditional LANs.

All personal computers and other devices connected to a LAN have a LAN card, and each such card has a unique address – a 6-byte number called a 'MAC address' burned into it by the manufacturer. (Each manufacturer is allocated a range of such addresses).

To send a message, the sending computer sends the data down through the TCP/IP stack where it is broken down into packets, as described earlier. Then the packets go to the LAN card, at the lowest network or datalink level (see Figure 15.3). There the packets are processed into 'frames' of not more than 1518 octets, and launched on to the network, or 'ether', with the MAC address of the destination. There are of course techniques and protocols that enable networked computers to find and match up the MAC addresses with the corresponding IP addresses. The receiving LAN card picks up the frames, and passes them up the TCP/IP stack to be reassembled.

All devices connected to the LAN receive the packet and decode the destination address. Each card is trusted to accept only packets sent to its own address, and to ignore all other packets (though 'sniffer' programs for diagnostic or possibly hacking purposes will eavesdrop on all packets).

In the case of an Ethernet LAN, rules define what happens if two devices try and send packets at the same time. Basically, they detect the collision, stop, and try again a randomly short time later (milliseconds). This is called CSMA/CD (Carrier Sense Multiple Access with Collision Detection).

LAN bridges can help solve this security problem (as well as that of distance) by learning the addresses of each device that exists on the LAN and filtering out those packets, which do not need to travel to other parts of the network; this also helps improve performance by reducing unnecessary traffic.

Switched Ethernet

There is also a newer LAN version called 'Switched Ethernet', in which each terminal has its own bandwidth, thus reducing or even eliminating data collisions. CSMA/CD is no longer needed. A central switch has a buffer to temporarily store packets in transit. These switches can also detect when new PCs are added to the network and automatically incorporate them into the LAN.

Standards in e-Business

Introduction

One useful benefit of the growth of the Internet is the matching growth in common or so-called 'open' standards. Just as reliable computer communications are a relatively new development, so are open standards. Although such standards had been available for some time, proprietary standards owned and developed by private corporations used to dominate the computer business, and even today are still in use. But the attractions of open standards in simplifying and reducing the cost of computing and computer communications have been so overwhelming that open standards now dominate. In this chapter, we shall take a more detailed look at some open standards in the TCP/IP suite and how they work – because of their importance in e-Business.

For e-Business, the three most important protocols in the TCP/IP suite are:

▷ SMTP   Simple Mail Transfer Protocol   To transfer E-mail

▷ FTP   File Transfer Protocol   To transfer files

▷ HTTP   HyperText Transfer Protocol   To transfer hypertext etc.

These protocols have several things in common:

▷ Based on a client-server model. In each case, the client (usually running browser software on a PC) prepares a request of some sort (such as to send an E-mail, to fetch a file, or to request a Web page of information), and receives a response from the server.

▷ As explained in Chapter 15, these protocols are at the application level. In terms of our postal parcel analogy, these protocols have a parcel of data to deliver, and they use TCP/IP for the transport. (Note that TCP/IP is not mandated; but in practice it is used almost universally).

▷ All the protocols therefore use the TCP/IP stack – in other words, they prepare their requests and pass them down to the transport layer, TCP, and TCP then passes the packets to the IP layer, which in turn sends them to the underlying networking infrastructure. Each layer adds protocol and addressing information – rather like adding an envelope to a letter.

▷ Although the three protocols do different things, the underlying design and methods are similar.

▷ Each has a small set of standardized commands for the dialogue across the network with a Web server.

▷ Each has a repertoire of three-digit reply codes to indicate success or failure. A typical example is the '404 not found' error message when you request a nonexistent Web page.

▷ In each case, on the receiving server there is a suitable responder program to deal with the client requests. Each responder listens on a different port number (see Chapter 18) so that client browsers can connect to the service they want.

In addition to these, we shall also look at other related protocols and systems:

▷ IMAP and POP. These are used mainly to retrieve E-mail from a server to a client.

▷ DNS – Domain Name System. An essential directory facility on the Internet, enabling users to use domain names instead of IP addresses.

▷ X.400. An E-mail system similar to SMTP, and still widely used.

Electronic Mail (E-mail)

E-mail for many people is the single most useful aspect of the Internet. E-mail systems follow closely the model of the familiar paper-based postal system – these days sometimes called 'snail mail' because it is so much slower than its electronic counterpart. Just as the postal system has an infrastructure consisting of sorting offices, where letters and parcels are sorted and forwarded according to the addresses on them, so E-mail has E-mail servers that perform similar functions. E-mail needs a set of rules or 'protocol' to keep the system running. The commonest E-mail system in the world today is SMTP – Simple Mail Transfer Protocol.

SMTP

The Simple Mail Transfer Protocol enables E-mail servers to do exactly what the name implies – exchange data simply and reliably. The flow of data is shown in Figure 16.1:

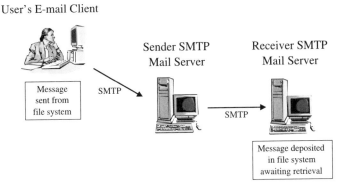

Figure 16.1 Sending E-mail using SMTP

Mail can therefore be sent either directly by the user, or by a program sending a file or files of data. At the receiving end, it is assumed that the message is stored in a file system until the recipient is ready to read it.

One specification (RFC 822) describes in detail what an E-mail consists of:

▷ Header fields (rigidly defined) such as E-mail addresses, subject, etc.

▷ Body part, free format text

SMTP E-mail Addresses

Just as a paper letter must have a valid postal address, an E-mail message must have an address that conforms to the SMTP specification – the familiar **name@domain** format such as **John.Smith@mail.webserver.com** – and like a postal address, this combination must be unique worldwide.

Incidentally, SMTP also specifies that each mail system must have a mailbox called 'Postmaster' to receive and handle any problem messages to that domain – for example with invalid addresses.

SMTP Commands

SMTP has a small number of short commands, some with parameters (specified in RFC 821). These are all issued by your E-mail software behind the scenes, so you never see them. The sending system must first resolve the recipient domain name into a numeric IP address, and then contact the remote mail server, using an IP address and port number (connecting to port number 25, reserved for SMTP). Once connected to port 25, SMTP uses a command 'HELO' to open an E-mail connection, with a parameter to define the client system where the message was prepared. If it gets a positive response from the mail server, SMTP continues with a 'MAIL FROM' command with the address of the sender, then a 'RCPT TO' command with the recipient. You can see in this small example below that SMTP works in much the same way as a human telephone call – first connect, then identify yourself, then give information and finally close the call. In the example below, the actual data is between the <> signs. Notice the single fullstop at the start of the second DATA line, shown here as <.> – that is how SMTP identifies the end of the mail data:

```
HELO mailserver.co.uk
MAIL FROM:   John.Smith@mailserver.co.uk
RCPT TO: Jane.Brown@othermailserver.com
DATA   <Dear Jane, the meeting time has changed
from 2:00 to 3:00 pm.>
<.>
QUIT
```

When defining the recipient, there are several possible replies:

▷ The recipient is known, so the remote server accepts the E-mail

▷ The recipient is unknown, so the server refuses the E-mail

▷ The server knows where the recipient is located, and offers to forward the E-mail

▷ The server may refuse the E-mail, but suggests another server or gateway to try

If all is well, SMTP sends the data, followed by a final QUIT.

SMTP Reply and Error Codes

At each stage, the E-mail server at the receiving end sends back reply or error codes. SMTP (and also FTP and HTTP) use a simple but effective set of such codes, consisting of three digits giving varying levels of detail. Success codes start with two, while failure codes start with 4 or 5. These codes enable the sending system to work out what has gone wrong, and if necessary convert the digits into more detailed error messages to the sender.

SMTP and MIME

SMTP was designed to send text messages – printable characters only. To meet the requirement to exchange any kind of file, another standard was developed – MIME, short for 'Multipurpose Internet Mail Extensions'. This enables you to attach one or more files to an SMTP message, and these files (unlike the text of the SMTP message itself) can contain any data. In order to enable the receiving system to handle such files, each file is given a 'MIME type' to identify what sort of data it holds. This MIME type consists of a type name and a sub-type name separated by a slash, for example 'text/plain' or 'text/html'. There are a limited number of type names, including 'text', 'image', 'audio', 'video', 'application', 'multipart' etc. and then a larger number of subtype names, including user-defined ones. In this way, the receiving system can work out what sort of file it is, and launch the corresponding application or 'plug-in' to display the data correctly.

This MIME type facility has proved very useful, and is also used outside SMTP – for example in HTTP. When you request a file, your browser tells the server what sort of files it will accept by quoting the MIME types such as 'text/html' or 'image/jpeg'.

The diagram below shows the structure of a typical E-mail message, and the various RFCs that define this structure:

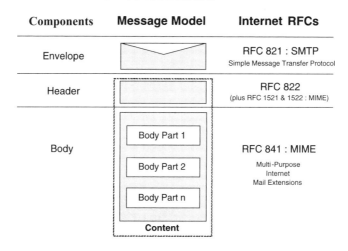

Figure 16.2   Message model

SMTP and e-Business

SMTP can be used in scripts or programs, thus making it possible to run automatic sessions to send or receive data to or from other systems without human intervention. But there are some disadvantages, at least when compared to FTP. Although SMTP requires a reply code from the receiving SMTP server to show that the message has arrived, this is generally not definite enough for e-Business purposes. The SMTP success code means that the message has been successfully delivered to the remote server, and has left the SMTP world. It does not prove that the recipient has actually received the message – it may, for example, be waiting on a POP server until collected by the recipient. For many non-commercial messages, this is adequate. But if you are sending an urgent order for perishable goods to a trading partner, standard SMTP is not definite enough – it does not give the end-to-end audit trail often needed in business. However, there are alternatives – the remote system can return an acknowledgement message confirming receipt, for example the EDIFACT CONTRL message, or the ANSI X12 997 message, and there are various initiatives to use SMTP for e-Business – see Chapter 6.

S/MIME (Secure MIME)

There is a variant of MIME called Secure MIME or just S/MIME. This adds encryption and digital signatures to standard MIME, and thus provides a much higher level of security (there is none in standard MIME). There is more about the use of MIME and S/MIME in the section on EDIINT in Chapter 6, and about encryption and digital signatures in Chapter 12.

The diagram below summarizes how business data (in this case, EDI data) to be exchanged by SMEs using dial-up could be handled using SMTP/MIME:

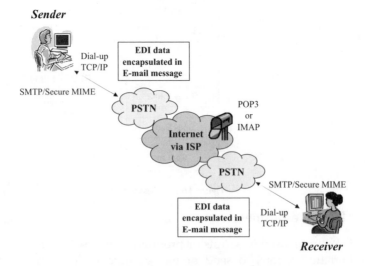

Figure 16.3 Sending EDI data using SMTP/MIME

IMAP and POP

As mentioned above, SMTP delivers E-mails to the recipient's system. But most E-mail users have PCs that are not always switched on, or not permanently connected to the Internet, and therefore cannot always receive E-mail directly. Often, therefore, E-mail is stored on a receiving E-mail server until the recipient wants it. This requires yet another protocol to enable the client to fetch waiting E-mails, and the two most popular ones are:

▷ IMAP   Internet Message Access Protocol, currently version 4

▷ POP   Post Office Protocol, currently version 3

The Post Office Protocol (POP3 defined in RFC 1725) is the oldest and the best known, designed to support off-line E-mail processing. E-mails are delivered using SMTP to a mail server (a mail drop), and the personal computer (PC) user periodically connects to the server to download E-mails to the PC. Behind the scenes, POP3 connects to the mail server, and using a simple command language, retrieves waiting E-mails back to the PC. Once this is completed the mail server deletes the E-mails. In its off-line mode, POP really provides a store and forward 'on demand' service to move E-mails from the mail drop to the user's PC, where they can be read when convenient using local E-mail client software.

There are two other modes of operation, namely 'online' and 'disconnected'. In the online mode, messages are left on the mail server and manipulated remotely using the E-mail client software. The 'disconnected' mode, means that the user's E-mail software connects to the mail server, retrieves selected E-mails and then disconnects, only to re-connect later to synchronize with the mail server. This synchronization with the mail server is important, to ensure that message status (Seen, Deleted and Answered) is updated.

IMAP Facilities

The Internet Message Access Protocol (IMAP4 defined in RFC 1730) supports all three modes of operation, namely off-line, online and disconnected, while POP only supports the off-line mode. IMAP permits users to optimize the communications path between the mail server and E-mail client software and is based on the principle that the mail server is the primary mail repository. E-mails are always retained on the mail server, until the user issues a command to delete them.

IMAP provides several facilities that can be used to reduce the data transmitted between the E-mail client and the mail server. Firstly, there is the facility to determine the E-mail message structure without downloading the entire message. This allows the E-mail client to display information about any MIME message attachments without transferring them. This means that if a two-line text message is received with a MIME attachment containing a 10MB video clip, using the E-mail client, the user can choose to transfer only the two lines of text. If connected via a slow dialup line, this can be a tremendous saving of time. A further important feature of IMAP is the ability to use server-based searching and selection as another way of minimizing data transfer and should not be underestimated.

FTP

One of the commonest requirements in computing is to send a file of data from one computer to another – in e-Business, for example to send an order for an invoice from one organization to another. Of course, this could be done using SMTP and MIME. But FTP is purpose-designed to get or send one or more files from or to a remote system, and has other advantages. It is defined in RFC 959.

FTP Facilities

The problem of incompatible computer systems and varying standards is particularly acute in FTP – but fortunately, FTP provides a variety of solutions:

▷ FTP converts lines of data automatically between operating systems with different conventions. For example, the carriage-return line-feed characters at the end of an ASCII DOS line are converted into UNIX line feeds.

▷ FTP has an option to send pure binary data with no character conversion.

▷ Because some networks intercept certain control characters, FTP can transmit binary files in a format consisting only of printable characters, and restore the original binary file correctly at the receiving end.

▷ Some FTP implementations try to adjust filenames to suit different systems – for example to translate long UNIX filenames into the DOS 8.3 format.

▷ Although FTP was designed to be used at the command line, there are versions that provide a graphical interface, and FTP can also be used with Web browsers.

▷ FTP is the commonest way of downloading files from the Web to a PC. Although HTTP can also be used, FTP is more efficient.

Other advantages of FTP:

▷ FTP can get or send multiple files using wildcards – e.g. *.GIF to get all *.GIF files.

▷ If enabled, FTP can move around in the directory structure of the remote system.

▷ FTP can easily be included in scripts or programs.

▷ FTP can verify that a file has been successfully delivered to and stored on a remote computer system.

FTP commands

Like SMTP, FTP has a set of simple commands. Below is an example of a typical short session :

OPEN ftpsite.co.uk	log on with username and password
BINARY	set binary mode
GET filename	copy file from remote system to local
BYE	quit FTP

FTP and e-Business

The advantages of FTP, and the ability to transfer either ASCII or binary files, make FTP a useful and attractive option for e-Business. FTP can be used in several ways:

▷ With a URL from a browser. If supported by the server, a user puts in an FTP URL instead of the more usual HTTP one, like this: **ftp://www.webserver.com**

▷ If supported, by direct connection at the client command line. You will generally need a user account and password on the receiving system, though some systems support what is called 'anonymous FTP'. You logon as a user called 'anonymous', and the convention is that you use your E-mail address as the password.

▷ FTP can easily be incorporated into scripts or programs, thus making it possible to run automatic sessions to send or receive data to or from other systems. This is a very convenient method for e-Business, and is quite widely used. An FTP script contains the same commands that would be used at the command line. One big attraction of FTP is that it is possible to detect whether a file has been successfully transferred to another system, for example by checking whether the file on the remote system is the same size as the file being sent. If that information is stored in a log, then it provides an 'audit trail' to show that the data (for example, an order or invoice) has been successfully delivered to a trading partner. This 'audit trail' has always been an important requirement in e-Business. It is easier to achieve in FTP than in other protocols like SMTP or HTTP, and explains the popularity of FTP in e-Business. However, some security-conscious organizations are unwilling to provide any kind of FTP access to trading partners, because it gives other people access to internal systems.

The diagram below summarizes how business data (in this case, EDI data) could be exchanged between an SME sender and a large trading partner connected to the Internet by a permanent leased line. Data can be sent either by FTP or HTTP (see next section):

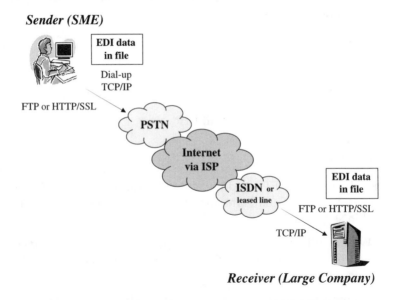

Figure 16.4 Sending EDI data using FTP or HTTP/SSL

HTTP

HTTP and FTP have a great deal in common – the basic purpose in both cases is file transfer. But hypertext (or more broadly hypermedia) has some different requirements, notably links between files, and it made sense therefore to develop a transfer protocol specifically geared to the requirements of hypertext and the Web. HTTP is defined in RFC 1945.

Hypertext users often want to browse through a series of files or services. This is achieved by entering a URL (Uniform Resource Locator), which identifies several things. Take for example a typical URL like

http://www.webserver.com/info/data.html – this identifies several values:

http:	Use HyperText Transfer Protocol to talk to server
//	What follows is a server, not a file or directory name
www.webserver.com	Name and domain of server
/info/	Sub-directory below the server root
data.html	file to fetch (default index.html if no filename specified)
:80	Use port 80 on the server (default 80 if no number specified)

In this way, a URL contains a lot of information in a convenient and compact form to send to a Web server. However, a filename by itself is often not enough. For example, if you want to search a Web site, you can usually fill in a small box with your search terms. Either way, HTTP needs to pass a request to the server with parameters.

GET, HEAD and POST

The main so-called 'methods' to request information are GET, HEAD and POST. GET is used to fetch a file from the server, as in the example above. GET is also used for sending the server a small amount of data, such as parameters for a search. If, for example, you were searching using the word 'airlines', on the Web server mentioned above, the URL you use might look something like this, telling the server to run a program called 'search' with a single parameter 'airlines':

    http://www.webserver.com/cgi-bin/search?q=airlines

At the server end, the 'search' program or script just has to untangle this command. In the jargon, it has to 'parse' the command, meaning to split it up into its component parts, just as in a human language you parse a sentence into nouns, verbs etc. This is where Perl with its powerful string handling really scores.

GET can include quite a lot of data for URL, but for even larger amounts, the POST method is better because it creates a small file that is sent back with the URL to the server for processing.

HEAD does the same as GET, but only the HTML head or 'meta-data' is returned, not the body part. This can be used, for example, to check whether a file has been modified recently or not.

Stateless HTTP

One fundamental aspect of HTTP is that it is 'stateless' or 'non-persistent'. This means that every time you interact with a Web server, for example by clicking on 'Submit' or on a URL, it is a one-off event, with nothing to connect it to any previous interactions.

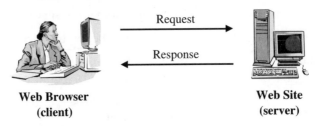

Web Browser
(client)

Web Site
(server)

Figure 16.5 HTTP protocol

HTTP was deliberately designed this way, for speed, efficiency and simplicity. If you are merely getting HTML files to read, it is a very quick and easy way of working for the server. However, if you are filling in a form spread over several pages, for example when filling a so-called 'shopping cart' with goods you are buying over the Internet, then the server needs to know about previous interactions – your history. In computer jargon, what is needed is 'persistence'.

There are several techniques for handling this, such as 'cookies' which are tiny files created by the server on your client, initially in memory, later on disk, to store information and keep track of where you are. When using scripts or other Web server programs, there are other techniques for keeping track of your history – for example, the script can generate hidden fields on the client's screen that are returned when the user clicks on 'Submit', thus enabling the script to keep track of who is doing what. The details are for Web programmers, and at this stage we just need to note that by default these HTTP interactions are stateless, and some programming work needs to be done if the client state or history needs to be preserved or 'persisted' during a session, or over subsequent sessions.

HTTP and e-Business

As HTTP is relatively new, and similar in many ways to both SMTP and FTP, it is mostly used for its intended purpose of handling URLs. But it can also be used for sending and receiving data (as explained in RFC 1945), and there are proposals in the Internet community for using HTTP for secure peer-to-peer EDI and XML over the Internet, using HTTP POST.

HTTP has one substantial advantage to do with Internet security. Many large organizations are a very concerned about computer security, and therefore keep tight control over Internet addresses and port numbers available for use. In some cases, they close off all ports but the bare minimum – which these days may mean closing off everything except HTTP and SMTP, because they are essential for any Web activity. Even FTP is regarded as potentially insecure. As a result, port 80, the standard 'well-known' port for HTTP, is bound to be open. (There is more about this in Chapter 17). Therefore it makes sense to use HTTP for exchanging data and commands between systems as well as for Web activity. A good example of such use is SOAP.

HTTP and SOAP

SOAP (Simple Object Access Protocol) is a recent development from Microsoft that provides an even more powerful and flexible mechanism than GET and POST, and indeed goes further than both, because it is designed not only to exchange structured data between systems, but also to provide a framework for what are called 'remote procedure calls' (RPC). This is a way of sending commands (in programming terms, function calls and parameters) to run programs on remote systems and thereby achieve decentralized distributed processing. There are already various existing techniques for doing this, such as CORBA (Common Object Request Broker Architecture), but SOAP has two big advantages:

▷ SOAP can use HTTP and therefore port 80, so any organization providing a Web service must leave this port open. Consequently SOAP is not affected by the security problems that affect other messaging techniques which often rely on special or user-defined port numbers.

▷ SOAP is written in XML, and therefore provides a popular, standard and non-proprietary way of exchanging information.

There is more about CORBA in Chapter 17.

HTTPS

HTTPS (Hypertext Transfer Protocol Secure) is a secure version of HTTP developed by Netscape. It provides authentication and encryption (see Chapter 12) in an additional software level, called SSL, or Secure Sockets Layer, before the data is passed to the TCP/IP stack. In addition, data does not go through the standard HTTP port 80, but through port 443 (reserved for HTTPS).

HTTPS provides end-to-end security between a browser and the Web server, and is widely used, particularly for financial transactions on the

Web. On some browsers, including of course Netscape, you can see a small padlock icon that is open for HTTP, but securely closed for HTTPS.

DNS – Domain Name System

In all the protocols mentioned above, you can identify a server either by its domain name or by its numeric IP address. However, for TCP/IP, a domain name is like a nickname or alias, and it has to be converted into the corresponding IP address bcause TCP/IP does not understand names.

There are two ways of doing this:

▷ TCP/IP can look up a 'hosts' file. This is a file that lists various hosts and their corresponding IP addresses.

▷ TCP/IP can consult the Domain Name System (DNS) – a service that avoids the need for a separate hosts file on every client.

Because of the difficulty of administering and updating hosts files, DNS is now widely used in preference, so much so that DNS is now critical to the operation of the Internet. Every time you send or receive an E-mail or file, or click on a URL, you are probably using DNS without realizing it. Usually, your ISP will be providing DNS for you.

Domains

The basic purpose of DNS is therefore to provide the 'mapping' or conversion of Web site names, properly called 'domain names', into their equivalent 32-bit IP addresses. Internet domains form the basis of the common Internet naming scheme. For example, **www.webserver.co.uk** identifies one particular server called 'www' within the domain webserver.co.uk. Domains are in the form of an inverted tree. Each branch or leaf on the tree is labelled with an alphanumeric string, and a complete domain name is written by stringing all the labels together, separated by periods. For the United Kingdom the root domain is 'uk'; 'co' means it is a commercial site in the UK, and 'webserver' identifies a particular domain within all the commercial sites in the UK. The allocation of domain names ending in 'webserver.co.uk' is solely at the discretion of the owner of 'webserver.co.uk' who manages that domain name space (note that at the time of writing, this site does not exist).

Top-level Domain Names

Top-level domain names (defined in RFC 1591) take one of two forms. They can either be generic domains and take the form of three-letter names, or they can be geographic, with a two-letter country code:

| **.com** | an international domain for commercial organizations |
| **.co.uk** | the UK version of .com |

Other options include:

.org	an international domain for non-commercial organizations
.org.uk	the UK version of .org
.ltd.uk	for UK Private Limited Companies. The name chosen must precisely match the name of the company registered at Companies House, with spaces either omitted or replaced by hyphens
.plc.uk	as above but for Public Limited Companies
.net	intended for Internet Service Providers, but can be used by anyone
.sch.uk	for schools
.gov.uk	or UK Local and National Government
.uk.com	another commercial domain for UK organizations

Country specific domain names using the UN two-character country code are also available, for example:

.fr	France
.de	Germany
.ie	Ireland

Additional qualifiers have been introduced including **.biz**, **.info** and **.name** but these do not seem to be quite as popular outside North America. It is possible to point more than one domain name at a Web site, and it is worth considering registering several variations of a domain name. For example if a company conducts business both in the UK and abroad, it will most probably register both the **.co.uk** and the **.com** variants of its domain name.

CENTR

CENTR is an association of Internet Country Code Top-Level Domain Registries such as **.uk** in the United Kingdom and **.es** in Spain. Full Membership is open to organizations managing an ISO 3166-1 country code Top-Level Domain (ccTLD) registry. The project that became CENTR was formed in March 1998, and in 1999 it was legally established as a not-for-profit company in the UK, limited by guarantee. Membership fees fund CENTR activities and a small secretariat is co-located with the UK national registry, Nominet UK. Whilst the organization has a European focus there are no geographical restrictions to membership and it provides a forum to discuss matters of policy affecting ccTLD registries and acts as a channel of communication to Internet governing bodies and other organizations involved with the Internet.

ICANN

The Internet Corporation for Assigned Names and Numbers (ICANN) is a non-profit corporation that has assumed responsibility from the US Government for co-ordinating certain Internet technical functions, including the management of the Internet domain name system. Only registrars accredited by ICANN are authorized to register **.biz**, **.com**, **.info**, **.name**, **.net** and **.org** names. Some of these accredited registrars offer their services through resellers, which may provide assistance in completing the registration process. Further information about ICANN can be found at **www.icann.org.**

Network Solutions, Inc.

NSI was the company that acted as the sole registry and registrar for the **.com**, **.net**, and **.org** top-level domains from 1993-1999, in accordance with a co-operative agreement with the US Government. NSI has since been acquired by VeriSign, Inc. and continues to operate the **.com**, **.net**, and **.org** top-level domain registries on a similar basis with ICANN and the US Government. NSI is also one of nearly 100 companies that have been accredited by ICANN to offer registrar services in these and other top-level domains. See **www.networksolutions.com** for further details.

Root Server System Advisory Committee RSSAC

The responsibility of the Root Server System Advisory Committee (RSSAC) is to advise ICANN about the operation of the root name servers of the domain name system. The RSSAC considers and provides advice on the operational requirements of root name servers, including host hardware capacities, operating systems and name server software versions, network connectivity, and physical environment. The RSSAC is also responsible for advising on the security aspects of the root name server system, and reviewing the number, location, and distribution of root name servers in light of the performance, robustness, and reliability of the overall system.

Overview of DNS

DNS is to computers and the World Wide Web what Directory Enquiries is to telephone users – a way of converting an easy-to-understand name into a hard-to-understand number. The most visible use of this is when you enter a URL into a browser – for example, **www.microsoft.com.** That name is easier to remember than the IP address. It also means that if Microsoft decide to change the IP address, they can do so by changing DNS. They don't have to tell everyone in the world to use the new IP address instead of the old one.

So, what happens when you type in a URL in your browser? In some cases, the corresponding IP address may already be stored or 'cached' locally. More often, your computer uses DNS. It sends a message to a computer that provides a DNS service, asking in effect: 'Tell me the IP address for **www.microsoft.com** This is exactly like phoning Directory Enquiries to ask 'Can you tell me Microsoft's telephone number? In the case of DNS, the DNS server may have the information already (cached), and sends back the IP address immediately. Your browser then uses this to send IP packets to that address, and back comes Microsoft's main page.

If your local DNS server does not know the address, it passes the request to another DNS server, and the process is repeated until an answer is returned either with the IP address, or a failure message, saying that name is not known. Note the search looks for an exact match – there is no fuzzy searching in DNS.

DNS Hierarchy

In effect, therefore, DNS is a worldwide, distributed, hierarchical database. At the top of the hierarchy is the top-level DNS server, known as 'root', and identified solely by a . (full stop). It points to the next level DNS servers, which are simply the next part of the URL name, for example 'com'. There are other top-level servers with the same sort of names – org, net, etc, and also the country-specific ones like uk. Somewhere in the hierarchy there is (hopefully) a DNS server, which does know the IP address that corresponds to the domain in the URL. This is why IP addresses and domain names must be registered – otherwise the worldwide DNS system would have no way of identifying an IP address and its location. In short, an IP address, like a telephone number, must be unique, and must be registered. If not, you get the infamous HTTP error code 404 – not found, the computer equivalent of 'number unobtainable' on a telephone.

However, this does not mean that every single computer in the world must be registered with a unique IP address. That used to be the case, but these days, particularly in large organizations, it is more common to use a firewall and proxy server, which must use registered addresses. But behind the firewall, it does not matter. Each computer must still have an IP address, but it no longer needs to be unique worldwide – only unique within the domain behind the firewall. Certain ranges of IP address are reserved for exactly this purpose, notably 10.0.0.0 (meaning all IP addresses starting with 10.). The proxy server keeps track of which local computer has sent a request, but forwards it to the Internet using a proper registered address. When the data is returned, the proxy server redirects it to the local computer.

DNS is defined in RFC 1034 and 1035.

X.400

Because of the focus these days on the Internet, most people are familiar only with Internet-style E-mail – addresses in the form **name@domain.com** and using SMTP. But there are other types of E-mail, and we will therefore also look briefly at another system, called X.400, still widely used in several countries round the world, though mainly in Europe.

X.400 is a complete internationally agreed E-mail standard, similar in concept to SMTP. It was adopted by the International Standards Organization ISO, and is therefore part of the OSI set. However, it seems to be suffering the same fate as other non-TCP/IP standards – getting squeezed out, in this case by the growth of SMTP. But X.400 is still in use and is also supported in E-mail systems such as Microsoft's Outlook (if configured), so it is useful to have a basic understanding of what it is. Some would argue that it is a more comprehensive and better thought-out E-mail system than SMTP. But that, sadly, is never a guarantee of commercial success.

Both SMTP and X.400 are application layer protocols and therefore independent of the underlying network protocol. Therefore X.400 based messages can be run over TCP/IP and indeed this is standardized in RFC 1006. Similarly, SMTP messages could be run over the X.400 normal networking infrastructure, namely X.25 (part of the OSI network architecture), but in practice rarely does (except where X.25 provides the physical layer for TCP/IP).

Overview of X.400

Just as SMTP has the concept of a user connecting to a mail server, so X.400 has the concept of a User Agent (UA) that prepares the message contents (including message header and message body) and is usually a desktop PC with suitable software. The body of the message can be broken up into a series of body parts each containing a different media type such as text, voice, facsimile, graphic, image, etc.

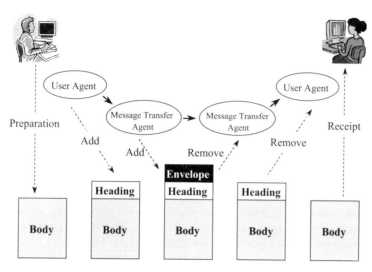

Figure 16.6 Sending E-mail using X.400

The message contents are then submitted by the user agent to the X.400 electronic post office (known in X.400 jargon as the 'Message Transfer Agent' or MTA, similar to an SMTP server), using the appropriate X.400 (P3) protocol. It is then sent to the destination X.400 electronic post office. This destination X.400 MTA presents the message to the recipient user agent (UA).

X.400 addressing

The X.400 addressing system is much closer to a normal postal address than SMTP. X.400 is hierarchical, and starts with the country, for example COUNTRY=GB. X.400 has the concept of 'management domains', which function very much like postal sorting offices. Within a country, there may be one or more top-level 'administrative management domains' or ADMDs, generally run by a PTT. Then there are 'private management domains' or PRMDs, generally run within a large organization. Below that are Organization names, optionally with up to four distinct Organization Units, and finally the name of an individual (usually surname and given name, though X.400 also supports Initials and even a Generational Qualifier, e.g. John Smith III). The five main ones – country, ADMD, PRMD, organization and name are usually enough. In some cases PRMDs can contact each other directly and bypass the ADMD; then the ADMD can be omitted.

So a typical X.400 address might be:

C=GB; P=ABC plc; O=Accounts Dept; S=Smith; G=John

For people familiar only with SMTP addresses, this addressing format looks at first complicated, even off-putting. But it does have advantages – such as the similarity with postal addresses, the flexibility, and the greater level of detail allowed. For example, if there are several people called John Smith, they can easily be distinguished from each other by other X.400 addressing details, such as Organizational Unit. In contrast, SMTP is less flexible, sometimes leading to very artificial and much less intuitive names in SMTP E-mail addresses.

X.400 and EDI

X.400 has proved to be a very robust E-mail system, once installed and configured. It is still quite widely used, particularly in Europe, for sending EDI data as well as E-mail. Standards and conventions have been agreed on how to use X.400 for EDI.

Another significant use of X.400 is for the exchange of EDI data between VANs. If you are a customer of one VAN, and your trading partner is registered on another VAN, there needs to be some way of forwarding the data between the VANs. That involves using some mutually agreed common standard, and for this purpose X.400 is often used.

Figure 16.7 – Standards can be confusing!

Server-side Technologies

Introduction

So far, most of our attention has been on the client side of e-Business, from a consumer's view of using a browser. However, the real value of the Internet lies in the hundreds of thousands of servers providing a huge range of information and services to millions of users. In this chapter, we look at what an e-Business server does and how it does it.

In the early days of the Web, many organizations dipped their toes into this new medium in a very cautious fashion – sometimes doing no more than putting up a few pages of marketing information on a Web server. In technical terms, this was very easy – just create a few reasonably attractive pages in the form of HTML files, and a few links between them. There was no attempt to connect these pages with any existing computer systems.

The limitations soon became obvious – for example, if a company put up product information, with stock availability, it was difficult to maintain that stock information manually, resulting either in excessive stock, or frustrated customers. The obvious answer was to connect the server in some way to the company's existing systems and databases. In today's jargon, this is called 'integration'. But this adds a whole new level of complexity. Over the years, various solutions have emerged, and more solutions are emerging every day.

In this chapter, we shall take a fairly non-technical look at these so-called 'server-side technologies'.

Client-server Model

The first step is to look at the underlying model, called client-server architecture, because it is the basis of the whole Internet and its protocols.

If you are not familiar with client-server architecture, the best way to understand this concept is to start by looking at a simple but common use – print servers. Because it is inefficient and expensive to provide one printer for every computer, most organizations have centralized printers used by a number of people in a workgroup. But what happens if two people want to print at the same time? That problem can be avoided by putting in a separate computer on the network called a 'print server' that receives files to be printed, puts them into a queue, and manages the printing operations. Optionally, it returns confirmation. That way, the various users can simply print and forget.

The key point is that a print server is a passive device that just sits there, waiting for users to connect and make requests. Similarly, a file server sits there passively waiting for requests for files from users, and a Web server waits for requests for HTML files or Web services from people using browsers. When you enter a URL into a browser, you are effectively requesting a file or a service from a Web server somewhere on the Internet. The client requests, the server responds. We do not know – and do not care – where the server is located. It is somewhere deep in cyberspace, where both the geography and time seem to be collapsed.

But cyberspace is a somewhat romantic, non-technical notion. In reality, we know that somewhere, probably in a dark air-conditioned basement, there is a decidedly unromantic computer running a Web server program that just loops continuously waiting for users to connect using some standard recognized protocol such as HTTP or FTP. In concept, it is like a human telephone switchboard operator who sits passively waiting for incoming calls, then routes them to specific phone extensions.

Other Models – Dumb Terminals and Peer-to-Peer

In some ways, client-server is similar to dumb terminals connecting to a traditional time-sharing mainframe, though today many mainframes are being used as Web servers. But there is an important difference between clients (typically a desktop PC) and dumb terminals. Today's PCs have powerful processors, plenty of memory and disk space. They can therefore do additional processing on any data received from a Web server. The most obvious example is the way that a browser will receive an HTML file and process the file to generate a multimedia display on the screen. Without that, a server would have to process and deliver over the network every detail to be displayed on the dumb terminal's screen, requiring very much more network traffic and taking much more time. However, dumb terminals have other advantages, and there are still plenty about.

One interesting development of dumb terminals is so-called 'thin clients' – PCs or workstations with plenty of processing power but no hard disk. They therefore do not need a fully-featured operating system like Windows, and they cannot store programs or data. Therefore, (like a dumb terminal) they must run programs on the server. But (unlike a dumb terminal), they have plenty of processing power to manage the local display. Some people believe that the future lies with such Java-based 'thin client' network computers, while others, notably of course Microsoft, favour 'fat' clients running Windows.

A third model that is growing in importance is peer-to-peer, in which each computer is equal and works as a server or client or both, with no central or controlling system, but as a distributed system. A common use of this is to share files, as in Windows workgroups, and for sharing things like music files over the Internet.

Client-server is the commonest model, because it enables the server to do what it does best – handle multiple users, security and large volumes of data, and the client to do what it can do easily – provide an attractive and useful display to the end user. To sum up – the client-server model provides the best compromise as an efficient and effective foundation for Web services and e-Business.

Servers

A server is simply a computer that is connected to a network, with:

▷ An operating system that can handle multiple users

▷ A TCP/IP stack to handle the communications

▷ Some sort of server software to process client requests

Such server software is usually called a 'responder', because it is passive, waiting for and responding to incoming requests. In Unix terminology, it is called a 'daemon', and in Windows, a 'service'. In programming terms, it is a program that just runs in a continuous loop, continually checking for any activity, and springing to life when needed.

Push or Pull

This basic server model can be described as 'pull technology', because the server is passive, and the browser is always pulling data from it. But a server can also be configured to 'push' data – for example, to send news or share prices automatically to browsers.

Operating Systems

From the earliest days of the Internet, UNIX systems have been very popular for servers because they are powerful, robust, come with TCP/IP networking as standard, and support multiple concurrent users. More recently, PCs running Linux or Microsoft operating systems and software have been a growing market. In addition, it is not unusual to find large mainframe computers being used as Web servers.

One widely used server package is Apache (pronounced 'a-patchee'). The name is supposed to derive from the large number of software modifications or 'patches' applied to it, hence 'patchy'.

Sockets

Before we look further into server-side technologies, we need to look at how a browser actually connects to a Web server, and how one Web server can support a large number of clients. If hundreds or even thousands of clients are connected simultaneously, how does the server keep all these connections separate, given that it has only one IP address? Also, the server needs to be able to talk back to your PC. To complicate things, your PC may be running more than one concurrent connection.

There are several aspects to this problem and first we shall look at one of the most important but least known technical features of TCP/IP – sockets and ports. They are fundamental to the whole Internet. Every time you surf the Internet, or use FTP, or send or receive E-mail, you are using sockets. They are an essential part of the technical infrastructure. For the average user, they are irrelevant and also mostly invisible. But for the serious student of e-Commerce, an understanding of sockets is valuable.

Telephone Analogy

To understand what happens, it is worth returning to our telephone analogy. Suppose you want to telephone someone in a large organization. Traditionally, you go through a two-stage process – first dial the organization's main switchboard, then ask the operator for the particular person you want to speak to. The operator then puts you through to a particular telephone extension number. We can illustrate this process by comparing what happens when you telephone the organization with what the browser does:

Telephone	Browser
Get organization's name e.g. SuperOrg	Obtain URL e.g. www.superorg.com
Pick up telephone	Start browser internet connection
Call Directory Enquiries to get SuperOrg's phone number e.g. 012 3456 7890	Browser calls DNS to get SuperOrg's numeric IP address
Dial number of SuperOrg's switchboard	Browser connects to IP address using HTTP
Reach operator	Connected OK to SuperOrg's Web server
Ask for extension e.g. 123	Port number (HTTP defaults to 80)
Reach person	Connect to responder on port 80
Caller ID tells SuperOrg what phone number you are calling from	Your browser tells SuperOrg's server how to reply to you (your IP address and temporary port number)

Table 17.1   Telephone and browser analogy

In computer terms, the IP address is like the telephone number for the organization's switchboard – it is a number that uniquely identifies the server you want (ignoring DNS for the moment). For the next stage, the port number is like the telephone extension – it is a short number that uniquely identifies the responder for the protocol you want. The combination of the two – IP address and port number – form a socket. Returning to our telephone analogy, a socket is therefore like the combination of an organization's telephone number plus an extension number.

Ports

We shall start by focusing on ports. These are not hardware ports like the comms ports COM1 and COM2 on a PC, but a software identifier – like that office telephone extension number. Each port is given a number in the range $1 - 65535$ (in binary $1 - 2^{16}$). Port numbers below 1024 are reserved. Some of these ports are called 'well-known' ports. For example, port 80 is reserved for HTTP, and 25 for SMTP. In TCP/IP, there are hundreds more services. However, many of them are specialised, or little used, and most of them are usually barred at any security-conscious Web site. Among the commonly barred ones are services like 'finger', which is designed to give you information about other users (as it were, to 'finger' them). For security reasons, that is high on the list of services not offered – it gives too much help to hackers. There are also some odd but occasionally useful ones, like 'daytime' on port 13. If you connect successfully to that port, it returns the date and time from the server – and only that. It can be useful, for example, when testing a connection because it proves that the remote computer system's TCP/IP stack is responding correctly, and that the operating system is functioning. A more common and useful command for that same purpose is 'ping', a name derived from the sonar systems in submarines that send out a 'ping' to detect other submarines. Similarly, this command detects whether a remote system is responding, but has the advantage of not needing a port number, just an IP address.

When you enter a URL in your browser, you do not need to define the port number (unless specially asked to do so). If you type just **www.Website.com** the browser defaults to HTTP, and therefore port 80, just as if you had typed the whole URL: **http://www.Website.com:80** and similarly, if you connect to a secure site using HTTPS as in **https://www.Website.com** then you will connect to port 443 because that port is reserved for HTTPS. If you want to make an ftp connection, you type ftp instead of http, as in **ftp://www.Website.com** and by default, your browser will ask for port 21. If you type: **ftp://www.Website.com:80** you will get an error, because the Web service responder on port 80 expects HTTP, not FTP.

The names and port numbers are held in a file called 'services', on systems that support TCP/IP, including most Windows PCs. If you look at this file, you will find that it contains all sorts of other often specialized services. However, if your PC is a client, not a server, it may not include ports like http and https. You will also find that some ports come in both a TCP and a UDP version (see glossary).

Sockets as Communications Endpoint

Like a port, a socket is not a physical entity. It is a logical concept, and is usually defined as a 'communications end-point' – the combination of an IP address and a port number, for example 192.168.73.122:80

From a programming point of view, a socket behaves rather like a file. In a program, you can open a file for reading and/or writing. Similarly, a program can open a socket for reading or writing over the network connection, and in return it will get a 'file descriptor' to handle the flow of data. So to read and write you need two sockets.

One of the attractions of sockets is that they can handle multiple connections on the same port. When connecting for example to an HTTP Web site, your PC will send the URL to port 80, but also nominate a unique port number on which it will accept data from the server back to your PC. This will normally be a much higher number selected at random (but not already in use), and well outside the range of those well-known ports. The basic principle is that for the duration of your connection, you have a socket (IP address plus port number) to the server (not necessarily unique), and the server has a unique socket back to you, and that combination is therefore unique during your session. No other pair of computers in the world will use exactly the same pair of IP addresses and port numbers. (If you are going through a proxy server, then of course that is where the sockets are unique). If your browser is running multiple concurrent TCP/IP sessions (not uncommon), it is using several different but unique socket combinations.

Winsock

Winsock (Windows Sockets) supports TCP/IP on Windows PCs. Programmers can use Winsock to communicate with other systems, typically a browser connecting to a Web server. It is usually implemented as a DLL (Dynamic Link Library) with functions that can be called from other programs. It is a good example of 'glue' software between Windows and TCP/IP, because it provides a toolkit of useful functions. In the jargon, it gives 'abstraction' by providing a high-level interface that programmers can use, thus sparing them from the low-level detail.

Raw Sockets

One issue that has caused some controversy in the Internet community is what is called 'raw sockets'. In many operating systems with TCP/IP, the only interface is via the TCP/IP stack. That limits what you can do to what is specified for TCP/IP. But if an operating system allows raw sockets, then you can send out IP packets directly, bypassing the TCP/IP stack. This is great for experimental and testing purposes, but also means that hackers can disguise their IP addresses, making it easier for them to launch attacks on other servers – for example the so-called 'distributed denial of service' or DDoS attacks, that flood a Web server with connection requests, thus overloading it and preventing it from providing a normal service.

Dynamic Data

Now that we have looked at the mechanics of connecting to a server, we need to move on to look at what sort of technologies are available on a server. To answer that, we need to start by looking first at the client side – to see what the client can do (which is usually what the user's desktop PC can do). The answer is – not that much. Most users will have some sort of browser software, and different versions can do different things. As we have seen earlier in this book, more recent browser versions can handle XML, but older ones cannot. Some browsers cannot display graphics, and some users prefer to disable graphics, for performance reasons. A server can only usefully provide what a browser will display. What all browsers have in common is that they can display HTML. This is therefore the lowest common denominator. A Web server must therefore deliver HTML data. (Of course, if the browser supports XML, then the server can deliver XML and HTML data to that browser.)

It does not matter to the client how the server generates that data. If you can run a program on the server to generate HTML data dynamically, the client does not know the difference, and the server can then also do other things in the process, such as connecting to a database. In that way, the server can fetch up-to-date information, merge it with other data, and dynamically generate a stream of data that, to the browser, is just HTML. Bear in mind that an HTML file can of course include colours, often graphics and animation, even audio and video, depending on the capabilities of the browser software and the preferences of the user. We should really be talking about hypermedia, not just hypertext. The key point here for the server side is summed up in the phrase 'dynamically-generated data'. This is the main objective of all these server-side technologies.

CGI

CGI, the 'Common Gateway Interface' provides a standard interface for generating dynamic data. It is simple and straightforward, and a good starting point for understanding the mechanics of dynamic data.

The standard way of using CGI on a server is to define a specific subdirectory (usually but not necessarily called 'cgi-bin') that holds scripts or programs instead of HTML files. Then you also tell the server software that if a request comes in for a file in that sub-directory, that file is to be run, not displayed – it is a program or script, not an HTML file.

Scripts and Programs

Incidentally, in this context, 'script' is a Unix term that simply means an executable file, or what in MS-DOS is called a 'batch file'. It is not easy to draw a hard and fast line between scripts and programs, because they are both executable files. But as a general rule, scripts are text files that are interpreted at runtime, while programs are compiled into a binary format before being run. However, it is also possible to compile scripts, and Java programs, as we'll see later, are semi-compiled.

CGI in Action

If a user clicks a link on a browser screen that points to a URL like **www.myWebserver.com/cgi-bin/welcome.pl** then the Web server will detect that it specifies sub-directory cgi-bin, and will therefore try to run the script 'welcome.pl'. The CGI interface also collects information about the browser and the whole environment – for example the exact browser version being used, and the various MIME types that the browser will accept (such as image/gif or image/jpeg for graphics files). This information is therefore available to the script, and it can react accordingly, and even prepare different outputs if required for different browser versions.

What happens next depends entirely on what the script is designed to do. CGI scripts are often used to process data from forms submitted by Web users. These scripts can also download small programs to the client, to give dynamic feedback (more about this below). The vital point here is that suddenly we have all the power and flexibility that a program can provide. We can do things dynamically, instead of just displaying a static file. This is why the technique is called a 'Gateway', because it provides a gateway to all the other facilities and resources on the system.

CGI Languages

A CGI script or program can be written in any computer language supported on the server, for example Java, C or C++ on Windows PCs, Macintosh and Unix systems. Visual Basic can be used on Windows PCs, and AppleScript on Macs. But the most popular language on all these CGI systems is Perl, because it has a number of features that are particularly useful for providing Web services. It is also highly portable between different systems. Another big attraction of Perl is that it is free, and can be downloaded from various sites under the GNU Public Licence. However, some large organizations, for security reasons, refuse to install Perl or indeed any software not supplied and supported directly by the hardware manufacturer. If you are running a mission-critical computer system, you may want expert 24-hour support seven days a week, even though that may be expensive. Nevertheless, plenty of large organizations are happy to use Perl.

Perl

A quick overview of Perl if you are not familiar with it: the name stands for 'Practical Extraction and Report Language', though its creator, Larry Wall, says Perl could also stand for 'Pathologically Eclectic Rubbish Lister'. However, it is always known just as Perl for the language, and perl for the interpreter that runs your Perl scripts – like welcome.pl (where the extension .pl indicates it is a Perl script). Perl is an interpreted language, and is particularly good at scanning text files and extracting information using sophisticated pattern matching techniques – far better for example than other languages such as C or Basic, and this is the main reason for its name and its popularity. It is particularly good at handling the complicated strings that are often returned from a Web browser to a server, for example after an on-screen form has been filled in by a user. In addition, there are add-ons that enable Perl to do a vast range of other things on a server, for example to connect to relational databases such as Oracle and Sybase. Because of that, a Perl script can do everything needed to communicate with a user on one side, and to collect information from a database on the other, and bring everything together. For that reason, it is sometimes called a 'glue' language because it provides the programming glue to integrate complex systems.

This tiny script will give you a quick idea what Perl looks like:

```
#!/usr/bin/perl

print "Hello world!\n";
```

The first line defines where to find the Perl interpreter (called 'perl') in the directory structure, and the second line just prints on the screen the words Hello world! The '\n' means start a new line, and the semi-colon indicates the end of the command. It is a complete program in its own right.

Using Perl with a Database

To give you some idea of what's involved when talking to a database, let's use this scenario: your company wants to sell widgets over the Internet, and you want a screen which shows the current number of widgets available in your warehouse. You already have an internal database, such as Oracle, which holds this information. The database may be on the same machine as the Web server, or more likely, on a separate machine connected over a local area network. In effect, therefore, the database itself is a server, waiting for queries from users or other systems.

In Oracle, as in all relational databases, information is stored in the form of tables, consisting of rows and columns. Data can be handled using a special language called SQL (Structured Query Language). It has commands such as INSERT to insert new data into a table, DELETE to delete data, and SELECT to select or retrieve values from the database. If you were doing this manually, you would first log on to Oracle, then type an SQL command something like this:

```
SELECT total FROM widgets;
```

Assuming you had logged on correctly, and that there was a table of data called widgets, with a column called total (in this case consisting of just one row), the database would return the current value of total.

Oraperl

To do the same in a Perl script, you could use Oraperl, an extension to Perl giving access to Oracle databases by means of a number of specialized functions. Your script would first contain a command to provide access to Oracle, with a command to log on to Oracle (here just shown as "$login"), and an SQL command to select the required data. The key parts of the script would look something like this:

```
use Oraperl;
$number = "SELECT total FROM widgets; "
&Oraperl::ora_do($login,$number);
```

In outline what the script is doing is:

▷ Calling the special separate Perl add-on for Oracle

▷ Setting up a variable called $number to hold the actual SQL command

▷ Calling a sub-routine in OraPerl called "ora_do", and passing two parameters to the sub-routine: first, to login to Oracle (not shown in full); then the SQL SELECT command itself (as $number).

This would return the current value of 'total' from the widgets table, in exactly the same way as if you had done it manually – except that instead of being displayed on the screen, the value is now held in Perl. Your Perl script can now use this value to build the HTML Web page to be displayed to the user.

In real life the script would be longer and more complex, with for example much more error-checking and logging. This short extract shows that it is relatively straightforward to use CGI and Perl as the glue between a Web page and a database.

ODBC

Another option, not language-specific, is Microsoft's ODBC (Open Database Connectivity). This provides an API (application programming interface) for database access by programs, and means that an application can access different database systems using special software modules called 'drivers' that isolate the programmer from needing to know the details about each database – summed up in the word 'interoperable'. It is the same idea as printer drivers that insulate a word processing program from printer-specific commands (another example of abstraction).

Java

Java is also a popular language on Web servers, because it is designed for the Web. This means, for example, that it is designed to run programs stored not necessarily on your own computer but elsewhere on the Internet, thus opening the way for all kinds of collaborative processing, for example interactive games. To do this, it must be portable to different operating systems, and we shall see in a moment how that is done.

To give you a flavour of this powerful but complex language, here is a short example of a Java program that does the same as the Perl "Hello World!" shown above:

```
public class HelloWorldApp {

    public static void main (String args [ ] ) {

        System.out.println ("Hello World!");

    }

}
```

Straight away you can see that this is more complex than the Perl example. If you are familiar with the C++ language, you will see that Java is similar, and likewise object-oriented, which means among other things that Java programs can be built from existing modules rather than being written from scratch each time - summed up in the word 'reusability'.

Another important aspect of Java is that it is compiled not into different programs for specific computers or platforms, as with C programs, but into a special semi-compiled form called Java bytecode that, in the jargon, is 'platform-independent' – that means it can be run on any computer and operating system that contains the software needed to interpret the Java bytecode. This includes various browsers (provided they are Java-enabled in user preferences or options).

What Does 'Object-Oriented' Mean?

If you are not familiar with the term 'object-oriented' here is a brief explanation.

Let's assume you are asked to write the software to manage a modern fly-by-wire aircraft. There are two obvious approaches:

▷ Procedural (the traditional way to write computer programs). You write programs that manage standard activities and procedures – for example one program to control aircraft takeoff, one for level flight, and one for landing.

▷ Object-oriented. You write separate program modules that control real-world things or 'objects' on the plane such as engines, rudder, wheels, wing flaps etc. Each module has data about the object it manages, and routines that use the data to control the object (for example to vary the angle of the flaps). You then write a top-level program that calls these modules as required with suitable parameters to control different stages of the flight.

Either set of software will fly the plane. The advantage of the object-oriented program is that each module is self-contained, with its own data and instructions, and therefore easier to write and test. You do not need different programs or modules to control the engines in different phases of flight – you just need to vary the parameters or 'messages' you pass to the engine module. Also, there is only one top-level program, again easier to write and test. In addition, and more importantly, you may be able to reuse or adapt object-oriented modules already developed for other planes, and later, you may be able to reuse the modules you have developed or improved.

An object is not necessarily a physical entity – it can also be a graphics object, such as a shape or box that appears on a PC screen, and can even be individual bits of software less tangible than an aircraft engine.

There are a number of jargon words in object-oriented, such as 'classes', 'inheritance', 'abstraction', 'encapsulation' and 'polymorphism'. A 'class' is like a template for related objects. For example, an aircraft has several varieties of flaps that have certain features in common. These features could go into a class, and then each separate flap module could inherit those common features from the class – that simplifies the programming.

Abstraction and encapsulation are related concepts – they are all about separating out the low-level detail of an object, and hiding or 'encapsulating' it in a module, to separate behaviour from implementation, so that the programmer can deal with it at a high level.

Polymorphism is from the Greek for 'many forms', and means the ability for an object belonging to one class to be treated as a member of other classes – again with the aim of increasing programming efficiency.

To sum up:

▷ An 'object' is self-contained; a programming module for an object consists of both data and the procedures to manipulate that data – in short, to control the object.

▷ You deal with objects, not with procedures, and you pass messages to the objects.

▷ The aim is to increase programming productivity.

Java Applets

Java can also be used to create small programs or applications called 'applets' that can be written, compiled into bytecode, and embedded in a Web page stored on the Web server. When the user selects that page, the page plus applets are downloaded to the client, and run automatically. Applets run in a special secure environment in the browser called a 'sandbox', by analogy with a garden sandbox for children that is a safe place to play. The Java sandbox is software that verifies that the applet is correctly written, and also restricts what it can do – applets, for example, cannot access or delete local files, or run other programs. Once used, they are thrown away. The idea of the sandbox is that because applets in theory cannot do any harm, you will be happy to download applets from any source. In the jargon, such applets are 'untrusted', but because of the sandbox they are deemed 'trusted', and therefore safe to run. However even so some users prefer to disable Java on their browsers, at the expense of losing the advantages of applets.

ASP – Active Server Pages

ASP is a technology developed by Microsoft to provide more dynamic Web pages. ASP makes it possible to include powerful features – such as ActiveX controls, and commands in scripting languages (such as JavaScript or VBscript) in HTML files stored on a Web server. Such files are stored with an .asp extension (for example 'welcome.asp'), and when requested by a browser, the server will run any scripts or programs in the file before sending it to the client computer. On the Net, you will often see URLs with .asp file extensions.

ActiveX

ActiveX controls are small programs that can provide animation and multimedia effects on client computers. Like Java applets, they are downloaded and run (provided the browser supports and enables ActiveX). Unlike applets, however, they can be stored locally and can be reused – so the next time your browser needs that control, it does not need to be downloaded again.

ActiveX controls are more powerful than Java applets, and therefore potentially more dangerous. To resolve that, Microsoft have adopted an approach very different from Java applets. ActiveX controls can have digital certificates to prove that they have been produced by a known and trusted source (typically a software publisher), and also that the controls have not been tampered with on their way to your browser. You can therefore pick and choose (in Microsoft Explorer's Internet options) which sites you trust and which you don't, and how to handle ActiveX (and Java). The technique is called 'Authenticode'. By default, Internet Explorer will only allow signed ActiveX controls, but some cautious users recommend disabling even that, though that means losing some attractive functionality.

Servlets

Just as applets are fragments of Java that run on a client, so 'servlets' are fragments of Java that run on a Web server. They are resident in memory (unlike a CGI script), and are executed when an HTTP command is received. Servlets can also be used to 'maintain state' or 'persist' – in other words, to keep track of a user's history, for example when ordering goods or services, particularly when using an Internet shopping cart.

Servlets have one important technical advantage over CGI scripts. In standard CGI, every time a new user connects, another copy of the CGI script has to be loaded and run. That is traditional 'multi-user' or 'multi-tasking' computing. If there are hundreds or thousands of users, this is a big overhead on the Web server. There are various solutions to this, even in CGI. Some languages, including Java, support what is called 'multi-threading'. This is a programming technique in which one program can look after multiple users at the same time, all using different parts or 'threads' in that program. The program automatically keeps track of each user's state, and saves or restores it as needed. Of course, such a program is more complex, and has much more work to do, than a script running on behalf of only a single user, but the advantage is that it is more robust and efficient – only one copy or 'instance' is loaded, and only one process runs. This avoids the considerable overhead of loading, running and closing separate programs or scripts.

Microsoft .NET

Microsoft .NET is an evolution from earlier technologies such as COM. The underlying aim is to make it easier for developers to create new programs by providing ready-made programming components – one of the goals of object-oriented. Such code reuse has long been a great idea in theory, but hard to achieve in practice, especially if different programming languages are used. Sometimes the reasons may seem remarkably trivial. One example is the use of arrays – widely used in programming to hold lists of variables. In some programming languages, arrays are numbered from 1 upwards, in others from zero. You can see straight away that a component written in one language can easily give the wrong results if called from another.

COM

One of the aims of COM therefore is to provide an interface that handles such differences automatically and invisibly, and spares the programmer from having to write extra code to handle this. That helps to make components reusable. Another aim is to make components 'location independent' so that a programmer does not need to know exactly where a component is located – whether locally or on a separate remote machine. COM sits in the middle and deals with it.

CORBA

Similarly, CORBA (Common Object Request Broker Architecture) provides the glue that enables computer programs on different systems to interwork over networks. A CORBA application consists of 'objects' (as explained above) – for example, the software to manage a Web site shopping-cart. Other programs can pass parameters to this object, and receive the results. Again, the advantage is that programmers can reuse existing objects.

.NET Web Services

In these ways, .NET and its precursors like COM provide a wide-ranging programming infrastructure that can vastly increase programmer productivity. .NET supports what are called XML Web services, like programming building blocks, for complex tasks like checking a Web buyer's credit rating and then charging the buyer's account for purchases. Among the advantages that .NET claims to have over other techniques like CORBA is that it is simpler, and that it uses existing Web protocols, namely XML and HTTP for passing messages (parameters) to other services.

Among the facilities provided by .NET are:

▷ Support for ASP

▷ Support for connecting to databases

▷ Support for distributed computing – using programs on other systems

▷ Web services can be written in various languages

▷ Web services are described and registered, so that users can find them using UDDI (Universal Discovery Description and Integration)

▷ Garbage collection (automatic memory management)

Memory Leaks

That last point (garbage collection) highlights a source of problems in computing that are particularly hard to detect and resolve called 'memory leaks'. It is mainly of interest to programmers, but is worth understanding. When a program runs, it occupies space in the computer's memory, and also needs additional space for processing and storing variables that by definition keep changing. Some programming languages, notably C, require the programmer to allocate such space and later to de-allocate it. But in a complex program, particularly a server program that needs to run continuously with 'high nines' (99.999%) availability, it can be tricky and error-prone to keep track of how and when to do this, so de-allocation may not always work as intended. The result is that a program may work fine when tested, and work fine for days or weeks – until suddenly it runs out memory and crashes. Or perhaps worse it may start reading random data accidentally left in memory. So an infrastructure that automatically manages memory and clears out unwanted data ('garbage collection') is a distinct plus, and this is one of Java's big plus points.

Other Web Languages

Various other scripting languages are also used, notably JavaScript, Jscript and VBscript. They are generally embedded in Web pages, downloaded and run on the client. Note that despite the names, JavaScript and Jscript have nothing much to do with Java. JavaScript is generic, and Jscript is Microsoft's implementation of JavaScript. VBScript, as the name implies, is based on Microsoft's Visual Basic. All three are scripting languages, much closer to MS-DOS batch files or UNIX scripts than they are to full-blooded programming languages like Java. They will work with any browser that can interpret the scripts.

JavaScript Example

Here is a short example of JavaScript embedded in an HTML page to give you an idea of what it looks like. The whole HTML file (including the script) is stored on the server and is downloaded to the browser and runs there in response to a client request:

```
<HTML>
  <HEAD>
    <TITLE>A title</TITLE>
  </HEAD>
<BODY>
  <H1>
```

```
<SCRIPT LANGUAGE=JAVASCRIPT TYPE="TEXT/JAVASCRIPT">
  document.write("Hello World!")
</SCRIPT>
</H1>
</BODY>
</HTML>
```

. . . and how it appears in a JavaScript-enabled browser:

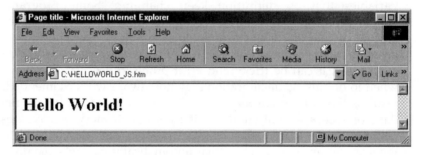

Two attractions of such scripting languages are:

▷ They reduce the need for processing on the server, and transfer it to the client – one of the key attractions of the client-server model

▷ Unlike Java or compiled programs, such scripts are human-readable, and can be seen by the user by viewing the HTML source in the browser – a good way to learn how to write them yourself.

A common use for such scripts is to add special effects, and to display forms on the screen etc. They are similar – for example, if you change the JavaScript above to 'Jscript' or 'VBScript' it will produce the same result – but only in Microsoft browsers, because Jscript and VBScript are both Microsoft products. JavaScript, on the other hand, works in both Microsoft and Netscape, and any browser that supports it.

Browser Incompatibility

That underlines a key point – you cannot assume that all browsers work in the same way. It is therefore usually necessary in CGI and other server-side processing to detect the version of the browser being used on the client, and to write additional code to handle any variations. To test CGI, you need a client or clients with multiple versions of browsers, and to test on each one. For example, in a browser that does not support JavaScript, the "Hello World!" example above would appear not as intended, but showing the text as it stands – something disagreeable like this: document.write("Hello World!") As you can see, the browser ignores the line starting <SCRIPT, and treats the next line as normal text.

Using Server-side Technologies

Now we have seen how server-side technologies work, it is time to look at the broader picture of how organizations use them, and the issues that arise in doing so. As we have seen, there is more to e-Business than just setting up a Web server and some HTML pages. There is also more to it than adding a bit of animation and multimedia. The real requirements for any serious attempt at e-Business can be summed up in the phrase Enterprise Application Integration – EAI for short.

These days most companies, and practically all major companies, have plans to expand their e-Business activities in several directions, such as the better management of the supply chain, better systems for customer service and Web-based commerce, and better internal management using Enterprise Resource Planning (ERP) systems. All these require integration with existing in-house systems, which in many cases means integration with databases and other stores of data.

Legacy Systems

Most organizations have what are called 'legacy' systems – computer systems developed years ago that pre-date these Web initiatives, but are essential to the running of the business. Some large organizations, particularly in financial services like insurance, have literally thousands of programs developed over the years. In some cases, the programmers who wrote the original programs are no longer available, or the programs were written in languages no longer used, or perhaps using old-fashioned techniques or databases. It is often risky, and sometimes impossible, to upgrade these. Therefore the only option is to develop an interface between the legacy systems and the Web servers. Even if more modern facilities are used, such as ERP (Enterprise Resource Planning) systems, most organizations still have very large amounts of data. The problem gets worse when companies grow by acquisition – buying other companies. It is then more than likely that the newly acquired companies will have different computer systems, different applications and different databases.

Middleware

One solution to the integration problem is to use so-called 'middleware', a layer of software placed between the network and programs that provides generic services such as security, authentication, permissions etc.

Middleware means that programmers do not have to reinvent the wheel each time they want to incorporate such services in new programs. Middleware often includes programs designed to extract data from an existing system, and re-format it into another format suitable for use with a Web server. Such software sits in the middle between the systems, and is usually described as 'translation' or 'mapping' software. However, such translation or 'mapping' often turns out to be more complex than expected. There are many reasons for this, ranging from simple problems like inaccurate file definitions, through to more serious and sometimes fundamental problems, some of which we saw in Chapter 15. The history of such commercial acquisitions is littered with the problems and occasional disasters of merged companies struggling with incompatible computer systems and the problems of transferring data between them.

EAI – Enterprise Application Integration

Nevertheless, these days it is becoming more and more important to connect a Web server with an organization's existing computer systems.

The same problem also arises when an organization needs to exchange data with other organizations. In order to speed up the supply chain, organizations need to exchange far more than just orders and invoices. Increasingly, they also need to exchange other business documents such as forecasts, production plans and schedules, prices, despatch advices and delivery notes. As it is pretty well certain that the trading partners will have different computer systems, applications, databases and ERP systems, designed in different ways, organizations need to extract data from their own systems, reformat it to some agreed standard, and then send it. At the receiving end, they need to do the reverse – accept data in the agreed standard format, translate it into their own in-house format, and then integrate it into their own systems. Even if organizations have the same brand of ERP system, it is more than likely that their own implementations will be different. And though this integration process is getting easier as the middleware gets better – the mapping or translation programs in the middle – many organizations report that such integration is still cumbersome, time-consuming and expensive.

This whole area has been given its own name – EAI or Enterprise Application Integration, and despite improvements in the software, it remains a complex and difficult area, and one very popular among management consultants because it remains a lucrative specialist field.

Acronyms and Glossary

.NET Microsoft's framework strategy for Web services. Enables a Web server to provide various generic services to Web applications, such as security and password control, to speed up and simplify software development.

A2A Application-to-Application. The transfer of data (XML, EDI) between separate application programs usually on separate computer systems, without human intervention. Vital for EAI. See also B2B, B2C.

ActiveX Microsoft's response to Java, used to extend the functionality of applications running within a browser.

ADSL Asymmetric Digital Subscriber Line (see DSL). Asymmetric because data is received more quickly than it is sent. See also broadband.

AFNOR Association Françaize de Normalization is the national standards body in France – other examples include BSI (UK), ANSI (US) and DIN (Germany).

Agents Software routines which personalize Web access.

AIAG The US Automobile Industry Action Group is an active EDI forum and has developed a sub-set of the ANSI ASC X12 standard for use in the US motor industry.

ANA UK Article Numbering Association. Affiliated to the European Article Numbering Association (EAN), now called 'e.centre'. See **www.eca.org.uk**

ANA Number Unique identifier for members of ANA. Usually a 13-digit number. Used in barcodes on products, and also as e-Commerce address. Same idea as DUNS number.

Analogue Where a signal is transmitted over a medium in a continuously varying waveform, like speech over an old-fashioned telephone line, or music in an old-fashioned vinyl gramophone record. See also digital and modem.

Anonymous FTP Facility on Internet sites that allow anyone to connect to them and transfer files using FTP.

ANSI American National Standards Institute represents the US in the International Standards Organization (ISO). See also ASCII and X12. See **www.ansi.org**

API Application Program Interface. A facility in a program that provides an interface (a set of commands and parameters etc.) that enables other programs to use it.

Applet A small computer program written in Java that runs inside a secure so-called 'sandbox' in a Java compatible Web browser.

Application A computer program intended for users, as opposed to a computer or "system" program designed for use by the operating system. ERP programs etc. are applications. See also EAI.

Application Integration (AI) AI, a business computing term for the plans, methods, and tools aimed at modernizing, consolidating, and co-ordinating the computer applications in an enterprise.

ARPA Internet suite of protocols developed by the Advanced Research Projects Agency (formerly DARPA).

AS2 Applicability Statement 2 is the draft standard by which vendor applications communicate EDI (EDIFACT or X12), binary or XML data over the Internet.

ASC X12 Accredited Sub-Committee X12 responsible for devising US national EDI standards. See X12.

ASCII American Standard Code for Information Interchange that assigns numeric values to characters, including letters, numerals and punctuation marks. Strictly speaking, ASCII is 7-bit, up to the decimal value 127, and therefore does not include special characters as found in many European languages.

The phrase 'ASCII text' implies that a file contains only printable characters (as opposed to 'binary').

ASN.1 Abstract Syntax Notation One is an OSI language for describing abstract syntax (description of data types).

ASP Application Service Provider. An organization that provides hosted or outsourced software services for other organizations over the Internet. Paid by subscription, rather than being bought and installed on a user's system. See also ISP.

ASP (Active Server Pages) Active Server Pages, part of Microsoft .NET. ASPs are pages generated on a Web server, which can call other programs, e.g. for database searches. Like CGI, it provides dynamic pages, but is more efficient than CGI.

Asynchronous Transfer Mode ATM is a means of transmitting data, voice and video over high speed networks – ATM is a connection-oriented protocol using a fixed-length packet or cell.

Asynchronous, Async dial-up A basic method of data communications that uses start and stop bits to separate individual characters, thus allowing data to be sent without strict timing, and with occasional pauses. Suitable for use over a telephone connection. Usually shortened to 'async' as in 'async dial-up' via a modem.

ATM Automated Teller Machines allow banking customers the ability to obtain cash and account information on a 24-hour basis.

Attachment, attached file A file attached to an E-mail message, for example a word-processed document, spreadsheet, or computer program. The MIME protocol is used to send such files over the Internet using SMTP.

Attribute In general, an attribute is a property or characteristic of an object. Colour, for example, is an attribute of your hair. In computing, an attribute is a changeable property or characteristic of some component of a program that can be set to different values.

B2B Business-to-Business e-Commerce – the exchange of data between businesses, not involving consumers. See also Supply Chain, Reverse Auction, A2A, B2C.

B2C Business-to-Consumer e-Commerce – the exchange of data between a business and consumers.

Backbone The portion of the network that manages the main traffic volume. In traffic terms, like a high-capacity motorway that feeds smaller routes.

Bandwidth The capacity of a medium (LAN, telephone line etc.) to carry traffic. The greater the bandwidth, the higher the speed. See broadband.

Basic Rate ISDN An Integrated Services Digital Network (ISDN) service that offers two bearer channels (64K bits/sec) and a control channel (16K bits/sec).

Baud Measurement of data communications speed that does not always correspond to bits per second.

Binary Raw data represented by a string of zeroes and ones, split into bytes, for example graphical images, compiled programs etc.

Biometric Security Security approaches that use human characteristics to distinguish individuals.

BIOS Basic Input/Output System. Software on a PC that interfaces directly with the hardware (e.g. manages the keyboard, screen etc.). 1 **Bit** Bit is a basic unit of information representing 0 or 1 in the binary system (BInary digiT). 1 **Bits per second (bps)** Number of binary digits transmitted each second. In normal async dial-up, each character is sent in 10 bits – a start bit, then the 8-bit byte, finally a stop bit.

BizTalk A Microsoft initiative for XML transfer of data. See **www.BizTalk.org**

Bluetooth A short-distance wireless-data standard, to enable devices like mobile phones to connect to other devices without cables. See also IEEE.

BPR Business Process Re-engineering – term coined by Michael Hammer to signify the radical redesign of business processes, often using innovative IT.

Bridge Hardware device to connect similar local area networks.

Broadband Describes a communications network capable of carrying large amounts of data at high speed using different frequencies to provide separate channels over the same physical connection (as opposed to a narrowband single-channel connection provided by a dial-up modem). See DSL, ADSL.

Browser Software running on a PC to navigate the World Wide Web, look at pages etc. – the client side of the client-server structure of the Web. Netscape Navigator/Communicator and Microsoft Internet Explorer are market leaders. Recent versions are XML-aware. See client-server.

Bulletin Board System A centralized database application that contains information to be 'pulled' off as required by end users.

Business Library An electronically available specification of the components that enable an XML application. In their simplest form, they contain dictionaries of

XML tags, XML elements, components of DTDs, or other XML schemas. However, they may be extended to include all other materials that support trading relationships e.g. legal agreements, guidance, etc.

Byte Usually a group of 8 bits (BinarY digiT Eight). But may be only 7, as in ASCII, which uses 7 bits plus a check bit, or less than 7. Represents some meaningful value (see octet).

CA A Certificate Authority is a trusted third party that attests to an individual's electronic identity (public key).

Cable modem Uses existing cable TV connection to provide high speed bandwidth to PC (usually via LAN card).

Campus Network A series of interconnect local area networks (LANs).

Card Services Software that allocates system resources as PCMCIA cards are inserted/removed.

CCITT Comité Consultatif International Télégraphique et Téléphonique forms part of the International Telecommunications Union (ITU) – CCITT has been renamed ITU-T. Responsible for international telecommunications recommendations (e.g. X.400).

CEFACT See UN / CEFACT.

CEN Comité Européen de Normalization – European standards organization. See **www.cenorm.be**

CERT The Computer Emergency Response Team monitors the Internet for illegal or fraudulent activities, and issues warnings. See **www.cert.org**

Certificate Means of exchanging an individual's public key (see X.509 and Digital Certificate).

Certificate Chain A collection of certificates, in which each in the chain certifies the next one down. The top certificate is issued by a Certificate Authority.

Certificate Revocation List A list of digital certificates that have been revoked, and therefore should not be relied on; or those withdrawn or cancelled. Maintained by a Certificate Authority.

CGI Common Gateway Interface. Enables a Web server to run a script or programme to generate HTML output to be sent to a Web browser. This means that instead of being held in a static file, the HTML output can be generated dynamically, for example from a database. See also ASP.

Checksum A procedure to verify the integrity of data and detect any changes made by an intruder. The sending system calculates this sum, and sends it to the receiving system. The receiving system calculates the checksum independently. If the two sums agree, the data is accepted. A very simple checksum just adds the ASCII value of all characters in a file. More complex ones use various algorithms. See hash function.

CIDR Classless Inter-Domain Routing. A way of allocating IP addresses that avoids the wasteful allocation of ranges of addresses to organizations that do not need them all.

Ciphertext Text that has been disguised through encryption technologies.

CISC Complex Instruction Set Computing processors support many assembler level language instructions, resulting in a more powerful but slower CPU. See also RISC.

Client The user of a network service. Usually an application on a client computer that makes use of services such as applications, files or printers running on a remote server.

Client/server architecture A computing architecture, where client applications request and receive information and services from server applications that provide responses. A typical example is a user with a browser (the client) connecting to a Web site (the server).

Clipper chip A low cost encryption device that the US Administration proposes to make available to the public.

Compound Document A document that

holds various types of data, with dynamic links to the data sources.

Computationally infeasible A term used in cryptography to indicate that though a code or hash function is not 100% secure, the time and effort to decrypt a message is too great for the reward.

Conference Call Facility that allows individuals at different locations to participate in a meeting by phoning into a conference bridge.

Connection For individuals, the commonest way to connect is over the telephone system, using a modem or cable connection. For larger organizations, a permanent or 'leased line' connection provides much higher speeds for multiple users, but is more expensive.

Connection-less Protocol A technique for sending data without establishing a connection first (unlike, for example, a telephone call). This involves sending packets of data with addressing information included. See datagram, Internet Protocol, packets.

Cookie A small file of information generated from a Web site and stored on a user's PC. Used to keep track of the user's visits and other details. See stateless.

CORBA Common Object Request Broker Architecture is designed to simplify the way applications interact with one another over a network, so they function more like a single program. See **www.corba.org**

CPFR Collaborative Planning, Forecasting and Replenishment is an industry initiative to improve the partnership between manufacturers and distributors (or retailers) through the sharing of information and processes.

CPU Central Processing Unit. A microprocessor (e.g. Intel Pentium) that handles computer instructions.

CRP Continuous Replenishment Programme is an initiative that involves the supplier taking replenishment action based upon knowledge of the retailer's

420

inventory data.

CRL Certificate Revocation Lists highlight certificates that should not be trusted, or those withdrawn or cancelled.

CRM Customer Relationship Management. Software to support customer service from a help desk.

Cryptography Art or science, which renders plaintext unintelligible or converts encrypted messages into intelligible text – used to protect messages and transactions to ensure they cannot be read without the right 'key'.

CSCW Computer Supported Collaborative Working

CSS Cascading Style Sheet. A way of adding style (colours, different fonts etc.) to Web documents (e.g. XML page).

See **www.w3.org/Style.CSS**

CSV Comma-Separated Values. A file format in which values are separated by commas, usually with several values and commas to a line. Used to import data into spreadsheets etc.

Cyberspace A term created by William Gibson in his novel 'Neuromancer' used to describe the collective world of networked computers.

Daemon Background program that runs unattended, for example on a Web server, waiting for requests from user clients. Pronounced 'dee-mon'.

Database Collection of related objects with data attributes, such that information can be extracted.

Datagram A single block or 'packet' of information sent from one IP address to another, using IP (Internet Protocol).

DES The Data Encryption Standard is a popular encryption algorithm adopted by the National Bureau of Standards in 1977 and is used extensively in the Financial Sector. There is an enhanced version called 'Triple DES'.

Digital Where signals are transmitted over a medium in the form of binary numbers that can then regenerate the original signal, like sounds from a CD. See also analogue.

Digital certificate A file from a Certificate Authority that vouches for the identity of an individual. It is signed with the CA's own public key, and stored on a Directory Server. See PKI.

Digital Signature See PKI.

Directory Services A listing of users and resources located on a network and designed to help locate them.

Dis-intermediation In e-Commerce, selling products and services direct to consumers without a middleman (e.g. shop, or broker).

Distributed Computing Processing spread over more than one computer, often using databases on other machines on the network in support of e-Commerce. See also Middleware, EAI.

Document Type Definition (DTD) Document Type Definition. Used with XML to define and validate the elements and their attributes used in the XML file. Not as versatile as schemas. See also XML, Schema., parse.

DOM Document Object Model. Allows programs to process the data (or 'objects') in XML pages, thus providing more intelligence than with plain HTML pages.

Domain Name System (DNS) The Domain Name System (DNS), is software than runs on a global network of servers which converts an Internet domain name like **www.roehampton.ac.uk** into its equivalent numerical IP address – required by the computers and routers that manage the connection, but harder for humans to remember. DNS is said to 'resolve' a Domain Name into an IP address. If a local DNS does not know the address, it will refer to a higher level DNS to get the answer, such as 'com' or 'org' or 'uk' in the hierarchy. See domain.

Domain, Domain Name A group of computer systems. The top-level or 'trailing;' domain (at the end of the name) must be a recognized one such as com, gov, mil, edu, net, org, or of the newer set. In addition each country has its own top-level domain, e.g. '.us' for United States, '.uk' for the United Kingdom, '.fr' for

France etc. Below that, an organization may have a domain, like 'tie.nl', and below that, there may be various computers with their own names, e.g. **www.tie.nl** – 'www' is often used as the name of a computer that provides a World Wide Web service. See also DNS and FQDN.

Domain is also used in MS Widows to denote a group of PCs whose security is administered by a central server.

DOS Disk Operating System termed MS-DOS was developed and marketed by Microsoft for use on personal computers and licensed to IBM as PC-DOS.

DoS, Denial of Service attack Technique used by hackers to cripple an Internet server by sending a flood of connection requests to the server, thus overloading it.

Dotted quad An Internet address, broken down into four decimal numbers, separated by dots (full stops) e.g. 127.0.0.1. Each number represents one byte of the full 4-byte (32-bit) number, so must be in the range 1-255. See also IP address.

DSL Digital Subscriber Line. A method of connecting a user over a telephone line, using frequencies above those normally used for speech, and thus providing much higher speeds than those available through a modem. Unlike phones, DSL can provide a permanent 'always on' connection. See also broadband, ADSL.

DTD See Document Type Definition.

DUNS Dun & Bradstreet D-U-N-S Number. A unique nine-digit identification for business. Used in e-Commerce as an address. Similar to ANA number. D&S provide business information services. See **www.dnb.com**

EAI Enterprise Application Integration. The task of integrating external data (XML, EDI) into internal ERP or legacy systems. See ERP, legacy.

EAN European Article Numbering Association, now EAN International. Responsible for the development of a set of standards enabling the efficient management of global, multi-industry supply chains by uniquely identifying products, shipping units, assets, locations and services.

EANCOM A simplified subset of EDIFACT defined by EAN, widely used for EDI in international trade.

EBCDIC Extended Binary-coded Decimal Interchange Code. Assigns numeric values to characters. Developed by IBM, and used in mainframe systems. Same concept as ASCII but uses different numbers. Pronounced "ebb-cee-dic".

e-Business Abbreviation for electronic business.

ebXML Electronic Business XML is a working group to bring together EDI and XML, with the aim of modelling business processes as well as defining business transactions standards over the Internet. Sponsored by various groups, including United Nations. See also UDDI. See **www.ebxml.org**

e-Commerce

Abbreviation often used for electronic commerce.

ECR Efficient Consumer Response eliminates inefficiency in the supply chain using a combination of technologies and business process redesign.

EDI See Electronic Data Interchange.

EDI address Unique identifier for an organization. In the UK, organizations often use their ANA number, in the US often the DUNS number.

EDI Internet Gateway Software that allows EDI messages to be securely exchanged on a point-to-point basis with trading partners over the Internet.

EDI VAN Service A Value Added Network service provider that facilitates the exchange of EDI messages between trading partners.

EDIFACT (UN/EDIFACT) United Nations/Electronic Data Interchange for Administration, Commerce and Trade is an EDI standard. Provides definitions for a wide range of commercial documents that can be exchanged electronically, such as orders and invoices.

EDIINT Working Group to define standards for sending EDI data over the Internet , using Internet protocols such as FTP, SMTP or HTTP, and sending data as MIME attachments.

EEMA An association that acts as the European Forum for Electronic Business.

Efficient Consumer Response (ECR) Efficient Consumer Response eliminates inefficiency in the supply chain using a combination of technologies and business process redesign.

EFT Electronic Funds Transfer used in the financial services sector.

Electronic Business Electronic business is the practice of performing and co-ordinating critical business processes such as designing products, obtaining supplies, manufacturing, selling, fulfilling orders, and providing services through the extensive use of computer and communication technologies and computerized data.

Electronic Business Communications Describes the use of computing and telecommunications technologies for the exchange of information within and between organizations. Largely replaced by the term electronic business.

Electronic Commerce Electronic commerce is the use of the Internet and other information and communications technologies for the marketing, buying and selling of products and services. However, with the publicity surrounding the use of the Web by consumers, e-Commerce is becoming more associated with B2C category.

Electronic Data Interchange (EDI) Electronic Data Interchange (EDI) is defined as "The transfer of structured data, by agreed message standards, from one computer system to another, by electronic means."

'Structured' means the data that follows a defined format (such as UN/EDIFACT) and is not 'unstructured' like a free text E-mail message. 'Commercial data' means orders, invoices etc.

Electronic Mail (E-mail) Electronic Mail (E-mail) is person-to-person electronic messaging also known as inter-personal messaging (IPM). An E-mail address consists of individual@domain, e.g. JohnSmith@ourWebsite.com. The sending and receiving of mail between systems is managed by SMTP.

Encryption Process of encoding information to make it secure.

Enterprise Application Integration (EAI) See Application Integration (AI) and A2A above. Enterprises have existing legacy applications and wish to continue with their use whilst migrating to new applications that exploit the Internet and other new technologies.

EPOS Electronic point of sale. Starting point for supply chain.

ERP System Enterprise Resource Planning Systems are fully integrated packaged software applications supplied by SAP, BAAN, Oracle, PeopleSoft, etc. Originally based on materials planning or other specific function, they have evolved to cover all aspects of an organization, such as production planning, sales, finance, human resources etc. See also EAI, A2A, B2B.

Ethernet Popular LAN network media access protocol. There are two types: DIX (from Digital/Intel/Xerox) and IEEE 802.3 (ISO 8802.3). Data is broadcast to all devices on the network, but accepted only by the device with the MAC address contained in the message header.

EWOS European Workshop for Open Systems.

Extranet Private internet-based messaging and information management system often used to disseminate information from a large 'hub' organization such as a stores group to a large number of suppliers. Some extranets are 'horizontal' (many similar suppliers across a range of industries), or 'vertical' (ranging from raw materials to finished goods in one industry). See also Intranet.

Facsimile (FAX) A system for the transmission of images (text/graphics), usually over a telephone line.

Facsimile Modem Modem adapter that fits into a PC providing the ability to send and receive Group 3 FAX (analogue).

FAQ Frequently Asked Questions – a list of answers to the most frequently asked questions in a system, e.g. a Web site. This glossary is like an FAQ.

FDDI Fibre Distributed Data Interface, a high speed media access protocol used in LAN backbones.

Firewall Computer that sits between an organization's network and the Internet, and protects the internal network from unwanted access by unauthorized users. For example, a firewall may disallow certain services, or connections to certain other networks or IP addresses, or even specific port numbers. See also proxy server.

FQDN Fully Qualified Domain Name. A name for a particular computer system (such as a Web site) within a domain. Similar in concept to a postal address, and usually gives a clear indication of the site, e.g. microsoft.com. See also Domain.

Frame A block of data suitable for communication as a single unit, also known as a packet or cell. Also, part of a Web page that can operate independently of other frames (e.g. to show a menu).

FTP File Transfer Protocol (part of the TCP/IP architecture) that enables a user to log onto another computer and upload or download files.

Gateway A device that interfaces two different environments or protocols, such as SMTP and X.400. Can also mean a front-end system, e.g. E-mail gateway.

GCI The Global Commerce Initiative consists of international manufacturing and retailing companies. The aim is to develop and endorse standards and business processes in order to improve the international supply chain for consumer goods. GCI have been running pilot schemes for interoperability based on ebXML.

GENCOD EDI standard used mainly in France.

Gigabyte A billion (thousand million) bytes (2^30).

GIGO Garbage In, Garbage Out.

GOSIP Government OSI Profile. Formerly required by US and UK governments when purchasing IT products/services.

GSM Global System for Mobiles is designed to replace all Europe's analogue cellular mobile systems by a digital system.

GUI Graphical User Interface with 'point and click' characteristics using a mouse.

Hash function Like checksum, but designed to detect any change in data. Using complex algorithms, a hash function produces a checksum based on the contents of a file, in such a way that the smallest change can be detected. It is also computationally infeasible to create another file with the same hash value.

HDLC High-Level Data Link Control is the ISO standard for the data link layer protocol – ITU-T adapted HDLC for its link access protocol (LAP) used with X.25 networks.

Header The start of a datagram, containing the source and destination IP addresses, plus error-checking fields.

High Nines Refers to 99.999% availability of a Web server, meaning only a few minutes downtime a year.

Home Page The initial starting page on the World Wide Web.

Host A particular computer (usually means a server, because it acts as a 'host' to multiple clients).

Host Name A name for a specific computer within a domain. Free format, defined by the system manager, for example 'saturn' or 'www'. Outside its domain, a host must be identified with its Fully Qualified Domain Name, e.g. **www.ourWebsite.com**

Hosts file File containing a list of IP addresses and their corresponding domain names, used by TCP/IP stack on a computer. Often replaced by DNS, to avoid updating every hosts file on many computers in a domain.

HTML HyperText Markup Language comprises a set of formatting commands used to build Web pages.

HTTP HyperText Transfer Protocol (part of the TCP/IP architecture) provides the session level protocol to access a Web site and exchange data. Similar to FTP. Used mainly to transfer HTML pages. Can also be used in e-Commerce to exchange business documents, e.g. orders, invoices, and even commands (see SOAP).

Hypertext A method of presenting information so that it can be displayed in a non-sequential way, particularly by using links between such information so that users can move around freely between different information sources.

Hypertext link, Hyperlink Navigation from a Web page to another information source. May be a different part of the same page, or other files, or files on other Web sites.

IA5 International Alphabet 5, specified for X.400. International version of ASCII, but allowing national variants.

IAB The Internet Architecture Board is the co-ordinating committee for the management of the Internet.

ICANN Internet Corporation for Assigned Names and Numbers. Authority that registers domain names and IP addresses, and controls DNS.

ICMP Internet Control Message Protocol. Handles error messages, tests and information packets in IP. See ping.

ICT Information and Communication Technology. See also IT.

IEEE Institute for Electrical and Electronics Engineers. American institute that defines standards, e.g. Ethernet, Token Ring. Pronounced "I triple E". See **www.ieee802.org**

IEEE 802 A range of standards to enable devices to interconnect. Modelled on OSI 7-layer model, and covers bottom two layers – Physical Layer and Data Link Layer.

802.2 – Logical Link Control

802.3 – CSMA/CD

802.4 – Token Bus

802.5 – Token Ring

802.11b – A short-distance wireless-data standard, used in m-Commerce. See also Bluetooth.

IETF The Internet Engineering Task Force is a large open community that specifies protocols and other related standards. See **www.ietf.org**

Imaging The process of capturing, storing, cataloguing, displaying, and printing graphical information, as well as scanning paper documents for archival storage.

IMAP Internet Message Access Protocol is used to move E-mails from a mail server/mail drop a PC. See also POP.

Information superhighway Originally meant a high-speed network connection for any purpose, such as long-distance medical training. Now often confused with the Internet.

Interchange A file of EDI messages transmitted between two trading partners in a single transmission. Equivalent to a paper envelope containing one or more commercial messages.

Interconnectivity First of two stages in a successful networking environment, providing the secure path to move digits around.

Internet Short for Internetwork; two or more networks connected together by bridges, routers or gateways; and the name of the World's largest computer network. A network of networks, with no centralized ownership. In theory can use any network protocol. In practice, TCP/IP predominates.

Internet Address See IP Address.

Internet Commerce Synonymous with the term electronic commerce.

Internet Name Unique registered domain name for an organization, e.g. Website.co.uk that must end with top-level name. In the UK, the Registry for Internet Names is managed by Nominet.uk, which registers all names ending .uk and resolves disputes. See **nominet.org.uk**

Internet Service Provider (ISP) An Internet Service Provider offers Internet access usually for a fixed monthly charge based on the access speed. Many provide E-mail and Web site space as well.

Interoperability Co-operation between applications distributed over a network, so that programs on one system can request or provide services from/to programs on other systems. One way of doing this is XML and SOAP.

Interworking Second stage in a successful network environment that adds meaning to the digits being moved around.

Intranet Internal (within the same company) messaging and information management environment based upon open Internet technologies.

IP Internet Protocol is part of the TCP/IP architecture providing a connection-less packet-switched service at the network layer. IP will attempt to deliver a datagram to the destination address, but does not guarantee delivery.

IP Address Internet Protocol address. A 32-bit (4-octet) number that identifies a unique network destination or system worldwide. It identifies both an individual computer, and the network or subnetwork in which that computer operates. Allocated by a central authority, or (in many countries) a local delegated authority. For the benefit of humans, it usually has a mnemonic equivalent, e.g. **www.ourWebsite.com** See also Dotted Quad.

IPv6 Internet Protocol version 6. A new version of Internet Protocol, intended to replace current version of IP (version 4). Provides 128-bit IP addresses and other enhancements, but limited adoption so far. The IPv6 address includes a unique serial number taken from the computer's network-connection hardware, thus preventing spoofing (using someone else's IP address).

IPX Internet Packet Exchange is part of the Novell protocol stack.

IRTF The Internet Research Task Force

researches new technologies to be referred to the IETF.

ISDN Integrated Services Digital Network capable of transporting voice, data and moving image (video). Often used as backup on a network whose main or backbone connections are over leased lines.

ISO International Organization for Standardization is responsible for a wide range of standards, including computing. ISO is not an acronym, but a name, derived from the Greek word *isos* meaning 'equal'.

ISO/OSI Model Open System Interconnection model consisting of 7 layers, adopted by ISO. Useful structure for understanding networking.

ISP Internet Service Provider. An organization that provides a connection to the Internet for individuals or companies.

IT Information Technology is an all-embracing term to describe the whole of the computing landscape.

ITU Internal Telecommunications Union is a UN umbrella organization for worldwide telecommunications.

ITU-T International Telecommunication Union – Telecommunication, a standards making body for telecommunications operators (previously CCITT).

Java A network-aware, multi-platform programming language created by Sun Microsystems.

Java Applet Small programs or "applications" to add functionality and special effects to Web browsers. On the browser, these applets are run in a safe environment called a 'sandbox' that cannot damage or change your system. See also Applet.

Java Beans Java's component architecture that can be parts of Java programs or self-contained applications.

JavaScript A programming language created by Netscape to add functionality to Web browsers. Not related to Java.

JPEG The Joint Picture Experts Group

standard is a lossy compression technique based upon the work of a French mathematician.

Just-in-Time (JIT) Term used to describe the close coupling of goods arriving at a factory and their use in the manufacturing process – Quick Response is a similar philosophy in Retail.

Kerberos A security system, developed at MIT, to enable a user to log in from any computer and establish an identity which then controls access to other systems.

Kernel The part of an operating system that contains the basic commands and functions, such as memory and disk management, device drivers.

Kilobyte Kilo = 1000, but in IT, strictly speaking 1 Kilobyte (Kb) is $2^{10} = 1024$ bytes. See also Megabyte.

LAN A Local Area Network is a series of connected computers / peripherals in a specific geographical location, usually within a few kilometres. Typically in a building.

Layer A layer in a network architecture is a discrete group of services, functions and protocols, that is one of several.

LDAP The Lightweight Directory Access Protocol has become a standard way to access directory services. Simplified version of X.500.

Leased line Permanent physical connections between two or more computers that can form the basis of a network – sourced from a private/public telecommunications operator.

Legacy System Computer applications that have been in use for a long time, but are essential to an organization. Integrating such systems with newer ones is often difficult. See EAI, ERP.

Linux A popular open-source (free) 32-bit multi-user, multi-tasking and networking alternative to Unix and Windows NT/2000.

Local Loop The connection between a private house or small organization and a local telephone exchange. 'Unbundling of local loop' means providing access to this connection to other service suppliers. See PTO.

Lossless Compression Data compression method where there is no loss of original data when the file is decompressed.

Lossy Compression Data compression method that discards certain unwanted data, such that original data is lost during decompression – used for shrinking audio and image files.

Lotus Notes Popular groupware product from Lotus (now part of IBM).

Lotus Smartsuite Popular software suite (word processing, spreadsheets, presentations, etc.) from Lotus.

MAC The Message Authentication Code is a check value appended to a message to ensure integrity – widely used in the financial services sector. Similar to digital certificates.

Mailbox An electronic storage area in which information sent to a particular recipient is stored until retrieved by them.

Mail-enabled Application Applications that use E-mail as a transportation function.

Man-in-the-middle attack Form of computer hacking where users are misrouted to a fake server masquerading as the intended server.

MAPI Messaging Application Programming Interface from Microsoft that defines how applications and E-mail systems relate to one another.

Mapper / Translator Computer application that maps (converts) data between an internal (application) data format and an EDI or XML standard. See EAI, legacy.

Markup Markup refers to the sequence of characters or other symbols that are inserted in a text document to indicate how the document should look when it is printed, displayed or to describe the document's logical structure. The markup indicators are often called 'tags'.

m-Commerce Electronic Commerce on a business-to-consumer basis, using mobile phones instead of computers. See WAP.

MD5 See Message Digest.

Media Access Protocol The rules that workstations use to avoid collisions when sending information over a local area network (LAN). A 'MAC address' means the unique 6-octet address of a LAN network interface card (NIC).

Megabyte Mega = 1,000,000, but strictly speaking, 1 Megabyte (Mb) is 2^20 = 1048576 bytes. See also Kilobyte, Gigabyte, and Terabyte.

Message Digest An algorithm for calculating a check sum for a particular file. The calculation is so designed that even a tiny change in the file will result in a different checksum, and thus show whether the file has been changed in any way in transit. See SHA-1, PKI.

Message Disposition Notification Official Internet format for sending back an acknowledgement of receipt for an Internet mail message. Optional.

Messaging Handling System The ITU-T X.400 standard protocol for global store and forward messaging.

Metadata Data about data (e.g. invisible comments etc. at top of a Web Page (viewable using View Source). Metadata is defined by ISO as "the information and documentation which makes data sets understandable and shareable for users".

Microsoft Office Very popular software suite from Microsoft comes as Small Office and Professional editions.

Microsoft Windows Graphical operating environment that runs under DOS and brings many of the features found in the Apple Macintosh environment.

Microwave Line of sight communications that use high frequency waves (1 to 33 gigahertz).

Middleware Software to help integrate computer systems and provide distributed computing. Usually involves reformatting or translating data between different formats. See also EAI.

MIME Multi-purpose Internet Mail Extensions enhancing basic Internet Mail (see SMTP). MIME enables attachments to

be added to a text message. These attachments can contain any kind of data – text, graphics, audio, video etc.

Mirroring Duplication of a Website at other locations/countries, to speed up access for users near those other sites.

MNP Microcom Networking Protocol is a set of data compression and error detection protocols.

Modem A MODulator/DEModulator is an electronic device used to transmit data over the public switched telephone network by converting a computer's digital signals into the analogue signals needed to send data over the telephone system. At the receiving end there is a modem to demodulate the signal (convert it back to digital).

MPEG Motion Picture Experts Group. Graphics file format.

MQ Series Messaging middleware from IBM.

MRO Maintenance, Repair and Operation stock classification covers everyday commodity parts used by an organization. They are highly adaptable to e-Procurement through the use of electronic auctions.

Multi-media Refers to the simultaneous usage of different media, such as text, sound, graphics and video.

Multiplexing A technique that allows two or more communications sessions to share a common physical connection. TCP/IP achieves this by splitting data into packets, and individually addressing each packet over the same network. Similarly, computer systems such as Unix and Windows NT allow multiple users to use the same server at the same time.

Multi-tasking A computer that can run multiple copies of programs concurrently. Less efficient than multi-threading, because more memory is needed, but simpler.

Multi-threading A technique that allows a program to handle multiple users at the same time, by dividing up the program into 'threads'. Each thread is initialized with details about a particular user, thus enabling different threads in the same program to handle different users.

Multi-user system A computer that supports multiple concurrent user connections (e.g. Windows NT, Unix, MVS etc.).

NADF The North American Directory Forum focuses upon the issues of public X.500 directory services.

Namespace The purpose of XML namespaces is to distinguish between duplicate element names. An XML namespace is a collection of XML element names. The namespace is identified by a unique name, which is a URL. Thus, any element in an XML namespace can be uniquely identified by a two-part name: the name of its XML namespace and its local name. See the following: **www.rpbourret.com/xml/NamespacesFAQ.htm#q1_1.**

NAT See Network Address Translation.

NC A Network Computer relates to a basic PC based machine.

Netiquette Etiquette (guidelines on polite conduct) when using the Net, e.g. using CAPITALS = SHOUTING.

Netscape Communications Company known for its popular World Wide Web browser and Internet commerce applications.

Netware A series of popular local area network operating systems from Novell.

Network Series of computers and associated devices connected by a communications channel enabling the sharing of file storage and other resources.

Network Address Translation (NAT) A technique used in firewalls etc., in which, on one side, the firewall has an official and unique IP address allocated by some network authority, and on the other side has unofficial addresses, used internally by an organization (which may be the same numbers as at other organizations). In this way, there is no direct access to internal systems from the outside, thus enhancing security. IP addresses in the range 10.0.0.0 are reserved for this purpose. Also called 'masquerading'.

NFS Network File System. Enables files to be shared between machines. One system can use files on another system as if they were local.

NII National Information Infrastructure is the US programme for an information superhighway.

NIST National Institute of Standards and Technology – US government agency involved in setting commerce related standards.

Nominet UK Organization in the UK that manages the Registry of Internet Names ending in .uk and runs a Dispute Resolution Service to mediate over name disputes.

Non-repudiation Process to prevent sender of a message from denying the origin, or the contents, of a message. Also to prevent recipient from denying receipt of message. See digital certificates and PKI.

NOS Network Operating System used by local area networks.

OASIS Organization for the Advancement of Structured Information Standards is a non-profit, international consortium dedicated to accelerating the adoption of product-independent formats based on public standards. Involved in XML initiatives like ebXML. See **www.oasis-open.org www.openapplications.org** and **www.xml.org**

OBI Standard The Open Buying on the Internet standard that aims to make purchasing over the Internet easier. See **www.openbuy.org**

Octet Eight bits, not necessarily meaningful in their own right (unlike a byte, which is not always 8 bits, but always represents a character or number). However, 'byte' is often used instead of the more correct 'octet'.

ODA Open Document Architecture is an internationally recognized standard for compound documents.

ODBC Open Database Connectivity is an application program interface from Microsoft.

ODETTE European Automotive Association active in developing EDI and communications standards for its members. See **www.odette.org**

Open Group Formed by the merger of X/Open and OSF organizations

Open Standards Standards developed by recognized international bodies that are freely available in the public domain.

Open Systems Those systems and components which provide true vendor independence for users, achieved by conformance to open standards.

OpenDoc Compound document specification from a group of suppliers including Apple, IBM and Novell – similar in concept to OLE from Microsoft.

Open-source Software that is developed by a global group of programmers that is freely available including the program source code e.g. Linux.

OSF Open Systems Foundation formed in 1988 to maintain the open nature of Unix development. See **www.opengroup.org**

OSI Open Systems Interconnection. Set of protocols defined by ISO to connect computers and networks. Includes E-mail (X.400). An agreed international standard, similar in concept to TCP/IP, but now less popular. OSI Reference Model defines a 7-layer structure for networking, used to describe other networking protocols such as TCP/IP.

OSITOP European OSI user organization.

Outsourcing To subcontract out all or part of an organization's information technology department.

P2P Peer-to-peer. A technology that enables users to share and exchange files over the Internet, as on Napster etc., or to share computing power among many PCs. In P2P, a PC operates both as client and server, requesting and supplying files or data.

Packet A block of data sent over a packet-switched network, complete with sending and receiving IP addresses. Usually the same as 'datagram'.

Packet Switched Network Any network that breaks data up into separate packets, and sends each packet individually across the network, to the destination address defined in each packet. Because it can handle packets from many different users, a PSN is much more efficient than a circuit-switched network (such as a traditional telephone network). TCP/IP and X.25 are both packet-switched.

PARADISE European pilot for X.500 directories.

Parse To analyze the structure of something into its component parts. An XML parser analyzes the contents of an XML file in relation to a DTD. See XML, DTD.

PCMCIA Personal Computer Memory Card International Association – formed in 1989 that developed standards for connecting devices to portable computers. Sometimes said to stand for "People Can't Memorize Computer Industry Acronyms".

PDA Personal Digital Assistant that usually fits on the palm of a hand and provides organizer/E-mail functions.

PEM Privacy Enhanced Mail is a popular security technology widely used on the Internet.

Pentium Range of 64-bit microprocessor produced by Intel.

PGP Pretty Good Privacy is a security technology developed by Phil Zimmerman and distributed freely on the Web.See **www.pgpi.org**

PGP/MIME Security for MIME messages using PGP. See also S/MIME.

Ping A command to check if a remote system is up and running. Derived from the sonar systems in submarines, it sends a short message (ICMP packets) to the remote computer. A positive reply means that the remote system's TCP/IP stack is functioning. See ICMP, TCP/IP, traceroute.

PIP Partner Interface Process. RosettaNet specification to align electronic business interfaces between trading partners using XML.

PKCS Public Key Cryptography Standards. Created by a consortium of major computer vendors. See PKI.

PKI Public Key Infrastructure. An environment for authenticating the identities of trading partners (using digital signatures) and encrypting the data they exchange.

PKZIP Popular PC-based compression utility that uses lossless techniques. WINZIP is a popular version.

Platform An operating system environment such as Unix, sometimes also used to refer to hardware such as RS6000.

Platform Independence The ability of programs to run on nearly any kind of computer.

POP Point of Presence. Network access point to a server or network service. Usually provided by an ISP.

POP3 Post Office Protocol (version 3) is designed to retrieve waiting E-mails from a mail server to a browser. Has fewer features than IMAP.

Port An access point used in TCP/IP to exchange data between computers. Some ports are 'well-known', reserved for particular protocols; for example, ports 20 and 21 for FTP, port 80 for HTTP. See also socket.

Portal A user's starting-point for the World Wide Web, offering a wide variety of choices.

POTS 'Plain Old Telephone System' – a jocular reference to the PSTN.

PPP Point to Point Protocol. An Internet standard for providing a TCP/IP connection to the Internet, by transmitting IP datagrams over a serial point-to-point connection (e.g. async dial-up over a telephone line).

Programmatic interface Same as API. A facility in a program that allows it to be controlled by another program rather than by a human being.

Proprietary Software & Standards Software and standards developed and owned by an organization that are not in the public domain.

Protocol A set of rules/conventions that need to be respected if communications are to be achieved between two parties. Low-level protocols define things such as the machine-to-machine interface, at the electrical level. While high-level protocols for example define the dialogue between programs that exchange data, e.g. FTP. See FTP, HTTP, SMTP.

Proxy Server Security device that sits between an organization's network and the Internet, and requests data on behalf of internal users. It replaces the internal user's IP address with its own, thus hiding the internal user from the Internet. This also means that an internal network can use any IP addresses, regardless of what other organizations are using, thus getting round the constraint of using unique Internet addresses. Many organizations use combined firewalls and proxy servers. See also firewall, NAT.

PSPDN or PDN The Packet Switched Public Data Network is a global infrastructure operated by Private Telecommunications Operators based upon the X.25 standard.

PSTN The Public Switched Telephone Network is a global infrastructure operated by licensed Telephone Operators based upon international standards.

PTO Private Telecommunications Operators emerged from the de-regulation of telecommunication services in Europe to introduce greater competition into service provision. This means giving them access to local telephone connections, often called "unbundling the local loop".

PTT The Postal, Telephone and Telegraph organizations were the original government agencies (affiliated to the ITU) established in each country providing monopoly services.

Public Key Encryption An encryption scheme that uses two keys – the public key encrypts the data and the corresponding private key decrypts the data (and vice versa). Anyone can encrypt the message, but only the intended recipient can decrypt it. See also RSA.

Raw Socket Facility in an operating system to send data directly through a socket, rather than through the TCP/IP stack. Can be misused, e.g. for spoofing.

Reverse Auction An e-Commerce procedure, usually internet-based, in which a large organization solicits bids from other organizations to supply goods, often raw materials or components. Unlike a normal auction, where prices rise, in a reverse auction suppliers will be tempted to lower their prices as the deadline approaches.

RFC Request For Comment. A working note from the Internet research and development community, always in the public domain, and freely downloadable. Most of them describe a proposed or accepted Internet standard sponsored by the IETF, or enhancements to it. See various Internet sites, e.g. **www.ietf.org/rfc.html**

RFID RFID stands for Radio Frequency Identification. An RFID tag consists of a small computer chip and radio antenna that can be hidden in products for sale in shops. They can be read from several feet away, and can therefore replace barcodes, and also deter theft. The chief barriers to adoption are: cost of tags and the lack of industry standards

RIP Regulation of Investigatory Power Act 2000. UK law about interception of communications.

RISC Reduced Instruction Set Computing processors usually only recognize a limited number of assembler level language instructions, resulting in a simpler and faster CPU. See also CISC.

RosettaNet A consortium of mainly electronics and IT companies developing open e-Business process standards. Named after the Rosetta Stone, which has a hieroglyphic message in three languages. RosettaNet defines a common language and standard processes for exchanging business information. See also PIP. See **www.rosettanet.org**

Router An intelligent communications device for receiving and forwarding data packets between networks, or gateways to other networks, and finding the optimum route. If one link is congested or broken, a router can find an alternative route to the destination. See switch.

RPC Remote Procedure Call. A technique for enabling an application on machine to run applications on remote machines, in a client-server relationship.

RSA Popular encryption algorithm named after the developers (Rivest, Samir and Adleman) that uses prime numbers and public/private keys.

S/MIME Secure Multipurpose Internet Mail Extension. Used to send E-mail attachments securely over the Internet by adding a cryptographic signature and/or encryption to a MIME message.

Sandbox See applet.

Schema Used in XML. Similar to a Document Type Definition (DTD) to define the elements and their attributes, but more powerful and flexible because it also defines types of data (e.g. string, number, date) occurrence and other attributes in a hierarchical structure. See also XML and DTD.

SDLC Synchronous Data Link Control is a predecessor to HDLC, developed by IBM and used for the data link layer in SNA networks.

Search Engine Application that uses intelligent agents to index information available on the Web – users can use search engines to locate information and then hyperlink to the selected home page.

Server A computer that provides services, or resources, such as applications, files, printers to other computers, FTP, DNS. Essentially passive, waiting for requests, unlike a 'client'. See client-server, NFS.

Service Provider Term used to describe companies that provide network-based services to user organizations.

Services file File containing a list of services (such as FTP), with the port number and protocol used (tcp or udp).

Used by TCP/IP stack. See also hosts file.

SET Secure Electronic Transaction is a standard particularly orientated towards credit card usage in an electronic commerce environment. See **www.setc.o.org**

SGML Standard Generalised Mark-up Language (ISO 8879, issued 1986) for defining digital document structure – HTML and XML are both derived from SGML.

SHA Secure Hash Algorithm. See Message Digest.

SHA-1 Secure Hash Algorithm 1. A message digest to ensure that a message has not been tampered with. See also Message Digest.

SITPRO UK Simplification of International Trading Procedures is a government agency that has recently simplified its name to 'Simpler Trade Procedures'.

SLA Service Level Agreement. A contractual agreement by an ISP, ASP, VANS or similar to provide an agreed level of service to users. See also High Nines.

SLIP Serial Line Internet Protocol. Used for point-to-point serial connections, using TCP/IP. See also PPP.

SME Acronym for 'Small and Medium Enterprise'.

SMTP Simple Mail Transfer Protocol (part of the TCP/IP architecture) is used to manage the sending and receiving of E-mail messages between servers over the Internet. See also IMAP, POP and MIME.

SNA IBM's proprietary System Network Architecture.

Sniffer Unauthorized program used by hackers to monitor network traffic and to detect passwords.

SNMP Simple Network Management Protocol (part of the TCP/IP architecture). Internet standards for the remote monitoring and management of hosts, routers etc. on a network.

SOAP Simple Object Access Protocol. Provides a simple and lightweight carrier for exchanging structured information and messages between peers in a decentralized, distributed environment using XML. Typically used to send commands or requests from a client to a server. SOAP has two advantages over other similar protocols – the commands are defined using XML, and the connections go over HTTP, because many corporate firewalls block other connection protocols and port numbers.

Socket A communications end-point. A combination of IP address and port number that uniquely identifies a particular service (for example, a Web service) on a particular host, anywhere in the world. See also port.

Socket Services Software that monitors PCMCIA slots to detect insertion/removal.

Spam Unsolicited E-mail, for example advertizements, special offers.

SPECint System Performance Evaluation Co-operative integer – relates to a standard benchmark used to measure CPU performance.

Spoke Term used in EDI for organizations that all trade with a large central 'hub'. Typical 'spokes' are suppliers to a retail stores group (the 'hub').

Spoofing Using someone else's IP address.

SQL Structured Query Language is an ANSI and ISO relational database query language standard.

SSL Secure Sockets Layer. A protocol developed by Netscape Communications providing security services for Web-based applications. It provides authentication between a browser (client) and an Internet Web site server, and an encrypted connection (to protect, for example, credit card numbers). SSL sits between HTTP and TCP.

Stateless A 'stateless' system is one where each request from a client to a server is treated individually, unrelated to any previous requests. Such a design is simpler, because the server does not need to retain any details about user sessions. HTTP sessions are stateless – the server just responds to the request in the URL. However, cookies are often used to store some details on a user's PC.

Store and forward Service provided by VANs. A VAN client can send in data to the VAN, where it is stored, and forwarded to the recipient's mailbox (local or remote).

Style sheet A file that defines how data (e.g. XML data) is to be displayed. See CSS, also XSLT.

Subnet, subnet mask A portion of a network that shares a network address with other parts of the network, but has a unique subnet address. Typical use is where an organization has different locations, with a number of PCs. Each location has its own subnet, identified by the subnet mask. This enables routers in the network to decide whether data is to go to a local or remote subnet. Only if remote is the data forwarded to that network, thus improving network efficiency.

Supply Chain The flow of goods, starting as raw materials through to finished products, from suppliers through to the retailer. Speeding up and improving the supply chain is one of the main aims of e-Commerce, because of the savings on stocks.

SWIFT Network Society for World-Wide Interbank Financial Telecommunication is a global network used by the financial services industry. See **www.swift.com**

Synchronous Communications Communications that use a clock/synchronization signals to control traffic flow. See also async.

Syntax In language: the correct sequence of words in a sentence. 'I like XML' is correct, 'XML like I' is bad syntax. Applied to EDI, means the correct sequence of elements in a line, segment or message. In XML, there is a root element, with a hierarchy of child elements.

T1, T3 Names for leased lines in USA.

TCP Transmission Control Protocol is part of the TCP/IP architecture providing end-to-end reliable transport of data sent in datagrams by IP (Internet protocol).

TCP/IP The Transmission Control Protocol/Internet Protocol (often called TCP/IP suite) provides interconnection / transport services across TCP/IP networks. Supports higher-level services such as FTP, telnet, SMTP, HTTP, and a large number of more specialized protocols and services. Supplied as standard with many operating systems, e.g. Unix, Windows.

TCP/IP stack The collection of software in a system that manages TCP/IP connections. Called a 'stack' because of the layers of software – IP to handle individual packets, TCP to manage the transfer, and a higher-level such as FTP to provide a specific service. See also socket and port.

Telecommunications The transmission of electronic signals over a distance that can be used for voice, data or image.

Telecommuting Working from home using a portable computer connected the office via a modem and the Public Switched Telephone Network.

Telnet Terminal emulation protocol and part of the TCP/IP architecture providing connections to a remote time-sharing host or server from user terminals.

Terabyte A million million bytes (2^40).

Thick Architecture The result of reducing choice of IT conventions, rules and standards in use throughout an organization.

Thick Client A PC or workstation with plenty of memory and disk space, thus providing local processing. See Thin Client.

Thin Client A PC or workstation that has no disks, and thus depends on a server. Provides centralized control over PCs.

TLA Three-Letter Acronym – poking fun at the IT industry's love of cryptic acronyms (many in this Glossary).

Token Ring Popular LAN network media access protocol, developed jointly with IBM as IEEE 802.5 standard (ISO 8802.5).

TQM Total Quality Management aims to optimize the internal working practices of an organization and eliminate unnecessary cost.

Traceroute A program used to trace the route used by a TCP/IP connection, to identify the routers used in the path and the endpoint. (On Windows, called 'tracert').

TRADACOMs An EDI standard developed and used mainly in the UK. Stands for TRAding DAta COMmunicationS. Same concept as EDIFACT, and similar in design, but developed earlier.

Tradanet EDI VAN service.

Trading Partner Companies with whom an organization does business.

Trading Relationship An agreement between two parties governing the exchange of business messages. May include exchange of public keys (see PKCS). Often used on VANS to control who can send what data to whom.

Trojan Horse A program installed by hackers that performs an official function, but also an unofficial one (e.g. to send all usernames and passwords to the hacker). May also be used to give unauthorized access and control to a hacker.

UDDI Universal Description, Discovery and Integration. A technique that enables an organization to describe the services and products it offers; enables other organizations to discover those services and products, and thus integrates those services worldwide over the Internet for e-Business. UDDI data is carried by SOAP.

Similar in concept to ebXML. See also UML. See **www.uddi.org**

UDP User Datagram Protocol. Transport layer connectionless protocol. Sends packets over IP quickly and efficiently, because it does not provide the error handling and recovery of TCP.

UML Unified Modelling Language –

graphical modelling technique adopted internationally by industry to describe business processes, and thus define requirements for EDI/XML exchange of business messages.

UN/CEFACT United Nations standards body responsible for UN/EDIFACT. Part of UNECE. **www.uncefact.org**

UN/EDIFACT United Nations/Electronic Data Interchange for Administration Commerce and Trade. Guidelines for electronic interchange of structured data between computer applications, such as orders and invoices. (See EDIFACT & **www.unece.org/trade/untdid/welcome.htm**

UNECE United Nations Economic Commission for Europe. Based in Geneva, with a mission to facilitate international trade. See **www.unece.org**

Unicode New standard for assigning numerical values to letters, digits etc. Unlike earlier standards (ASCII, EBCDIC) uses 2 bytes for each character, thus allowing many additional characters – particularly non-Latin such as Japanese – to be uniquely identified. Aim is to provide "unambiguous encoding of the content of plain text, covering all languages in the world" (W3C).

Bottom part of range overlaps with ASCII. See also UTF-8, EBCDIC. See **www.unicode.org**

Unix A 32-bit multi-user, multi-tasking, portable operating system and very popular together with Windows NT in a client/server environment. See also Linux.

URL Uniform Resource Locator identifies a specific object or resource on the Web, such as a file or program, at a specific location (e.g. server), able to generate an HTML or XML page (text or graphics or audio etc.) to be displayed. Examples of various types of URL:

HTTP **http://www.Website.com/default.htm**

FTP **ftp://ftp.Website.com/info.txt**

MAIL **mailto:jsmith@Website.com**

URN Uniform Resource Name. Identifies a persistent and specific Web resource, independent of location. Little used as yet. A URN is like a mobile phone number, location independent, whereas a URL is like a phone number in a home or office, with a static location.

User Agent Official term for a user's terminal, e.g. browser on a PC.

UTF-8 Unicode Transformation Format-8. Encoding of Unicode characters, compatible with ASCII. Each Unicode character is encoded as a variable number of 1 or more octets. Used in XML. Known in ISO 10646 as "UCS transformation format". See also Unicode, ASCII.

UUCP Unix-to-Unix Copy Program. A protocol for exchanging data between Unix systems.

V.n standards ITU-T recommendations (e.g. V.32, V.90) that define how modems are to encode, modulate and transmit data over a communications link (typically an analogue dial-up connection over the PSTN).

VANS Value Added Network Services. Service providers that provide additional services e.g. E-mail, EDI, Applications, etc. rather than just networking. Often called just 'VAN'.

VICS Voluntary Interindustry Commerce Standard. A subset of ANSI X12 EDI standard, used in US retail industry.

Videoconference Use of voice and video linked by communications to allow individuals at different locations to participate in a meeting – groupware products provide desktop video and chalkboards to help people work together.

Virtual In IT, used to describe things that exist logically, but have no separate physical existence. An example is a 'virtual circuit' – a connection between two computer systems, but the actual physical network connections may vary from one session to another. See VPN.

Virus Program that can infect a computer by attaching itself to an existing program, or to code such as a macro that is run automatically when certain types of file are opened (such as E-mail attachments).

A virus can replicate itself in order to infect other computers. See also Trojan Horse and worm.

VoicE-mail Computerized store and forward system for voice messages.

VoIP Voice over IP. Emerging technology to handle telephone voice traffic over IP networks, by breaking speech down into multiple IP packets sent over high-speed networks.

VPN Virtual Private Network. Uses the public Internet to provide a private encrypted network for an organization.

VSAT Very Small Aperture Terminals provide a physical connection service via satellite links.

W3C World Wide Web Consortium. Main standards body for World Wide Web. Its director is Tim Berners-Lee, who invented the Web. See **www.w3.org**

WAN A Wide Area Network is a series of connected computers/ peripherals (or LANs) in dispersed geographically separate locations.

WAP Wireless Application Protocol. Provides Internet-style information and services for mobile phones.

Web Browser A computer program or 'client' that enables a user to connect to the Internet and access information from Web Servers.

Web Page Information (text, images and sound) stored on a Web server for subsequent display using a Web browser.

Web Server A computer connected to the Internet that sits passively waiting to provide Web services such as files to Web browsers.

Webcasting Allows Web broadcasting of events as they happen with video and sound.

Windows 2000 Evolution of Windows NT, incorporating Active Directory (similar to Novell NDS).

Windows 3.1 Graphical operating environment developed by Microsoft that runs under DOS and brings many of the features found in the Apple Macintosh environment. Replaced by Windows 95.

Windows 95, 98 & ME A 32-bit multitasking operating system with attractive GUI interface and strong networking capabilities.

Windows NT A 32-bit New Technology multitasking portable operating system from Microsoft running on a wide range of hardware platforms.

Windows XP Evolution of Windows client software with emphasis upon a reliable and robust operating system environment for both business and home users.

Word Several bytes together (usually 4). CPUs often process data a word at a time. See also byte, octet.

Workgroup Group of PCs linked together for browsing files. See also domain.

World Wide Web, WWW A killer application that has done much to accelerate the growth of the Internet – hypertext links connect information stored in separate files on servers, that can be explored using a Web browser. See W3C.

A URL like **www.Website.com** identifies a specific computer (Web Server) called www in the domain Website.com, and that the Web Browser (the client) wants to use the HTTP protocol to communicate.

Worm Program similar to a virus that can also spread itself, usually by E-mail. See also Trojan Horse and virus.

X Windows Windowing environment developed in the US by MIT for Unix workstations. Also available on PCs to access Unix systems and provide a Windows-like GUI (Graphical User Interface).

X.25 ITU-T recommendation that provides support for the physical, data link and network layers of the OSI model (X.n refer to digital standards for PSPDNs).

X.400 ITU-T recommendation for inter-personal messaging (IPM) that may run over a number of network protocols. Similar in principle to SMTP.

X.435 ITU-T recommendation that enhances X.400 to cater for the rather special requirements of EDI.

X.500 ITU-T recommendation for private and public electronic directory services. See also LDAP.

X.509 ITU-T recommendation defining digital certificates.

X/Open Company Founded in 1984 by a group of vendors and very active in open systems matters.

X12 (ANSI ASC X12) X12 is an EDI standard developed by the US American National Standards Institute Accredited Sub-committee.

XHTML Combination of HTML and XML, proposed by W3C in 2000. Follows XML rules for well-formedness etc.

Xlink Standard for adding hyperlinks to an XML file.

XML The eXtensible Markup Language is a powerful markup language for structuring, storing and exchanging data, for Web publishing, EDI etc. Defined by W3C in1998.

XML/EDI Working group on integrating XML and EDI.

Xpath XML Path Language. A facility for addressing a specific part of an XML file.

XSL eXtensible Stylesheet Language. Defines how to display and/or transform XML data. See XSLT.

XSLT XSL Transformer enables an XML document to be converted or transformed into another document or format – for example into an XHTML document.

Index